Spiritual Direction And Spiritual Directors:

St. Francis de Sales, St. Teresa of Avila, Thomas a Kempis, and St. John of the Cross

By
Joseph Paul Kozlowski

Library of Congress #:97-065318

Published by:
Queenship Publishing
P.O. Box 42028
Santa Barbara, CA 93140-2028
(800) 647-9882 • (805) 957-4893 • Fax: (805) 957-1631
email: qship@impulse.net

Printed in the United States of America

ISBN 1-882972-85-6

Dedicated To

Jesus, Mary, Joseph

And To

My Wife Helen, and My Children
Paul, Pamela, Joseph Gary, Sharon Lisa

Table of Contents

Foreword

The Second Vatican Council of the Roman Catholic Church has had wide-spread repercussions. One of the very helpful results of that Council is the impetus given to *all Catholics* to have an active role in the Church. It is encouraging, therefore, to see the interest of Mr. Joseph Kozlowski, a lay person, in the important area of spiritual direction. His interest represents a long and deep commitment. This commitment has resulted in his own personal development, of course, but has also led to benefits for many others. He has already published several articles in the field of spiritual direction. He has now prepared an extensive work to highlight the lives and writing of four very special persons, namely St. Francis de Sales, St. Teresa of Avila, Thomas a Kempis, and St. John of the Cross.

Another strong thrust of the Second Vatican Council was the insistence that the Church return to ideas and practices that are basic to her life. Here, too, Mr. Kozlowski has performed a true service in calling his readers back to the great roots of spiritual development in the Catholic tradition.

In a world where materialism, selfishness, violence, and similar evils seem to run rampant, this book offers a truly healing remedy. The reader is encouraged to go back to the writings of these great spiritual directors. To whet the appetite for such study the book provides not only helpful facts and insights about the four authors, but also provides a large selection of texts from these writings listed by subject, a very helpful procedure. He has concentrated in his fifth chapter on the person and writings of St. John of the Cross, truly a "man for all seasons." In addition to supplying text with some interpretation from this great writer, the author has also included a general survey of his life, an appreciation of his spiritual development abilities, and his continuing value for our own times.

As the author himself notes, "I have attempted to present the material in this book in such a way, that it will, hopefully, inspire the readers of this book to refer to that spiritual director whom they believe attracts them most at their particular stage of spiritual development in life... I have structured my presentation of materials in such a way that, hopefully, it will appeal to a very broad spectrum of persons who do prayerfully, and with concentrated effort, read works of spiritual direction. I fervently hope that my contribution will be especially referred to by all those religious and laity who themselves will seriously undertake an 'Apostolate of Spiritual Direction' as an essential part of their daily life activity." The book clearly provides ample material to make it possible that the author's hopes for it will become a reality!

Everyone will benefit from a tour of this book, from the opportunity to meet St. Francis de Sales, St. Teresa of Avila, Thomas a Kempis, and St. John of the Cross, but especially from the opportunity to study carefully the wonderful insights of these authors as one tries to walk the road to spiritual perfection. Continued study of these great authors can produce more women and men who will be competent to bring the values of Jesus Christ into the market place of this troubled world.

The Second Vatican Council has also emphasized the role of the laity in transforming the secular world in the image of Christ. The Council envisions men and women "working in harmony, should renew the temporal order and make it increasingly more perfect: such is God's design for the world." (Decree of the Apostolate of Lay People, n.7) But this same Decree insists that the laity will not succeed in transforming the world without true spiritual development (cf. No. 4) This book holds out one very valuable path to spirituality for all dedicated persons, both religious and lay.

Monsignor Ralph J. Kuehner, S.S.L. *
Washington Archdiocese and
Priest in Residence at St. Francis
of Assisi Church, Derwood, MD.

*Licentiate in Sacred Scripture.

Author's Preface

God willing, may this book inspire more and more persons in the religious life and the laity in all their professions, wherever they may be, to take up the subject of spiritual direction either as an additional vocation or a vocation during their lifetime. In doing so may they always be guided by the Holy Spirit, as expressed by St. John of the Cross who stated that God guides each individual soul: 1) kindly; 2) in a orderly way; and 3) according to the mode of the spiritual receptivity of each soul.

I express my personal gratitude to His Eminence James Cardinal Hickey, Archbishop of Washington for the continuing support, inspiration, and encouragement which he has given me over the past years during my work on this book. He has been a true friend and a wonderful pastor.

I

Introduction

My objective in preparing this work on spiritual direction and spiritual directors is to provide a guide for those persons (laity and clergy) who are either seeking further spiritual direction, or are striving themselves to become more competent spiritual directors, and, who hopefully, will make an "Apostolate of Spiritual Direction" one of the main focal spiritual tasks to be accomplished in their lives. St. John of the Cross, as I state in Chapter V specifically oriented his own life towards carrying out an "Apostolate of Spiritual Direction. He did this despite the many heavy responsibilities he carried out at the same time as an administrator, teacher, planner, religious superior, and organizer. As a spiritual director he gave of himself completely to all of his brothers and sisters in Christ in the religious community, and among the faith (all classes - poor, middle class, and rich) who sought him out for spiritual guidance.

It would indeed be an ideal luxury if each of us could have a personal spiritual director to whom we could turn to at will; persons who could guide our soul in its spiritual development, and give us useful constructive advice when we are confronted with serious problems of a spiritual situation as regards receiving good prudent counsel. The reality, however, is that it is not achievable, especially in today's complex and too frenetic pace of life. In our everyday life when we have problems of a technical nature beyond our competence, we seek out the best professionally competent advice we can obtain. If our car needs repair, we try to find an excellent, reliable mechanic. If the roof of our house leaks, we seek out a good roofing specialist. When the plumbing or electrical system breaks down, we look for a qualified plumber or electrician. If we are in need of spiritual advice we go to our priest, rabbi, or minister, or perhaps to a trusted, devout, and hopefully, learned friend or friends. However, in these our times such religious or clergy, ministers, and other servants of God are frequently so occupied, or overburdened with so many spiritual and temporal responsibilities, that they simply do not have the time to devote to each individual person, and to give the serious consideration or attention needed concerning their spiritual and temporal problems. The problem becomes more complex as regards consulting spiritual directors, when we see clearly that at times a number of various spiritual directors may need to be consulted because of the unique individual nature of the particular spiritual problems one may be facing. St. John of the Cross points this out very clearly in his discussion of spiritual directors in his *Collected Works* which I will briefly discuss later in this chapter.

It is true that we always have God ready at hand - closer to us than we are to ourselves - to turn to in prayer when we are confronted with spiritual problems, as well as other perplexities, troubles and confusion encountered in our daily living. Moses himself, a man very close to God's heart, when reason was no longer a recourse, and spiritual counselors were not able to counsel him, frequently then turned prayerfully with an open heart directly to God for guidance and wisdom. However, God Who guides us in a kindly and orderly way, according to the receptivity of our soul to Him, most frequently acts through the instrumentality of other persons. Thus, Moses at certain critical times of decision-making was inspired by God to consult with his brother Aaron. In the medical profession, for example, God very frequently makes use of very skilled, competent, and trustworthy surgeons, doctors, and so forth, to restore to health persons with painful, serious illnesses. Thus, each person endowed with unique gifts by God can always offer a useful service to us, or always teach us something valuable and important which we could not bring about ourselves. Conversely, we, with whatever gifts God has endowed us with, can similarly share them with others. John Donne, the English poet, expressed this spiritual wisdom so eloquently: "No man is an island unto himself" in this world. This is especially true as regards the spiritual life, and in many other aspects of life where serious decision-making is needed. Consultation with others who have been proven to be trustworthy, experienced, honest and reliable is a sign of a prudent, wise person, and quite often of a humble person who knows his limitations. Each of us, in terms of the gifts God has given to us can be considered to be at the same time, either inferior, or superior to one another. Wherefore we become mutually bound to lovingly, selflessly share our gifts with one another; never forgetting Who the Giver of such gifts is, and always expressing our gratitude to God for them.

I have brought together in this work materials extracted from the works of four persons who for many centuries have unquestioningly been considered to be truly outstanding spiritual directors. Their works can be prayerfully read and studied with considerable profit. Three of them have been canonized as saints in the Catholic Church: St. Francis of Sales, St. John of the Cross, and St. Teresa of Avila. The fourth person is Thomas a Kempis whose authorship of his much admired classic of spiritual direction *My Imitation of Christ* appears to be somewhat shrouded in some mystery. Regardless of the true authorship, however, the work of Thomas a Kempis, although small in size, contains many valuable, very concise principles of spiritual direction which are truly gems of spiritual direction and profundity.

Although throughout this work I have presented very extensively the principles of spiritual direction of all four of the spiritual directors cited above, I personally have chosen St. John of the Cross as the spiritual director to whom I would refer persons who would be able to derive effective spiritual direction from a prayerful reading and diligent study of the actual written works of the persons cited above. I state this, not to emphasize any special superiority of St. John of the Cross as compared to the others as regards spiritual direction, but rather because of my personal conviction that his spiritual direction is presented in a very systematic, very detailed, well-organized form, guiding the directee, with St. John of the Cross being the spiritual director, to the highest form of spiritual development of the soul possible on this earth before death, namely: "the spiritual marriage", "the union of love", or the "mystical union of love" with God; also sometimes referred to as the "state of likeness" (participatory) with God. For St. John of the Cross explicitly chose an "Apostolate of Spiritual Direction" to be his main preoccupation in life, while still fulfilling many other religious responsibilities and performing many other tasks. This is a state in which the soul may be compared to an exquisitely lovely diamond facet of indescribable beauty; a diamond facet of an incomprehensibly, indescribable large lovely diamond (GOD), brilliant and beautiful beyond all of our human understanding, or of the understanding of any angelic supra-human beings, for only God alone always knows Himself perfectly in His divine essence. In other words, the spiritual direction of St. John of the Cross contains something for the guidance of each soul, although as St. John of the Cross states explicitly, not everything in his *Collected Works* of spiritual direction is applicable to each soul. It is in this sense that St. John of the Cross may be considered to be "A Spiritual Director for All Times for All" as I refer to him in Chapter V where I present a summary interpretation of his entire *Collected Works*. He is especially unique as a spiritual director, and brilliantly so. A study of his *Collected Works* reveals that he was a keen student of the works of St. Thomas Aquinas * and many other outstanding theologians who were also very devout in addition to being very learned. Among these may be cited, Father Mancio de Corpus Christi, a Dominican who held the Chair of Theology, the most important one at the University of Salamanca in Spain* and who with others taught the *Summa Theologica* to St. John of the Cross.

I wish to suggest to the readers of this book that if at all possible, prior to reading the *Collected Works of St. John of the Cross*, that, in conjunction with the reading of this book, they consult the outstanding work of that renowned theologian and expositor of the *Summa Theologica* of St. Thomas Aquinas, the brilliant good Rev. Father Walter Farrel of blessed memory whom I had the pleasure of meeting in the late 1940's at the Dominican House of Studies in Washington, D.C. during a lecture series he was conducting on the *Summa Theologica*. In his classic four-volume work *A Companion to the Summa* he made the *Summa Theologica* of St. Thomas Aquinas so very clear, easy to understand, not only for many a religious in many faiths, but also for a vast number of laity here in this country and throughout the world wherever his work was published. He was a founder of the Thomistic Institute, and had devoted a lifetime to bringing the profound thoughts of St. Thomas Aquinas to a sharpness, clarity, and simplicity of written exposition, which, in my opinion, some of the works available today on the *Summa Theologica* have in many respects, unfortunately, failed to do, as I personally learned through hard experience. He accomplished this through a simplicity of style in writing and clarity and organization of thought intelligible to persons with various degrees of education.

---

* *Collected Works of St. John of the Cross;* p.18.

I personally owe him a great debt of gratitude for this achievement. He devoted almost twenty-five years of his life to the study and very prayerful analysis of the brilliant work and profound spiritual, and theological truths of the original work of the *Summa Theologica* of St. Thomas Aquinas, one of the most highly respected, outstanding theologians in the Catholic Faith and in many faiths throughout the world. Fr. Farrel also through his lecturing and preaching gave these same profound truths, which his brilliant intellect had extracted from the original work of the *Summa Theologica* to all throughout our nation, as well as throughout the world who were willing to invest the time and prayerful study in a quest for understanding some of the most profound theological truths ever explained by man.

St. Thomas Aquinas was an extremely keen student of human nature. During the 13th Century when he lived (1225-1274) his travels throughout Europe, many of them considerable on foot, took him into the life of all strata of society, from the merest scullery maids, servants, and laborers of diverse types to the palaces of kings and queens, and into the company of intellectuals of academia (religious and laity) of some of the most famous universities of Europe, especially of Paris where he spent many of his years of academic life. As a result of these numerous human encounters throughout many countries, spanning broad spectrums of all stratas of society, his knowledge of human nature became extraordinarily profound. He very effectively interwove this profound knowledge of human nature accumulated through first-hand experiences with his academic training, and above all with a perseveringly devout prayerful life into an architectonic symphonic harmony of theological knowledge.

As one studies the spiritual direction of St. John of the Cross one can discern the very powerful influence of St. Thomas Aquinas especially, and that of many other theologians and teachers who taught him in subjects such as: the passions (joy, hope, sorrow, fear), the emotions, habits, the appetites of the will, the intellect, the memory, the senses (internal and external); the superior (spiritual) and inferior (sensory) aspects of the soul; the imagination, the vegetative, animal and spiritual aspects of the human person; the inter-action of the will with the memory and the intellect, the role of the imagination as regards our soul and prayer life; the role of good and evil spirits (that is the good and the fallen angels), the various hierarchies of angels, and so many other profound subjects too numerous to discuss here. It is for this reason that I would again urge the reader of this work to, if at all possible, take the time to prayerfully study the Rev. Fr. Farrel's *A Companion to the Summa*, the complete reference of which I have cited below for the benefit of the reader. I believe I can say with complete confidence that it will bring untold spiritual treasures and joy to the heart and to the mind, or to express it in another way it will provide a real "short-cut" to a better understanding of theological truths, of our own soul, and of human nature in general. The reference:

A Companion to the Summa (Vol. I - The Architect of the Universe) pp. 1 - 457, 1945. (Vol. II - The Pursuit of Happiness); pp. 1- 467, 1945. (Vol III - The Fullness of Life); pp. 1-530, 1956; (Vol IV - The Way of Life); pp. 1- 464, 1949 by Walter Farrel, O.P., S.T.D., S.T.M., Member of the Thomistic Institute. New York, Sheed & Ward.

It is very revealing and significant in writing about St. John of the Cross as a spiritual director to note that he had been selected by St. Teresa of Avila - when she was already fifty-two years of age and he a mere twenty-five years of age - to be the spiritual director of her and for many of the sisters in the Foundations of the Carmelite Order under her supervision. She had been very instrumental in founding many of these, by the grace and love of God, throughout Spain. St. John of the Cross graciously honored her request to perform this service of spiritual direction, even though he was at the same time carrying out his own multiplicity of duties in the Carmelite Order as spiritual director, administrator, organizer, planner, and teacher. During this same time he performed many works of mercy for people in need: poor, middle class, or the rich. He frequently extended a helping hand to many persons whom others had turned down as regards their seeking spiritual direction or assistance, including many among the poor. We can find a clear congruity of a profoundly, intimate spiritual development shared by these two great saints; St. John of the Cross and St. Teresa of Avila. Both were outstanding for their proven competence as spiritual directors for others, and their undying deep devotion to God, despite their undergoing extremely severe spiritual and physical suffering throughout their lives.

There are many persons eagerly seeking spiritual direction who, for a variety of reasons, are not as receptive to obtaining spiritual direction from a number of books or from other literary devices, which have to be prayerfully and diligently studied over long periods of time, perhaps for many years. I therefore fervently hope that the materials I have presented here will prove useful to such persons.

The principal works of these remarkable saints and spiritual directors which I have made use of in preparing this book are quite lengthy: St. Teresa of Avila (2200 pages); St. John of the Cross (800 pages); St. Francis of Sales (367 pages); and Thomas a Kempis (474 pages). I have attempted to so compose the materials presented here in such a way that the readers of this book, have seriously prayed and studied the spiritual teaching of these spiritual directors, will then be inspired to go directly to consult their original works. An index arranged alphabetically is provided at the end of the book to show the specific subjects covered. The reader can simply refer directly to the chapter devoted to each spiritual director and very quickly select the subject which is of immediate or more direct interest to him. For those who wish to further study the works of these devout and learned spiritual directors which I have used as references, I have provided specific and explicit references for all the direct quotations and summarized sayings. In reference to this last statement, I wish to explain briefly the system of references which I have used, thusly. I have attempted throughout this study to provide as explicitly and concisely as I could the spiritual principles of direction, as well as a few devotional prayers collected from the works of these brilliant four spiritual directors and beautiful saints of God. Some of them are quite lengthy, for example, those by St. Francis de Sales. Some are very brief, but very cogent in their expression. However, as I prepared them I found that, although in very many instances, I could quote the saints exactly in their own words, in some instances I had to formulate the spiritual principle of direction in such a way as would make it more intelligible to the reader. For example, because Thomas a Kempis had used a style which was the mode of writing in his time, his choice of words here and there would tend sometimes to obscure the clarity of the meaning intended. In such instances, being certain of the meaning truly intended from having studied his entire work intensively, I added a word or two, or perhaps a phrase to sharpen the clarity of meaning intended. In the instance of St. Teresa of Avila, I would sometimes include a parenthetical note, usually in brackets, to more sharply bring into focus the saint's original thinking on a particular spiritual principle of direction In some of the points of spiritual direction being presented I found repetitiveness of the same thought throughout various places in the three volumes of St. Teresa of Avila. Also, I would find a clear coincidence of a similar thought shared by all three or four of the saints, as well as that shared with St. Thomas Aquinas. When such repetitiveness or recurrence of thought occurred I marked in the place of reference an asterisk, thistle: (*). This indicated that I drew that specific material from varied sources from among the works of several of these saints. In some instances I summed up considerable material found in many pages of the same source in order not to burden the reader with reading too much extraneous material not of serious import as regards to spiritual direction. I believe when the readers of this work read the original works of the saints cited, they will agree that I have faithfully adhered very closely to the truth of what each saint said exactly regarding principles of spiritual direction. In some instances I have repeated a principle of spiritual direction because it could be categorized under two different subject headings, for example, "Mystical Theology" and "Prayer".

For the majority of persons, religious or laity, our daily life responsibilities, tasks trials, and tribulations simply do not leave us enough time, or the luxury to prayerfully study and absorb the spiritual direction provided in the works of these saints - works which would so enrich the spiritual development of their lives. Having this in mind, therefore, I have attempted to provide insights into the spiritual direction offered by these beautiful saints which would be of sufficient value for such persons until such time as they can devote more intensive prayerful study to their original collected works. To use a metaphor, I have attempted to provide a springboard whereby the persons who have read this book will then perhaps "plunge" deeper into the deep waters of the rich pool of spiritual direction which they have provided us in their original works. The works cited have been beautifully translated into the English language from the Latin, French, and Spanish languages by very competent translators. If I have succeeded in providing such a springboard, I thank God.

St. John of the Cross has stated that each soul will differ from another sometimes by as much as one half. He also states, as remarked above, that God leads souls to Him: 1)kindly; 2) in an orderly way; and 3) according to the soul's unique mode of receptivity to his love and grace which He freely gives to all who ask for it. He also states that God, in raising a soul from sin to a purity of heart which He so lovingly and strongly desires, that is, a soul filled with His love and grace, performs a far greater act of His divine powers than He does in creating the soul itself.

I have attempted to present the material in this book in such a way, that it will, hopefully, inspire the readers of this book to refer to that spiritual director whom they believe attracts them most at their particular stage of spiritual development in life. As stated earlier above, there are many persons who simply do not easily take to reading works of spiritual direction with the intensity of concentration required, and thereby profiting from them as they would desire. These are persons who are more readily instructed through good, competent priests, theologians, teachers or preachers, or through well-prepared religious tapes of instructions, audio-visual media of communication such as television, discussion groups, spiritual counseling sessions, person-to-person spiritual direction from qualified spiritual directors, specially designed video programs, Bible study groups, and other various modern means of communication available today in such great abundance. If so, perhaps, these are the paths of spiritual direction they should take instead. However, I have structured my presentation of materials in such a way that, hopefully, it will appeal to a very broad spectrum of persons who do prayerfully, and with concentrated effort, read works of spiritual direction. I fervently hope that my contribution will be especially referred to by all those religious and laity who themselves will seriously undertake an "Apostolate of Spiritual Direction" as an essential part of their daily life activity.

As stated earlier above I highly recommend the spiritual direction of St. John of the Cross because of its very systematic and thorough orderly guidance of the directee by the spiritual director through the various stages of spiritual development. St. John of the Cross refers to the stages of spiritual development the directee proceeds through as: 1) Beginners; 2) Proficients; and 3) Advanced or Perfected.

Therefore, I would strongly recommend to all the readers of this book to additionally read the *Collected Works* (one volume) of *St. John of the Cross* cited in the bibliography. They will thereby, I am confident, profit much more as regards their spiritual development. I state this, because the "Sanjuanist Spirituality," that is, the spiritual direction of St. John of the Cross, *while it recognizes the importance of external actions and conduct,* at the same time very systematically, and in considerable, specific detail focuses its spiritual direction upon the internal purification, by the grace and love of God, of the soul itself.

In the material presented here on St. Francis of Sales, I have presented his practical wisdom of spiritual direction which he so brilliantly provides for all persons as they go through their daily lives, regardless of the state of life they may find themselves in. Although the various occupations and professions of life of his day vary considerably, his principles of spiritual direction are still very applicable to all persons (clergy or laity) in whatever occupations in life they may be working, no matter how menial or exalted they may be, whether it be a pope, cardinal, bishop, priest, brother, sister in the Catholic religious life, a rabbi in the Jewish faith, a minister of the Christian faiths, or Muslim, Buddhist, or Taoist religious. They will prove useful to the president of a nation, a governor of a state, a mayor of a city; or to a plumber, electrician, carpenter, a ditch digger, bus driver, refuse collector, janitor, bookkeeper, secretary, psychologist, social worker or a president of a corporation. St. Francis of Sales, if he were living today, would, I am certain, provide excellent, personal loving spiritual direction to all of the people, for he wrote for all of them.

Throughout the book I have presented as explicitly as I could the principles of spiritual direction of St. Francis of Sales, St. Teresa of Avila, and those of Thomas a Kempis in the same format. However, as regards St. John of the Cross, I have, of necessity, employed a different form of presentation. Thus, in Chapter V which is devoted entirely to St. John of the Cross, I have included three articles, one published earlier in the *Carmelite Digest* (Vol. 4, No. 4, Autumn 1989; pp. 19-32: "A Spiritual Director for All Time for All"). This article is the result of a six year prayerful effort of study of which the final objective was to prepare a very condensed summary of the main underlying principles of the spiritual direction and mystical theology of St. John of the Cross as found in his *Collected Works* (one volume); published and sold by ICS Publications, The Institute of Carmelites Studies, Washington, D.C. The second part of Chapter V is a summarized narrative of his personal life experiences, academic background, as well as some personal observation of my own as an admirer of this great saint and brilliant spiritual director. The third part of Chapter V consists of St. John of the Cross' clear, classic explanation of how persons can determine if they have entered the stage of the pure contemplative life, as compared with a stage of spiritual development in which a person is prayerfully engaged in a spiritual life of meditation, or else is alternating between a meditative and contemplative life of prayer to God. I was indeed very fortunate to have the good and wonderfully cooperative Daughter of St. Paul publish the third part as an article in their fine publication *Inner Horizons, a Magazine of Spirituality* (Fall Issue, 1989, pp 42-44; "Spiritual Development and St. John of the Cross") I am grateful to them and to all those fine people of the *Carmelite Digest* staff who have so generously assisted me in my Apostolate of making more available to a wider public of all faiths the works of this brilliant spiritual director.

The material in Chapter V on St. John of the Cross has been arranged in a way so as to encourage the reader to go directly to the *Collected Works of St. John of the Cross* (one volume), and to personally, prayerfully study them in the original, translated form. I believe that in this way the full benefit of the spiritual direction of this remarkable person will be most effectively absorbed, understood, and then, hopefully, put into actual daily practice. Because the principles of spiritual direction of this brilliant spiritual director are already so explicitly elaborated upon in his *Collected Works,* I decided that this was the most desirable form for presenting his teachings of spiritual direction in this book. Many of the principles of the other three spiritual directors whose spiritual wisdom is presented throughout this book are also those of St. John of the Cross. However, in the spiritual direction of St. John of the Cross he explicitly describes the important role which the operative faculties (the senses, the memory, intellect, the will, the imagination, and the vegetative, or animal, the psychological and the spiritual) of the soul play in the spiritual development of the soul, that is, the whole person; for the soul, a pure spirit permeates the entire body. St. John of the Cross also shows the clear interaction between the inferior (or lower, sensory part of the soul), and of the superior (or upper, spiritual part of the soul). The word *part* is used here only as a fragile, stylistic instrument of human description, for the soul is a pure spirit, without parts.

In the *Collected Works of St. John of the Cross* the "Sanjuanist Spirituality" as it is commonly referred to is presented in very great detail. Not only are the principles of spiritual direction explained, but underlying, fundamental reasoning for them is also given. As stated earlier above, the "Sanjuanist Spirituality" has as its principal objective the internal purification of the soul (heart) from which proceed all of its appetites for all un-Godly things whatever they may be, whether they originate from the world, the flesh, or the devil. However, it needs to be emphasized that *in this "Sanjuanist Spirituality" external actions or conduct are not de-emphasized,* on the contrary, in this form of spirituality we see clearly that our external actions are in reality clear reflection of what lies deep within our soul (heart). Thus, any selfish self-love which exists in the soul, contrary to the love of God and therefore of our neighbor and our own very selves, will be reflected in our external actions. Self-love can very subtly deceive ones own soul and make it believe that is a true love for God. Self-love thus can be one of the worst enemies we face in striving to achieve a true, pure love of God. It is only God whose omniscience encompasses a perfect knowledge of what lies deep in each soul who can truly interpret every single external action of ours and our innermost thoughts - external actions which are often very confusing or deceptive indeed to those around us, and even to those intimately in daily contact with us, when we attempt to understand them; or to ourselves judge our own personal actions in order to better understand them.

The entire structure underlying the "Sanjuanist Spirituality" owes its origin to a keen analysis of the manner in which God purifies the soul. It offers us very keen insights, therefore, into our own very soul, thanks to the grace and love of God, and to persons such as St. John of the Cross who have been endowed with such remarkable gifts in sharing partially in God's omniscience of seeing the soul as it truly is at all times. In this regard it can be truly said that St. John of the Cross in his great devotion to God, in his saintliness, and in his brilliance as an interpreter of Holy Scripture has made a tremendous contribution to Mystical Theology (that is, secret divine wisdom, secret divine understanding, or secret divine knowledge):

St. John of the Cross, in his *Collected Works*, devotes considerable reference to the heavy responsibilities of those who are by virtue of their responsibilities (clergy and laity) assigned the serious tasks at one time or another of acting as the spiritual directors of other persons. He stresses the serious nature of such responsibilities entrusted to such spiritual directors, and calls attention to the fact that God will hold them responsible for the way in which they utilize the gifts and talents of spiritual direction which he has given them. He points out in the passage cited below how diversified such spiritual directors may be in gifts and talents given to them:

> "Not everyone capable of hewing the wood knows how to carve the statue, nor does everyone able to carve know how to perfect and polish the work, nor do all who know how to polish know how to paint it, nor do all who can paint it know how to put the finishing touches on it and bring the work to completion. No man can do more with the statue than what he knows how to do, and were he to try to do more than this he would ruin it" (See p.632, *Collected Works*).

Despite his many varied responsibilities in the religious community St. John of the Cross did specifically choose as his true life's vocation an "Apostolate of Spiritual Direction." In this vocation he offered his services to all who came to him regardless of their status in life. Often he would give his attention to those persons who had been to others seeking help, including many among the poorer classes. Having died at the relatively young age of forty-nine, during the last fourteen years of his life (from age thirty-six to age forty-nine) he had already formulated in the fiery crucible of his soul his "Sanjuanist Spirituality", which, by the grace and love of Jesus Christ, he was able to bring to fruition in writing as found in his *Collected Works* before he died. He thereby gave to all of his followers in the religious community and to those among the laity in the secular world great riches of his spiritual direction. He is truly "A Spiritual Director for All Time for All."

Some General Remarks

Although the materials presented in this book have been taken from authors who, coincidentally, were all Catholics, and three of whom, as stated above were canonized as Saints in the Catholic Church, it should not be assumed by readers of this book that it has been written exclusively for Catholic readers. On the contrary, much of the subject matter on the subjects of: "Spiritual Development," "Spiritual Directors", and "Spiritual Direction" contained here can be utilized and practically applied by persons of all other faiths throughout the world; by the Muslims, Buddhists, Taoists, Jewish, or others. I state this unhesitatingly, for many of the principles of spiritual direction presented here are applicable to each human soul throughout the world regardless of their faith. Each human being wherever he or she exists in this world is very profoundly affected by the religious, educational, cultural, economic, geographical, social, and so forth, milieus, or environment of life into which he or she have been born, raised, and educated in. However, the basic and fundamental make-up of each of their souls is the same, even though souls will vary considerable in their operation as regards performing actions of good or evil. They also have the same enemies in this warfare of life that all human beings have: the world, the flesh and the devil. Therefore, the principles of spiritual direction presented here, except where they specifically refer to sacred dogma or articles of faith of the Catholic Church, can be used in practical everyday application by every person, that is, spiritually speaking by every soul throughout the world.

When the spiritual directors cited above were in the process of formulating their thought during their educational, working, or life experiences, lives of persevering prayer, and suffering of all kinds, they borrowed generously in many instances from fundamental basic truths relating to human beings; from their activities in the world they lived in, and their knowledge of the whole world, this earth, and eternal world beyond it of the universe as we know it physically. Thus is was that St. Thomas Aquinas filtered through his brilliant mind the best and the most true knowledge of that, also brilliant, great Greek philosopher and somewhat of a scientist in his own right, Aristotle, a pagan, and then synthesized it with the best tested truths of the outstanding Christian philosophers and theologians, both learned and devout of his time, to formulate his *magnum opus,* the *Summa Theologica.* Aristotle, himself had, of course, build upon the best knowledge of the learned philosophers or other learned persons who had either preceded him, or who had been contemporaries of his intellectual philosophical community. St. John of the Cross, in turn, throughout his formative early years of education had been exposed to the best writings, teachings, and thinking available in some of the best Catholic educational institutions operating in Spain during the 16th Century in which he lived. In addition to his studies at the Carmelite College, he studied at the University of Salamanca, which at that time (about the 1560's) ranked with the great universities of Bologna, Paris, and Oxford. Thus, when we study the *Collected Works* of St. John of the Cross, we see reflected in the work of this brilliant spiritual director, a coalescing, or a coming together of the thinking, the reasoning, the natural knowledge of the Christian and pagan intellectuals, philosophers, theologians, educators, and other who preceded him.

Of these four spiritual directors cited it was St. John of the Cross who, to a large extent, had, despite his many other serious responsibilities in the religious community, so specifically chosen as his true life's work and "Apostolate of Spiritual Direction." However, the other three persons were in their own unique way also excellent spiritual directors, as I believe a prayerful study of their spiritual wisdom presented here will clearly attest to. For example, St. Francis de Sales had the unique gift of presenting his spiritual direction in such an effective way that it could be applied remarkably well to the particular state of life or profession each person was actually living in or working at. He had a unique gentle touch in guiding souls. St. Teresa of Avila, on the other hand, was remarkable in her ability to give sound practical advice as regards a persevering prayer life and its penetrating influence upon the soul, and the great value of suffering in imitation of our Saviour, Our Redeemer, Jesus Christ. She also, just as did St. John of the Cross, stressed the vital importance of unrelenting, persistent prayer and a resolute determination to love God. Thomas a Kempis in his turn had the unique facility to set forth our Lord and Saviour Jesus Christ constantly before our mind and soul as the unfailing model Whom we should always strive to imitate and follow. He was also a penetrating analyst of human nature, of the human soul, and the workings of God's grace in our lives. St. John of the Cross combined in his unique way all of these gifts and talents of these excellent spiritual directors referred to, while at the same time he made available to us a unique form of a very systematic spiritual direction: the "Sanjuanist Spirituality" which I have attempted to clearly explain in Chapter V of this book - a chapter devoted to St. John of the Cross exclusively.

St. John of the Cross in his spiritual direction stresses the importance of having good spiritual directors in our lives, and he emphasizes the serious responsibility which persons (religious or laity) have before God for the spiritual direction of others. I cited above a quotation of his in which he points out, so to speak, that there are "spiritual directors" and there are spiritual directors, just as today there are "doctors" and there are doctors, "economists" and economists. Some spiritual directors have competence in providing spiritual direction as regards certain problems of a spiritual nature, while these very same spiritual directors may prove to be incompetent as regards giving proper spiritual direction regarding other spiritual problems to persons at various stages of spiritual development. This is why in seeking out spiritual direction it is very necessary to exercise considerable prudence as to whom we go to when seeking spiritual direction. We may quite often, more often than we would wish, have to find different persons to consult with for spiritual direction, depending on the nature of the spiritual problems we are confronted with. The selection of the wrong spiritual director may lead us into many a serious error as regards our personal spiritual development.

I have attempted to present the best of the principles of spiritual direction of these very devout and learned persons. Their principles of spiritual direction cover such a very broad spectrum of spiritual situations and problems encountered by people in all walks of daily life, that each person prayerfully reading this book, will hopefully, find here principles of spiritual direction relevant to their spiritual needs at various particular stages in their lives. In the instance of St. John of the Cross, the special uniqueness of his mode of spiritual direction made me decide, as regards my description of his life's background and of his spiritual direction, to summarize for the reader the entire *Collected Works of St. John of the Cross* (one volume) in a way so as to capture the fundamental or basic themes of his spiritual direction, which are the foundation of the "Sanjuanist Spirituality." My main objective in doing this was to, hopefully, inspire the readers to themselves prayerfully study the original *Collected Works* of his. The reason for this mode of treatment was mainly that I could not extract the principles of St. John of the Cross in such an encapsulated or abbreviated form as I did with the other three spiritual directors mentioned. For his principles of spiritual direction are interwoven amidst considerable specific, very detailed, but vitally necessary explanatory material. Some of the principles of spiritual direction of St. John of the Cross have already been presented by the other spiritual directors cited in this book - but in a very simplified, more quotable form of presentation.

I have intentionally, with the exception of St. John of the Cross, not included any descriptive material within this book on the lives of St. Francis of Sales or of St. Teresa of Avila. So many excellent works on their lives have already been written that I could add but very little other than what I have already stated about them here. As regards Thomas a Kempis, because his work *My Imitation of Christ* is shrouded in such mystery as to its true authorship, there is nothing to say regarding him except that this beautiful inspirational spiritual work speaks to us so eloquently of a very devout and indeed very learned person; of a truly beautiful soul and outstanding spiritual director. In Chapter IV I have provided a brief biographical sketch of his life according to one of the most recent historical accounts available.

It is necessary that the readers of this book keep in mind that some of the spiritual direction cited clearly reflects an earlier, middle, or later period in the life of the authors as they progressed in their spiritual development. This important point is particularly true as regards St. Teresa of Avila, and very much less so as regards the other three spiritual directors. Thus, St. John of the Cross, for example, had written his work of spiritual direction as contained in his *Collected Works* (one volume) looking back upon his life, when he had by the grace and love of God, attained to a very high stage of spiritual development before his death. The last fourteen years of his life, therefore, indicate clearly a steady, spiritual path and pattern of spiritual development which he was following guided by the Holy Spirit.

In my interpolations where I have used the word "NOTE", I very often am drawing on the spiritual direction of all four of the spiritual directors cited in this book, and upon the theology of St. Thomas Aquinas, as found in his work the *Summa Theologica* so brilliantly interpreted by the great scholar and interpreter of the *Summa*, the good Rev. Fr. Walter Farrel of blessed memory whose complete four volume works I have cited above. Although I may not always name all four spiritual directors specifically, if there had existed a contradiction among them regarding some spiritual principles, theology, or advice given, I would state the contradiction (which it was rarely necessary to do). I would try to elaborate on the contradiction as best I could in my "NOTE" of interpolation. A few of these "NOTES" have actually been taken from explanatory footnotes to be found at the end of the three-volume works of St. Teresa of Avila. In the instance of Teresa it needs to be clearly understood that there existed certain most extraordinary qualities relating to saintliness; extraordinary in that she had received many profound Revelations from God, or His intercessors. Only God knows how they were transmitted to her. These Revelations which transcend any natural or even supernatural knowledge reveal some of the most profound communications as regarding, for example: the Holy Trinity, Angels, Saints, living and deceased; as well as on subjects such as heaven, purgatory, and hell. From my experience in prayerfully studying the works of all four spiritual directors, I would strongly recommend that is would be prudent to first study the *Collected Works of St.*

John of the Cross before undertaking the prayerful study of the *Collected Works of St. Teresa of Avila.* The readers would thereby spare themselves much confusion in understanding, and much false or deceptive interpretation of St. Teresa of Avila's unique form of spirituality found there.

In order to more precisely identify, describe, and discuss such important subjects of the spiritual life as, for example: humility, fear, prayer, self-love, God, grace, suffering, mystical theology, Holy Scripture (the Bible), virtues, vices, the senses, the memory, intellect, will, the supernatural virtues of faith, hope, and love, trust, the imagination, and so forth, I have placed them under specific subject categories arranged alphabetically for quick easy reference. The category "Spiritual Direction" quite frequently is somewhat of a general category, which contains treatment of not only a number of these subjects collectively, but also contains spiritual direction in terms of suggested courses of action to be taken as regards one's own personal spiritual development.

Unlike the presentation of the principles of the spiritual direction of St. Francis de Sales, I have presented the spiritual direction of St. Teresa of Avila quite differently. Whereas I presented the principles of spiritual direction of St. Francis de Sales as they were actually taught by him in the style of a teacher, that is, St. Francis de Sales speaking to the soul in love with God (*Philothea,* * as he calls her - a soul aspiring to achieve a greater devotion in her love for God, in a series of instructions), I have presented the spiritual direction of St. Teresa of Avila and of Thomas a Kempis in a somewhat different form of exposition.

In the presentation of the principles of spiritual direction of St. Teresa of Avila, I have stylistically composed them in accordance with the narrative of her life and its spiritual development. Unlike St. Francis de Sales, Teresa does not provide us with a systematic, smooth flowing spiritual body of knowledge as regards spiritual direction as St. Francis de Sales did in his excellent book of spiritual direction: *Introduction to a Devout Life.* Instead, Teresa's principles of spiritual direction had to be drawn forth by me from the narrative of her entire life as it develops, with its spiritual "ups and downs", its trials and tribulations, its joys and

---

* It is conjectured by some authors that Philothea is actually St. Jane de Chantal to whom St. Francis de Sales gave much spiritual direction; they were very close friends.

sufferings; also from her many narratives of her spiritual and other temporal experiences of life as she progressed throughout her life. They were drawn from the three volumes of her life which present a vivid account of the resolute, determined persevering warfare which she wages, by the grace and love of God, against those powerful enemies of the soul - the world, the flesh, and the devil. The world conquered by unyielding hope, the flesh conquered by the supernatural virtue of love, and the devil conquered by an unshakable faith. As St. John of the Cross teaches us in Chapter V, the world is the enemy most easily conquered, the devil the most difficult to conquer because he is so difficult to understand in his lies, deceptions, and deceits, and the flesh, the most tenacious enemy to conquer for it clings to us fighting us unto the end.

St. Francis de Sales lived from 1563 to 1622 and reportedly reclaimed to the Catholic Faith seventy-two thousand persons according to the source cited in the bibliography. Many of these persons were inhabitants of Chablais, and other areas bordering on Geneva who had fallen away into the serious errors of Calvinism. His bishop at the time, Grenerius, had chosen him to preach to them, having recognized in him the brilliance of an excellent evangelist and spiritual director.

In the spiritual direction which St. Francis de Sales handed down to us, to our good fortune, he states that his advice may seem hard in theory, but will be sweeter than honey or sugar when put into actual practice. I personally certainly agree with his evaluation of his own spiritual direction. In describing his spiritual direction I have presented the material basically, exactly as he wrote it, with a few exceptions. My presentation may be termed as the do's and don'ts as regards the spiritual life and the attainment of a great devotion of love for God. The main emphasis is on the do's while the few don'ts serve as precautions or warnings to the soul. I have attempted to present as accurately as I could each of his principles or precepts of spiritual direction. My main reference source for the material presented is one which I have chosen from among others of St. Francis de Sales as being most suitable for this publication. This is the work:

Introduction to a Devout Life. From the French of *St. Francis de Sales, Bishop and Prince of Geneva,* to which is prefixed an abstract of his life. Frederick Postet & Co. Printers to the Holy Apostolic See and the Sacred Congregation of Rites. Ratisbon, Rome, New York, Cincinnati:

pp. 1-367 (With Table of Contents, But Without An Index; No Date).

My main, sole focus here has been upon his principles of spiritual direction, or as he himself refers to them as his theories of spiritual direction, or precepts. As the reader will note, some few of his precepts or teachings appear as pithy, short, but very meaningful and instructive maxims among his longer precepts of spiritual direction. Some of his spiritual direction, for example, on love, friendship, marriage, humility, and so forth, although quite lengthy is full of profound spiritual advice. His analogies, metaphors, comparisons, and other literary devices of instruction are so strikingly unique, as the reader will perceive, that I decided to retain them in their entirety. While they are very pertinent for today's times, they at the same time provide the readers with very interesting, piquant insights into the historical period of the time in which he lived.

As the reader prayerfully reads and studies the spiritual direction of St. Francis de Sales certain points should be kept in mind. Although much of what will be read of his direction here can be readily applied by persons in the religious life, this wonderful spiritual director adroitly designed his instructions , having in mind, common, ordinary people in all walks of life both within the religious communities and outside of them. Thus, it has a broad application to the masses of people going about their daily occupations in the secular world, while at the same time it is extremely valuable to both religious and laity who are seriously involved in providing spiritual direction or counsel to others in whatever state of life they may be working in. St. Francis de Sales states that as the fire-fly can pass often through flames without burning its wings, so a resolute and devout soul can by applying his precepts, fly through the flames of earthly temptations and sins without burning its wings of a holy desire to lead a devout life. By a devout life, he means a soul which aspires to not only climb the mountain of God's love in order to draw closer and closer to Him with a pure heart, but also on which actually aspires to reach the pinnacle of that mountain, that is, to penetrate deep into the most Sacred Heart of Jesus, Who is closer to us than we are to ourselves. He is in the depths of our own very soul. However, as St. John of the Cross counseled, He is a hidden God Whom we must search for and seek out in our own very soul here upon earth, rather than to look for Him in heaven. For we ourselves are the living temple of God where He always resides, never moving, although by the mysterious comings and goings of His grace it would seem that He does move within the soul.

Some very scientific observations made by St. Francis de Sales designed to bring out more pointedly, graphically, the principles of spiritual direction he is explaining may conceivably be erroneous, this is especially applicable to those relating to the botanical and biological sciences. Not being a scientist, I was in no position to challenge such scientific observations. They do provide an intriguing historical flavor. The readers of this book can use their own judgment as to their truth in the light of the fantastic new scientific developments and findings which have occurred since his times of over 300 years ago. They were so picturesque and interesting in giving the flavor of the life of his times, that I decided they should be retained, there are but a few of these accounts. Perhaps many of them are scientifically true according to our present state of knowledge in the sciences mentioned. The readers of this work can draw their own conclusions in this regard.

St. Francis de Sales included in his spiritual direction so much of the wisdom of Holy Scripture references and interpretation, and cited as well the wisdom of various saints and persons of extraordinary knowledge and wisdom, that I decided to retain as much of this richness in this work as possible. Some passages may therefore be lengthy for this reason, but they contain considerable penetrating wisdom - I believe the readers will agree - if one meditate or contemplates over them carefully. Some of these passages in their profound love for and observation of God's creatures, for example, bring out some unique spiritual lessons. There occurs a very subtle inculcation within the soul as one reads the counsels of St. Francis de Sales of the gently, but at the same time, firm manner in which he treated the soul and, so to speak, spoke to it.

I personally recommend to all readers of this book that they refer directly in prayerful study to the works of all the spiritual directors I have cited here. This includes also the work of the *Summa Theologica* of St. Thomas Aquinas from whom the four spiritual directors cited in this book have drawn considerably in formulating their own thoughts on spiritual direction. In this regard, I can not express sufficient gratitude to the beloved Rev. Fr. Walter Farrel of blessed memory of the Dominican Order who did so much during his relatively brief lifetime to make the *Summa Theologica* available to all those (religious and secular) in such a simple, clear, easily understood presentation. It contains so many well-chosen analogies, examples, metaphors, comparisons, and other literary devices of style which thereby make it so clearly intelligible to all who are willing to expend a reasonable effort of prayer and study.

As regards the arrangement of the book, I have arranged the largest part of this book so that the reader can refer by subjects, alphabetically arranged, to hundreds of specific various subjects which are of direct interest as regards spiritual development. Under each subject heading (referenced to as the source) will be found what these learned and devout spiritual directors had to say regarding each specific subject. By utilizing an orderly alphabetical arrangement of the material I have thereby composed a very simple index by subject. This will enable readers to quickly refer to the specific subject of interest listed under each name of the spiritual director who has provided spiritual direction on that subject.

Finally, I wish to express my considerable gratitude to the good Revs. Frs. Kieran Kavanaugh, O.C.D. and Otilio Rodriquez, O.C.D. who did such excellent work in translating from the *Collected Works of St. John of the Cross*★ (one volume), and of *St. Teresa of Avila*★★ (three volumes).

I could never have prepared this book without the tremendous contribution, the great labor of love of these wonderful priests, and especially of course without the grace and love of God, the Holy Spirit guiding me. For God does it all but without our humble cooperation

---

★ *THE COLLECTED WORKS OF ST. JOHN OF THE CROSS.* Translated by Kieran Kavanaugh, O.C.D. and Otilio Rodriguez, O.C.D. ICS Publications, Institute of Carmelite Studies, Washington, DC; 1979, pp 1-774.

★★ *THE COLLECTED WORKS OF ST. TERESA OF AVILA.* (Volume One - the Book of Her Life, Spiritual Testimonies, Soliloquies), 1976: pp. 1- 406. (Volume Two - The Way of Perfection, Meditations on the Song of Songs, The Interior Castle), 1980; pp. 1- 554. (Volume Three - The Book of Her Foundations, Minor Works), 1985' pp 1-483. All three volumes translated by Kieran Kavanaugh, O.C.D. and Otilio Rodriguez, O.D.D. ICS Publications, Institute of Carmelite Studies, Washington, DC, Washington Province of Discalced Carmelite.

with His grace and love nothing is done. I also wish to express my gratitude to my brothers and sisters in Christ of the Confraternity of the Precious Blood for the book on Thomas a Kempis.*

Finally, I wish to thank the Rev. Monsignor Ralph J. Kuehner (now in the 43rd year of his priesthood) for his graciousness in reviewing the entire manuscript for me, despite his many work responsibilities in the Washington Archdiocese, and his additional priestly duties at the St. Francis of Assisi Church in Derwood, Md. where he is a resident priest. He undertook to read the entire work carefully and to write the FOREWARD. I am especially indebted to him because he brought to the review of what is now a completed book a profound knowledge of Holy Scripture, and a very intimate knowledge of the work of the four spiritual directors cited. At the same time while reviewing the work he encouraged and inspired me to continue on to bring it to completion. I am grateful for this and for his subsequently agreeing to write the FOREWARD after having spent considerable time reading the manuscript.

I fervently hope that the readers of this book will be inspired to delve more deeply into the original works of these brilliant spiritual directors and faithful devoted friends of God, whose friendship with God and their expression of it has enriched our resources of spiritual direction, and hopefully will stimulate among both the clergy and laity the serious undertaking of choosing an "Apostolate of Spiritual Direction" as one of their life's principal vocations just as St. John of the Cross did.

**My Imitation of Christ* by Thomas a Kempis. Revised Translation. Confraternity of the Precious Blood. Rt. Rev. Msgr. Joseph B. Frey, Director: Brooklyn, 19, N.Y., May 1954: pp. 1-474.

St. Francis de Sales

SPIRITUAL DIRECTION OF
ST. FRANCIS DE SALES

Source: *Introduction to a Devout Life*

From the French of

St. Francis de Sales

Bishop and Prince of Geneva

To Which is Prefixed
An abstract of His Life; pp. 1-367
Frederick Postet & Co.
Printers to the Holy Apostolic See and
the Sacred Congregation of Rites
Ratisborn, Rome, New York, Cincinnati
Printed in USA [No Publication Date]

ANGELS: As Intercessors

"Make yourself familiar with the angels, and behold them frequently in spirit; for, without being seen, they are at present with you. Always bear a particular love and reverence towards the angel of the diocese wherein you dwell, and of the persons with whom you live;

but especially towards you own guardian angel. Address yourself to them, honor and praise them, and make use of their assistance and succor in all your affairs, spiritual or temporal, that they may cooperate with your intentions." (ST. FRANCIS DE SALES; p.98)

ANGER: Discussion of Remedies Against and
The Cultivation of Meekness.

"The holy chrism, which, by apostolic tradition, we use in the Church of God for confirmations and consecrations, is composed of oil of olives mingled with balm, which, amongst other things, represents to us the two favorite and well-beloved virtues which shone forth in the sacred person of our Lord, and which he has strenuously recommended to us; as if by them our hearts ought to be in a particular manner consecrated to his service, and dedicated to his imitation. 'Learn of me,' says He 'for I am meek and humble of heart.' Humility perfects us with respect to God; and meekness with regard to our neighbor. The balm, which, as I have before observed, always sinks beneath all other liquors, represents humility; and the oil of olives, that swims above, represents meekness and mildness, which surmount all things, and excel amongst virtues as being the flower of charity, which, according to St. Bernard is then in its perfection, when it is not only patient, but also meek and mild. But take care, that this mystical chrism, compounded of meekness and humility, be within your heart, for it is one of the great artifices of the enemy to make many deceive themselves with the expressions and exterior appearance of these two virtues, who, not examining thoroughly their interior affections, think themselves to be humble and meek; whereas, in effect, there are no virtues to which they have less pretensions. This may be easily discovered for, notwithstanding all their ceremonious mildness and humility, at the least cross word, or smallest injury, they exhibit an unparalleled arrogance. It is said that these who have taken the preservation which is commonly called, 'the grace of St. Paul', do not swell when they are bitten and stung by a viper, provided the preservation be of the best sort; in like manner, when humility and meekness are good and true, they preserve us from that swelling and burning heat which injuries are wont to raise in our hearts. But if, being stung and bitten by detractors and enemies, we swell, and are enraged, it is a certain sign that neither our humility nor meekness is true and sincere, but only apparent and artificial."

"That holy and illustrious patriarch Joseph, sending back his brethren from Egypt to his father's house, gave them this only advise: 'Be not angry with one another by the way.' I say the same to you. This wretched life is but a journey to the happy life to come; let us not, then, be angry with each other by the way, but rather march on with the troop of our brethren and companions, meekly, peaceably, and lovingly; nay, I say to you, absolutely and without exception, be not angry at all if it be possible, and admit no pretext whatsoever to open the gate of your heart to so destructive a passion; for St. James tells us positively, and without reservation, 'The anger of man works not the justice of God.' We must indeed resist evil, and restrain the vices of those that are under our charge constantly and courageously but yet with meekness and compassion. Nothing so soon appeases the enraged elephant as the sight of a little lamb, and nothing so easily breaks the force of a cannon shot as wool. We do not value so much the correction which proceeds from passion though it be accompanied with reason, as that which proceeds from reason alone; for the reasonable soul, being naturally subject to reason is never subject to passion but through tyranny; and, therefore, when reason is accompanied by passion she makes herself odious, her just government being debased by the fellowship of tyranny. Princes do honor to their people, and make them rejoice exceedingly, when they visit them with a peaceable train; but when they come at the head of armies, though it be for the common good, their visits are always disagreeable; for although they cause military discipline to be rigorously observed among their soldiers, yet they can never do it so effectually but that some disorders will always happen, by which the peasant will be a sufferer. In like manner as long as reason rules and peaceably exercises chastisements, corrections and reprehensions, although severely and exactly, every one loves and approves it; but when she brings anger, passion, and rage which St. Austin calls her soldiers, along with her, she rather makes herself feared than loved and even her own disordered heart is always the sufferer. 'It is better,' says the same St. Austin, writing to Profuturus, 'to deny entrance to just and reasonable anger, than to admit to it, be it every so little; because, being once admitted, it with difficulty is driven out again; for it enters as a little twig, and in a moment becomes a beam; and if it can but once gain the night of us, and the sun set upon it, which the apostle forbids, it turns into a hatred, from which we have scarce means to rid ourselves, for it nourishes itself under a thousand false pretexts, since there was never an angry man that thought this anger unjust.'"

"It is better then, to attempt to find the way to live without anger, than pretend to make a moderate and discreet use of it, and when, through our imperfections and frailty, we find ourselves surprised, it is better to drive it away speedily than enter into a parley; for, if we give it ever so little leisure, it will become mistress of the place, like the serpent, who easily draws in his whole body where he can once get in his head."

"But how shall I banish it? you may say. You must at the first alarm speedily muster your forces; not violently, not tumultuously, but mildly, and yet seriously; for as we hear the ushers in public halls and courts of justice crying Silence, make more noise than the whole assembly; so it frequently happens that, by endeavoring with violence to restrain our anger, we stir up more trouble in our heart than wrath has excited before; and the heart, being thus agitated, can be no longer master of itself. After this meek effort practice the advice which St. Austin, in his old age, gave the young Bishop Auxilius. 'Do, says he, 'that which a man should do, if that befall you of which the man of God speaks in the Psalms; My eye is troubled with wrath.' Have recourse to God crying out, 'Have mercy on me, O Lord!' that he may stretch forth his right hand to repress your anger. I mean we must invoke the assistance of God, when we find ourselves excited to wrath, in imitation of the apostles when they were tossed by the wind and the storm upon the waters; for he will command our passions to cease, and a great calm shall ensue. But the prayer which is made against present and pressing anger must always be performed calmly, and not violently; and they must be observed in all the remedies against this evil. Moreover, as soon as ever you perceive yourself guilty, perform an act of meekness towards the same person against whom your were angry. For, as it is a sovereign remedy against a lie to contradict it upon the spot as soon as we perceive we have told it, so we must repair anger instantly by a contrary act of meekness; for fresh wounds are most easily cured."

"Again, when your mind is in a state of tranquillity, supply yourself with meekness, speaking all your words, and doing all your actions, little and great, in the mildest manner possible, calling to mind, that as the Spouse in the Canticles has not only honey in her lips, on her tongue, and in her breast, but milk also, so we must not only have our words sweet towards our neighbor, but also our whole breast; that is to say, the whole interior of our soul; neither must we have the aromatic and fragrant sweetness of honey only, viz., the sweetness of civil conversation with strangers, but also the sweetness of milk amongst our family and neighbors; in which those greatly fail, who in the street seem to be angels, and in their houses demons." (ST. FRANCIS DE SALES; pp 152-157)

ANXIETY: Excessive Worry and Concern

"The care and diligence with which we should attend to our concerns must never be confounded with anxiety and solicitude. The angels are careful of our salvation and procure it with diligence, yet they are never agitated by anxiety and solicitude; for care and diligence naturally result from their charity, whereas solicitude and anxiety are utterly incompatible with their felicity; because the former may be accompanied by a calm and tranquil state of mind, whereas the latter never can."

"Be careful and attentive then to all those affairs which God has committed to your care, for such a disposition in you is agreeable to the will of his divine Majesty, without suffering your care and attention to degenerate into inquietude or anxiety; be not flurried about them, for an over-solicitude disturbs the reason and judgment, and prevents us from doing that properly for the execution of which we are so eager and anxious."

"When our Lord reprehended Martha, He said: 'Martha, Martha, thou are solicitous, and art troubled about many things.' You must here observe, that she would not have been "troubled" had she been but merely diligent; but, being over-concerned and disquieted, she hurried and troubled herself, and therefore received this reprehension from our Lord. As rivers, that flow slowly through the plains bear large boats and rich merchandise; and the rain, which falls gently in the open fields, makes them fruitful in grass and corn; or, as torrents and rivers, which run rapidly, and overflow the grounds, ruin the bordering country, and render it unprofitable for culture; so, in like manner, vehement and tempestuous rains spoil the fields and meadows. That work is never well executed which is done with too much eagerness and hurry. We must listen leisurely, according to the proverb, 'He that is in haste,' says Solomon, 'is in danger of stumbling.' We perform our actions soon enough when we perform them well. As drones, although they make more noise, and are more eager at work than bees, make only wax, and no honey, so they that hurry themselves with a tormenting anxiety, and eager solicitude, never do much, and the little they do perform is never very profitable."

"As flies do not trouble us by their strength, but their multitudes, so affairs of importance give us not so much trouble as trifling ones, when they are in great number. Undertake, then, all your affairs with a calm and peaceable mind, and endeavor to dispatch them in order, one after another; for if you make an effort to do them all at once, or in disorder, your spirit will be so overcharged and depressed, that it will probably sink under the burden without effecting anything."

"In all your affairs rely wholly on Divine Providence, through which you alone must look for success; labor, nevertheless, quietly on your part, to cooperate with its designs, and then you may be assured, if you trust as you ought in God, the success which shall come to you shall be always that which is the most profitable for you, whether it appear good or bad, according to your private judgment. Imitate little children, who, as they with one hand hold fast by their father, with the other gather strawberries or blackberries along the hedges; so you, gathering and handling the goods of this world with one hand, must with the other always hold fast the hand of your heavenly Father, turning yourself towards him, from time to time, to see if your actions or occupations be pleasing to him; but, above all things, take heed that you never leave his protecting hand, nor think to gather more; for, should he forsake you, you will not be able to go a step further without falling to the ground. My meaning is that amidst those ordinary affairs and occupations, that require not so earnest an attention, you should look more on God than on them; and when they are of such importance as to require your whole attention, that then also you should look from time to time towards God like mariners, who, to arrive at the port to which they are bound look more towards heaven than down on the sea which they sail; thus will God work with you, in you, and for you, and your labor shall be followed with consolation." (ST. FRANCIS DE SALES pp. 161-164)

BODY OF CHRIST OR BLOOD OF CHRIST: The Blessed Sacrament, Its Reception.

"It is not advisable to dissuade generally from it, but it is better to leave it to be regulated by the consideration of the inward state of each individual. Wherefore, as it would be imprudent to advise every one, without distinction, to frequent communion, so it would be imprudent also to blame any one for it, especially if he followed the advice of a prudent director. When daily communion was objected against St. Catherine of Sienna, she returned this modest and graceful answer, 'Since St. Austin blamed it not I pray do not you blame it, and I shall be content.'...to communicate every day, it is necessary we should overcome the greatest part of our evil inclinations, and that it should be by the advice of our spiritual director."

"...for your part, being imperfect, weak and sick, you have need to communicate frequently with Him who is your perfection, your strength, and your physician. Tell them that those who have not many worldly affairs to look after ought to communicate often, because they have leisure; that those who have much business on hand should also communicate often, for he who labors much and is loaded with pains ought to eat solid food, and that frequently. Tell them that you receive the holy sacrament to learn to receive it well; because one hardly performs an action well which he does not often practice."

"Communicate frequently, then, as frequently as you can, with the advice of your ghostly father {NOTE: Spiritual Director};...If wordlings ask you why you communicate so often, tell them it is to learn to love God, to purify yourself from your imperfections, to be delivered from your miseries, to be comforted in your afflictions, and supported in your weaknesses." (ST. FRANCIS DE SALES; pp. 111-115)

CHASTITY: The Necessity, and Various Observations Regarding This Virtue.

"Chastity, the lily of virtues, makes men almost equal to angels. Nothing is beautiful but what is pure, and the purity of men is chastity. Chastity is called honesty, and the possession of it honor; it is also named integrity, and the opposite, vice, corruption. In short, it has its peculiar glory, to be the fair and unspotted virtue of both soul and body."

" It is never lawful to draw an impure pleasure from our bodies in any manner whatsoever, except in lawful marriage, the sanctity of which may, by a just compensation, repair the damage we receive in that delectation; and yet, even in marriage itself, the honesty of the intention must be observed, to the end that, if there be any indecency in the pleasure that is taken, there may be nothing but honesty in the will that takes it."

"The chaste heart is like the mother-pearl, that can receive no drop of water but such as comes from heaven; for it can accept of no pleasure but that of marriage, which is ordained from heaven; out of which it is not allowed so much as to think of it, so as to take a voluntary and deliberate delight in the thought."

"For the first degree of this virtue, beware of admitting any kind of forbidden pleasure, as all those are which are taken out of, or even in, marriage, when they are taken contrary to the rule of marriage. For the second, refrain as much as is possible from all unprofitable and superfluous delights, although lawful and permitted. For the third, set not your affection on pleasures and delights which are ordained and commanded; for though we must take these delectations that are necessary, I mean those which concern the end and institution of holy matrimony, yet we must never set our heart and mind upon them."

"As to the rest, every one stands in great need of this virtue. They that are in the state of widowhood ought to have a courageous chastity, to despise not only present or future objects, but to resist also the impure imaginations which former pleasures, lawfully received in marriage, may produce in their minds, which on this account are more susceptible of unclean allurements. For this cause St. Austin admires the purity of his friend Alipius, who had wholly forgotten and despised the pleasures of the flesh, of which, nevertheless, he had some experience in his youth."

"In effect, as when fruits are entire and sound, they may be preserved, some in straw, some in sand, and some in their own leaves, but being once cut or bruised, it is almost impossible to preserve them but by honey and sugar, in the form of sweetmeats, so untainted chastity may many ways be kept; but, after it has once been violated, nothing can preserve it but an extraordinary devotion, which, as I have often repeated, is the true honey and sugar of the spirit."

"Virgins have need of a chastity extremely sincere, nice, and tender, to banish from their hearts all sorts of curious thoughts, and to despise, with an absolute contempt, all sorts of unclean pleasures; which in truth deserve not to be desired by men, since they are better enjoyed by swine. Let, then, these pure souls be careful never to doubt but that chastity is incomparably better than all that which is incompatible with it; for, as the great St. Jerome says, the enemy violently tempts virgins to desire to make a trial of these pleasures, representing them as infinitely more agreeable and delightful than indeed they are, which often troubles them very much, whilst, as this holy father says, they esteem that more sweet of which they know nothing."

"For as the little butterfly, seeing the flame, hovers with a curiosity about it, to try whether it be as sweet as it is fair, and, being borne away with this fancy, ceases not till it is destroyed at the very first trial; so young people suffer themselves frequently to be so possessed with the false and foolish opinion they have formed of the pleasure of voluptuous desire, that after many curious thoughts they at length ruin themselves, and perish in the flames; more foolish in this than the butterflies, for these have some cause to imagine that the fire is sweet, because it is so beautiful; but those knowing that which they seek to be extremely dishonest, cease not, nevertheless, to set a value of that brutish pleasure."

"But as for those who are married, it is most true, though the vulgar cannot conceive it, that chastity is very necessary, also, for them; because, in respect of them, it consists not in abstaining absolutely from carnal pleasures, but in containing themselves in the midst of pleasures. Now at this commandment, 'Be angry and sin not', is, in my opinion, more difficult to be observed than this, Be not angry; and as one may more easily abstain from anger than regulate it; so it is easier to keep ourselves altogether from carnal pleasures than to preserve a moderation in them. It is true, that the holy liberty of marriage has a particular force to extinguish the fire of concupiscence, but the frailty of them that enjoys this liberty passes easily from permission to dissolution, and from use to abuse; and as we see many rich men steal, not through want but avarice, so also we may observe many married people fall into excess by mere intemperance and incontinence, notwithstanding the lawful object to which they ought and might confine themselves; their concupiscence being like wildfire, which runs burning here and there, without resting in any one place. It is always dangerous to take violent medicines, for if we take more than we would, or if they be not well prepared, they may be attended with fatal consequences. Marriage was blessed and ordained in part as a remedy for concupiscence, and, doubtless, it is a very good remedy, but yet violent, and consequently very dangerous, it if be not used with discretion."

"I add, that the variety of human affairs, besides long diseases, oftentimes separates husbands from their wives; and therefore married people have need of two kinds of chastity; the one for absolute abstinence, when they are separated upon the occasions of which I have been speaking; the other for moderation, when they are together in the ordinary course. St. Catherine of Sienna saw, amongst the damned, many souls grievously tormented for having violated the sanctity of marriage, which happened, said she, not for the enormity of the sin, for murders and blasphemies are more enormous, but because they that commit it make no conscience of it, and thereof continue long in it."

"You see, then, that chastity is necessary for all classes of people: 'Follow peace with all men,' says the Apostle, 'and holiness, without which no man shall see God:' by holiness is here understood 'chastity': as St. Jerome and St. Chrysostom observe. No one shall see God without chastity; no one shall dwell in his holy tabernacle, that is not clean of heart; and, as our Saviour Himself says, 'the unchaste shall be banished thence,' and 'Blessed are the clean of heart, for they shall see God.' (ST. FRANCIS DE SALES: pp 167-172)

CONVERSATION: Advice and Suggestions as Regards the Spiritual Life.

"As physicians discover the health and sickness of a man by looking on his tongue, so our words are true indications of the qualities of our souls. 'By thy words,' says our Saviour, 'thou shalt be justified, and by thy words thou shalt be condemned.' We readily move our hand to the pain that we feel, and the tongue to the love we entertain."

"If, then you are in love with God, you will often speak of him in your familiar discourses with those of your household, your friends, and your neighbors: 'For the mouth of the just will meditate on wisdom and his tongue will speak judgment.' As bees, with their little mouths, touch nothing but honey: so should your tongue be always sweetened with its God, and find no greater pleasure than in the sweet praises and blessings of His name flowing between your lips, like St. Francis who used to apply his tongue to his lips, after pronouncing the holy name of the Lord, to draw thence the greatest sweetness in the world."

"But speak always of God as of God; that is, reverently and devoutly; not with ostentation or affectation, but with a spirit of meekness, charity, and humility, distilling as much as you can, as it is said of the things of God, imperceptibly, into the ears sometimes of one, and sometimes of another, and pray secretly to God, in your soul, that it would please him to make this holy dew sink deep into the heart of those that hear you."

"Above all things, this angelical office must be done meekly and sweetly; not by way of correction, but inspiration; for it is surprising how powerfully a sweet and amiable manner of proposing good things attracts the hearts of the hearers."

"Never therefore, speak of God or devotion, in a light or thoughtless manner, but rather with the utmost attention and reverence. I give you this advice, that you may avoid that remarkable vanity which is found in many false devotees, who upon every occasion speak words of piety and godliness by way of entertainment, without ever thinking of what they say, and afterwards falsely imagine themselves to be very devout."

Of Modesty in Our Words, And The Respect We Owe to Persons.

"'If any offend not in words,' says St. James, 'he is a perfect man.' Be careful never to permit an indecent word to escape from your lips; for, although you do not speak it with an ill intention, yet it may be hurtful to those that hear it. An evil word falling into a weak heart spreads itself like a drop of oil falling on linen; nay, it sometimes seizes on the heart in such a manner as to fill it with a thousand unclean thoughts and temptations to lust; for, as the poison of the body enters by the mouth, so the poison of the heart enters by the ear, and the tongue which utters an indecent word is a murderer. For, although perhaps the poison, which it has cast forth, has not produced its effect, because it found the hearts of the hearers guarded by some preservative, yet there wanted no malice in the tongue to occasion their death. Let no man, therefore, tell me that he has no evil intention; for our Lord, the Searcher of hearts, has said, 'That out of the abundance of the heart, the mouth speaketh.' But if we intend no evil on such occasions, yet the enemy, who is of a contrary opinion, secretly uses immodest words to pierce the heart of some one. As they that have eaten the herb angelica have always a sweet and agreeable breath, so they that have honesty and chastity, which is an angelical virtue, in their hearts, have their words always modest and chaste. As for indecent and obscene things the apostle will not have them even named amongst us; assuring us, 'that nothing so much corrupteth good manners as wicked discourse.'"

"When immodest words are disguised with affectation and subtlety, then they become infinitely more poisonous; for; the more pointed the dart is, the more easily it enters our bodies; so, also, the more pointed an obscene word is, the more deeply does it penetrate the heart; and if they who esteem themselves men of gallantry for speaking such words were convinced that in conversation they should be like a swarm of bees, convened together to collect honey from some sweet and virtuous entertainment, they certainly would not thus imitate a nest of wasps, assembled together to such corruption. If some impudent person should address you in a lascivious manner, convince him that your ears are offended, either by turning yourself immediately away, or by such other mark of resentment as your discretion may direct."

On Modesty In Our Words

"To become a scoffer is one of the worst qualities of a wit. God, who detests this vice, has therefore inflicted remarkable punishment on it perpetrators. Nothing is so opposite to charity or devotion as despising and condemning our neighbor. As derision and mockery is never without scoffing, therefore divines consider it is one of the worst offenses of which a man can be guilty against his neighbor, by words; for other offenses may be committed with some esteem of the party offended, but by this he is treated with scorn and contempt."

"As for certain good-humored jesting words, spoken by way of modest and innocent mirth, they belong to the virtue called Eutrapelia by the Greeks, which we may denominate good conversation; and by these we take an honest and friendly recreation from those frivolous occasions with which human imperfections furnish us. We must be careful, however, not to pass from honest mirth to scoffing; for scoffing excites laughter in the way of scorn and contempt of our neighbor: whereas innocent mirth and drollery cause laughter by an unoffencing liberty, confidence and familiar freedom, joined to the sprightly wit of some ingenious conceit. St. Lewis, when the religious offered to speak to him, after dinner of high and sublime matter, told them: 'It is not now a time to allege texts, but to recreate ourselves with some cheerful conceits; let every man say whatever innocent things come to his mind,' this he said when any of the nobility were present, to receive marks of kindness from his majesty. But let us remember to pass our time of recreation in such a manner that we may never lose sight of the greatest of all concerns, Eternity."

"Let your language be meek, open, and sincere without the least mixture of equivocations, artifice, or dissimulation; for although it may be not be always advisable to say all that is true, yet it is never allowable to speak against the truth. Accustom yourself, therefore, never to tell a deliberate lie, either by way of excuse or otherwise; remembering always that God is the God of truth. Should you tell a lie inadvertently, fail not to correct it upon the spot by some explanation or reparation; an honest excuse has always more grace and force to bear one harmless then a lie."

"Though one may sometimes prudently disguise the truth by some equivocation, yet it must never be done but when the glory and service of God manifestly requite it; in any other case, such artifices are dangerous. The Holy Spirit dwells not in a deceitful soul. No artifice is so good and desirable as plain-dealing, worldly prudence and artifice belong to the children of the world; but the children of God walk uprightly and their heart is without guile. 'He that walketh sincerely,' says the wise man, 'walketh confidently.' Lying, double-dealing, and dissimulation, are always signs of a weak and mean spirit. St. Austin had said, in the fourth book of his Confessions, that his soul and that of his friend were but one soul; and that he had a horror for his life after the death of his friend, because he was not willing to live by halves; and yet that for the same reason he was unwilling to die, lest his friend should die wholly. These words seemed to him afterwards so artful and affected, that he recalled them, and censured them in his book of Retractions. Observe the exactness of this holy soul with respect to the least artifice in his words. Fidelity, plainness, and sincerity of speech are the greatest ornaments of a Christian life: "I will take heed," says holy David, "to my ways, that I may not sin with my tongue. Set a watch, O Lord, before my mouth, and a door round about my lips." It was the advice of St. Lewis, in order to avoid contention not to contradict any one in discourse unless, it were either sinful or very prejudicial to acquiesce to him. But should it be necessary to contradict any one, or oppose our own opinion to his, we must do it with much mildness and dexterity, so as not to irritate his temper; for nothing is ever gained by harshness and violence."

"To speak little, a practice so much recommended by all wise men, does not consist in uttering few words, but in uttering none that are unprofitable; for in point of speaking one is not to regard the quantity so much as the quality of the words; but in my opinion we ought to avoid both extremes. For to be too reserved, and refuse to join in conversation, looks like disdain, or a want of confidence; and, on the other hand, to be always talking, so as to afford neither leisure nor opportunity to others to speak when they wish, is a mark of shallowness and levity."

"St. Lewis condemned whispering in company, and particularly at table, lest it should give others occasion to suspect that some evil was spoken of them. 'He that is at table,' said he, 'in good company, and has something to say that is merry and pleasant, should mention it so that all the company may hear him; but if it be a thing of importance, let him reserve it for a more suitable occasion.' (ST. FRANCIS DE SALES; pp 239-241)

DEPRESSION: Melancholy, Inquietude ofThe Soul.

"As inquietude is not only a temptation, but the source of many temptations, it is therefore necessary that I should say something concerning it. Inquietude, or sadness, then, is nothing else but that grief of mind which we conceive for some evil which we experience against our will, whether it be exterior as poverty, sickness, contempt; or interior, as ignorance, avidity, repugnance, and temptation. When the soul, then, perceives that some evil has befallen her, she becomes sad, is displeased and extremely anxious to rid herself of it; and thus far she is right, for every one naturally desires to embrace good, and fly from that which he apprehends to be evil. If the soul, for the love of God, wishes to be freed from her evil, she will seek the means of her deliverance with patience, meekness, humility, and tranquillity, expecting it more from the providence of God than from her own industry or diligence. But if she seeks her deliverance, from a motive of self-love then will she fatigue herself in quest of these means, as if the success depended more on herself than on God. I do not say that she thinks so, but that she acts as if she thought so. Now, if she succeeds not immediately according to her wishes, she falls into inquietude, which, instead of removing, aggravates the evil, and involves her in such anguish and distress, with so great loss of courage and strength, that she imagines her evil incurable. Thus, then, sadness, which in the beginning is just, produces inquietude, and inquietude produces an increase in sadness, which is extremely dangerous."

"Inquietude is the greatest evil that can befall the soul, sin only excepted. For, as the seditious and intestine commotions of any commonwealth prevent it from being able to resist a foreign invasion, so our heart, being troubled within itself, loses the strength necessary to maintain the virtue it had acquired, and the means to resist the temptations of the enemy, who then uses his utmost efforts to fish, as it is said, in troubled waters."

"Inquietude proceeds from an inordinate desire of being delivered from the evil which we feel, or of acquiring the good which we desire; and yet there is nothing which tends more to increase evil, and to prevent the enjoyment of good, than an unquiet mind. Birds remain prisoners in the nets, because, when they find themselves caught, they eagerly flutter about to extricate themselves, and by that means entangle themselves the more. Whenever, then, you are pressed with a desire to be freed from some evil, or to obtain some good, be careful both to settle your mind in repose and tranquillity, and to compose your judgment and will; and then gently procure the accomplishment of your desire, taking in regular order the means which may be most convenient; when I say gently, I do not mean negligently, but without hurry, trouble, or inquietude; otherwise, instead of obtaining the effect of your desire, you will mar all, and embarrass yourself the more."

"'My soul is continually in my hands, O Lord, and I have not forgotten thy law.' said David. Examine frequently in the day or at least in the morning and evening, whether you have your soul in your hands, or whether some passion or inquietude has not robbed you of it. Consider whether you have your heart at command, or whether it has not escaped out of your hands, to engage itself to some disorderly affection of love, hatred, envy, covetousness, fear, uneasiness, or joy. If it should be gone astray, seek after it before you do anything else, and bring it back quietly to the presence of God, subjecting all your affections and desires to the obedience and directions of his divine will. For as they who are afraid of losing anything which is precious hold it fast in their hands; so, in imitation of this great king, we should always say, "O my God! my soul is in danger, and therefore I carry it always in my hands; and in this manner I have not forgotten thy holy law."

"Permit not your desires, how trivial soever they may be, to disquiet you, lest afterwards those that are of greater importance should find your heart involved in trouble and disorder. When you perceive that inquietude begins to affect your mind recommend yourself to God, and resolve to do nothing until it is restored to tranquility, unless it should be something that cannot be deferred; in that case, moderating the current of your desires as much as possible, perform the action, not according to your desire but your reason."

"If you can disclose the cause of your disquietude to your spiritual director, or at least to some faithful and devout friend, be assured that you will presently find ease; for communicating the grief of the heart produces the same effect on the soul as bleeding does in the body of him that is in a continual fever; it is the remedy of remedies. Accordingly the holy king St. Lewis gave this counsel to his son: 'If thou hast any uneasiness in thy heart, tell it immediately to thy confessor, or to some good person, and then thou shalt be enabled to bear thy evil very easily, by the comfort he will give thee.'

"'The sadness that is according to God,' says St. Paul, 'worketh penance steadfast unto salvation; but the sadness of the world worketh death.' Sadness, then, may be good or evil, according to its different effects. It is true it produces more evil effects than good, for it has only two that are good, compassion and repentance; but it has six that are evil, viz., anxiety, sloth, indignation, jealousy, envy, and impatience which caused the wise man to say, 'sadness kills many and there is no profit in it;' because, for two good streams which flow from the source of sadness, there are six very evil."

"The enemy makes use of sadness and temptation against the just; for, as he endeavors to make the wicked to rejoice in their sins, so he strives to make the good grieve in their good works; as he cannot procure the commission of evils but by making it appear agreeable, so he cannot divert us from good but by making it appear disagreeable. The prince of darkness is pleased with sadness and melancholy, because he is and will be sad and melancholy to all eternity; therefore, he desires that every one should be like himself."

"The sadness which is evil troubles and perplexes the soul, excites inordinate fears, creates a disgust for prayer, stupefies and oppresses the brain, deprives the mind of counsel, resolution, judgment and courage, and destroys her strength. In a word, it is like a severe winter, which demolishes all the beauty of the country, and devours every living creature; for it takes away all sweetness from the soul, and renders her disabled in all her faculties. If you should at any time be seized with the evil of sadness apply the following remedies."

"'Is any one sad,' says James, 'let him pray.' Prayer is a sovereign remedy, for it lifts up the soul to God, our only joy and consolation. But, in praying, let your words and affections, whether interior or exterior, always lend to a lively confidence in the divine goodness, such as 'O God of mercy! O infinite goodness! O my sweet Saviour! O God of my heart, my joy and my hope! O my divine Spouse, the well-beloved of my soul!'"

"Oppose vigorously the least inclination to sadness, and, although it may seem that all your actions are at that time performed with tepidity and sloth, you must, nevertheless, persevere; for the enemy, who seeks by sadness to make us weary of good works, seeing that we cease not on that account to perform this, and that, being performed in spite of his opposition, they become more meritorious, will cease to trouble us any longer."

"Sing spiritual canticles for the devil by this means has often desisted from his operations, witness the evil spirit with which Saul was afflicted, whose violence was repressed by such music. It is also necessarily serviceable to employ ourselves in exterior works, and to vary them as much as possible, in order to divert the soul from the melancholy object, and to purify and warm the spirits, sadness being a passion of a cold and dry complexion."

"Perform external actions of fervor, although you may perform them without the least relish; such as embracing the crucifix, clasping it to your breast, kissing the feet and the hands, lifting up your eyes and your hands to heaven, raising your voice to God by words of love and confidence like these: 'My beloved is mine, and I am his. My beloved is to me a posy of myrrh, he shall dwell between by breasts. My eyes have fainted after thee, O my God!' Say also: 'When wilt thou comfort me? O Jesus, be thou a Jesus to me! Live, sweet Jesus, and my soul shall live! Who shall ever separate me from the love of God'?"

"But frequently the holy communion is the best remedy because this heavenly bread strengthen the heart and rejoices the spirit."

"Disclose to your confessor, with humility and sincerity, all the feelings, affections, and suggestions which proceed from your sadness. Seek the conversation of spiritual persons, and frequent their company as much as you can. In a word, resign yourself into the hands of God, preparing yourself to suffer this troublesome sadness." (ST. FRANCIS DE SALES, pp. 306-309)

DEVOTION: Prayer and Meditation, Commentary

"St. Lewis was a prince admirable both in war and peace, and one who administered justice, and managed his affairs with the most assiduous attention, yet he heard two masses every day, said vespers and compline with his chaplain, made his meditation, visited hospitals every Friday, confessed and took the discipline, heard sermons frequently, and held very often spiritual conferences; yet, notwithstanding all this, he never saw an occasion of promoting the public good which he did not improve and diligently put in execution; and his court was more splendid and flourishing than it had even been in the time of his predecessors. Perform then, these exercises as I have marked them out for you and God will give you sufficient leisure and strength to perform all your other duties, although he should make the sun stand still for you, as he did for Josua. We always do enough when God works with us."

"The world will perhaps say that I suppose, almost throughout the whole work, that some souls have the gift of mental prayer; and, yet every one has it not; so that this introduction will not serve for all. It is true I have made this supposition; it is also true that every one has not this gift; but it is no less true that almost all, even the most ignorant, may have it, provided they have good guides, and are willing to take as much pains to obtain it as it deserves. But, should there be some who have not this gift in any degree whatever, which I think almost impossible, a prudent spiritual director will easily supply that defect, by teaching them to read, or to hear others read, the considerations included in the meditations with profound and close attention."

"On the first day of every month repeat, after your meditations....saying, with David, 'No, my God, thy justifications I will never forget, for by them thou hast given me life.' When you feel any disorder in your soul take your protestation in hand, and, prostrate in the spirit of humility, recite it with your whole heart, and you will find great ease and comfort."

"Make an open confession not of being devout but of desiring to become devout. Be not ashamed to practice those necessary actions which conduct the soul to the love of God. Acknowledge frankly that you would rather die than commit a mortal sin; that you are resolved to frequent the sacraments, and to follow the counsels of your director, though sometimes it may not be necessary to name him; for this candid profession of our desire to serve God, and of consecrating ourselves entirely to his love is very acceptable to his divine Majesty, who commands us not to be ashamed either of Him or of His cross. Besides, it presents many proposals and invitations which the world might make to draw us into the contrary way, and oblige us in honor to act according to what we profess. As the philosophers professed themselves philosophers, that they might be suffered to live like philosophers; so we must profess ourselves to be desirous of devotion, that we may be suffered to live devoutly. If any one tells you that you may live devoutly without practicing these advises and exercises, answer him mildly, that, your weakness being so great, you stand in need of more help and assistance than others."

"In fine, I conjure you be all that is sacred in heaven and on earth, by the baptism which you have received by the breasts with which Jesus Christ was nourished, by the charity with which He loved you, and by the bowels of that mercy in which you hope, continue to persevere in this blessed enterprise of a devout life. Our days glide away, and death is at the gate. 'The trumpet sounds, retreat,' says St. Gregory Nazianzen; 'let every man be ready, for judgment is near.' St. Symphorian's mother, seeing him led to martyrdom, cried after him, 'My son! remember eternal life, look up to heaven, and think upon Him who reigns there; your approaching end will quickly terminate the short career of this life.' I also will say to you, look up to heaven, and do not forfeit it for this despicable earth, look down into hell, and do not cast yourself into it for transitory joys; look at Jesus Christ, and do not renounce Him for this world; and, when the labors of a devout life seem painful to you, sing with St. Francis:

How sweet are all those momentary toils
which lead to never-ending heavenly joy!

"Live Jesus! to whom, with the Father and Holy Ghost, be all honor and glory, now and throughout the endless ages of eternity. - Amen."

(ST. FRANCIS DE SALES; pp. 361-364)

DEVOTION: Positive and Negative Aspects, Manifesting an Imbalance of Virtues

"As Aurelius painted all the faces of his pictures to the air and resemblance of the woman he loved, so every one paints devotion according to his own passion and fancy. He that is addicted to fasting thinks himself very devout if he fasts, though his heart be at the same time filled with rancor, and scrupling to moisten his tongue with wine, or even with water, through sobriety, he makes no difficulty to drink deep of his neighbor's blood, by detraction and calumny. Another considers himself because he recites daily a multiplicity of prayers, though immediately afterwards he utters the most disagreeable, arrogant, and injurious words amongst his domestics and neighbors. Another cheerfully draws an alms out of his purse to relieve the poor, but he cannot draw meekness out of his heart to forgive his enemies. Another readily forgives enemies, but never satisfies his creditors but by constraint. These, by some are esteemed devout, while, in reality, they are by no means so." (ST. FRANCIS DE SALES; p. 2)

DEVOTION: Observations, The Worldly View

"The world defames holy devotion representing devout persons as a peevish, gloomy, and sullen race of men, pretending that devotion begets melancholy and insupportable humors, however, the contrary is true, a devout life is a life of all others, the most sweet, happy and amiable. Devout souls, it is true, find much bitterness in their exercises of mortification, but in performing them they convert them into the most delicious sweetness." (ST. FRANCIS DE SALES; p.5)

FORGIVENESS: As Regards Others

"Depending on the person we are in contact with, we should not be offended at what this or that person may say of us, nor should we resent any affront they may render us. We should, with prudence, embrace every opportunity to gain their affection, and to appease them." (ST. FRANCIS DE SALES: pp. 72-73)

FRIENDSHIP: True and False, Friendship Which is Evil and Frivolous

"Love holds the first place among the several passions of the soul; it is the sovereign of all the motions of the heart; it directs all the rest towards it, and makes us such as it is the object of its love. Be careful, then, to entertain no evil love, for, if you do, you will presently become evil. Friendship is the most dangerous love of all; because other loves may be without communication; but friendship, being wholly grounded upon it, we can hardly hold a communication of friendship with any person without partaking of its qualities."

"All love is not friendship; for when one loves without being again beloved, then there is love, but not friendship; because friendship is a communication of love, therefore, where love is not mutual, there can be no friendship. Nor is it enough that it be mutual, but the parties that love each other must know their mutual affection, for, if they know it not, they have love, but not friendship. There must be also some kind of communication between them, which may be the ground of friendship. Now, according to the diversity of the communication, the friendship also differs, and the communications are different according to the variety of the things which they communicate to each other; if they be false and vain, the friendship is also false and vain; if they be true, the friendship is likewise true; and the more laudable the goods may be the more laudable also is the friendship. For as that honey is best which is gathered from the blossom of the most exquisite flowers, so that love which is founded upon the most exquisite communication is the most noble. And as there is honey in Heraclea of Pontus, which is poisonous, and deprives those of reason that eat it, because it is gathered from the aconite, which abounds in that country; even so the friendship, grounded upon the communication of false and vicious goods, is altogether false and vicious."

"The communication of carnal pleasures is a mutual inclination and brutish allurement, which can no more bear the name of friendship among men that that of beasts for the like effects; and if there was no other communication in marriage there would be no friendship at all; but because, besides that, there is a communication in matrimony of life, of industry, of goods, of affections, and of an indissoluble fidelity, therefore the friendship of matrimony is a true and holy friendship. As friendship that is grounded on the communication of sensual pleasures is utterly gross, and unworthy of the name of friendship; and so is that which is founded on virtues which are frivolous and vain; because the virtues also depend on the senses. I call those pleasures sensual which are immediately and principally annexed to the exterior senses; such as the pleasure to behold a beautiful person, to hear a sweet voice, to touch and the like. I call certain vain endowments and qualities frivolous accomplishments, which weak minds call virtues and perfections. Observe how the greater part of silly maids, women, and young people talk; they hesitate not to say: Such a gentleman has many virtues and perfections, for he dances gracefully, he plays well at all sorts of games, he dresses fashionably, he sings delightfully, speaks eloquently, and has a fine appearance; it is thus that mountebanks esteem those, in their way, the most virtuous who are the greatest buffoons."

"But as all these things regards the senses, so the friendships which proceed from them are termed sensual, vain, and frivolous, and deserve rather the name of foolish fondness than of friendship; such are the ordinary friendships of young people which are grounded on curled locks, a fine head of hair, smiling glances, fine clothes, affected countenances, and idle talk; a friendship suited to the age of those lovers whose virtue is, as yet, only in the blossom, and their judgment in the bud, and indeed, such amities being but transitory melt away like snow in the sun."

"When these foolish friendships are maintained between persons of different sexes, without pretensions of marriage, they are called fond love; for being but embryos, or rather phantoms of friendship, they deserve not the name either of true friendship or true love, by reason of their excessive vanity and imperfection. Now, by means of these fondnesses, the hearts of men and of women are caught and entangled with each other in vain and foolish affections, based upon these frivolous communications and wretched complacencies of which I have been just speaking."

"And although these dangerous loves, commonly speaking, terminate at last in carnality and downright lasciviousness, yet that is not the first design or intention of the persons between whom they pass; otherwise they would not be merely fond loves, but absolute impurities and uncleanesses. Sometimes even many years pass before anything directly contrary to the chastity of the body happens between them, whilst they content themselves with giving their hearts the pleasure of wishes, desires, sighs, amorous entertainments, and such like fooleries and vanities; and this upon different pretensions."

"Some have no other design than to satisfy their hearts with loving and being loved, following in this their amorous inclination; and these regard nothing in the choice of their loves but their instinct; so that at the first meeting with an agreeable object, without examining the interior, or the comportment of the person, they begin this fond communication, and entangle themselves in these wretched nets, from which afterwards they find great difficulty to disengage themselves. Others suffer themselves to be carried to fond loves, by the vanity of esteeming it no small glory to catch and bind hearts by love. Now these aiming at glory in the choice they make set their net and lay their snares in spacious, high, rare, and illustrious places. Others are let away at the same time, both by their amorous inclination and by vanity; for though their hearts be altogether inclined to love, yet they will not engage themselves in it without some advantage of glory. These loves are always criminal, foolish, and vain; criminal because they end at length, and terminate in the sin of the flesh, and because they rob God, the wife and the husband, of that love, and consequently of that heart, which belonged to them; foolish, because they have neither foundation nor reason; pain, because they yield neither profit, honor, not content; on the contrary, they are attended by a loss of time, are prejudicial to honor, and bring no other pleasure than that of an eagerness in pretending and hoping, without knowing what they would have, or to what they would make pretensions. For these wretched and weak minds still imagine they have something to expect from the testimonies which they receive of reciprocal love; but yet they cannot tell what this is; the desire of which can never end, but goes on continually, pressing their hearts with perpetual distrusts, jealousies, and disquietudes.

"St. Gregory Nazianzen, in his discourse, addressed indeed to vain women, but applicable also to men, says: 'Thy natural beauty is sufficient for thy husband; but if it be for many men, like a net spread out for a flock of birds, what will be the consequence? He shall be pleasing to thee who shall please himself with thy beauty; thou wilt return him glance for glance, look for look; presently will follow smiles and little amorous words, dropped by stealth at the beginning, but soon after they will become more familiar, and pass to an open courtship. Take heed, my tongue! of telling what will follow: yet will I say this one truth: nothing of all those things which young men and women say and do together in these foolish complacencies is exempted from grievous stings. All the links of wanton loves depend on one another, and follow one another as one piece of iron, touched by the loadstone, draws many others after it.'"

"How wisely has this great bishop spoken! What is it you think to do? To give love? No; for no one gives love voluntary, that does not receive it necessarily. He that catches in this chase is likewise caught himself. The herb apoxis receives and conceives fire as soon as it sees it, our hearts do the like; as soon as they see a soul inflamed with love for them they are presently inflamed with love for it. But some one will say, I am willing to entertain some of this love, but not too much. Alas! you deceive yourselves, the fire of love is more active and penetrating than you imagine; you think to receive but a spark, and will wonder to see it in a moment take possession of your whole heart, reduce all your resolutions to ashes, and your reputation to smoke. "Who will have pity on a charmer struck by a serpent? And I also, after the wise man, cry out, O foolish and senseless people! think you to charm love in such a manner as to be able to manage it at pleasure? You would play with it, but it will sting and torment you cruelly; and do you know that every one will mock and deride you for attempting to charm or tie down love, and on a false assurance put into your bosom a dangerous serpent, which has spoiled and destroyed both your soul and your honor?"

"Good God! what blindness is this, to play away thus at hazard, against such frivolous stakes, the principal power of our soul! Yes, for God regards not man, but for his soul, nor his soul, but for his will; nor his will, but for his love. Alas! we have not near so much love as we stand in need of; I mean to say that we fall infinitely short of having sufficient wherewith to love God; and yet, wretched as we are, we lavish it away foolishly on vain and frivolous things, as if we had some to spare. Ah! this great God who hath reserved to himself the whole love of our souls, in acknowledgment of our creation, preservation, and redemption, will exact a strict account of all these criminal deductions we make from it; for, if he will make so rigorous an examination into our idle words, how strictly will he not examine into our impertinent, foolish, and pernicious loves!

"The walnut-tree is very prejudicial to the vines and fields wherein it is planted; because, being so large, it attracts all the moisture of the surrounding earth, and renders it incapable of nourishing the other plants; the leaves are also so thick that they make a large and close shade; and lastly, it allures the passengers to it, who, to beat down the fruit, spoil and trample upon all about it. These fond loves do the same injury to the soul, for they posses her in such manner, and so strongly draw her motions to themselves, that she has no strength left to produce any good work: the leaves, viz., their idle talk, their amusements, and their dalliance, are so frequent, that all leisure time is squandered away in them; and, finally, they engender so many temptations, distractions, suspicions, and other evil consequences, that the whole heart is trampled down and destroyed by them. In a word, these fond loves not only banish heavenly love, but also the fear of God from the soul; they waste the spirit and ruin reputation; they are the sports of courts, but the plague of hearts.

"Love every one with a strenuous love of charity, but have no friendship, except for those that communicate with you the things of virtue; and the more exquisite the virtues are, which shall be the matter of your communications, the more perfect shall your friendship also be. If this communication be in the sciences, the friendship is certainly very commendable; but still more so if it be in the moral virtues: in prudence, discretion, temperance, fortitude, and justice. But should your reciprocal communications relate to charity, devotion, and Christian perfection, good God! how precious will this friendship be! It will be excellent, because it comes from God; excellent, because it tends to God; excellent, because it shall last eternally in God. Oh, how good it is to love on earth as they love in heaven; to learn to cherish each other in this world, as we shall do eternally in the next!"

"I speak not here of that simple love of charity which we must have for all men; but of that spiritual friendship, by which two, three, or more souls communicate one to another their devotion and spiritual affections, and make themselves all but one spirit. Such happy souls may justly sing: "Behold how good and pleasant it is for brethren to swell together in unity!" For the delicious balm of devotion distills out of one heart into another, by so continual a participation, that it may be said that God has poured out upon this friendship "his blessing and life everlasting." I consider all other friendships as but so many shadows in respect to this, and that their bonds are but chains of glass or of jet, in comparison of this bond of holy devotion, which is more precious than gold."

"Make no other kind of friendship than this: I speak of such friends as you choose yourself; but you must not, therefore, forsake or neglect the friendships which nature or former duties oblige you to cultivate with your parents, kindred, benefactors, neighbors, and others."

"Many perhaps may say: 'We should have no kind of particular affection and friendship, because it occupies the heart, distracts the mind, and begets envy;' but they are mistaken, because having seen, in the writings of many devout authors, that particular friendships and extra-ordinary affection are of infinite prejudice to religious persons, they therefore imagine that it is the same with regard to the rest of the world; but there is a material difference, for, as in a well-ordered monastery, where the common design of all tends to true devotion, it is not requisite to make these particular communications of friendship, lest by seeking among individuals for that which is common to the whole, they should fall from particularities to partialities. But for those who dwell among worldlings, and desire to embrace true virtue, it is necessary for them to unite themselves together by a holy and sacred friendship, since by this means they encourage, assist, and conduct each other to good: for, as they that walk on plain ground need not lend each other a hand, whilst they that are in a rugged and slippery road hold one by the other, to walk more securely; so they that are in religious orders stand in no want of particular friendships: but they that are in the world have need of them, to secure and assist each other amidst the many dangerous passages through which they are to pass. In the world all are not directed by the same views, nor actuated by the same spirit; we must therefore separate ourselves, and contract friendships according to our several pretensions. This particularity causes indeed a partiality; but is a holy partiality, which creates not other division but that which of necessity should always subsist betwixt good and evil, sheep and goats, bees and hornets."

"No one surely can deny but that our Lord loved St. John, Lazarus, Martha, and Magdalen, with a more sweet and more special friendship. We know that St. Peter tenderly cherished St. Mark and St. Petronilla, as St. Paul did Timothy and St. Thecla. St. Gregory Nazianzen boasts a hundred times of the incomparable friendship he had with the Great St. Basil, and describes it in this manner: 'It seemed that in us there was but one soul dwelling in two bodies, and if those are not to be believed, who say that all things are in all things, yet of us two you may believe, that were both in each other; we had each of us one only pretension to cultivate virtue, and to accommodate all the designs of our life to future hopes; going in this manner out of mortal earth before we died in it.' St. Austin testifies that St. Ambrose loved St. Monica entirely for the real virtue he saw in her, and that she reciprocally loved him as an angel of God. But I am blamable in detaining you so long on so clear a matter. St. Jerome, St. Austin, St. Gregory, St. Bernard, and all the greatest servants of God, have had very particular friendships, without any prejudice to their perfection. St. Paul, reproaching the disorders of the gentiles, accuses them that they were people without affection; that is to say, that they had no true friendships. And St. Thomas, with all the wisest philosophers, acknowledges that friendship is a virtue; and he speaks of "particular friendship" since as he says "perfect friendship cannot be extended to a great many persons." Perfection therefore consists, not in having no friendship but in having none but with such as are good and holy."

"Observe, this important admonition. As the poisonous honey of Heraclea is so similar to the other that is wholesome, that there is a great danger of mistaking the one for the other, or of taking them mixed together (for the goodness of the one cannot destroy the poison of the other); so he must stand upon his guard who would not be deceived in friendships, particularly when contracted betwixt persons of different sexes, under what pretext soever. The devil often effects a change in those that love; they begin with virtuous love, with which, if not attended to with the utmost discretion, fond love will begin to mingle itself, then sensual love, and afterwards carnal love; yea, there is even danger in spiritual love, if we are not extremely upon our guard, though in this it is more difficult to be imposed upon, because its purity and whiteness make the spots and stains which Satan seeks to mingle with it more apparent, and therefore when he takes this in hand he does it more subtlety, and endeavors to introduce impurities by almost insensible degrees."

"...worldly friendship ordinarily produces a great profusion of endearing words, passionate expressions, with admiration of beauty, behavior, and other sensual qualities. Holy friendship, on the contrary, speaks a plain and sincere language, and commends nothing but virtue and the grace of God, the only foundation on which it subsists. As the honey of Heralcea, when swallowed, occasions a giddiness in the head, so false friendship produces a vertigo in the mind, which makes persons stagger in chastity and devotion, hurrying them on to affected, wanton, and immodest looks, sensual caresses, inordinate sighs, and ridiculous complaints of not being beloved, to a studied and enticing carriage, to gallantries, to interchanging of kisses, with other familiarities and indecent favors, the certain and unquestionable presages of the approaching ruin of chastity. But the looks of holy friendship are simple and modest; its caresses pure and sincere; its sighs are but for heaven; its familiarities are only spiritual; its complaints but when God is not beloved. These are infallible marks of a holy friendship . As the honey of Heraclea affects the sight, so this worldly friendship dazzles the judgment to such a degree, that they who are infected with it think they do well when they act wrongly, and believe their excuses and pretexts for two reasons: they fear the light, and love darkness. But holy friendship is clear-sighted, and never conceals herself, but appears willingly before those that are good. In fine, as the honey of Heraclea leaves a great bitterness in the mouth, so false friendships change into lewd and carnal words and demands; and, in case of refusal, into injuries, slanders, imposture, sadness, confusion, and jealousies, which often terminate in madness. Chaste friendship is always equally honest, civil, and amiable, and changes only into a purer union of spirits; a lovely image of the blessed friendship existing in heaven."

"St. Gregory Nazianzen says, that as the cry of the peacock, when he struts and spreads his feathers, excites the peahens to lust, so, when we see a man dressed in his best apparel, approaching to flatter, and whisper in the ears of a woman, without pretension to lawful marriage, then no doubt it is to incite her to impurity; and every virtuous woman will stop her ears against the cry of this peacock, the voice of the enchanter, who seeks thus subtlety to charm her; but, should she hearken to him, good God! what an ill presage of the future loss of her heart!"

"Young people who use gestures, glances, and caresses, or speak words in which they would not willingly be surprised by their fathers, mothers, husbands, wives, or confessors, testify hereby that they are treating of something contrary to honor and conscience. Our Blessed Lady was troubled when she saw an angel in the shape of a man, because she was alone, and because he gave her extraordinarily though heavenly praises. O Saviour of the world! if purity itself be afraid of an angel in the shape of a man, why should not impurity fear a man, even though he should come in the shape of an angel, especially when he praises her with sensual and earthly commendations?"

"But what remedies must we take against this multitude of filthy loves, fondnesses, and impurities? As soon as you perceive the first approach of them, turn suddenly away, with an absolute horror and detestation, run to the cross of your Saviour, take the crown of thorns, and press it to your heart, so that the evil spirit may not come near it. Beware of coming to any kind of compromise with this enemy: do not say I will hearken to him, but will do nothing of what he shall say to me: I will lend him my ears, but will refuse him my heart. Oh, no! For God's sake, be resolute on these occasions: the heart and the ears correspond with each other; and, as it is impossible to stop a torrent that descends by the brow of a mountain, so it is hard to prevent the love which has entered in at the ear from falling suddenly down into the heart."

Alemaeon pretended that goats breathe by the ears, but Aristotle denies it; as for myself I cannot decide the question: but I know that our heart breathes by the ear, and as it sends forth its own thoughts by the tongue, so it receives the thoughts of others by the ear. Let us, then, keep a diligent guard over our ears that we may not inhale the corrupt air of filthy words, for otherwise our hearts will soon be infected. Hearken to no kind of propositions, under what pretext soever: in this case alone there is no danger of being rude or uncivil."

"Remember that you have dedicated your heart to God, and that your love having been sacrificed to Him it would be a sacrilege to alienate the least part of it from Him. Rather sacrifice it to Him anew by a thousand resolutions and protestations; and keeping yourself close within, as a deer within its cover, call upon God, and He will help you, and take you under His protection, that you may live for Him alone."

"But if you are already entangled in the nets of filthy loves, good God! how difficult will it be to extricate yourself from them! Place yourself before the divine Majesty, acknowledge , in His presence, the excess of your misery, frailty and vanity. Then, with the greatest effort of which your heart is capable, detest them; abjure the vain professions you have made of them; renounce all the promises received, and, with the most generous and absolute resolution, determine in your heart never to permit them to occupy the least thought for the remainder of your life."

"An excellent remedy would be to withdraw yourself from the object; for as they that have been bitten by serpents cannot easily be cured in the presence of those who were before wounded by the same animal, so the person stung with love will hardly be cured of this passion as long as he is near the other who has been similarly wounded. Change of place contributes very much to allay the heat and pain of grief of love. The youth to whom St. Ambrose speaks, in his second book of Penance, having made a long journey, returned home altogether delivered from those fond loves he had formerly entertained, and so much changed that his foolish mistress meeting him, and saying, "Dost thou not know me? am I not the same that I was?"—"Yes," answered he, "but I am no longer the same." Absence has wrought in him this happy change. St. Austin also testifies that, to mitigate the grief he suffered for the death of his friend, he withdrew himself from Tagasta, the place in which his friend died, and went to Carthage."

"But what must he do who cannot withdraw himself? Let him absolutely retrench all particular familiarity, all private conversation, amorous looks, smiles, and, in general, all sorts of communication and allurement, which may nourish this dangerous passion; if he must speak to the other party, let it be only to declare, with a bold, short, and serious protestation, the eternal divorce which he has sworn. I call upon every one who has fallen into these wretched snares: cut them - break them - tear them; do not amuse yourself in unravelling these criminal friendships; you must tear and rend them asunder; do not untie the knots, but break or cut them, so that the cords and strings may be rendered useless; do not enter into any compromise with a love which is contrary to the love of God."

"But after I have broken the chains of his infamous bondage there will still remain some vestiges: the marks and prints of the irons will still be imprinted in my feet; that is, my affections. No, they will not, provided you have conceived as great a detestation of the evil as it deserves; you will now be excited with no other motion but that of an extreme horror for this base love and all its appendages, and will entertain no other affection towards the forsaken object but that of a pure charity, for God's sake. But if through the imperfection of your repentance, there should remain in you any evil inclinations, procure a mental solitude for your soul, according to what I have taught you before, and retire thither as often as you can, and by a thousand reiterated ejaculations renounce all your criminal inclinations, and reject them with your whole force. Read pious and holy books with more than ordinary application; go to confession and communion more frequently; treat humbly and sincerely with your director, or some prudent and faithful friend, concerning all the suggestions and temptations of this kind which may befall you, and doubt not but God will deliver you from those criminal passions, provided you continue faithfully in these good exercises."

"Ah, will it not be ingratitude to break off a friendship so unmercifully? Oh, how happy is that ingratitude which makes us pleasing to God! But no I tell you, in the name of God, this will be no ingratitude but a great benefit, which you shall confer upon your lover; because, in breaking your own bonds asunder, you shall also break his since they were common to you both; and though for the present he may not be sensible of his happiness, yet he will soon acknowledge it, and exclaim with you in thanksgiving: 'O Lord thou hast broken my bonds. I will sacrifice to thee a sacrifice of praise, and call upon thy holy name'."

"I have another important advice to give you on this subject. Friendship requires great communication between friends, otherwise it can neither grow nor subsist. Wherefore it often happens, that with this communication of friendship many other communication insensibly glide from one heart to another, by a mutual infusion and reciprocal intercourse of affections, inclinations and impressions. This happens especially when we have a high esteem for him whom we love; for then we open our heart in such manner to this friendship that with it his inclinations and impressions, whether good or bad, enter rapidly. Certainly the bees, that gather the honey of Heraclea, seek nothing but honey; yet with the honey they insensibly suck the poisonous qualities of the aconite, from which they gather it. Good God! on these occasions we must carefully practice what the Saviour of our souls was accustomed to say: 'Be ye good bankers,' or changers of money: that is to say, 'Receive not bad money with the good, nor base gold with the fine'; separate that which is precious from that which is vile; for there is scarcely any person that has not some imperfections. For why should we receive promiscuously the imperfections of a friend, together with his friendship? We must love him indeed, notwithstanding his imperfections; but we must neither love nor receive his imperfections; for friendship requires a communication of good, not of evil. Wherefore as they that draw gravel out of the river Tagus separate the gold which they find, to carry it away, and leave the sand on the banks; so they, who have the communication of some good friendship ought to separate it from the imperfections, and not suffer them to enter their souls. St. Gregory Nazianzen testifies, that many, loving and admiring St. Bazil, were brought insensibly to imitate him, even in his outward imperfections, as in speaking slowly, and with his spirit abstracted and pensive, in the fashion of his beard, and in his gait. And we often see husbands, wives, children, and friends, who, having a great esteem for their friends, parents, husbands, and wives, acquire either by condescension or imitation a thousand little ill humours in their communication of friendship. Now this should not be so by any means, for every one has evil inclinations enough of his own, without charging himself with those of others; and friendship is so far from requiring it, that, on the contrary, it obliges us mutually to aid and assist one another, in order to free ourselves. But I speak only of imperfections; for as to sins, we must neither occasion them, nor tolerate them in our friends. It is either a weak or a wicked friendship to behold one's friend perish, and not help him; - to see him die of an imposthume and not dare to save his life by opening it with the lancet of correction. True and living friendship cannot subsist in the midst of sins. As the salamander extinguishes the fires in which he lies, so sin destroys the friends in which it lodges. If it be but a transient sin, friendship will presently put it to flight by correction; but if it be habitual, and up its habitation, friendship immediately perishes; for it subsists upon the solid foundation of virtue. We must never, then commit sin for the sake of friendship. A friend becomes an enemy when he would lead us to sin; and he deserves to lose his friend when he would destroy his soul. It is an infallible mark of false friendship to see it exercise towards a vicious person, be his sins of what kind soever; for, if he whom we love be vicious, without doubt our friendship is also vicious, since, seeing it cannot regard true virtue, it must needs be grounded on some frivolous virtue, or sensual quality. Society formed for traffic among merchants is but a shadow of true friendship; since it is not made for the love of the person, but for the love of gain."

"Finally, the following divine sentences are two main pillars, upon which reposes a Christian life; the one is that of the wise man: 'He that feareth God shall likewise have a good friendship': the other is that of the Apostle St. James: 'The friendship of this world is the enemy of God.' (ST. FRANCIS DE SALES; pp. 186-208)

GOD His Omnipresence

"Wherever we go or wherever we are, we shall always find God present. Everyone may acknowledge this truth, but few consider it with a lively attention. When therefore you come to prayer, you must say with your whole heart, and in your heart: Oh, my heart, be attentive, for God is truly here. God is not only in the place in which you are, but that He is in a most particular manner in your heart, that is, your soul. The soul being...God of his heart the very center of your spirit, which He enlivens and animates by His divine presence, being there as the heart of your heart, and the spirit of your spirit; for, as, the soul, being diffused through the whole body is present in every part thereof, and yet resides in a special manner in the heart, so likewise God is present to all things, yet He resides in a more particular manner in our spirit for which reason David calls Him 'the God of his heart.' And St. Paul says, 'that it is in God we live, and we move, and we are.' In consideration, therefore, of this truth, excite in your heart a profound reverence towards God, who is there so intimately present." (*ST. FRANCIS DE SALES;* pp 65-67)

HUMILITY: How We are to Preserve Our Good Name In The Practice Of Humility

"Praise, honor, and glory are not given to men for every degree of virtue, but an excellence of a virtue; for by praise we endeavor to persuade others to esteem the excellency of those whom we praise; by honor we testify that we ourselves esteem them; and glory, in my opinion, is only a certain lustre of reparation that arises from the concurrence of praise and honor, so that honor and praise are like precious stones, from a collection of which glory proceeds like a certain enameling. Now, humility not enduring that we should have any opinion of our own excellence, or think ourselves worthy to be preferred before others, cannot permit that we should seek after praise, honor, and glory, which are only due to excellence; yet she consents to the counsel of the wise man, who admonishes us to be careful of our good name, because a good name is an esteem, not of an excellence, but only of an ordinary honesty and integrity of life, which humility does not forbid us either to acknowledge in ourselves, or to desire the reputation of it. It is true, humility would despise a good name if charity did not need it; but, because it is one of the foundations of human society, and that without it we are not only unprofitable, but prejudicial to the public, by reason of the scandal it would receive, charity requires, and humility consents, that we should desire, it, and carefully, preserve it."

"Moreover, as the leaves, which, in themselves, are of little or no value, are, nevertheless, necessary, not only to beautify the tree, but also to preserve its young and tender fruits; so a good reputation, which, though of itself not very desirable, is, notwithstanding very profitable, not only for the ornament of life, but also for the preservation of virtue, especially of those virtues which are as yet but weak and tender."

"The obligation of preserving our reputation, and of being actually such as we are thought to be, urges a generous spirit forward with a strong and agreeable impulse. Let us, then, preserve our virtues, because they are acceptable to God, the sovereign object of all our actions. But as they who desire to preserve fruits are not content to cover them with sugar, but also put them into vessels that are proper to keep them so, although the love of God be the principal preserver of our virtues, yet we may further employ our good name as very profitable for that purpose."

"Yet we must not be over-nice in regard to the preservation of our good name; for those who are too tender and sensible in this point are like those persons who, for every slight indisposition, take physic, and, thinking to preserve their health, quite destroy it. Thus, persons, by endeavoring to maintain their reputation so delicately, entirely lose it; for by this tenderness they become whimsical, quarrelsome and insupportable, and thus provoke the malice of detractors."

"The overlooking and despising of an injury or calumny is, generally speaking, by far a more effectual remedy than resentment, contention, and revenge; for contempt causes them to vanish; whereas, if we are angry, we seem to own them. Crocodiles hurt only those that fear them, and detraction, those that are vexed by it. An excessive fear of losing our good name betrays a great distrust of its foundation, which is the truth of a good life. The inhabitants of towns that have wooden bridges over great rivers fear lest they should be carried away by every little flood, but they that have bridges of stone only apprehend extraordinary inundations; so they that have a soul solidly grounded on Christian virtue despise the overflowing of injurious tongues; but those that find themselves weak are disturbed with every discourse. In a word, he that is too anxious to preserve his reputation loses it; and that person deserves to lose honor who seeks to receive it from those whose vices render them truly infamous and dishonorable."

"Reputation is but a sign to point out the residence of virtue; it is virtue, then, that must be preferred in all and through all; wherefore, should any one call you a hypocrite because you are devout, or a coward because you have pardoned an injury, laugh at him; for although such judgments are passed on us by the weak and foolish, we must not forsake the path of virtue, even if we were to lose our reputation, because we must prefer the fruit before the leaves, viz., interior and spiritual graces before all external goods. It is lawful to be jealous, but not an idolater of our reputation; and, as we should not offend the eyes of the good, so we must strive to satisfy those of the wicked. The beard is an ornament to the face of a man, and the hair to that of a woman; if the beard be plucked from the chin, and the hair from the head, it will hardly grow again, but if it be only cut, nay, though it be shaved close, it will soon be renewed, and grow stronger and thicker than ever; so although our reputation be cut, or even shaved by the tongues of detractors, which David compares to sharp razors, we must not make ourselves uneasy, for it will soon shoot forth again, not only as fair as before, but much more firm and durable. But if our vices and wicked course of life take away our reputation, it will hardly return, because it is pulled up by the root; for the root of a good name are virtue and probity, which, as long as they remain in us, can always recover the honor due to it."

"If any vain conversation, idle habit, fond love, or custom of frequenting improper company blast our reputation, we must forsake these gratifications because our good name is of more value than such vain contentments. But if, for the exercise of piety, the advancement of devotion, or our progress towards heaven, men grumble, murmur, and speak evil of us, let us leave these, like curs, to bark at the moon; for should they, at any time, be able to cast an aspersion on our good name and by that means cut and shave the beard of our reputation, it will quickly spring up again, and the razor of detraction will be as advantageous to our honor as the pruning-knife to the vine, which makes it abound and multiply in fruit."

"Let us incessantly fix our eyes on Jesus Christ crucified, and proceed in his service with confidence and sincerity, but yet with wisdom and discretion; He will be the protector of our reputation; and, should He suffer it to be taken from us, it will be either to restore it with advantage, or to make us profit in holy humility, one ounce of which is preferable to ten thousand pounds of honors. Are we blamed unjustly, let us peaceably oppose truth against calumny; does the calumny continue, let us also continue to humble ourselves, resigning our reputation, together with our soul, into the hands of God; we cannot secure it better. Let us serve God in evil and in good report, according to the example of St. Paul, that we may say with David: 'For thy sake, O Lord, I have borne reproach, and shame hath covered my face.' I except, nevertheless, certain crimes, so horrid and infamous, that no man ought to suffer the false imputation of them, if he can justly acquit himself; and also certain persons, on whose reputation depends the edification of many; for, in these cases, according to the opinion of divines, we must quietly seek a reparation of the wrong received." (ST. FRANCIS DE SALES; pp. 147-152)

HUMILITY: Observations on the Noblest of the Moral Natural Virtues

"'Borrow empty vessels, not a few,' said Eliseus to the poor widow, 'and pour oil into them.' To receive the grace of God into our hearts they must be emptied of vainglory."

"As the Castrel of Kestrel, a bird of the hawk kind by crying and looking on the birds of prey, affright them by a secret property peculiar to itself, which makes the doves love her above all other birds, and live in security with her; so humility repels Satan, and preserves the grace and gift of the Holy Ghost within us. All the Saints, but particularly the King of Saints and His Mother, have always honored and cherished this blessed virtue more than any amongst the moral virtues. We call that glory vain which we assume to ourselves, either for what is not in us, or for what is in us, and belongs to us, but deserves not that we should glory in it. The nobility of our ancestors, the favor of great men, and popular honor, are things, not in us, but either in our progenitors, or in the esteem of other men. Some become proud and insolent, either by riding a good horse, wearing a feather in their hat, or be being dressed in a fine suit of clothes; but who does not see the folly of this? for if there be any glory in such things, the glory belongs to the horse, the bird, and the tailor; and what a meanness of heart must it be, to borrow esteem from a horse, from a feather, or some ridiculous new fashion! Others value themselves for a well-trimmed beard, for curled locks, or soft hands; or because they can dance, sing, or play; but are not these effeminate men, who seek to raise their reputation by so frivolous and foolish things? Others, for a little learning, would be honored and respected by the whole world, as if every one ought to become their pupil, and account them his master. These are called pedants. Others strut like peacocks, contemplating their beauty and think themselves admired by every one. All this is extremely vain, foolish, and impertinent; and the glory which is raised on so weak foundations is justly esteemed vain and frivolous."

"True goodness is proved like true balm; for as balm, when dropped into water, if it sinks and rests at the bottom, is so accounted the most excellent and precious; so, if you would know whether a man be truly wise, learned, or generous, observe whether his qualifications tend to humility, modesty, and submission; for then they shall be good indeed; but if they swim on the surface, and strive to appear above water, they shall be so much the less true, in the same proportion as they appear. As pearls, that are conceived and nourished by the wind, or by the noise of thunder, have nothing in the substance of pearls, but merely the external appearance; so the virtues and good qualities of men that are bred and nourished by pride, ostentation, and vanity, have nothing but the appearance of good."

"Honors, rank, and dignities, are like saffron, which thrives best, and grows most plentifully, when trodden under foot. It is no honor to be beautiful when a man prizes himself for it; beauty, to have a good grace, should be neglected; and learning is a disgrace to us when it degenerates into pendantry."

"If we stand upon the punctilio for places, precedence, and titles, besides exposing our qualities to be examined, tried, and contradicted, we render them vile and contemptible; for as honor is beautiful when freely given, so it becomes base when exacted or sought after. When the peacock spreads his tails to admire himself, in raising up his beautiful feathers he ruffles all the rest and discovers his deformities. Flowers that are fair whilst they grow in the earth wither and fade when handled; and as they that smell the mandrake at a distance perceive a most agreeable fragrance, whilst they that approach become sick and stupefied, so honors give a pleasant satisfaction to those that view them afar off, without stopping to amuse themselves with them, or being earnest about them. Those who affect them, or feed on them, are exceedingly blamable and worthy of reprehension."

"The pursuit and love of virtue begin to make us virtuous; but the pursuit and love of honor make us contemptible and worthy of blame. Generous minds do not amuse themselves about the petty toys of rank, honor, and salutation; they have other things to perform; such baubles only belong to degenerate spirits."

"He that may have pearls never loads himself with shells; and such as aspire to virtue trouble not themselves about honors. Every one indeed may take and keep his own place without prejudice to humility, so that it be done carelessly, and without contention. For as they that come from Peru, besides gold and silver, bring also thence apes and parrots, because they neither cost much, nor are burdensome; so they that aspire to virtue refuse not the rank and honor due to them, provided it cost them not too much care and attention, nor involve them in trouble, anxiety, disputes, or contentions. Nevertheless, I do not here allude to those whose dignity concerns the public, nor to certain particular occasions of important consequences; for in these every one ought to keep what belongs to him, with prudence and discretion, accompanied by charity and suavity of manners."

"But if you desire to penetrate still deeper into humility; for what I have hitherto said rather concerns wisdom than humility. Let us, then, proceed. Many neither will not and dare not consider the particular favors God has done them, lest it might excite vainglory and self-complacency; but in doing so they deceive themselves; for since the best means to attain the love of God (says the great Angelical Doctor) is the consideration of his benefits the more we know them the more shall we love him; and as the particular benefits he has conferred on us more powerfully move us than those that are common to others, so ought they to be more attentively considered. Certainly nothing can so effectually humble us before the mercy of God as the multitude of His benefits; nor so much humble us before His justice as the enormity of our innumerable offenses. Let us, then, consider what He has done for us, and what we have done against Him; and as we reflect on our sins, one by one, so let us consider His favors in the same order. We must not fear lest the knowledge of His gifts make us proud, so long as we are attentive to this truth 'That whatsoever there is of good in us is not from ourselves.' Do mules cease to be disgusting beasts, because they are laden with the precious and perfumed goods of the prince? 'What has thou which thou has not received?' says the apostle. And if thou hast received it, why dost thou glory? Nay, on the contrary, the lively consideration of favors received makes us humble, because a knowledge of them excites gratitude. But if, in considering the favors that God has conferred on us, any thought of vanity should attack us, it will be an infallible remedy to recur to the consideration of our ingratitudes, imperfections, and miseries. If we consider what we did when God was not with us, we shall easily be convinced that what we do while He is with us is not of our own exertion; we shall indeed rejoice in it, because we enjoy it, but we shall glorify God, because He alone is the author of it. Thus, the Blessed Virgin confesses that God had done great things for her, but it is only to humble herself, and to glorify God: 'My soul', says she, 'doth magnify the Lord because he has done great things for me'."

"We often confess ourselves to be nothing, nay, misery itself, and the refuse of the world; but would be very sorry that any one should believe us, or tell others that we are really such miserable wretches. On the contrary, we pretend to retire, and hide ourselves, so that the world may run after us, and seek us out. We feign to wish ourselves considered as the last in the company, and sit down at the lowest end of the table; but it with a view that we may be desired to pass to the upper end. True humility never makes a show of herself, nor uses many humble words; for she desires not only to conceal all other virtues, but principally herself; and, were it lawful to dissemble, or scandalize her neighbor, she would perform actions of arrogancy and haughtiness, that she might conceal herself beneath them and remain altogether unknown."

"My advice, therefore, is that we should either not accustom ourselves to words of humility, or else use them with a sincere interior sentiment conformably to what we pronounce outwardly. Let us never cast down out eyes but when we humble our hearts; let us not seem to desire to be the lowest, unless we sincerely desire it. I think this rule so general as to admit of no exception; I only add, that civility requires we should sometimes offer precendency to those who will doubtless refuse it, and yet this is neither duplicity nor false humility; for in this case, as the offer of precedency is only the beginning of honor, and since we cannot give it them entirely, we do well to give them the beginning. I say, though some words of honor or respect may not seem strictly conformable to the truth, yet they are sufficiently so, provided the heart of him that pronounces them has a sincere intention to honor and respect him to whom they are addressed, for although the words signify with some excess that which we would say, yet we do not act wrongly in using them when common custom requires it; however, I wish our words were always as nearly as possible suited to our affections, that so we might follow; in all and through all, a cordial sincerity and candor. A man that is truly humble would rather another should say to him that he is miserable, and that he is nothing, than to say it himself; at least, if he knows that any man says so he does not contradict it, but heartily agrees to it; for, believing it himself firmly, he is pleased that others entertain the same opinion."

" Many say that they leave mental prayer to those that are perfect; that, as for themselves, they are unworthy to use it. Others protest they dare not communicate often, because they find themselves not sufficiently pure. Others fear they should bring disgrace upon devotion if they meddled with it, by reason of their great misery and frailty. Others refuse to employ their talents in the service of God and their neighbor, saying they know their own weakness, and fear they should become proud if they proved instruments of any good; and that, in giving light to others, they should consume themselves in the flames of vanity. All this is nothing but an artificial kind of humility, false and malicious whereby they tacitly and subtlety seek to find fault with the things of God; or, at the best, to conceal the love of their own opinion, humor , and sloth, under the pretext of humility...The Desire of God is, that we should be perfect uniting ourselves to Him and imitating Him as nearly as possible. The proud man, who trusts in himself, has just reason not to attempt anything; but he that is humble is so much the more courageous, by how much the more he acknowledges his own inability; and the more wretched he esteems himself the more confident he becomes; because he places his whole trust in God, who delights to display His omnipotence in our weakness, and to elevate His mercy upon our misery. We may then humbly and devoutly presume to undertake all that may be judged proper for our advancement by those that conduct our souls."

"To imagine we know what we do not know is folly; to desire to pass for knowing that of which we are ignorant is an intolerable vanity. For my part, as I would not make a parade of the knowledge even of that which I know; so, on the other hand, I would not pretend to be ignorant thereof. When charity requires it we must freely and mildly communicate to our neighbor, not only what is necessary for our instruction, but, also, what is profitable for our consolation; for humility; which conceals virtues, in order to preserve them, discovers them, nevertheless, when charity requires it, in order that we may enlarge, increase, and perfect them. In this respect humility imitates a certain tree in the Isles of Tylosk that at night closes up her beautiful carnation flowers, and only opens them to the rising sun; and as the inhabitants of the country say that those flowers sleep by night, so humility covers all our virtuous and human perfections, and never unfolds them except for the sake of charity, which, being not a human and moral but a divine and heavenly virtue is the true son of all other virtues, over which she ought always to have dominion. Hence we may conclude that the humilities which are prejudicial to charity are assuredly false."

"I would neither pretend to be a fool nor a wise man; for if humility forbids me to conceal my wisdom, candor and sincerity also forbids me to counterfeit the fool; and as vanity is opposite to humility, so artifice affectation, and dissimulation are contrary to sincerity. But, if some great servants of God have pretended to be fools to render themselves more abject in the eyes of the world, we must admire, but not imitate them; for having had peculiar and extraordinary motives that induced them to this excess, no one ought thence to draw any consequence for himself. David, when he danced and leaped before the Ark of the Covenant with an excess that ordinary decency could not admire, had no design to make the world believe him foolish; but, with all simplicity and openness, he made use of those exterior motions to express the extraordinary and excessive joy he felt in his heart; and when Michol, his wife, reproached him for it, as an act of folly, he did not regret to see himself vilified, but, continuing in a true and sincere manifestation of his joy, he testified that he was glad to be reproached for his God. Remember that if, for acts of a true and sincere devotion, the world shall esteem you mean, abject, or foolish, humility will make you rejoice at his happy reproach, the cause of which is not in you, but in those that reproach you."

"In all, and through all, you should love your own abjection. But you will ask me what it is to love your own abjection. In Latin 'abjection' signifies 'humility,' and 'humility' signifies 'abjection'; so that when our Lady, in her sacred canticle, says, that 'all generations shall call her blessed,' because our Lord had regarded the 'humility of His handmaid,' her meaning is, that our Lord had graciously looked down on her abjection, her meanness, and lowliness, to heap His graces and favors upon her. Nevertheless, there is a difference between the virtue of 'humility' and our 'abjection': for our 'abjection' is the lowliness, meanness, and baseness that exist in us, without our knowledge; whereas, the virtue of 'humility' is a true knowledge and voluntary acknowledgment of our abjection. Now, the main point of this humility consists in being willing not only to acknowledge our abjection, but in loving and delighting in it; and this, not through want of courage and generosity, but for the great exaltation of the divine Majesty and holding our neighbor in greater estimation than ourselves. To this I exhort you; and, that you may comprehend me more clearly, I tell you that among the evils which we suffer some are abject, and others honorable; many can easily accommodate themselves to those evils that are honorable; but scarce any one to such as are abject. You see a devout old hermit covered with rages; every one honors his tattered habit, and compassionates his sufferings; but if a poor tradesman, or a poor gentleman, be in the like case, the world despises and scoffs at him; and thus you see how his poverty is abject. A religious man receives a sharp reproof from his superior, or a child from his father, with meekness, and every one calls this mortification, obedience and wisdom; but should a gentlemen or lady suffer the like from another, and although it were for the love of God, it is then called cowardice and want of spirit. Behold, then, here another evil that is abject. One has a canker in his arm, and another in his face; the first has only the disease, but the other, together with the disease has contempt, disgrace, and abjection. I say, then, that we must not only love the evil which is the duty of patience, but also embrace the abjection, by virtue of humility. There are, moreover, virtues which are abject, and virtues which are honorable. Patience, meekness, simplicity, and even humility itself, are virtues which worldlings consider as mean and abject; whilst, on the contrary they hold prudence, fortitude, and liberality, in the highest estimate. There are also action of one and the same virtue, some of which are both acts of charity; and yet the first is honored, whilst the latter is despised in the eyes of the world. A young gentlemen or lady who refuse to join in the disorders of a debauched company, or to talk, play , dance, drink, or dress, as the rest do, will incur their scorn and censure. and their modesty will be termed bigotry or affection: to love this is to love your own abjection."

"Behold an abjection of another kind. We go to visit the sick; if I am sent to the most miserable, it will be to me an abjection according to the world, for which reason I will love it. If I am sent to a person of quality, it an abjection according to the spirit, for there is not so much virtue or merit in it, and therefore I will love this abjection. There are even faults which have no other ill in them besides abjection; and humility does not require that we should deliberately commit them, but that we should not vex ourselves when we have committed them. Such are certain follies, incivilities, for the sake of civility and discretion; so when they are committed, we ought to be content with the abjection we meet with, and accept it willingly, for the sake of practicing humility."

"I say yet more: should I, through passion or anger, have spoken any unbecoming words, wherewith God and my neighbor may have been offended, I will repent, and be sorry for the offense, and endeavor to make the best reparation I can, but yet will admit of the abjection, and the contempt which it has brought upon me; and could the one be separated from the other, I would most cheerfully cast away the sin, and humbly retain the abjection."

"But though we love the abjection that follows the evil, yet we must not neglect, by just and lawful means, to redress the evil that caused it, especially when it is of consequence; as, for example, should I have some disagreeable disorder in my face, I will endeavor to have it cured, but not with the intention of forgetting the abjection I received by it. If I have been guilty of some folly, which has given no one offence, I will give no apology for it; because, although it were an offence, yet it is not permanent; I could not, therefore, excuse it, but only with a view to rid myself of the abjection, which would not be agreeable to humility. But if, through inadvertence or otherwise, I should have offended or scandalized any one, I will repair the offence by some true excuse; because the evil is permanent, and charity obliges me to remove it. Besides, it sometimes happens that charity requires we should remove the abjection for the good of our neighbors to whom our reputation is necessary; but in such a case, though we remove the abjection from before our neighbor's eyes, to prevent scandal, yet must we carefully shut it up in our heart for its edification."

"But would you know which are the best abjections? I tell you plainly that these are most profitable to our souls and most acceptable to God which befall us by accident, or by our condition of life; because we have not chosen them ourselves, but received them as sent by God whose choice is always better than our own. But were we to choose any, we should prefer the greatest, and those are esteemed such as are most contrary to our inclinations, provided that they be conformable to our vocation; for, as I have already said, our own choice spoils or lessens almost all our virtues. Oh, who will enable us to say: 'I have chosen to be an abject in the house of God, rather than to dwell in the tabernacles of sinners'? No one certainly, but he who, to exalt us, lived and died in such a manner as to become the reproach of men, and the abjection of the people. I have said many things to you which may seem hard to you in theory, but believe me, they will be more agreeable than sugar or honey when you put them in practice." (ST. FRANCIS DE SALES; pp. 133-147)

JUDGEMENTS: Precautions and Avoidance of, and When to Judge

"'Judge not, and you shall not be judged,' says our Saviour of our souls; 'Condemn not, and you shall not be condemned. 'Judge not,' says the holy apostle, 'before the time; until the Lord come, who both will bring to light the hidden things of darkness, and will make manifest the counsels of the hearts.' Oh, how displeasing are rash judgments to God! The judgements of the children of men are rash, because they are not the judges of one another, and therefore usurp to themselves the office of our Lord. They are rash, because the principal malice of sin depends on the intent in the heart which is an impenetrable secret to us. There are not only rash, but also impertinent, because every one will find sufficient employment in judging himself, without taking upon him to judge his neighbor. To avoid future judgment it is as necessary to refrain from judging others as to be careful to judge ourselves. For as our Lord forbids the one so the apostle enjoins the other, saying, that if we judged ourselves we should not be judged. But we act quite the contrary; for, by judging our neighbor on every occasion we do that which is forbidden; and by not judging ourselves, we neglect to practice that which we are strictly commanded."

"The remedies against rash judgements must be according to their different causes. There are some hearts naturally so bitter and harsh as to make everything bitter and harsh that they receive, converting judgement, as the prophet Amos says, into wormwood, by never judging their neighbors except with all rigor and harshness. These must seek the advice of a good spiritual physician, because this bitterness of heart, being natural to them, is subdued with difficulty; and though it be not in itself a sin, but an imperfection only, yet it is dangerous, because it introduces and causes rash judgment and detraction to reign in the soul. Some judge rashly, not through harshness but through pride, imaging that in the same proportion as they depress the honor of other men, they raise their own. Arrogant and presumptuous spirit who admire and place themselves so high in their own esteem, look on all others as mean and abject. 'I am not like the rest of men,' said the foolish Pharisee. Others, who have not altogether this manifest pride, indulge a certain satisfaction in considering the evil qualities of other men, the more agreeable to contemplate, and make others admire the contrary good qualities wherewith they think themselves endowed; for this complacency is so secret and imperceptible as not to be discovered even by those of their own consciences, very willingly judge others to be guilty of the same vices to which they themselves are addicted, or of some other vices equally as great; thinking that the multitude of offenders diminishes the guilt of the sin. Many take the liberty of judging others rashly, merely for the pleasure of delivering their opinion and conjectures on their manners and humors, by way of exercising their wit; and if, unhappily, they sometimes happen not to err in their judgment, their rashness increases to so violent an excess as to render it in a manner impossible ever to effect their cure. Others judge through passion and prejudice, always thinking well of what they love, and ill of that which they hate; excepting in one case only, not less wonderful than true, in which the excess of love incites them to pass an ill judgment on that which they love, - a paradoxical effect, which always proceeds from an impure and distempered love; and this is jealousy, which, as every one knows, on account of a mere look, or the least smile, condemns the person beloved of disloyalty or adultery. In fine, fear, ambition, and other similar weaknesses of the mind, frequently contribute towards the breeding of suspicious and rash judgments."

"But what is a remedy: As they who drink the juice of the herb of Ethiopia, called ophiusa, imagine that they everywhere behold serpents and other frightful objects; so they who have imbibed pride and ambition, and hatred, think everything they see evil and blamable. The former, to be healed must drink palm wine; and I say to the latter, drink copiously of the sacred wine of charity, and it will deliver you from those noxious humors that engender rash judgment. As charity is afraid to meet evil, so she never seeks after it, but whenever it falls in her way she turns her face aside, and does not notice it. At the first alarm of evil she closes her eyes, and afterwards believes, with an honest simplicity, that it was not evil, but only its shadow or apparition; and if she cannot avoid sometimes acknowledging it to be real evil she quickly turns from it and endeavors to forget even its shadow. Charity is that sovereign remedy for all evils, but for this especially. All things appear yellow to the eyes of those who are afflicted with the jaundice; and it is said, that to cure this evil they must wear celandine under the soles of their feet. The sin of rash judgment is indeed a spiritual jaundice, and causes all thing to appear evil to the eyes of those who are infected; he that would be cured must apply the remedies to such an action. We must always do the same, judging as much as possible in favor of our neighbors; and if one action could bear a hundred faces we should always consider that which is the fairest."

"Our blessed Lady was with child, and St. Joseph plainly perceived it; but, on the other hand, as he saw her holy, pure, and angelical, he could not believe she became pregnant in an unlawful manner; so that he resolved to leave her privately, and commit the judgment of her case to God; and though the argument was well calculated to make him conceive an ill opinion of his virgin spouse, yet he would never judge her; and why? Because, says the spirit of God 'he was a just man'." A just man when he can no longer excuse either the action, or the intention, of him whom otherwise he sees to be virtuous, nevertheless will not judge him, but endeavors to forget it and leaves the judgment to God. Thus, our blessed Saviour on the cross, not being able to excuse entirely the sin of those that crucified Him, extenuated the malice of it by alleging their ignorance. When we cannot excuse the sin, let us at least render it worthy of compassion, attributing it to the most favorable cause, such as ignorance or infirmity."

"But can we never judge our neighbor? No, verily, never. It is God that judges malefactors in public justice. It is true that He uses the voice of judges to make Himself intelligible to our ears; are His interpreters, and ought to pronounce nothing but what they learn of Him, as being His oracles; if they act otherwise, by folly their own passions, then, indeed, it is they that judge, and who consequently shall be judged; for it is forbidden to men, in quality of men, to judge others."

"To see or know a thing is not to judge it; for judgment, at least according to Scripture, presupposes some difficulty, great or small, true or apparent, which is to be decided, it says, 'He who not is already judged,' because there is no doubt of his damnation. It is not, then, a sin to doubt of our neighbor? No, for we are not forbidden to doubt, but to judge; however, it is only allowable to doubt or suspect as far as reason and arguments may constrain us, otherwise our doubts and suspicions will be rash."

"If some evil eye had seen Jacob when he kissed Rachel by the well, or had seen Rebecca receive bracelets and ear-rings from El a man unknown in that country, he would no doubt have thought ill of these two patrons of chastity; but without reason or foundation; when an action is in itself indifferent, it is a rash suspicion of an ill consequence from it, unless many circumstances give strength to the argument from an action, in order to blame the person; but I shall hereafter explain more clearly."

"In fine, those who have tender consciences are not very subject to rash judgment; for, as the bees in misty or cloudy weather keep in their hives to arrange their honey; so the thought of good souls do not venture in search of objects that lie concealed amidst the cloudy actions of their neighbors; but, to avoid meeting them, they retire into their own hearts, to arrange the good resolutions of their own amendments."

"It is natural to an unprofitable soul to amuse itself with examining the loves of other persons; I except spiritual directors, fathers of families, magistrates, etc., because a considerable part of their duty consists in watching over the conduct of others; let them discharge their duty with love and, having done this, they must then attend to their own advancement in virtue."

"Rash judgment engenders uneasiness, contempt of our neighbor, pride, self-complacency, and many other most pernicious effects. Oh, that I possessed one of the burning coals of the holy altar to touch the lips of men, so that their iniquities might be taken away, and their sin cleansed, in imitation of the seraphim that purified the mouth of the prophet. He that would deliver the world from detraction would free it from a great number of sins."

"Whoever robs his neighbor of his good name is not only guilty of sin, but is also bound to make reparation; for no man can enter into heaven with the goods of another; and, amongst all exterior goods, a good name is the best. Detraction is a kind of murder; for we have three lives, viz., the spiritual, which consists in the grace of God; the corporal, which depends on the soul; and the civil, which consists in our good name; sin deprives us of the first, death takes away the second, and detraction robs us of the third. But the detractor by one blow of his tongue commits three murders; he kills not only his own soul, and the soul of him that hears him, but also, by a spiritual murder, takes away the civil life of the person detracted; for, as St. Bernard says, both he that detracts and he that hearkens to the detractor have the devil about them; the one in his tongue, and the other in his ear. David, speaking of detractors, says, 'They have sharpened their tongues like a serpent.' Now, as the serpent's tongue, according to Aristotle, is forked, and has two points, so is that of the detractor, who at one stroke stings and poisons the ear of the hearer, and the reputation of him against whom he is speaking."

"I earnestly conjure you, then, never to detract any one, either directly or indirectly; beware of falsely imputing crimes and sins to your neighbor; of discovering his secret sins, or of aggravating those that are manifest; or of making an evil interpretation of his good works; or of denying the good which you know that he possesses, or dissembling it maliciously, or diminishing it by words; for in all these ways you will highly offend God, but, most of all, by false accusations, and denying the truth to the prejudice of a third person; for it is a double sin to calumniate and injure your neighbor at the same time."

"They who preface detraction by protestations of friendship and regard for the person detracted, or who make apologies in his favor, are the most subtle and venomous of all detractors. 'I protest,' say they, 'I love him; in every other respect he is a worthy man; but yet the truth must be told, he was wrong to commit so treacherous an action. She was very virtuous, but, alas! she was surprised,' etc., Do you not perceive the artifice? As the dexterous archer draws the arrow as near as possible to himself, that he may shoot the dart away with greater force, so, when these detractors seem to draw the detraction towards themselves, it is only with a view to shoot it away with more violence, that it may pierce more deeply into the hearts of their hearers. But the detraction which is uttered by way of a witty jest is still more cruel than all the rest. For, as hemlock is not of itself a very quick, but rather a slow, poison, which may be easily remedied, yet being taken with wine is incurable; so detraction, which of itself might pass lightly in at one ear and out at the other, remains in the minds of the hearers, when it is couched under some subtle and merry jest. 'The venom of asps,' says David, 'is under their lips.' The bite of the asp is almost imperceptible, and its venom at first produced a delightful itching, by means of which the heart and the bowels are expanded and receive the poison; again which there is afterwards no remedy."

"Say not such a one is a drunkard, because you have seen him drunk; nor that he is an adulterer, because he has been surprised in that sin; nor that he is incestuous, because he has been guilty of that abominable action; for one act alone is not sufficient to constitute a vice. The sun stood still once in favor of the victory of Josue, and was darkened another time in favor of that of our Savior; yet none will say that the sun is either immovable or dark. Noah was once drunk, and Lot another time, and this latter also committed a great incest; yet neither the one nor the other was a drunkard, nor was the latter an incestuous man. St. Peter had not a sanguinary disposition, because he once shed blood, nor was he a blasphemer, though he once blasphemed. To acquire the name of a vice or a virtue the action must be habitual; one must have made some progress in it. It is, then, an injustice to say that such a man is passionate, or a thief, because we have seen him once in a passion, or guilty of stealing. Although a man may have been a long time vicious, yet we are in danger of accusing him falsely if we call him vicious. Simon, the leper, called Magdalen a sinner, because she had been so not long before; yet he accused her falsely, for she was then no longer a sinner, but a most holy penitent; and therefore our Saviour took her cause under His protection. The proud Pharisee considered the humble publican as a great sinner, or even perhaps an unjust man, an adulterer, an extortioner; but was greatly deceived, for at that very time he was justified. Alas! since the goodness of God is so immense, that one moment suffices to obtain and receive His grace, what assurance can we have that he who was yesterday a sinner is not a saint today? The day that is past ought not to judge the day present, or the present day judge that which is past; it is only the last day that judges all. We can, then, never say a man is wicked without exposing ourselves to the danger of lying; all that we can say, if we must speak is, that he did such bad actions, or lived ill at such a time; that he does ill at present; but we must never draw consequences from yesterday to this day, nor from this day to yesterday, much less to tomorrow."

"Now, though we must be extremely cautious of speaking ill of our neighbor, yet we must avoid the contrary extreme, into which some fall, who, to avoid the sin of detraction, commend and speak well of vice. If a person be, indeed, a detractor, say not, in his excuse, he is a frank and free speaker; if a person be notoriously vain, say not that he is genteel and elegant; never call dangerous familiarities by the name of simplicity and innocence; nor disobedience by the name of zeal; nor arrogance by the name of freedom; nor lasciviousness by the name of friendship, No, dear Philothea, we must not, in order to avoid the vice of detraction, favor, flatter, or cherish vice; but we must openly and freely speak of evil, and blame that which is blamable; for in doing this we glorify God, provided we observe the following conditions:-

"To speak commendably against the vices of another it is necessary that we should have in view the profit either of the person spoken of, or of those to whom we speak. For instance, when the indiscreet or dangerous familiarities of such or such persons are related in the company of young maids; or the liberties taken by this or that person, in their words or gestures, are plainly lascivious, if I do not freely blame the evil but rather excuse it, these tender souls, who hear of it, will perhaps take occasion to allow themselves some such like liberties. Their advantage, then, requires that I should freely reprehend these liberties upon the spot, unless I could reserve this good office to be done better, and with less prejudice to the persons spoken of, on some other occasion."

"It is, moreover, requisite that it should be my duty to speak on this occasion, as when I am one of the chief of the company; for, if I should keep silence, I would seem to approve of the vice; but if I be one of the least, I must not take upon me to pass my censure. But, above all, it is necessary that I should be so cautious in my remarks as not to say a single word too much. For example, if I blame the familiarity of this young man, and that young maid, because it is apparently indiscreet and dangerous, good God! Philothea, I must hold the balance so even as not to make the matter a single grain heavier. Should there be but a slight appearance, I will call it no more; if a mere indiscretion, I would give it no worse name; should there be neither indiscretion, nor real appearance of evil, but only a probability that some malicious spirit may take from thence a pretext to speak ill, I will either say nothing at all, or say this only, and no more. My tongue, whilst I am speaking of my neighbor, shall be in my mouth like a knife in the hand of a surgeon, who would cut between the sinews and the tendons. The blow I shall give shall be neither more nor less that the truth. In fine, it must be our principal care in blaming any vice to spare, as much as possible, the person in whom it is found."

"It is true, we may speak freely of infamous public and notorious sinners, provided it be in the spirit of charity and compassion, and not with arrogance and presumption, nor with complacency in the evils of others, which is always the part of a mean and abject heart. Amongst these, however, the declared enemies of God and his Church, such as the ringleaders of heretics and schismatics, must be excepted, since it is charity to cry out against the one, wherever he is, more especially when he is among the sheep."

"Every one takes the liberty to censure princes and to speak ill of whole nations, according to the different affections they bear them, Philothea, avoid this fault; besides the offence against God, it may bring you into a thousand quarrels,"

"When you hear any one spoken ill of, make the accusation doubtful, if you can do it justly; if you cannot, excuse the intention of the party accused: if that cannot be done, express a compassion for, change the topic of conversation, remembering yourself, and putting the company in mind, that they who do not fall owe their happiness to God alone; recall the detractor to himself with meekness, and declare some good action of the party offended, if you know any." (ST. FRANCIS DE SALES: pp. 226 - 239)

LOVE: On Loving God

"It is well to lament the painful death and passion of our Blessed Redeemer, but why then, do we not give Him the apple which we have in our hands, for which He so earnestly asks? Why do we not give Him our heart the only token of love which our Saviour requires of us? Why do we not resign to Him so many petty affections, delights, and complacencies, which He wants to pluck out of our hands but cannot, because we feel more affection for these trifles than His heavenly grace? Ah, these are the friendships of little children; tender, indeed, but weak, capricious, and of no effect. Devotion, then, consists not in these sensible affections, which sometimes proceed from a soft nature, susceptible of any impression we may wish to give it; sometimes from the enemy, who, to amuse us, stirs up our imagination to conceive these effects."

"Yet these tender and delightful affections are sometimes good and profitable, for they excite the affections of the soul, strengthen the spirit, and add to the promptitude of devotion a holy cheerfulness, which makes our actions lovely and agreeable even in the exterior. This relish which we find in the things of God is that which made David exclaim: 'O Lord, how sweet are thy words to my palate! More than honey to my mouth.' Doubtless the least consolation of devotion that we receive is in every respect preferable to the most agreeable recreations of the world. The breasts of the heavenly Spouse are sweeter to the soul than the wine of the most delicious pleasures on earth. He that has once tasted this sweetness esteems all other consolations no better than gall and wormwood. There is a certain something here, the taste of which is said to impart such sweetness as to prevent hunger and thirst; so they to whom God has given the heavenly manna can neither desire nor relish the consolations of the world, so far at least as to fix their affections on them; they are little foretastes of those immortal delights which God has in reserve for the souls that seek Him; they are little delicacies which He gives to His children to allure them; they are the cordials with which He strengthens them, and they are also sometimes the earnest of eternal felicity. It is said that Alexander the Great, sailing on the ocean, discovered Arabia Felix, by perceiving the fragrant odors which the wind bore thence, and thereupon encouraged both himself and his companions, so we oftentimes receive these sweet consolations in the sea of our mortal life, which doubtless must give us a certain foretaste of the delights of that heavenly country to which we tend and aspire."

"But you will perhaps say, since there are sensible consolations which are good, because they come from God; and others unprofitable, dangerous, and even pernicious, that proceed either from nature, or from the enemy, - how shall I be able to distinguish the one from the other, or know those that are evil or unprofitable, from those that are good? It is a general doctrine with regard to the affections and passions of our souls, that we must know them by their fruits. Our hearts are the trees and those affections and passions are good which produce in us good effects and holy actions. If this sweetness, tenderness and consolation make us more humble, patient, tractable, charitable, and compassionate towards our neighbor; more fervent in mortifying our concupiscence and evil inclinations; more constant in our exercises; more pliant and submissive to those whom we ought to obey; more sincere and upright in our lives, - then, doubtless they proceed from God. But if these consolations have no sweetness but for ourselves; if they make us curious, harsh, quarrelsome, impatient, obstinate, haughty, presumptuous and rigorous towards our neighbor, when we already imagine ourselves to be saints, and disdain to be any longer subject to direction or corrections, they are then, beyond all doubt, false and pernicious; for a good tree cannot bring forth bad fruit."

"Whenever we experience these consolations we must humble ourselves exceedingly before God, and beware of saying. 'Oh, how good am I!' No, these considerations, as I have already said, cannot make us better; devotion does not consist in them; but let us say: 'Oh, how good is God to such as hope in Him, to the soul that seeks Him!' As the bare perception of something sweet cannot be said to render the palate itself sweet; so although this principal sweetness be excellent, and though God who gives it is sovereignty good, yet it follows not that he who receives it is also good. Let us acknowledge that we are as yet but little children, who have need of milk, and that these dainties are given to us because our tender and delicate spirit stands in need of some, allurement to entice us to the love of God. Let us afterwards humbly accept these extraordinary graces and favors, and esteem them, not so much on account of their excellence, as because it is the hand of God which puts them into our hearts, as a mother would do who the more to please her child, puts the dainties into his mouth with her own hand, one by one; for if the child has understanding he sets a greater value on the tenderness of his mother than the delicious morsels which he receives and thus, it is a great matter to taste the sweetness of sensible consolations, but it is infinitely more sweet to consider that it is His most loving and tender hand that puts them, as it were, into our mouth, our heart , our soul, and our spirit. Having thus humbly received them, let us carefully employ them according to the intention of the donor. Now, to what end, think you, does God give us these sweet consolations? To make us sweet towards every one, and excite us to love Him. The mother gives little presents to her child to induce him to embrace her; let us, then, embrace our blessed Saviour who grants us these favors. But to embrace Him is to obey him, to keep His commandments, do His will, and follow His desires, with a tender obedience, and fidelity. Whenever, therefore, we receive any spiritual consolation, we must be more diligent in doing good and in humbling ourselves. Besides all this we must from time to time, renounce those sweet and tender consolations, by withdrawing our heart from them and protesting that, although we humbly accept them and love them because He sends them and that they excite us to His love yet it is not these we seek but God Himself and His holy love; not the consolations, but the comforter, not their deliciousness, but the sweet Saviour; not their tenderness, but Him that is the delight of heaven and earth. It is in this manner we ought to dispose ourselves to persevere in the holy love of God, although throughout our whole life we were never to meet with any consolation and be ready to say as well upon Calvary as upon Thabor: 'Lord! it is good for me to be with thee, whether thou be upon the cross, or in thy glory.' To conclude, I admonish you, that should you experience any great abundance of such consolations, tenderness, tears, sweetness, etc., you must confer faithfully with your spiritual director, that you may learn how to moderate and behave yourself under them...." (ST. FRANCIS DE SALES: pp 317-321)

LOVE: Faithfulness to God in Things Great and Small

"The sacred Spouse in the canticle says, that his Spouse has wounded 'his heart with one of her eyes, and with one hair of her neck.' Now among all the exterior parts of the human body, none is more noble, either for its construction or activity, than the eye, and none more inconsiderable than the hair. Wherefore the divine Spouse would give us to understand, that He is pleased to accept not only the great works of devout persons, but also the least and most trivial; and that, to serve Him as He desires, we must take care to serve Him well, not only in great and important things, but in those that are small and unimportant; since we may equally by the one and the other wound His heart with love."

"Prepare yourself, then, to suffer many great afflictions, even martyrdom itself, for our Lord; resolve to surrender to Him whatever is most dear to you, when it shall please him to take it; father, mother, husband, wife, brother, sister, children, yea, even your eyes, or your life;

for to all these sacrifices you ought to prepare your heart. But as long as divine Providence sends you not afflictions so sensible or so great since He requires not your eyes, give Him at least your hair. I mean, suffer meekly those small injuries, trifling inconveniences, and inconsiderable losses, which daily befall you; for by means of such little circumstances as these, managed with love and affection, you will engage His heart entirely, and make it all your own. These little daily charities; this headache, or toothache, this cold; this perverse humor of a husband or wife; this breaking of a glass; this contempt of scorn; this loss of a pair of gloves, of a ring, or a handkerchief; those little inconveniences which we suffer by retiring to rest at an early hour, and rising early to pray or communicate; that little bashfulness we have in performing certain acts of devotion in public; in short, all these trivial sufferings, being accepted, and embraced with love, are highly pleasing to the divine goodness, who for a cup of cold water only has promised an eternal reward to His faithful servants. Wherefore as these occasions present themselves every moment, to employ them to advantage will be a great means to heap up a store of spiritual riches."

"When I saw in the life of St. Catharine, of Sienna, her many raptures and elevations of spirit, so many words of wisdom, nay, even profound instructions uttered by her, I doubted not but that, with the eye of contemplation, she had ravished the heart of her heavenly Spouse. But I was no less comforted when I found her in her father's kitchen humbly turning the spit, kindling the fire, dressing the meat, kneading the bread, and performing the meanest offices of the house, with a courage full of love and affection towards her God; for I esteem no less the little and humble meditations she made in the midst of these menial and abject employments than the ecstasies and raptures she so often enjoyed, which were perhaps granted to her only in recompense of her humility and abjection. Her manner of meditating was as follows: whilst she was dressing the meat for her father she imagined that, like another St. Martha, she was preparing it for our Saviour, and that her mother held the place of the blessed Virgin, and her brothers that of the apostles; exciting herself in this manner to serve the whole court of heaven in spirit, whilst she employed herself with great delight in these humble services, because she knew that such was the will of God. I have adduced this example that you may know of what importance it is to direct all your actions, how inconsiderable soever they may be, with a pure intention to the service of his divine Majesty."

"Wherefore I earnestly advise you to imitate the valiant woman whom the great Solomon so highly commends; 'she hath put out her hands,' he says, 'to strong things'; that is, to high, generous, and important things, and yet disdained not to 'take hold of the spindle.' Put out your hand to strong things, exercise yourself in prayer and meditation, in frequenting the sacraments, in exciting souls to the love of God, and infusing good inspirations into their hearts, and, in a word, in the performance of great and important works, according to your vocation: but never forget your distaff or spindle, or in other words, take care to practice these low and humble virtues, which grow like flowers at the foot of the cross; such as serving the poor, visiting the sick, taking care of your family, and attending to all your domestic concerns with that profitable diligence which will not suffer you to be idle; and, amidst all these occupations, mingle consideration similar to those I have related above of St. Catharine."

"Great occasions of serving God present themselves seldom, but little ones frequently. 'Now he that shall be faithful in small matters,' says our Saviour, 'shall be set over great things.' Perform all things, then, in the name of God, and you will do all things well, whether you eat, drink, sleep, recreate yourself, or turn the spit provided you will profit much in the sight of his divine Majesty." (ST. FRANCIS DE SALES; pp 249-253)

MARRIAGE: Instruction ofValue to Married Persons

"Matrimony is a great Sacrament, but I speak in Christ, and in the Church." It is honorable to all persons, in all persons, and in all things, that is, in all its parts. To all persons, because even virgins ought to honor it with humility; in all persons, because it is equally holy in the rich and poor; in all things, because its origin, its end, its advantages, its form, and its matter are all holy. It is the nursery of Christianity, which supplies the earth with faithful souls, to complete the number of the elect in heaven; in a word the preservation of marriage is of the highest importance to the commonwealth for it is the origin and source of all its streams."

"Would to God that his most beloved Son were invited to all marriages as He was to that of Cana; then the wine of consolations and benedictions would never be wanting; for the reason why there is commonly a scarcity of it at the beginning is, because Adonis is invited instead of Jesus Christ, andVenus instead of his blessed Mother. He that would have his lambs fair and spotted as Jacob's were, must, like him, set fair rods of diver colors before the sheep when they meet to couple; and he that would have a happy success in marriage ought in his espousals to represent to himself the sanctity and dignity of this sacrament. But, alas! instead of this there are a thousand disorders committed in diversions, feasting, and immodest discourse; it is not surprising , then, that the success of marriages should not correspond. Above all things, I exhort married people to that mutual love which the Holy Ghost so much recommends in the Scripture. O you that are married! I tell you not to love each other with a natural love, for it is thus that the turtles love; nor do I say, love one another with a human love, for the heathens do this; but I say to you, after the great Apostle, 'Husbands, love your wives, as Christ also loved the Church. And you, wives, love your husbands, as the Church loveth her Savior.' It was God that brought Eve to our first father, Adam, and gave her him in marriage; it is also God, O my friends who, with his invisible hand, has tied the knot of the holy bond of your marriage, and given you to one another; why do you not, then, cherish each other with a holy, sacred, and divine love?"

"The first effect of this love is an indissoluble union of your hearts. Two pieces of fir glued together, if the glue be good, cleave so fast to each other that they can be more easily broken in any other place than that in which they were joined. But God joins the husband to the wife with his own blood; for which cause this union is so strong that the soul must sooner separate from the body of the one or the other, than the husband and the wife. Now, this union is not understood principally of the body, but of the heart, of the affection, and of the love."

" The second effect of this love ought to be the inviolable fidelity of one part to the other. Seals were anciently graven upon rings worn on the fingers, as the holy Scripture itself testifies. Behold, then, the mystery of this ceremony in marriage. The Church, which by the hand of the priest blesses a ring, and gives it first to the man, testifies that she puts a seal upon his heart by this sacrament, to the end that henceforward neither the name nor the love of any other woman may enter therein, so long as she shall live who has been given to him; afterward the bridegroom puts the ring on the hand of the bride, then she reciprocally may understand that her heart must never admit an affection to any other man, so long as he shall live upon earth whom our Lord here gives her for a husband."

"The third fruit of marriage is the lawful production and education of children. It is a great honor to you that are married, that God, designing to multiply souls, which may bless and praise Him to all eternity, makes you cooperate with Him in so noble a work, by the productions of the bodies, into which He infuses immortal souls like heavenly drops, as He creates them."

"Preserve, then O husbands! a tender, constant, and cordial love for your wives; for the woman was taken from that side of the first man which was nearest his heart, to the end she might be loved by him cordially and tenderly. The weaknesses and infirmities of your wives, whether in body or mind, ought never to provoke you to any kind of disdain, but rather to a mild and affectionate compassion; since God has created them such, to the end that, depending upon you, you should receive from them more honor and respect, and that you should have them in such manner for your companions, that nevertheless you should be their heads and superiors. And you, O wives! love tenderly and cordially the husbands whom God has given you, but with a respectful love, and full of reverence; for therefore did God create them of a sex more vigorous and predominant; and was pleased to ordain that the woman should depend upon the man being bone of his bone, and flesh of his flesh, and that she should be made of a rib taken from under his arm, to show that she ought to be under the hand and guidance of her husband. The holy Scripture, which strictly recommends to you this subjection, renders it also agreeable, not only prescribing that you should accommodate yourselves to it with love, but also by commanding your husbands to exercise it over you with charity, tenderness and complacency. 'Husbands,' says St. Peter 'dwell with your wives according to knowledge giving honor to the woman as to the weaker vessel.'"

"But while I exhort you to advance more and more in this mutual love, which you owe one another, beware lest it degenerate into any kind of jealousy; for it often happens, that as the worm is bred in the apple which is the most delicate and ripe, so jealousy grows in that love of married people which is the most ardent and affectionate, of which nevertheless it spoils and corrupts the substance, breeding by insensible degrees, strifes, dissensions, and divorces. But jealousy is never seen where the friendship is reciprocally grounded on solid virtue; it is, therefore, an infallible mark that the love is in some degree sensual and gross, and has met with a virtue imperfect, inconstant, and subject to distrust. Jealousy is an absurd means of proving the sincerity of friendship. It may, indeed, be a sign of the greatness of the friendship, but never of its goodness, purity, and perfection; since the perfection of friendship presupposes an assurance of the virtue of those whom we love, and jealousy presupposes a doubt of it."

"If you desire, O husbands! that your wives should be faithful to you, give them a lesson by your example. 'How,' says St. Gregory Nazianzen, 'can you exact purity of your wives, when you yourselves live in impurity? How can you require of them that which you give them not? Do you wish them to be chaste? behave yourselves chastely towards them'; and, as St. Paul says, 'let every man know how to possess his vessel in sanctification.' But if, on the contrary, you yourselves teach them not to be virtuous, it is not surprising if you are disgraced by their perdition. But you, O wives! whose honor is inseparably joined with purity and modesty, be zealous to preserve this your glory, and suffer no kind of loose behavior to tarnish the whiteness of your reputation."

Fear all kinds of assaults, how small soever they may be; never suffer any wanton addresses to approach you; whoever presumes to praise your beauty, or your general behavior, ought to be suspected; for he that praises the ware which he cannot buy is strongly tempted to steal it, but if to your praise he adds the dispraise of your husband, he offers you a heinous injury; for it is evident that he not only desires to ruin you, but accounts you already half lost, since the bargain is half made with the second merchant when one is disgusted with the first."

"'Ladies formerly, as well as now, were accustomed to wear ear-rings or pearl, for the pleasure': says Pliny, 'which they derive from hearing them jingle against each other.' But for my part, as I know that the great friend of God, Isaac, sent ear-rings, as the first earnest of his love, to the chaste Rebecca, I believe that this mysterious ornament signifies that the first part which a husband should take possession of in his wife, and which his wife should faithfully keep for him, is her ears; in order that no other language or noise should enter there but only the sweet and amiable music of chaste and pure words, which are the orient pearls of the gospel; for we must always remember that souls are poisoned by the ear, as the body is by the mouth."

"Love and fidelity joined together always produce familiarity and confidence; and therefore the saints have used many reciprocal caresses in their marriage; caresses truly affectionate, but pure, tender, and sincere. Thus, Isaac and Rebecca, the most chaste married couple of antiquity, were seen through a window caressing one another in such manner that, though there was no immodesty, Abimelech was convinced that they could be no other than man and wife. The great St. Lewis, equally rigorous to his own flesh, and tender in the love of his wife, was almost blamed for the abundance of such caresses; though indeed, he rather deserved praise to being able to bring his martial and courageous spirit to stoop to these little duties so requisite for the preservation of conjugal love; for, although these demonstrations of pure and free affection bind not the hearts, yet they tend to unite them, and serve for an agreeable disposition to mutual conversation."

"St. Monica, being pregnant of the great St. Augustine, dedicated him by frequent oblations to the Christian religion, and to the service and glory of God, as he himself testifies, saying, that 'he had already tasted the salt of God in his mother's womb.' This is a great lesson for Christian women, to offer up to His divine Majesty the fruit of their wombs, even before they come into the world; for God, who accepts the offerings of a humble and willing heart, commonly at that time seconds the affections of mothers; witness Samuel, St. Thomas of Aquinas, St. Andrew of Fiesola, and many others. The Mother of St. Bernard, a mother worthy of such a son, as soon as her children were born, took them in her arms, and offered them up to Jesus Christ; and, from that moment, she loved them with respect as things consecrated to God and entrusted by Him to her care. This pious custom was so pleasing to God that her seven children became afterwards eminent for sanctity. But when children begin to have the use of reason, both their fathers and mothers ought to take great care to imprint the fear of God in their hearts. The devout queen Blanche performed this duty most fervently with regard to St. Lewis, her son. She often said to him, 'I would much rather, my dear child, see you die before my eyes, than see you commit only one mortal sin.' This caution remained so deeply engraved in his soul that, as he himself related not one day of his life passed in which he did not remember it, and take all possible care to observe it faithfully. Families and generations are in our language, called houses and even the Hebrews called the generations of children the building up of a house; for, in this sense, it is said that God built houses for the midwives of Egypt. Now, this is to show that the raising of a house, of family, consists not in storing up a quantity of worldly possessions, but in the good education of children in the fear of God, and in virtue, in which no pains or labor ought to be spared; for children are the crown of their parents. Thus, St. Monica fought with so much fervor and constancy against the evil inclination of her son St. Augustine, that, having followed him by sea and land, she made him more happily the child of her tears, by the conversion of his soul, than he had been of her blood, by the generation of his body."

"St. Paul leaves to wives the care of the household concerns and their portion, for which reason many think with truth that their devotion is more profitable to the family than that of the husband, who, not residing among the domestics, cannot of consequence so easily form them to virtue. On this consideration Solomon, in his Proverbs, makes the happiness of the whole family depend on the care and industry of the valiant woman whom he describes."

"It is said, in the book of Genesis, that Isaac, seeing his wife Rebecca barren, prayed to the Lord for her; or, according to the Hebrews prayed to the Lord opposite to her, because the one prayed on the one side of the oratory, and the other on the other; and the prayer of the husband offered in this manner was heard. Such union as this of the husband and wife, in holy devotion, is the best and most fruitful of all; and to this they ought mutually to encourage and to engage each other. There are fruits, as, for example, the quince, which, on account of the bitterness of their juice, are not agreeable unless they are preserved with sugar; there are others, which, on account of their tenderness, cannot be long kept, unless they are preserved in like manner, such as cherries and apricots, thus, wives ought to wish that their husbands should be preserved with the sugar of devotion; for a man without devotion is severe, harsh, and rough. And husbands ought to wish that their wives should be devout, because without devotion a woman is very frail, and liable to obscure, and perhaps to lose, her virtue. St. Paul says 'that the unbelieving husband is sanctified by the believing wife; and the unbelieving wife is sanctified by the believing husband'; because, in this strict alliance of marriage, the one may easily draw the other to virtue; but what a blessing is it when the man and wife, being both believers, sanctify each other in the true fear of God!"

"As to the rest, their mutual bearing with each other ought to be so great that they should never be both angry with each other at the same time, so that a dissension or debate be never seen between them. Bees cannot stay in a place where there are echoes or rebounding of voices; nor can the Holy Ghost remain in a house in which there are reboundings of clamor, strife, and contradictions. St. Gregory Nazianzen tells us, that in his time married people made a feast on the anniversary of their wedding. For my part, I should approve of the reviving of this custom, provided it were not attended with preparation of worldly and sensual recreations; but that the husband and wife should confess and communicate on that day, and recommend to God, with a more than ordinary fervor, the happy progress of their marriage; renewing their good purposes to sanctify it still more and more by mutual love and fidelity, and recovering breath, as it were, in our Lord, in order to support with more ease the burdens of their calling."

"The marriage bed ought to be undefiled, as the Apostle says, that is to say, exempt from uncleanness and all profane filthiness. Holy marriage was first instituted on the earthly paradise, where, as yet, there never had been any disorder of concupiscence, or of anything immodest. There is some resemblance between lustful pleasures and those that are taken in eating, for both of them have relation to the flesh, though the former, by reason of their brutal vehemence, are called simply carnal. I will, then, explain that which I cannot say of the one by that which I shall say of the other."

"1. Eating is ordained for our preservation: as, the, eating, merely to nourish and preserve health, is a good, holy, and necessary thing; so that which is requisite in marriage for bringing children into the world and multiplying mankind is a good thing and very holy, as it is the principal end of marriage.

2. As to eat, not for the preservation of life, but to keep up that mutual intercourse and condescension which we owe to each other, is a thing in itself both lawful and just; so the mutual and lawful condescension of the parties united in holy marriage is called by St. Paul a debt of so obligatory a nature that he allows neither of the parties exemption from it, without the voluntary consent of the other, not even for the exercises of devotion... How much less, then, may either party be dispensed from it through a capricious pretense of virtue, or through anger or disdain?

3. As they that eat to maintain a mutual intercourse of friendship with others ought to eat freely, and endeavor to show an appetite to their meat; so the marriage debt should always be paid as faithfully and freely as if it were in hopes of having children, although on some occasions there might be no such expectation.

4. To eat for neither of these reasons, but merely to satisfy the

appetite, may, indeed, be tolerated, but cannot be commended; for the mere pleasure of the sensual appetite cannot be a sufficient object to render an action commendable. To eat not merely for the gratification of the appetite, but also with excess and irregularity, is a thing more or less blamable as the excess is more or less considerable.

5. Now, excess in eating consists not only in eating too much, but also in the time and manner of eating. It is surprising that honey, which is so proper and wholesome a good for bees, may, nevertheless, become so hurtful to them as sometimes to make them sick; for in the spring, when they eat too much of it, being overcharged with it in the forepart of the head and wings, they become sick, and frequently die. In like manner, nuptial commerce which is so holy, just, and commendable in itself, and so profitable to the commonwealth, is, nevertheless, in certain cases dangerous to those that exercise it; for it frequently debilitates the soul with venial sin, as in cases of mere and simple excess; and sometime it kills it effectually by mortal sin, as when the order appointed for the procreation of children is violated and perverted; in which case according as one departs more of less from it, the sins are more or less abominable, but always mortal; for the procreation of children being the principal end of marriage one may never lawfully depart from the order which that end requires; though, on account of some accident or circumstance, it cannot at that time be brought about, as it happens when barrenness, or pregnancy, prevents generation. In these occurrences corporal commerce may still be just and holy, provided the rules of generation be followed: no accident whatsoever being able to prejudice the law which the principal end of marriage has imposed. Certainly the infamous and the execrable action of Onan in his marriage was detestable in the sight of God, as the holy text of Genesis testifies; for although certain heretics of our day, much more blamable that the Cynics, of whom St. Jerome speaks in his commentary on the Epistle to the Ephesians, have been pleased to say it was the perverse intention only of that wicked man which displeased God, the Scripture positively asserts the contrary, and assures us that the act itself which was committed was detestable and abominable in the sight of God."

"It is a certain mark of a base and abject spirit to think of eating before meal time, and still more, to amuse ourselves afterwards with the pleasure which we took in eating, keeping it alive in our words and imagination, and delighting in the recollection of the sensual satisfaction we had in swallowing down those morsels; as men do who before dinner have their minds fixed on the spit, and after dinner on the dishes; men worthy to be 'scullions' of a kitchen, 'who,' as St. Paul says, 'make a god of their belly.' Persons of honor never think of eating but at sitting down at table, and after dinner wash their hands and their mouth, that they may neither retain the taste nor the scent of what they have been eating. The elephant, although a gross beast, is yet the decent and most sensible of any other upon earth. I will give you a specimen of his chastity; although he never changes his female, and hath so tender a love for whom he hath chosen, yet he never couples with but at the end of every three years, and then only for the space of five days, but so privately that he is never seen in the act. On the sixth day afterwards, when he makes his appearance, the first thing he does is to go directly to some river, where he washes his body entirely, being unwilling to return to the herd till he is quite purified. May not these modest dispositions in such an animal serve as lessons to married people, not to keep their affections engaged in those sensual and carnal pleasures which, according to their vocation, they have exercised; but when they are past to wash their heart and affections, and purify themselves from then as soon as possible, that afterwards, with freedom of mind, they may practice other actions more pure and elevated. In his advice consists the perfect practice of that excellent doctrine of St. Paul to the Corinthians. 'The time is short,' said he: 'it remaineth that they who have wives be as though they have none.' For, according to St. Gregory, that man has a wife as if he had none, who takes corporal satisfaction with her in such a manner as not to be diverted from spiritual exercises. Now, what is said of the husband is understood reciprocally of the wife. 'Let those that use the world', says the same apostle, 'be as though they used it not.' Let every one, then, use this, world according to his calling, but in such manner that, not engaging his affection in it, he may be as free and ready to serve God as if he used it not. 'It is the great evil of man,' says St. Austin 'to desire to enjoy the things which he should only use.' We should enjoy spiritual things, and only use corporal, of which when the use is turned into enjoyment our rational soul is also changed into a brutish and beastly soul. I think I have said all that I would say to make myself understood, without saying that which I would not say."

(ST. FRANCIS DE SALES: pp. 259-273)

MASS, THE HOLY SACRIFICE: A Mystery of Divine Love

"St. Francis of Sales offers these brief perspectives on a mystery so indescribable as to comprise within itself the very depths of divine love:

"Endeavor, therefore, to assist at Mass every day, that you may jointly, with the priest offer up the holy sacrifice of your Redeemer, to God his Father, for yourself and the whole Church 'The angels,' says St. John Chrysostom 'always attend in great numbers to honor this adoration mystery;...'. And, indeed, to speak once for all there is always more benefit and comfort to be derived from the public offices of the Church than from private devotions, God having ordained this communion of prayer should always have the preference." (ST. FRANCE DE SALES; pp. 93-96)

MAXIMS: Important Principle of Learning

"To study is a good way to learn; to hear is still better, but to teach is the best of all." (ST. FRANCIS DE SALES; P xx)

MAXIMS: Faults, Their Damaging Progressive Effect

"Small faults committed in the beginning of any undertaking, grow in the progress infinitely greater." (ST. FRANCIS DE SALES: p 1.)

MAXIMS: Charity and Devotion

"As it is the business of charity to make us observe all of God's commandments, generally and without exception, so it is the part of devotion to observe them more fully and with diligence." (ST. FRANCIS DE SALES p. 3)

MAXIMS: Charity and Devotion

"Charity is a spiritual fire, which, when inflamed, is called devotion. (ST. FRANCIS DE SALES: p. 4)

MAXIMS: Spiritual Exercises, Appropriate Time

"The morning is the best time for spiritual exercises, which can then be meditated on and contemplated on the rest of the day." (ST. FRANCIS DE SALES: p.21)

MAXIMS: Gratitude to God

"Think on this ingratitude, that God having run so often after you, to save you, you have always run from him to lose yourself." (ST. FRANCIS DE SALES; p.30)

MAXIMS: Warfare of Life

"It is happy for us that in this warfare we shall always be victorious provided we do but fight." (ST. FRANCIS DE SALES; p. 15)

MAXIMS: Purification

"The exercise of purifying the soul neither can nor ought to end but with our life. Let us not then be disturbed at the sight of our imperfections, for perfection consists in fighting against them." (ST. FRANCIS DE SALES; p. 15)

MAXIMS: The Views of Saints

"The saints assure us that the way to heaven is not so difficult as the world, our enemy, would persuade us to think." (ST. FRANCIS DE SALES; p.44)

MAXIMS: Resolutions

"Good resolutions are vain and dangerous when they are not reduced to action."

(ST. FRANCIS DE SALES; p.75)

MAXIMS: When You Can't Sleep

"Should you awake in the night, raise your heart to God immediately in prayer." (ST. FRANCIS DE SALES; p.114)

MAXIMS: Trust in God

"Courageous souls continue firm and unmoved under all kinds of storms. (ST. FRANCIS DE SALES; P. 89)

MAXIMS: Spiritual Daily Life

"St. Gregory Nazianzen advised that we should attempt to place all things that we do daily in life by applying to them this question. How much spiritual profit will this bring me.?" (ST. FRANCIS DE SALES; p.92)

MAXIMS: On Sin

"St. Basil said that the rose which is a fair flower made him sorrowful because it reminded him of his sin for which the earth has been condemned to bring forth thorns." (ST. FRANCIS DE SALES; p. 91)

MEEKNESS: Exercising It Towards Ourselves

"One of the best exercises of meekness we can perform is that of which the subject is within ourselves, in never fretting at our own imperfections, for though reason requires that we should be sorry when we commit any fault, yet we must refrain from that bitter, gloomy, spiteful and passionate displeasure, for which many are greatly to blame, who, being overcome by anger, are angry for having been angry, and vexed to see themselves vexed; for by this means they keep their heart perpetually steeped in passion; and, though it seems as if the second anger destroyed the first, it serves, nevertheless, to open a passage for fresh anger on the first occasion that shall present itself. Besides, this anger and vexation against ourselves tend to pride, and flow from no other source than self-love, which is troubled and disquieted to see itself imperfect. We must be displeased at our faults, but in a peaceable, settled, and firm manner; for, as a judge punishes malefactors much more justly when he is guided in his decision by reason, and proceeds with the spirit of tranquillity, than when he acts with violence and passion (because, judging in passion, he does not punish the faults according to their enormity, but according to his passion), so we correct ourselves much better by a calm and steady repentance, than by that which is harsh, turbulent, and passionate; for repentance exercised with violence proceeds not according to the quality of our faults, but according to our inclinations. For example, he that affects chastity will vex himself beyond all bounds at the least fault he commits against that virtue, and will but laugh at a gross detraction he shall have been guilty of; on the other hand, he that hates detraction torments himself, for a slight murmur, and makes no account of a gross fault committed against chastity; and so of others. Now, all this springs from this source, that these men, in the judgement of their conscience are not guided by reason, but by passion."

"Believe me, Philothea, as the mild and affectionate reproofs a father have far greater power to reclaim his child than rage and passion; so when we have committed any fault, if we reprehend our heart with mild and calm remonstrances, having more compassion for it than passion against it, sweetly encouraging it to amendment, the repentance it shall conceive by this means will sink much deeper, and penetrate it more effectually, than a fretful, injurious, and stormy repentance."

"If, for example, I had formed a strong resolution not to yield to the sin of vanity, and yet had fallen into it, I would not reprove my heart after this manner: 'Art thou not wretched and abominable, that, after so many resolutions, has suffered thyself to be thus carried away by vanity? Die with shame; lift up no more thy eyes to heaven, blind, impudent traitor as thou art, a rebel to thy God;' but I would correct it thus, rationally saying, by way of compassion: 'Alas, my poor heart, behold we are fallen into the pit we had so firmly resolved to avoid! Well, let us rise again, and quit it forever; let us call upon the mercy of God, and hope that it will assist us to be more constant for the time to come, and let us enter again the path of humility. Let us be encouraged; let us from this day be more upon our guard; God will help us; we shall do better;' and on this reprehension I would build a firm and constant resolution never more to relapse into that fault, using the proper means to avoid it by the advice of my director."

"However, if any one should find his heart not sufficiently moved with this mild manner of reprehension, he may use one more sharp and severe to excite it to deeper confusion, provided that he afterwards closes up all his grief and anger with a sweet and consoling confidence in God, in imitation of that illustrious penitent, who, seeing his soul afflicted, raised it up in this manner, 'Why art thou sad, O my soul and why does thou disquiet me? Hope in God, for I will still give praise to him, who, is the salvation of my countenance and my God'."

"Raise up your heart, then, again whenever it falls, fairly and softly; humbling yourself before God, through the knowledge of your own misery, but without being surprised at your fall, for it is no wonder that weakness should be weak, or misery wretched...." (ST. FRANCIS DE SALES; pp. 158-160)

MORTIFICATION: Exercises in Mortification

"They who treat of agriculture tell us that if any word be written upon a very sound almond, and it be again enclosed in the shell and planted, all the fruit which that tree shall produce will have the same word engraved upon it. As for myself, I could never approve of the method of those who, to reform a man, begin with his exterior, such as his gestures, his dress, or his hair; on the contrary, I think we ought to begin with his interior. 'Be converted to me,' said God, 'with your whole heart. Son, give me thy heart.' For, the heart being the genuine source of our actions, our works will always correspond to our heart. The divine Spouse, inviting the soul, 'Put me,' says he, 'as a seal upon thy heart, as a seal upon thy arm.' Yes verily; for whoever has Jesus Christ in his heart will quickly show him in all his exterior actions. I desire, therefore, above all thing also to engrave upon your heart this sacred motto, 'Live Jesus,' begin assured that your life, which proceeds from the heart as an almond tree from its kernel, will afterwards produce the same words of salvation written upon all your actions; for, as this sweet Jesus lives within your heart, so will He also live in all your exterior, in your eyes, your mouth, your hands, and even the hair on your head, so that you will be able to say, with St. Paul, 'I live now not I but Christ liveth in me.' In a word, he that has gained the heart has gained the whole man; but even this heart, by which we would begin, required to be instructed how it should frame its exterior behavior, so that men may not only behold holy devotion therein, but also wisdom and discretion; for this end I desire your serious attention to the following short admonitions: -

"If you are able to endure fasting, you would do well to fast some days besides those which are commanded by the Church; for besides the usual effects of fasting, viz., to elevate the spirit to keep the flesh in subjection, to exercise virtue, and acquire a greater reward in heaven, it is a great means to restrain gluttony, and keep the sensual appetite and body subject to the law of the spirit; and although we may not fast much, yet the enemy fears us when he discovers that we know how to fast. Wednesdays, Fridays, and Saturdays are the days in which the ancient Christians chiefly exercised themselves in abstinence; choose, then, some of these days to fast, as far as your devotion and the discretion of your director shall advise you."

"I would willingly say to you, as St. Jerome said to the pious Laeta: 'Long and immoderate fastings displease me greatly, especially in those that are yet in their tender age.' I have learned, by experience, that young people, who become infirm through excess of fasting, easily give way to delicacies. We are greatly exposed to temptations, both when our body is too much pampered, and when it is too much weakened; for the one makes it insolent with ease, and the other desperate with affliction. The want of this moderation in the use of fasting, disciplines, and hair-shirts, and other austerities, renders the best years of many unprofitable in the service of charity as it did even in St. Bernard who repented that he had used so much austerity; and the more cruelly they ill-treated their bodies in the beginning, the more were they constrained to favor them in the end. Would they not have done better to have mortified their bodies moderately, and in proportion to the offices and labors which their condition obliged them?"

"Labor, as well as fasting serves to mortify and subdue the flesh. Now, provided the labor you undertake contributes to the glory of God and your own welfare, I would prefer that you should suffer the pain of labor rather than that of fasting. This is the intention of the Church which exempts those labors that contribute to the service of God and our neighbor even from the fasts commanded. Some find it painful to fast, others to serve the sick, or visit prisoners; others to hear confession, to preach, to pray and to perform similar exercises; for, besides subduing the body, they produce fruits much more desirable, and therefore, generally speaking, it is better to preserve our bodily strength more than may be necessary, in order to perform these functions, than to weaken it too much; for we may always abate it when we wish, but we cannot always repair it when we would."

"We should attend with great reverence to the admonition given by our blessed Saviour to his disciples, 'Eat the things that are set before you.' It is, in my opinion, a greater virtue to eat, without choice, that which is laid before you, and in the same order as it is presented, whether it be more or less agreeable to your taste, than always to choose the worst; for although this latter way of living seems more austere, yet the former has, notwithstanding, more resignation, since by it we renounce not only our own taste, but even our own choice; and it is no small mortification to accommodate our taste to every kind of meat, and keep it in subjection to all occurrences. Besides, this kind of mortification makes no parade, gives no trouble to any one, and is happily adapted to civil life. To set one kind of meat aside to eat another - to eat of every dish - to think nothing well dressed, or sufficiently exquisite - bespeak a heart too much attached to delicacies and dainties. I esteem St. Bernard in drinking oil instead of water or wine, more than if he had drunk designedly the most bitter draught; for it was a sure sign that he did not consider what he drank; in this indifference respecting our good consists the perfection of the practice of that sacred rule, 'Eat that which is set before you.' I except, however, such meats as may prejudice the health, or incommode the spirit, such as hot and high-seasoned meats; as also certain occasions, in which nature requires recreation and assistance in order to be able to support some labor for the glory of God. A continual and moderate sobriety is preferable to violent abstinences, practiced occasionally, and mingled with great relaxations."

"We must dedicate the night to sleep, every one as much as his constitution requires, so that he may be able to watch and spend the days profitably; and also because the Holy Scriptures, the examples of the saints, and reason itself, strenuously recommend the morning to use as the most fruitful part of time, and our Lord himself is named the Orient, or rising sun, and our blessed Lady the dawning of the day. I think it a point of virtue to retire to rest early in the evening that we may be enabled to awake and rise early. In the morning which is certainly of all other times, the most favorable, the most agreeable, and the least exposed to disturbance and distractions; when the very birds invite us to awake and praise God; so that early-rising is equally serviceable to health and holiness."

"Balaam, mounted on his ass, was going to King Bala; but because he had not a right intention, the angel waited for him in the way, with a sword in his hand to kill them. The ass, on seeing the angel, stood still three times, and became restive, Balaam in the meantime beat her cruelly with his staff to make her advance forward, until the beast at the third time, falling under Balaam, by an extraordinary miracle spoke to him, saying, "What have I done to thee? why strikest thou me, lo now this third time?' Balaam's eyes were soon opened, and he saw the angel, who said to him, 'Why beatest thou thy ass? if she had not turned out of the way giving place to me, I had slain thee, and she should have lived.' Then Balaam said to the angel, 'I have sinned, not knowing that thou didst stand against me.' Behold, although Balaam be the cause of the evil, yet he strikes and beats his poor beast, that could not prevent it. It is often the same case with us; for example, a woman sees her husband or child sick, and presently betakes herself to fasting, haircloth, and the discipline, dear friend, you beat the poor beast, you afflict your body; but it cannot remedy the evil, nor is it you; correct your heart, which is an idolator of this husband, and which, having tolerated a thousand vices in this child, has destined it to pride, vanity, and annition. Again, a man perceives himself frequently to relapse in shameful manner into the sin of impurity; an inward remorse assails his conscience, and his heart returning to itself, he says, 'Ah. wicked flesh! ah, treacherous body! thou hast betrayed me;' and immediately he inflicts great blows on his flesh, with immoderate fasting, excessive discipline, and insupportable hair-shirts. O poor soul! if thy flesh could speak, as Balaam's beast did, she would say to thee, 'Why, o wretch! doest thou strike me?' It is against thee, O my soul! that God arms his vengeance; it is thou that are the criminal; why dost thou lead me into bad company? why doest thou employ my eyes, my hands, and my lips in wantonness? why dost thou trouble me with impure imaginations? Cherish good thoughts, and I shall have no evil motions; keep company with those that are modest and chaste, and I shall not be provoked to lust. It is thou, alas, that throwest me into the fire, and yet thou wouldst not have me burn; thou castest smoke into my eyes, and yet wouldst not have them inflamed. And God, without doubt, says to you in these cases. Beat, break, bend, and crush your heart to pieces, for it is against it principally that my anger is excited. Although to remedy our vices it may be good to mortify the flesh, yet it is still more necessary to purify our affections and refresh our hearts." (ST. FRANCIS DE SALES; pp. 208-214)

OBEDIENCE: Its Exercise and Its Value

"Charity alone can place us in perfection, but obedience, chastity, and poverty, are the three principal means to attain it. Obedience consecrates our heart; chastity, our body, and poverty, our means to the love and service of God. These three branches of the spiritual cross are grounded on a fourth, viz., humility. I shall say nothing of these three virtues, as they are solemnly vowed, because this subject concerns the religious only; nor even as they are simply vowed: for though a vow gives many graces and merits to virtues, yet, to make us perfect, it is not necessary they should be vowed, provided they be observed. For though being vowed and especially solemnly, they place a man in the state of perfection; yet to arrive at perfection itself, if suffices that they be observed: there being a material difference betwixt the state of perfection and perfection itself, since all bishops and religious are in the state of perfection; and yet, alas! all are not arrived at perfection itself, as is too plainly to be seen. Let us endeavor, then Philothea, to practice well these virtues, each one according to his vocation; for though they do not place us in the state of perfection, yet they will make us perfect; and indeed, every one is obliged to practice them, though not all after the same manner."

"There are two sorts of obedience, the one necessary, the other voluntary. By that which is necessary, you must obey your ecclesiastical superiors, as the pope, the bishop, the parish priest, and such as are commissioned by them; as also your civil superiors, such as your prince, and the magistrates he has established for administering justice; and, finally, your domestic superiors, viz., your father and mother, master and mistress. Now, this obedience is called necessary, because no man can exempt himself from the duty of obeying his superiors. God having placed them in authority to command and govern each in the department that is assigned to him. You must, then, of necessity obey their commands; but, to be perfect, follow their counsels also, nay, even their desires and inclinations, so far as charity and discretion will permit. Obey them when they order that which is agreeable, as to eat, or to take your recreation; for though there seems no great virtue to obey on such occasions, yet it would be a great vice to disobey. Obey them in things indifferent, as to wear this or that dress; to go to one or another; to sing or to be silent; and this will be a very commendable obedience. Obey them in things hard, troublesome, and disagreeable; and this will be a perfect obedience. Obey, in fine, meekly, without reply, readily, without delay; cheerfully, without repining; and, above all, obey lovingly, for the love of Him, who, through His love for us, made Himself obedient unto death, even to the death of the cross, and who, as St. Bernard says, rather chose to part with His life than His obedience."

"That you may learn effectually to obey your superiors, condescend easily to the will of your equals, yielding to their opinions in what is not sin without being contentious or obstinate. Accommodate yourself cheerfully to the desires of your inferiors, as far as reason will permit, never exercise an imperious authority over them so long as they are good. It is an illusion to believe that we should obey with ease if we were religious, when we feel ourselves so backward and stubborn in what regards obedience to those whom God has placed over us." NOTE: The word inferior is used here not as a degrading term. It simply means, as St. Thomas Aquinas clearly points out (see bibliography) that some persons are gifted by God with certain gifts which others do not posses and vice-versa. To a degree that a person is not gifted with gifts which another person possesses, he is considered "inferior" only as regards lacking such gifts. In the eyes of God all His people, His children, are equal, each individual person, each soul. In the giving of love we share whatever superior gifts we may posses which God has given to us with others, while at the same time we would hope that, similarly, they would share whatever superior gifts they have been given to them by God with us. In the spiritual life this a very important principle, it is also a very important principle in the assignment of tasks and responsibilities by management of any kind involving human beings."

"We call that obedience voluntary to which we oblige ourselves by our own choice, and which is not imposed on us by another. We do not commonly choose our prince, our bishop, our father or mother; and even wives, many times, do not choose their husbands; but we choose our confessor and director. If, then, in choosing we make a vow to obey, as the holy Mother Teresa did, who, as has been already observed, besides her obedience, solemnly vowed to the superior of her order, bound herself by a simple vow, to obey Father Gratian; or if , without a vow we dedicate ourselves to the obedience of any one, this obedience is always called voluntary, on account of its being grounded on our own free will and choice." NOTE: The reference is to St. Teresa (of Jesus) of Avila.

"We must obey every one of our superiors, according to the charge he has over us. In political matters we must obey our prince; in ecclesiastical, our prelates; in domestic, our father, master, or husband; and, in what regards the private conduct of the soul, our ghostly (spiritual) father, or director."

"Request your ghostly father to order you all the actions of piety you are to perform, in order that they may acquire a double value; the one of themselves, because they are works of piety; the other of obedience to his commands, and in virtue of which they are performed. Happy are the obedient, for God will never suffer them to go astray."

(ST. FRANCIS DE SALES; pp. 164-167)

PATIENCE: Its Great Value and Proper Exercise

"'Patience is necessary for you; that, doing the will of God, you may receive the promise.' If our Saviour himself has declared, 'In your patience you shall posses your souls,' should it not be a great happiness for man to posses his soul? - and the more perfect our patience, the more absolutely do we possess them. Let us frequently call to mind, that as our Lord has saved us by patient sufferings, so we also ought to work out our salvation by sufferings and afflictions; enduring injuries and contradictions with all possible meekness."

"Limit not your patience to this or that kind of injuries and afflictions, but extend it universally to all those that it shall please God to send you. Some are unwilling to suffer any tribulations but those that are honorable; for example, to be wounded in battle, to be a prisoner of war, to be persecuted for religion, or impoverished by some lawsuit determined in their favor; now these people do not love the tribulation, but the honor wherewith it is accompanied; whereas he that is truly patient suffers, indifferently, tribulations whether accompanied by ignominy or honor. To be despised, reprehended, or accused by wicked men is pleasant to a man of good heart; but to suffer blame and ill-treatment from the virtuous or from our friends and relations, is the test of true patience. I admire the meekness with which the great St. Charles Borromeo suffered a long time the public reprehensions that a great preacher of a strictly reformed order uttered against him in the pulpit, more than all the assaults he received from others; for as the sting of a bee is far more painful than that of a fly, so the evils we suffer from good men are much more insupportable than those we suffer from others; and yet it often happens that two good men, having each of them the best intentions, through a diversity of opinion, foment great persecutions and contradictions against each other."

"Be patient, not only with respect to the subject of the affliction which may befall you, but also with regard to its accessories or accidental circumstances. Many could be content to encounter evils, provided they might not be incommoded by them. I am not vexed, says one, at being poor, if it had not disabled me to serve my friends, to give my children proper education; or to live as honorable as I could wish. It would give me no concern, says another, were it not that the world would think it happened through my own fault. Another would be content to suffer the scandal patiently, provided no one would believe the detractor. Others are willing to suffer some part of the evil, but not the whole; they do not complain on account of their sickness, but for the want of money to obtain a cure, or because they are so troublesome to those about them. Now, I say, we must not only bear sickness with patience, but also be content to suffer sickness under any disorder, and in any place, among those persons, and with those inconveniences, which God pleases; and the same must be said of other tribulations, which God pleases; and the same must be said of other tribulations. When any evil befalls you, apply the remedies that may be in your power, agreeably to the will of God; for to act otherwise would be to tempt divine Providence Having done this, wait with resignation for the success it may please God to send; and, should the remedies overcome the evil, return Him thanks with humility, but if, on the contrary, the evils overcome the remedies, bless Him with patience.

"The following advice of St. Gregory is useful: whenever you are 'justly accused' of a fault, humble yourself, and candidly confess that you deserve more than the accusation which is brought against you; but, if the charge be false, excuse yourself meekly, denying your guilt, for you owe this respect to truth, and to the edification of your neighbor. But if, after your true and lawful excuse, they should continue to accuse you, trouble not yourself nor strive to have your excuse admitted; for, having discharged your duty to truth, you must also do the same to humility, by which means you neither offend against the care you ought to have of your reputation, nor the love you owe to peace, meekness of heart, and humility."

"Complain as little as possible of the wrongs you suffer; for, commonly speaking, he that complains sins, because self-love magnifies the injuries we suffer, and makes us believe them greater than they really are. Make no complaint to choleric or censorious persons; but if complaints be necessary, either to remedy the offense or restore quiet to your mind, let them be made to the meek and charitable, who truly love God; otherwise, instead of easing your heart, they will provoke it to greater pain; for instead of extracting the thorn, they will sink it the deeper."

"Many, on being sick, afflicted, or injured by others, refrain from complaining or showing a sensibility of what they suffer, lest it should appear that they wanted Christian fortitude, and resignation to the will of God; but still they contrive divers artifices, that others should not only pity and compassionate their sufferings and afflictions, but also admire their patience and fortitude. Now this is not true patience, but rather a refined ambition and subtle vanity. 'They have glory,' says the apostle, 'but not with God.' The truly patient man neither complains himself nor desires to be pitied by others; he speaks of his sufferings with truth and sincerity, without murmuring, complaining, or aggravating the matter. He patiently receives condolence, unless he is pitied for an evil which he does not suffer, for then he modestly declares that he does not suffer on that account, and thus he continues peaceable betwixt truth and patience, acknowledging, but not complaining of the evil."

"Amidst the contradiction which shall infallibly befall you in the exercise of devotion, remember the words of our Lord, 'A woman when she is in labor, hath sorrow because her hour is come; but when she has brought forth her child, she remembereth no more the anguish, for joy that a man is born into the world.' For you have conceived Jesus Christ, the noblest child in the world, in your soul, and until He is quite brought forth, you cannot but suffer in your labor; but be of good courage, these sorrows once past, everlasting joy shall remain with you for having brought Him forth. Now you shall have wholly brought Him forth, when you have entirely formed Him in your heart and in your works by an imitation of His life."

"In sickness offer up all your griefs and pains as a sacrifice to our Lord and beseech Him to unite them with the torments He suffered for you. Obey your physician, take your medicines, food, and other remedies, for the love of God, remembering the gall He took for your sake; desire to be cured, that you may serve Him, but refuse not to continue sick, that you may obey Him; and dispose yourself for death, if it be His pleasure, that you may praise and enjoy Him forever."

"Remember, that as bees, whilst making their honey, live upon a bitter provision, so we can never perform acts of greater sweetness, nor better compose the honey of excellent virtues, than whilst we eat the bread of bitterness, and live in the midst of afflictions. And as the honey that is gathered from the flowers of thyme, a small bitter herb, is the best, so the virtue which is exercised in the bitterness of the meanest and most abject tribulations is preferable."

"Consider frequently Christ Jesus crucified, naked, blasphemed, slandered, forsaken, and overwhelmed with all sorts of troubles, sorrows, and labors; and remember that all your sufferings, either in quality or quantity are not comparable to His, and that you can never suffer anything for Him equal to that which He has endured for you."

"Consider the torments the martyrs have suffered, and those which many at present endure more grievous without any comparison that yours, and then say: Alas! are not my sufferings consolations, and my pains pleasures, in comparison of those, who, without relief, assistance, or mitigation, live in a continual death, overcharged with affliction infinitely greater than mine?" (ST. FRANCIS DE SALES; pp 127-132)

POVERTY: How to Practice It

"Deprive yourself, then, frequently of some of your property, by bestowing it on the poor with a willing heart; for to give away what we have is to impoverish ourselves in proportion as we give; and the more we give the poorer we become. It is true, God will repay us not only in the next world, but even in this; for nothing makes us so prosperous in this world as alms, but till such time as God shall restore it to us we remain so much the poorer by as much as we have given. Oh, how holy and rich is that poverty which is occasioned by giving alms!"

"Love the poor and poverty, and you shall become truly poor, since as the Scripture says, 'we are made like the things which we love.' Love makes the lovers equal. 'Who is weak,' saith St. Paul,' with whom I am not weak?' He might have likewise said, Who is poor, with them I am not poor? For love made him resemble those whom he loved; if, then, you love the poor you shall be truly a partaker of their poverty, and poor like them. Now, if you love the poor, be often in their company, be glad to see them in your house, and to visit them in theirs, converse willingly with them, be pleased to have them near you in the church, in the streets, and elsewhere. Be poor in conversing with them, speaking to them as their companion; but be rich in assisting, by imparting your goods to them, since you have more abundance."

"Besides, content not yourself to be as poor, but poorer than the poor themselves; but how may this be effected? The servant is lower than his master; make yourself, then, a servant of the poor; go and serve them in their beds when they are sick; serve them with your own hands; prepare their food for them yourself, and at your own expense; be their seamstress and laundress. O Philothea! This service is more glorious than a kingdom."

"I cannot sufficiently admire the ardor with which this counsel was practiced by St. Lewis, one of the greatest kings that ever graced a throne; great in every kind of greatness. He frequently served at table the poor whom he maintained, and caused three poor men to dine with him almost every day, and may times ate the remainder of the food with an incomparable love. When he visited the hospitals, which he frequently did, he commonly served the leprous, ulcerous, and such as had the most loathsome diseases, kneeling on the ground, respecting in their persons the Saviour of the world, and cherishing them as tenderly as any fond mother cherishes her child. St. Elizabeth, daughter of the king of Hungary, often visited the poor, and, for her recreation, sometimes clothed herself like a poor woman among her ladies, saying to them, 'If I were poor, I would dress in this manner.' Good God, Philothea, how poor were this prince and princess in the midst of their riches, and how rich in their poverty! Blessed are they who are poor in this manner, for to them belongs the kingdom of heaven. 'I was hungry, and you gave me to eat; I was naked, and you clothed me; come, possess the kingdom prepared for you from the foundation of the world.' He who is the King of the poor, as well as of kings, will say, when He addresses Himself to the elect at the day of general judgement."

"There is no one, who, on some occasion or other, does not feel a want of some convenience. Sometimes we receive a visit from a guest, whom we would entertain very well, but at present have not the means; at other times, our best clothes are in one place when we want them in another, where we must be seen. Again, sometimes all the wines in our cellar ferment and turn, so that there remain only those that are bad or green: at another time we happen to stop at some poor village, where all things are wanting; where we have neither bed, chamber, table, nor attendance; in fine, it is very often easy to suffer the want of something, be we ever so rich. Now, this is to be poor in effect, with regard to the things we want. Rejoice on these occasions, accept them with a good heart, and suffer them cheerfully."

"But should you meet with losses which impoverish you, more or less, as in the case of tempests, fires, inundations, dearths, robberies, or lawsuits, then is the proper season to practice poverty, receiving those losses with meekness, and submitting with patience and constancy to your impoverishment. Esau presented himself to his father with his hands covered with hair, and Jacob did the same; but as the hair on Jacob's hands belonged not to his skin, but his gloves, one might take away the hair without injuring the skin; on the contrary, the hair on the hand of Esau adhered to his skin, so that if any one would attempt to pluck off his hair it would have caused excessive pain. Thus, when our worldly goods cleave to our heart, if a tempest, a thief, or an imposter, should take any part of them from us, what complaints, trouble, and impatience do we not fall into? But when our goods do not cleave to our hearts, and are only considered on account of the care God would have us take of them should they be taken form us, we lose neither our peace nor our senses. Hence the difference betwixt beasts and men, as to their garments; for as the garments of the former, viz., their skin, adhere to their flesh, those of the latter are only put upon them, so that they may be taken off at pleasure."

"But if you be really poor, dear Philothea, be likewise, for God's sake, actually poor in spirit; make a virtue of necessity, and value this precious jewel of poverty at the high rate it deserves; its lustre is not discovered in this world, and yet it is exceedingly rich and beautiful."

"Be patient; you are in good company; our Lord Himself, His blessed mother, the apostles, and innumerable saints, both men and women, have been poor; nay, even when they might have been rich, they refused to be so. How many great personages have there been, who, in spite of contradictions from the world, have gone to seek after holy poverty in cloisters and hospitals, and took indefatigable pains to find her! Witness St. Alexius, St. Paula, St. Paulinus, St. Angela, and so many others; and behold Philothea, this holy poverty, more gracious towards you, comes to present herself to you in your own lodging; you have met her without being at the trouble of seeking after her; embrace her, then, as the dear friend of Jesus Christ, who was born, who lived, and who died in poverty; poverty was his nurse during the whole course of his life."

"Your poverty, Philothea, enjoys two great privileges, by means of which you may considerably enhance its merits. The first is, that she came not to you by choice, but by the will of God, who has made you poor, without any concurrence of your own will. Now, that which we receive purely from the will of God is always very agreeable to Him, provided that we receive it with a good heart, and through a love of His holy will; where there is least of our own there is most of God; the simple and pure acceptance of God's will makes our offerings extremely pure."

"The second privilege of this kind of poverty is that it is truly poverty. That poverty which is praised, caressed, esteemed, secured and assisted is nearly allied to riches; at least, it is not altogether poverty; but that which is despised, rejected, reproached and abandoned, is poverty indeed. Such is ordinary poverty; for, as the poor are not poor by their own choice, but from necessity, their poverty is not much esteemed, for which reason their poverty exceeds that of the religious; although otherwise the poverty of the religious has a very great excellency, and is much more commendable, by reason of the vow, and of the intention for which it is chosen."

"Complain not, then, my dear Philothea, of your poverty; for we never complain but of that which displeases us; and if poverty displease you, you are no longer poor in spirit, but rich in affection."

"Be not disconsolate for your not being so well assisted as might appear necessary; for in this consists the excellence of poverty. To be willing to be poor, and not to feel the hardships of poverty, is to desire the honor of poverty with the convenience of riches."

"Be not ashamed to be poor, nor to ask alms in charity. Receive with humility what shall be given you, and bear the denial with meekness. Frequently remember the journey our blessed Lady undertook into Egypt, to preserve the life of her dear Son, and how much contempt, poverty, and misery she was obliged to suffer, provided you live thus, you will be very rich in your poverty." (ST. FRANCIS DE SALES; pp. 180-186)

PRAYER: Aspirations

"As St. Gregory Nazianzen says, 'I am wont to refer all things to my spiritual profit.' Read the devout epitaph of St. Paula, composed by St. Jerome. How agreeable to behold it interspersed with those aspirations and holy thoughts, which she was accustomed to draw from occurrences of every nature!"

"Now, as the great work of devotion consists in the exercise of spiritual recollection and ejaculatory prayers, the want of all other prayers may be supplied them; but the loss of these can scarcely be repaired by any other means. Without them we cannot lead a good active life, much less a contemplative one." (ST. FRANCIS DE SALES: p 92)

PRAYER: In The Solitude of One's Heart

"ST. FRANCIS DE SALES elaborated on the spiritual point that even when engaged in business or conversation that one retire occasionally into the solitude of one's heart:

"Remember then, Philothea, to retire occasionally into the solitude of your heart while you are outwardly engaged in business or conversation. This mental solitude cannot be prevented by the multitude of those who surround you; for, as they are not about your heart, but your body, your heart may remain in the presence of God alone. This was the exercise which the holy King David practiced amidst his various occupations, as he testifies in the following, as well as in several other places of his psalms; 'O Lord! as for me, I am always with thee. I beheld the Lord always before me, I have lifted up my eyes to thee, O my God! who dwellest in heaven. My eyes are always toward God.' And indeed our occupations are seldom so serious as to prevent us from withdrawing our heart occasionally from them in order to retire into this divine solitude."

"When the parents of St. Catherine of Sienna had deprived her of the opportunity of a place, and of leisure to pray and meditate, our Lord directed her, by His inspirations to make a little interior oratory within her soul into which retiring mentally, she might, amidst her exterior occupations, enjoy this holy spiritual solitude; and when the world afterwards assaulted her, she received no inconvenience from it, because, as she said, she had shut herself up in her interior closet, where she comforted herself with her heavenly Spouse. From her own experience of the utility of this exercise, she afterwards counseled her spiritual children to practice it." (ST. FRANCIS DE SALES; pp. 84-85)

PRAYER: Forms of Meditation

"A third means is to consider our Saviour in His humanity looking down from heaven on all mankind, but especially on Christians, who are His children; and more particularly on such as are at prayer, whose actions and behavior He minutely observes. This is by no means a mere flight of the imagination, but a most certain truth; for although we see Him not, yet it is true that He beholds us from above. So that we may truly say with the Spouse: 'Behold He standeth behind our wall, looking through the windows, looking through the lattices.'"

"A fourth method consists in making use of the imagination by representing to ourselves our Saviour in His sacred humanity, as if He were near us, as we sometimes image a friend to be present, saying. "Methinks I see Him...." (ST. FRANCIS DE SALES: p.67)

PRAYER: After Eating

"It is imprudent to take up prayer after eating, because by doing so, immediately after, before digestion is advanced, besides being heavy and drowsy, the health may be injured.." (ST. FRANCIS DE SALES; p.64)

PRAYER: Suggestions

"Begin all your prayers whether mental or vocal, with a lively sense of the presence of God, by attending strictly to this rule, you will soon become sensible of its salutary effect." (ST. FRANCIS DE SALES: P.6)

PRAYER: Suggestions on Meditation

"There is nothing that so effectually purges our understanding of its ignorance or our will from its depraved affections as prayer. Above all I recommend to you mental prayer or the prayer of the heart, and particularly that which has for its object the life and passion of our Lord. By making Him the frequent subject of your meditation, your whole soul will be replenished with Him; you will imbibe His spirit, and frame all your actions to the model of His...We could never contemplate the divinity of this world, had we not been united to the sacred humanity of our Saviour, whose life and death is the most delightful, sweet, and profitable object we can select for our ordinary meditation. It is not without reason that our Saviour called Himself the bread that came down from heaven; for, as bread is to be eaten with all sorts of meat, so our Saviour should be the subject of our meditation." (ST. FRANCIS DE SALES: pp. 93-94)

PRAYER: Types of Prayer

"The Sacraments and prayer, especially the Holy Sacrifice of the Mass are great means by which the soul may unite itself to his divine Majesty, God." (ST. FRANCIS DE SALES: pp. 93-94)

PRAYER: Short Spontaneous Prayers (Ejaculations)

"Short expressions of love can be sent forth to God from the heart during the day, for example: Live Jesus, Live Jesus, Live Jesus; Jesus, Mary and Joseph, I Love You; Thou has made me, O Lord for Thyself, and for the external enjoyment of Thy incomprehensible glory. Stand near my guardian angel dear. These prayers (Ejaculations) were highly recommended by the great St. Austin who was a spiritual adviser to St. Catherine of Sienna." (ST. FRANCIS DE SALES: pp. 86-87)

PRAYER: Avoiding Haste

"Only one Our Father, said with feeling and affection, is of infinitely more worth and value than ever so great a number run over in haste."(ST. FRANCIS DE SALES: p.63)

PRAYER: Mental Prayer

"If, however, you have the gift of mental prayer, you should always give it the preference, so that if, either through multiplicity of business, or some other cause, you cannot say your vocal prayers, you must not be troubled on that account, but rest contented with saying, either before of after your meditation, the Pater, Ave, and Credo."

"If, whilst at vocal prayer you feel your heart inclined to mental prayers, refuse not the invitation, but let your mind turn gently that way without being concerned at not finishing the vocal prayer you purpose to say; for the choice you have made is more pleasing to God, and more profitable to your soul: with this exception however, that if you are bound to say the office of the Church, you must fulfill your obligations." (ST. FRANCIS DE SALES; p. 64)

PRAYER: Consolation Need Not Be Present

"One need not seek to receive consolation in prayer, for sometimes, in the spiritual life it may happen that we will not receive it. It is prudent not to be concerned about this whatsoever, continuing in prayer to the glory of God. St. Francis of Sales, expresses it thus: ...God always hears our prayers and answers us in his good time, without us knowing it and having awareness of it." (ST. FRANCIS DE SALES; pp. 77-79)

PRAYER: Varieties of Prayer

St. Francis of Sales said many things on the subject of forms or varieties of prayer, in the following paragraph I will briefly summarize a few of his statements, as follows: Short spontaneous prayers (ejaculatory, meditative, contemplative, and others) should be an integral part of our prayer life throughout each day. They should be supplemented by any other prayers, such as our daily professional work itself which being offered up for the honor, greater glory, and love of God can become a prayer all of its own throughout each day. (ST. FRANCIS DE SALES; pp. 86-87)

PURGATION: Types of, by the Grace and Love of God

"This ordinary purification or healing of the body or soul is not instantaneously effected, but takes place gradually, by passing from one degree to another, with labor and patience. There have been miraculous purgations: St. Paul in a moment, was cleansed with a perfect purgations, so was St. Catherine of Genoa, St. Mary Magdalene, St. Pelalia, and some others. These kinds of purgations, however, were as miraculous and extraordinary in the order of grace as the resurrection of the dead is in that of nature." (ST. FRANCIS DE SALES; p.14)

RECREATION: A Medicine for the Soul

"It is necessary sometimes to relax our minds, as well as our bodies, by some kind of recreation. St. John the Evangelist, as Cassian related, amusing himself one day with a partridge on his hand, was asked by a huntsman, how such a man as he could spend his time in so unprofitable a manner? To whom St. John replied: 'Why does thou not carry thy bow always bent?' 'Because,' answered the huntsman, 'were it always bent, I fear it would lose its spring and become useless.' 'Be not surprised then,' replied the apostle, 'that I should sometimes remit a little of my close application and attention of mind to enjoy some little recreation, that I may afterwards employ myself more fervently in divine contemplation.' It is doubtless a defect to be so rigorous and austere as neither to be willing to take any recreation ourselves, nor allow it to others."

"To take the air, to walk, to entertain ourselves with cheerful and friendly conversations, to play on the lute or any other instrument, to sing to music, or go hunting, are recreations so innocent, that, in a proper use of them, there is needed but that common prudence which gives to everything its due order, time, place, and measure."

"Those games in which the gain serves as a recompense for the dexterity and industry of the body or of the mind, such as tennis ball, pall-mall, running at the ring, chess, and backgammon, are recreations in themselves good and lawful; provided excess, either in the time employed in them, or in the sum that is played for, be avoided; because, if too much time be spent in them, they are no longer an amusement, but an occupation, in which neither the mind nor the body is refreshed, but on the contrary stupefied and oppressed. After playing five or six hours at chess, the spirits are altogether fatigued and exhausted. To play long at tennis is not to recreate, but fatigue, the body; and if the sum played for be too great, the affections of the players become irregular; besides, it is unjust to hazard so much upon skill of so little importance, as that which is exercised at play. But, above all take particular care not to set your affections upon these amusements; for how innocent soever any recreation may be, when we set our hearts upon it, it becomes vicious. I do not say that you must take no pleasure whilst at play, for then it would be no recreation; but I say you must not fix your affection on it, nor spend too much time in it, nor be too eager after it." (ST. FRANCIS DE SALES: pp 241-243)

RESOLUTIONS: Their Value for Spiritual Renewal

"The first point of these exercises consists in our being thoroughly sensible of their importance. Human nature easily falls off from its good affections, on account of the frailty and evil inclinations of the flesh, which depress the soul, and draw her always downwards, unless she often raise herself up by fervent resolutions; just as birds which fall suddenly to the ground if they do not multiply the strokes of their wings to support themselves in the air. For this reason, dear Philothea, you must repeat very often the good resolutions you have made to serve God, lest, by neglecting to do so, you should relapse into your former state, or rather into a worse one; for spiritual falls always cast us down to a lower state than that from which we ascended up to devotion."

"As every watch, no matter how good it may be, must be daily wound up, and now and then taken asunder, to remove the rust and dust, and to mend and repair what may be broken or out of order; so he that is careful of his soul ought to wind it up daily to God by the foregoing exercises, and at least once a year take it asunder to redress, rectify, and examine diligently all its affections and passions, that all it defects may be repaired. And as the watchmaker anoints the wheels, the springs, and all the works, with some delicate oils, that the motion of the wheels may be more easy, and the whole of the watch less subject to rust; so a devout person, after taking this review of his heart in order to renovate it, must anoint it with the Sacraments of Confessions and the Holy Eucharist. This exercise will fortify your spirit, impaired by time, warm your heart, reanimate your good resolutions, and make your virtues flourish with fresh vigor. The primitive Christians were careful to practice this devotion on the anniversary day of the baptism of our Lord, when, as St. Gregory Nazianzen relates, they renewed those professions and protestations which are usually made in baptism. Let us, also, my dear Philothea, seriously dispose ourselves to follow their example. Having, then, for this purpose, chosen the most convenient time, according to the advice of your spiritual father, and withdrawn yourself into a little more solitude than ordinary, make one, two, or three meditations. (ST. FRANCIS DE SALES; pp. 334-335)

SAINTS: Their Imitation

St. Francis of Sales gives some advice regarding saints, that is, that there are certain saints that can be used as models, or at least partially imitated, however, there are others more to be admired than imitated, he expresses it this way:

"Read, also, the histories and lives of the saints, in which as in a looking-glass, you may behold the portraiture of a Christian life, and accommodate their actions to your state of life; for, although several actions of the saints cannot absolutely be imitated by such as live in the midst of the world, yet they may, in some degree, be followed. For example, we may imitate the solitude of St. Paul, the first hermit [NOTE: Not St. Paul the Apostle] in our spiritual and real retirements, of which we shall hereafter speak, and have already spoken; the extreme poverty of St. Francis, by the practices of poverty, and so of the rest. It is true, there are some of their histories that give more light for the conduct of our lives than others, such as the life of the blessed mother Teresa, the lives of the first Jesuits, that of St. Charles Borromeus, archbishop of Milan; of St. Lewis; of St. Bernard; the Chronicles of St. Francis; and several others."

"There are others again, which contain more matter of admiration than of imitation; as the life of St. Mary of Egypt, of St. Simeon Stylites, of the two St. Catherines of Sienna and of Genoa, of St. Angela, and like; which, nevertheless, fail not, in general, to give us a great relish for the love of God." (ST. FRANCIS DE SALES; pp. 100-101)

SELF-LOVE: Its Deceptive Nature and Damaging Effects

"It is reason alone that makes us men truly reasonable, because self-love ordinarily puts us out of the paths of reason, leading us insensibly to a thousand small, yet dangerous, injustices, and partialities which, like the little foxes spoken of in the Canticles, destroy the vines; for, because they are little, we take no notice of them; but, being great in number, they fail not to injure us considerably."

"Are not the things of which I am about to speak unjust and unreasonable? We condemn every trifle in our neighbors, and excuse ourselves in things of importance; we want to sell very dearly and to buy very cheaply; we desire that justice should be executed in another man's house, but mercy and connivance in our own; we would have everything we say taken in good part, but we are delicate and touchy with regard to what others say of us; we would insist on our neighbor parting with his goods, and taking our money; but is it not more reasonable that he should keep his goods, and leave us our money? We take it ill that he will not accommodate us; but has he now more reason to be offended that we should desire to incommode him?"

"If we love one particular exercise we despise all others, and set ourselves against everything that is not according to our taste. If there be any of our inferiors who is not agreeable, or to whom we have taken once a dislike, we find fault with all that he does, and we cease not on every occasion to mortify him. On the contrary, if the conduct of any one be agreeable to us, he can do nothing that we are not willing to excuse. There are some virtuous children, whom their parents can scarcely abide to see, on account of some bodily imperfections; and there are others that are vicious, who are favorites, on account of some corporal gracefulness. On all occasions we prefer the rich before the poor, although they be neither of better condition, nor more virtuous; we even prefer whose who are best clad. We rigorously exact our own dues, but we desire that others should be gentle in demanding theirs; we keep our own rank with precision, but would have others humble and condescending; we complain easily of our neighbor, but none must complain of us; what we do for others seems always very considerable, but what others do for us seems as nothing. In a word, we like the partridges in Paphlagonia, which have two hearts; for we have one heart, mild, favorable, and courteous towards ourselves and another hard, severe, and rigorous towards our neighbor. We have two balances; one to weight out to our own advantage and the other to weigh in to the detriment of our neighbor. 'Deceitful lips,' says the Scripture, 'have spoken with a double heart,' viz., two hearts; and to have two weights, the one greater, with which we receive , and the other less, with which we deliver out, is an abominable thing in the sight of God."

"Philothea, in order to perform all your actions with equity and justice, you must exchange situations with your neighbor; imagine yourself the seller whilst you are buyer, and the buyer whilst you are selling; and thus you will sell and buy according to justice and equity; for, although small injustices, which exceed not the limits of rigor, in selling to our advantage, may not oblige to restitution; yet being defects contrary to reason and charity, we are certainly obliged to correct and amend them; at best, they are nothing but mere illusions; for, believe me, a man of a generous, just, and courteous disposition is never on the losing side. Neglect not then, Philothea, frequently to examine whether your heart by such with respect to your neighbor as you would desire his to be with respect to you were you in his situation; for this is the touchstone of true reason. Trahan, being blamed by his confidants for making the imperial majesty, as they thought, too accessible, said, 'Ought I not to be such an emperor towards private men as I would desire an emperor to be towards me were I myself a private man?'" (ST. FRANCIS DE SALES; pp. 253-255)

SINS: Purgation from Sins

"I do not say that you shall discover the venial sins themselves, but your affections and inclinations to them; because the one is very different from the other; for although we can never be altogether so pure from venial sins as to continue for a long time without committing them, yet we need not entertain any voluntary affection for them. Surely it is one thing to tell a lie now and then in jest, or in matter of small importance, and another to take pleasure in lying, and retain an affection for it on every occasion.

"I therefore say that we must purge the soul from every affection to venial sins; that is to say, we must not voluntarily nourish the desire of persevering in any kind of venial sin, be it ever so small; because it displeases God, though not to that degree as to cause Him to cast us off and damn us for it. Now, if venial sin offends Him, the will and affection which we retain to venial sin is no better than a resolution to entertain the desire of displeasing His divine Majesty; but is it possible that a generous soul should not only consent to offend her God, but also to retain with affection the desire of offending Him?"

"Such affections, Philothea, are as directly opposite to devotion as an affection to mortal sin is contrary to charity; they depress and weaken the spirit, prevent divine consolations, open the gate to temptations, and although they kill not, yet they make the soul extremely sick. 'Dying flies,' says the wise man, 'spoil the sweetness of the ointment.' His meaning is, that flies which stay not long upon the ointment, but only taste it in passing by spoil no more than they take, the rest remaining sound; but those which die in the ointment, deprive it of its sweetness. Thus venial sins, which come upon a devout soul, and stay not long there, do it no great damage; but if they dwell in it by affections, they make it lose the sweetness of ointment, that is, holy devotion."

"Spiders kill not the bees, but they spoil and corrupt their honey, and so entangle the honeycombs with their web that the bees cannot go forward in their work; no this is to be understood, when venial sin continues to dwell in our hearts, by the affection with which we cherish it."

"It is not a matter of great consequence, Philothea, to tell some trifling lie, to fall into some little irregularity in words, in actions, in looks, in dress, in mirth, in play, in dancing, provided that as soon as these spiritual spiders are entered into our conscience we chase and drive them away, as the bees do the corporal spiders; but if we permit them to remain in our hearts, if we cherish the desire of retaining and multiplying them, we shall soon find our honey destroyed, and the hive of our conscience corrupted and ruined." (ST. FRANCIS DE SALES; pp. 55-56)

SIN: Affections to Sin

"Who does not see, that although he be delivered from the sin, he is still entangled by an affection to it. To undertake to lead a devout life you must not only cease to sin, but also cleanse your heart from all affections to sin."

"...To undertake a devout life you must not only cease to sin but also cleanse your heart from all affections to sin; for, besides the danger of a relapse, these wretched affections will so perpetually weaken and depress your spirits, that they will render you incapable of practicing good works with alacrity and diligence, in which, nevertheless, consists the very essence of devotion. Souls that are recovered from the state of sin, and still retain these affections, are, in my opinion, like minds in the green-sickness; though not sick, yet all their actions are sick; they eat without relish, sleep without rest, laugh without joy, and rather drag themselves along than walk. This is exactly the case with those here described; they do good, but with such a spiritual heaviness that it takes away all the grace from their good exercises, which are few in number and small in effect."

"....When a penitent hates sin only with a weak, though true contrition, he not only detests the sin, but also the affections, connections, and occasions which lead towards it. We must, then, Philothea, enlarge our contrition as much as possible; we must extend it to everything that has the least relation to sin. Thus, Magdalen, in her conversion, lost so effectually the taste of the pleasure she had taken in her sins as never to think of them more." (ST. FRANCIS DE SALES; pp. 19-20)

SIN: Venial, Root Causes and Their Eradication

"In rooting them out it is important to discover what are the affections and inclinations which lead you to commit them. In other words the root causes, the vices you are prone to, or the virtues in which you are weak. One must strive to purge oneself completely of, of course, any mortal sin, but also of all venial sins, as well as imperfections, impurities, and weaknesses of the soul which are not sins but which if neglected could lead to sin."

SOCIAL LIFE: Aspects of Conversation and Solitude

"To seek and avoid conversation are two extremes equally blamable in the devotion of those that live in the world, which is that of which we are now treating. To shun all conversations savors of disdain, and contempt of our neighbor; and to be addicted to them is a mark of sloth and idleness. We must love our neighbor as ourselves, and to prove that we love him we must not flee his company; and to testify that we love ourselves we must remain with ourselves when we are alone by ourselves. 'Think first of thy self,' says St. Bernard 'and then of others.' If, then, nothing obliges you to go abroad into company, or to receive company at home, remain with yourself, and entertain yourself with your own heart; but if company visits you, or any just cause invites you into company, go in God's name, Philothea, and see your neighbor with a benevolent heart and a good intention."

"We call those conversations evil which are held with an evil intention, or when the company is vicious, indiscreet, and dissolute; and must abide them as bees shun wasps or hornets. For, as when persons are bitten by mad dogs, their perspiration, their breath, and their very spittle, become infectious, especially for children, and those of tender complexions; so vicious and dissolute persons cannot be visited without the utmost hazard and danger, especially by those whose devotion is a yet young and tender."

"There are some unprofitable conversations held merely to recreate and divert us from our serious occupations, to which we must not be too much addicted, although we may allow them to occupy the leisure destined for recreation. Other conversation have civility for their object, as in the case of mutual visits, and certain assemblies made to do honor to our neighbor. With respect to these, as we ought not to be superstitious in the practice of them, so neither must we be uncivil in condemning them, but modestly comply with out duty in their regard, so that we may equally avoid both ill-breeding and levity."

"It remains for us to speak of the profitable conversation of devout and virtuous persons. To converse frequently, Philothea, with such persons will be to you of the utmost benefit. As the vine that is planted amongst olive trees produces oily grapes, which have the taste of olives, so the soul which often in the company of virtuous people cannot but partake of their qualities. As drones cannot make honey without the assistance of the bees, so it is of great advantage to us in the exercise of devotion to converse with those that are devout."

"In all conversations, sincerity, simplicity, meekness, and modesty should be preserved. There are some persons who make no gesture or motion without so much affectation as to trouble the company; and as he who cannot walk without counting his steps, or speak without singing, would be troublesome to the rest of mankind, so they who affect an artificial carriage and do nothing without affectation, are very disagreeable in conversation, for in such persons there is always some kind of presumption. Let a moderate cheerfulness be ordinarily predominant in our conversation. St. Romuald and St. Anthony are highly commended, that, notwithstanding all their austerities, they had always both their countenance and their discourse adorned with joy, gayety, and courtesy. 'Rejoice with that, rejoice'. And again I say to you, with the Apostle, 'Rejoice always, but in the Lord. Let your modesty be known to all men.' To rejoice in our Lord., the subject of your joy must not only be lawful, but also decent; and, that your modesty may be known to all, keep yourself free from insolence, which is always reprehensible. To cause one of the company to fall down, to disfigure another's face, are foolish and insolent merriment's.

"But, besides that mental solitude to which you may retreat, even amidst the greatest conversation, as I have hitherto observed, you ought also to love local and real solitude; not that you should go into the desert, as St. Mary of Egypt, St. Paul, St. Anthony, St. Arsenius, and the other ancient solitaries, did; but that you should remain for some time alone by yourself in your chamber or garden, or in some other place, where you may at leisure withdraw your spirit into your heart, and recreate your soul with pious meditations, holy thought, or spiritual reading. St. Gregory Narianzen, speaking of himself, says, 'I walked with myself about sunset, and passed the time upon the sea-shore; for I am accustomed to use this recreation to refresh myself, and to shake off a little my ordinary troubles;' and afterwards he relates the pious reflections he made, which I have already mentioned. St. Austin relates, that often going into the chamber of St. Ambrose, who never denied entrance to any one, he found him reading, and that after having remained awhile, for fear of interrupting him, he departed again without speaking a word, thinking that the little time that remained to this great pastor for recreating his spirit, after the hurry of his various affairs, should not be taken from him. And when the apostles one day had told our Lord how they had preached, and how much they had done, He said to them, 'Come ye apart into a desert place, and rest a little.'" (ST. FRANCIS DE SALES; pp 215-218).

SOUL: The State of Our Soul and God

"How stands your heart with respect to mortal sin? Are you firmly resolved not to commit it, on any account whatever? Has this resolution continued from the time of your protestation till the present moment? In this resolution consists the foundation of the spiritual life."

"How is your heart disposed with regard to the commandments of God? Do you find them good, sweet, and agreeable? Ah!, my child, he whose taste is in good order, and whose stomach is sound, loves good meat and rejects bad."

"How is your heart affected with regard to venial sin? We cannot keep ourselves so pure as not to fall now and then into such sins; but is there none to which you have a particular inclination; or, what would be still worse, is there none to which you bear an affection and love?"

"How is your heart affected with regard to spiritual exercises? Do you love them? Do you esteem them? Do they not make you uneasy? Are you not disgusted with them? To which of them do you find yourself more or less inclined? To hear the word of God, to read it, to discourse of it, to meditate, to aspire to God, to go to confession, to receive spiritual counsel, to prepare yourself for communion, to communicate, to restrain your affections, - in all this, what is there to which you feel repugnance? If you find anything to which your heart has less inclination, examine the cause whence this dislike arises, and apply the remedy."

"How stands your heart towards God himself? Does it delight in the remembrance of God? Does this remembrance leave an agreeable sweetness behind it? 'Ah!' said David, 'I remembered God, and I was delighted.' Does your heart feel an inclination to love God, and a particular satisfaction in relishing this love? Does not your heart love to reflect on the immensity of God, on the goodness, on His sweetness? If the remembrance of God comes to you amidst the occupations and vanities of the world, do you not willingly receive it? Does it not seize upon your heart? Does it not seem to you that your heart turns towards that side, and, as it were, runs to meet her God? Certainly there are such souls to be found."

"When the husband of an affectionate wife returns home from a distant country, as soon as she is sensible of his approach, or hears his voice, although she be ever so much engaged in business, or forcibly detained from him by some urgent occupation, yet her heart is not withheld from him, but leaps over all other thoughts to think on her husband, who is returned. It is the same with souls that love God well; let them be ever so busy, when the remembrance of God comes near them, they lose almost the thought of all things else, so rejoiced are they that this dear remembrance is returned; and this is a very good sign."

"How is your heart affected towards Jesus Christ, God, and man? Do you place your happiness in Him? As bees find pleasure in their honey, and wasps in corrupted things, so good souls seek their happiness in thinking on Jesus Christ and feel a tender affection towards Him; but the wicked please themselves about vanities."

"How is you heart affected towards the blessed Virgin, the saints, and your good angel? Do you love them? Have you a special confidence in their patronage? Are you pleased with their pictures, their lives, and their praises?"

"As to your tongue: do you speak of God? Do you find pleasure in speaking well of Him, according to your condition and ability? Do you love to sing His praises?"

"As to works: consider whether you take the exterior glory of God to heart, and are emulous of doing something for His honor; for such as love God love, like David, the adorning of His house."

"Can you discover that you have forsaken any affection, or renounced anything for the sake of God? for it is a good sign of love to deprive ourselves of anything in favor of Him whom we love. What, then, have you hitherto forsaken for the love of God?"

"How do you love yourself? Do you not love yourself too much for this world? If so, you will desire to live always here and be very solicitious to establish yourself of this earth; but if you love yourself for heaven, you will desire or at least be willing, to depart hence at whatever hour it shall please our Lord."

"Do you observe due order in the love of yourself? For the inordinate love of ourselves is the only thing that will cause our ruin. Now, a well-ordered love requires that we should love the soul more than the body; that we should be solicitous to acquire virtue than anything else; that we should set a higher estimation on the favor of heaven than on the honor of this low and perishable world. A well-ordered heart will oftener say within itself, 'What will the angels say, if I think upon such a thing?' than, 'What will men say?'"

"What kind of love have you for your own heart? Are you not willing to serve it in its infirmities? Alas! you ought to assist it, and procure assistance for it, whenever passions torment it, and for this purpose to neglect every other consideration."

"What do you esteem yourself before God? Doubtless nothing. It is no great humility in a fly to esteem herself nothing in comparison of a mountain: nor for a drop of water to hold itself for nothing in comparison of the sea; nor for a spark of fire to hold itself nothing in respect to the sun; but humility consists in not esteeming ourselves above others and in not desiring to be so esteemed by others. How are you disposed in this respect?"

"As to your tongue: Do you not sometimes boast of yourself in one way or another? Do you not flatter yourself in speaking of yourself?"

"As to recreation. Do you allow yourself pleasure contrary to your health - I mean vain or unprofitable pleasure; such for example, as that which prevents you from retiring to bed at a proper hour and like?

An Examination of the State of Our Soul Towards Our Neighbor

"The love of husband and wife ought to be sweet and tranquil, constant and persevering, and this principally because the will of God requires it. I say the same of the love of our children, our near relations and our friends, every one according to his rank."

"But, to speak in general, how is your heart affected towards your neighbor? Do you love him from your heart, and for the love of God? To discern this well you must represent to yourself troublesome and disagreeable persons, for it is among them that we exercise the love of God towards our neighbor, and much more among those who injure us, either by their actions or words. Examine well whether your heart be well disposed towards them, or whether you do not find a greater repugnance to love them."

"Are you not apt to speak ill of your neighbor, and especially of such as do not love you? Do you refrain from doing evil to your neighbor, either directly or indirectly? Provided you be reasonable, you will easily perceive it."

An Examination of The Affections of Our Soul

"I have thus protracted these points, in the examination of which consists the knowledge of our spiritual advancement; for the examination of sin is rather for the confessions of such as think not seriously of advancing in devotion."

"We must not, however, delay too long on any of these points, but consider gently in what state our heart has been with regard to them, and what considerable faults we have committed."

"But, to abridge the whole, we must reduce the examen to search into our passions; and if it be inconvenient to consider every point in particular, as has been said, we may examine in general what have been our dispositions, and how we have behaved ourselves in our love to God, our neighbor, and ourselves; in our hatred for our own sins, and for those of others, - for we desire the extirpation of both; in our desires relating to riches, pleasures, and honors; in our fear of the dangers of sin, and in that of the loss of our worldly goods, - for we are apt to fear the one too much, and the other too little; in our hope, placing too much reliance on the world and creatures, and too little on God and things eternal; in an inordinate sadness, or excessive joy for vain things. In a word, we must examine what affections entangle our heart, what passions possess it, in what it has principally strayed out of the way; for by the passions we may judge of the state of the soul, by examining them one after the other; and, as he that plays on the lute, by touching all the strings finds which are out of tune, and makes them accord either by winding them up, or letting them down; so if after having examined the passions of love, hatred, desire, hope, sadness, and joy in our soul, we find them out of tune for that harmony which we desire to make to the greater glory of God, we may accord them by means of his grace, and the counsel of our spiritual director."

Affections to be Formed After This Examination

"After having quietly considered each point of the examination into the state of your soul, you must afterwards proceed to the affections in this manner:

1. Return thanks to God for the little amendment you may have found in your life since your resolution, and acknowledge that it has been His mercy alone that has wrought it in and for you.

2. Humble yourself exceedingly before God, acknowledging that, if you have not advanced much, it has been through your own fault, because you have not faithfully, courageously and constantly corresponded with the inspirations, graces, and affections which He has given you in prayer, and at other times.

3. Promise that you will eternally praise Him for the graces which He has bestowed on you, and for having withdrawn you from your evil inclinations, to make this little amendment.

4. Ask pardon for your infidelity and disloyalty in not corresponding with His graces.

5. Offer him your heart, that He may make Himself the sole master of it.

6. Beseech Him to make you forever faithful to Him.

7. Invoke the saints, the blessed Virgin, your good angel, your holy patron, St. Joseph, and the whole court of heaven."

Considerations Proper to Renew Our Good Resolutions

"After having made your examination, and conferred with some worthy director concerning your defects, and the proper remedies for them, make use of one of the following considerations every day, by way of meditation, employing in it the time of your mental prayer, observing always the same method with regard to the preparation and the affections as you did in the meditations of the first part, by placing yourself first in the presence of God, and then imploring His grace to establish you in His holy love and service."

The First Consideration - The Excellence Of Our Soul

"Consider the worth and excellence of your immortal soul, which is endued with an understanding capable of knowing, not only this visible world, but also that there are angels, an eternity, a heaven, and a most high sovereign, and ineffable God, and which, moreover, knows the means of living well in this visible world, that she may one day be associated with the angels of heaven, and enjoy God for all eternity."

"Consider, also, that your soul has a will capable of loving God, and cannot hate Him in Himself. Take a view of your heart, and behold how generous it is; and that, as bees can never stay upon any corrupt thing, but only stop among the flowers, so no creature can ever satisfy your heart, for it can never rest but in God alone. Recall to your remembrance the dearest and strongest affections that have hitherto engaged your heart, and judge in truth, whether, in the midst of them, it was not full of anxious inquietudes, tormenting thoughts, and restless cares."

"Our heart, alas! runs eagerly in pursuit of creatures, thinking that they will satisfy its desires; but as soon as it has overtaken them it finds its satisfaction still afar off, God being unwilling that our heart should find any resting-place, like the dove which went out of Noah's ark, that it may return to Himself, from whom it proceeded. Ah! what natural beauty is there in our heart! Why, then, do we detain it against its will in the service of creatures?"

"Since, then, O soul! thou are capable of knowing and loving God, why wilt thou amuse thyself about anything less than God? Since thou mayest advance thy claim to eternity, why shouldst thou amuse thyself about transitory moments? It was one of the most sorrowful reflections of the prodigal son that he might have been faring deliciously at his father's table, whilst he was feeding amongst the filthy swine. Since, O my soul! thou are capable of God, woe be to thee if thou content thyself with anything less than God."

"Elevate your soul cheerfully with this consideration: remind her that she is immortal and worthy of eternity; animate her with courage of this subject."

The Second Consideration - The Excellence of Virtue

"Consider that nothing but virtue and devotion can satisfy your soul in this world. Behold how beautiful they are, and draw a comparison between the virtues and their contrary vices. How amiable is patience, when compared with revenge! Meekness, compared with anger and vexation! Humility, compared with arrogance and ambition! Liberality, compared with covetousness! Charity, in comparison with envy! Sobriety, compared with revellings! For virtues have this admirable quality, that they delight the soul with an incomparable sweetness and satisfaction after we have practiced them; whereas vices leave the soul exceedingly fatigued and disordered. Why, then, do we not endeavor to acquire this satisfaction?"

"With respect to vices, he that has but little of them is uneasy, and he that has more of them is more discontented; but as for virtues, he that has but a little has already some contentment, which, increases as the virtues themselves increase."

"O devout life! how fair, how lovely, how sweet and delightful art thou! thou alleviates our tribulations, and addest sweetness to our consolations; without thee good is evil, and pleasures are full of restlessness, trouble and deceits. Ah! he who would know thee well might exclaim, with the Samaritan woman. 'Lord! give me this water!' an aspiration frequently used by the holy mother Theresa, and St. Catherine of Genoa, although upon different occasions."

The Third Consideration - The Example Of The Saints

"Consider the examples of the saints in every condition of life. What have they not done to devote themselves entirely to the love and service of God? Look on the invincible resolution of the martyrs; what torments have they not suffered in defense of the faith? But, above all, behold that innumerable train of holy virgins, whiter than the lilies in purity, fairer than the roses in charity; of whom, some at twelve, others at thirteen, fifteen, twenty, and twenty-five years of age, have endured a thousand kinds of martyrdom, rather than renounce their resolution, not only with regard to the profession of their faith, but, also, their protestation of devotion; some dying rather than forsake their virginity; others rather than desist from the service of their companions in torments, from comforting the afflicted, and burying the dead. O good God! what fortitude have they not evinced on these occasions!"

"Consider the unshaken constancy with which so many holy confessors have despised the world; how invincible have they shown themselves in their resolutions, from which nothing could ever divert them; they have embraced them without reserve, and practiced them without exception. Good God! what admirable things does St. Augustine relate of his holy mother, St. Monica? With what constancy did she pursue her determination of serving God, both in marriage and in widowhood? How admirably does St. Jerome speak of his dear daughter Paula, in the midst of so many oppositions, in the midst of such a variety of accidents? What is there that we might not do after such excellent patterns? They were what we are; they served the same God, and practiced the same virtues; why, then, should not we do as much, according to our condition and vocation, to preserve our resolution and holy protestation?"

The Fourth Consideration - The Love That Jesus Christ Bears Us

"Consider the incomparable love with which Jesus Christ our Lord has suffered so much in this world, but especially in the Garden of Olives and upon Mount Calvary, for your sake. By all these pains and sufferings He obtained of God the Father good resolutions and protestations for your heart; and by the same means He also obtained whatever is necessary to maintain, nourish, strengthen, and fulfill them. O resolution, how precious art thou, being the daughter of such a mother, as in the passion of my Saviour! Oh, how tenderly ought my soul to cherish thee, since thou has been so dear to my sweet, Jesus! Alas, O Saviour of my soul! though didst die to purchase for me these resolutions. Oh, grant me the grace rather to suffer death than to lose them!"

"Observe, my Philothea, it is certain that the heart of Jesus beheld your heart from the tree of the cross, and, by the love which He bore towards it, obtained for it all the good you shall ever have, and among the rest your resolutions. Yes, Philothea, we may all say, with the prophet, Jeremias: 'O Lord, before I had a being thou didst behold me, and called me by my name': since the divine goodness did actually prepare for us all the general and particular means of salvation, and consequently our good resolutions. As a pregnant woman prepared the cradle, the linen, and swathing-clothes, and even a nurse for the child which she hopes to bring forth, although it is not yet in the world; so our Saviour, who designed to bring you forth to salvation, and make you His child, prepared all that was necessary for your happiness. Such are all those graces by which He seeks to attract your soul and bring it to perfections."

"Ah, my God! how deeply ought we to imprint this thy love in our memory! It is possible that I could have been so tenderly beloved by my Saviour as that He should think of me in particular even in all these little occurrences, by which He has drawn me to Himself? How much, then, ought we to love, cherish, and convert them all to our own profit! O consoling reflection! the amiable heart of God has thought of Philothea, loved her, and procured her a thousand means of salvation, even as many as if there had been no other souls in the world to think of. As the sun shining upon one place of the earth enlightens it no less than if it shined on no other, so in the very same manner is our Lord solicitous for all her dear children, thinking on each of them as though He had forgotten the rest, 'He loved me,' says St. Paul, 'and delivered Himself for me.' He says for me alone, as if He had done nothing for the rest. O Philothea, let this sacred truth be imprinted in your soul, in order to cherish and nourish your resolution, which has been so precious to the heart of our Saviour."

The Fifth Consideration - The Eternal Love of God Towards Us

"Consider the eternal love which God has borne towards you: for, before our Lord Jesus Christ, as man, suffered on the cross for you, His divine Majesty, by His omniscience, already foresaw your being, and loved you exceedingly. But when did His love for you begin? Even when he began to be God. But when did He begin to be God? Never, for he has always been without beginning or end, so also has He always loved you from all eternity, and in consequence of this love He prepared for you these graces and favors. Hence, speaking to you as well as others, by the prophet Jeremias, He says, 'I have loved thee with an everlasting love, therefore have I drawn thee, taking pity on thee'; and amongst other things He caused you to make firm resolutions to serve Him."

"O God! what resolutions are these on which thou has thought and meditated from all eternity. Ah, how dear and precious should they be to us! What ought we not to suffer, rather than forget the least of them! Though the whole world should be destroyed in consequence, yet we must observe them faithfully; for the whole world is not worth one soul, and a soul is worth nothing without these resolution."

General Affections on the Preceding Considerations and a Conclusion of These Exercises

"O Dear resolution! fair tree of life, which God, with His own hand has planted in the midst of my heart, and which my Saviour desires to water with His blood to make thee fruitful: I will rather endure a thousand deaths than suffer any wind of prosperity or adversity to pluck thee up. No; neither vanity, delights, riches, nor tribulations, shall every withdraw me from my design."

"Alas! O Lord, it is thou thyself that hast planted and eternally preserved in thy fatherly bosom this fair tree for the garden of my heart. Alas! how many souls are there who have not been favored in this manner; and how, then, can I ever sufficiently humble myself beneath thy mercy?"

"O fair and holy resolutions! if I preserve you will preserve me; if you live in my soul, my soul will live in you. Live, then, forever, O resolutions, which are eternal in the mercy of God; live eternally in me, and let me never forsake you!"

"After these affections you must consider the particular means necessary to maintain these cherished resolutions, and determine to be faithful in making good use of them; such as frequent prayer, the sacraments, good works, the amendment of your faults discovered in the examination, retrenching the occasions of evil, and following the counsels which shall be given you for this purpose."

"Afterwards, by way of recruiting your strength, make a thousand protestations that you will persevere in your resolutions; and as if you held your heart, soul, and will in your hands, dedicate, consecrate, sacrifice, and immolate them to God, protesting never to take them back again, but leave them in the hands of His divine Majesty, to follow on all occasions His holy ordinances."

"Pray to God to renovate you entirely, and to bless and strengthen this your protestation. Invoke the blessed Virgin, your guardian angel, and your holy patron."

"In this disposition of heart go to your spiritual father, and accuse yourself of the principal faults which you may have remarked since your general confession, and, receiving absolution in the same manner as the first time, pronounce and sign your protestation before him; and, in conclusion, unite your renovated heart to its first principle, your Saviour, in the most holy sacrament of the Eucharist."

Of Our Sentiments After This Exercise

"On the day on which you have made this renovation, and the days immediately following, you ought frequently to repeat from your heart those inflamed words of St. Paul, St. Austin, St. Catherine of Genoa, etc; 'No, I am no more my own; whether I live, or whether I die, I am my Saviour's. I have no longer anything of me or mine; my me is Jesus, and my mine is to be wholly his. O world! thou are always thyself, and I have hitherto been always myself, but from henceforth I will be myself no more.' No, we shall be no more ourselves, for we shall have our heart changed, and the world which has so often deceived us shall be deceived in us; for, perceiving our change only by degrees, it will think us still Esaus, but we shall find ourselves to be Jacobs. All these exercises ought to remain fixed in the heart, and when we finish our considerations and meditation we must turn gently and quietly towards our ordinary affairs and conversations, lest the precious liquor of our resolutions should be suddenly spilt; for it must penetrate through all parts of the soul, without, however, any effort of mind or body."

An Answer to Two Objections Which May be Made to This Introduction

"The world will perhaps tell, Philothea, that these exercises and advices are so numerous, that he who would practice them must apply himself to nothing else. Alas! Philothea, should we do nothing else, we should do enough, since we should do all that we ought to do in this world. But do not you perceive the delusion? If they were all to be necessarily performed every day, they would then, indeed, constitute our whole occupation; but it is not requisite to perform them otherwise than in their proper time and place, as occasions may present themselves. How many civil laws and regulation there are which must be observed, but it is universally understood that they are to be executed on proper occasions, and no one imagines that they are all to be put in force every day. David was a king charged with the most difficult affairs, yet he performed many more exercises than I have prescribed for you..." (ST. FRANCIS DE SALES; pp.341-360)

SOUL: Imperfections, Purgation of, and Various Manifestations of

"We have, moreover, Philothea, certain natural inclinations, which, though they spring from our particular sins, yet are not properly sins, either mortal or venial, but are called imperfections; and the acts which proceed from them are termed defects and failings. For example, St. Paula, according to St. Jerome had so great an inclination to sadness that at the death of her children and husband she was in danger of dying with grief. This was an imperfection but not a sin, because she had it against her will."

"There are some people who are naturally of a light, others of a morose temper; some of an obstinate disposition, others inclined to indignation; some prone to anger, others to love, in short, there are few in whom we may not observe some of these imperfections. Now although they are peculiar and natural to each of us, yet by care and a contrary affection, we may not only correct and moderate them, but even altogether free ourselves from them; and I tell you, Philothea, it is necessary that you should do so. As a means has been discovered to change bitter almond trees to sweet, by piercing them at the bottom to let out the juice, why may not we let out the juice of our perverse inclinations and become better?" (ST. FRANCIS DE SALES; p 59)

SPIRITUAL DIRECTION: Spiritual Development and Spiritual Dryness, Contending With Some Fundamental Causes

"...Sometimes you shall find yourself so absolutely destitute of all feeling of devotion that your soul shall seem to be a wild, fruitless, barren desert, in which there is no trace of a pathway to find her God, nor any water of grace to refresh her, on account of the dryness which seems to threaten her with a total and absolute desolation. Alas! how much does a poor soul in such a state deserve compassion; but especially when the evil is vehement; for then, in imitation of David, she feeds herself with tears night and day; while the enemy, to cast her into despair, mocks her by a thousand suggestions of despondency, saying 'Ah! poor wretch, where is thy God? By what path shalt thou be able to find him? Who can ever restore to thee the joy of his holy grace?'"

"What shall you then do, Philothea? Examine the source whence this evil has flowed to you; for we ourselves are often the cause of our spiritual dryness.

1. As a mother refuses to gratify the appetite of her child, when such gratification might increase its indisposition, so God withholds consolations from us, when we take a vain complacency in them, and are subject to the spiritual maladies of self-conceit and presumption. 'It is good for me that thou has humbled me'; yes, 'for before I was humbled I offended.'

2. When we neglect to gather the sweetness and delights of the love of God at the proper season He removes them for us in punishment of our sloth. The Israelite, who neglected to gather the manna betimes, could gather none after sunrise, for it had then all melted.

3. We are sometimes pleased in the bed of sensual consolations, as the sacred Spouse was in the Canticles; the Spouse of our soul comes and knocks at the door of our heart, and invites us to return to our spiritual exercises; but we put them off, because we are unwilling to quit these vain amusements, and false satisfactions; for this reason He

departs, and permits us to slumber. But afterwards, when we desire to seek Him, it is with great difficulty that we find Him; and it is no more than what we have justly deserved, since we have been so unfaithful and disloyal as to refuse the participation of His love, to enjoy the consolations of the world. Ah! if you still keep the flour of Egypt, you shall not have the manna of heaven. Bees detest artificial odors; and the sweetness of the Holy Spirit is incompatible with the counterfeit delights of the world."

4. "The double-dealing and subtlety which we use in our spiritual communications with our director may also produce spiritual dryness; for, since you lie to the Holy Ghost, it is no wonder He should refuse His consolations. If you will not be as sincere and plain as a little child, you shall not, then, have the sugar-plums of little children."

5. " If you have glutted yourself with worldly pleasure it is no wonder that you should find an unsavory taste in spiritual delights. When birds have once satiated their appetite the most delicious berries appear to them distasteful. 'He hath filled the hungry with good things,' says our blessed Lady. 'And the rich he hath sent away empty.' They that are glutted with the pleasures of the world are not capable of the delights of the Spirit."

6. "If you have been careful to preserve the fruits of the consolations which you have received, you shall receive new ones; for, to him that has, more shall be given; but he that has not kept, but lost, what was given him, through his own fault, shall never receive those graces which had been prepared for him. Rain enlivens green plants, but it destroys those that have lost their verdure."

"There are several causes which occasion our fall from the consolations of devotion into dryness and barrenness of spirit. Let us, then, examine whether we can find any of them in ourselves; but observe, Philothea, that this examination is not to be made either with inquietude or too much curiosity; but if, after having faithfully considered our comportment, we find the cause of the evil to originate in ourselves, let us thank God for the discovery; for the evil is half cured when the cause of it is known; but if, on the contrary, you can find nothing in particular which may seen to have occasioned this dryness, trouble not yourself about making any further inquiry, but with all simplicity do as I shall now advise you."

1. "Humble yourself very much before God, by acknowledging your own nothingness and misery. Alas! O Lord, what am I when left

to myself but a dry, parched soil, which, far from receiving those showers, of which it stands in so great need, is exposed to the wind, and thus reduced to dust."

2. "Call upon God, and beg comfort from Him. 'Restore unto me the joy of thy salvation. Father, if it be possible, let this chalice pass from me.' Away, thou barren north wind, that witherest my soul; and blow, gentle gale of consolations, upon the garden of my heart, that is good affections may diffuse the odor of sweetness."

3. "Go to your confessor, and opening to him the several plaits and folds of your soul, follow his advice with the utmost simplicity and humility; for God, who is well pleased with obedience, frequently renders the counsels we take from others, but especially from those who are the guides of our soul, profitable, when otherwise there might be no great appearance of success; as He imparted healing qualities to the waters of Jordan, the use of which Eliseus had, without any appearance of human reason, prescribed to Naaman."

4. "But, after all this, there is nothing so profitable, so fruitful, in a site of spiritual dryness, as not to suffer our affections to be too strongly fixed upon the desire of being delivered from it. I do not say that we ought not simply to wish for a deliverance, but that we should not set our heart upon it; but rather yield ourselves up to the pure mercy and special providence of God, that He make use of us to serve Him as long as He pleases. In the midst of these thorns and deserts, let us say, 'Father, if it be possible, let this chalice pass from me'; but let us also add, courageously, 'nevertheless, not my will but thine, be done.' But here let us stop with as much tranquillity as possible; for God, beholding this holy indifference, will comfort us with many graces and favors; as was the case with Abraham when he resolved to deprive himself of his son Isaac. God, who contented himself with seeing him in this disposition of a pure resignation, comforted him with a most delightful vision, accompanied by the most consolatory benedictions. We ought then, under all kinds of afflictions, whether corporal or spiritual, and amidst all the distractions or subtractions of sensible devotion which may happen to us, to say from the bottom of our heart, with profound submission, 'The Lord gave, and the Lord hath taken away; blessed be the name of the Lord.' For, if we continue in this humility, He will restore us His delightful favors as He did to Job, who constantly used the like words in his desolations."

"Finally, Philothea, in the midst of our spiritual dryness, let us never lose courage, but wait with patience for the return of consolation. Let us not omit any of our exercises of devotion, but if possible, let us multiply our good works, and not being able to present to our dear Spouse the most exquisite dishes, let us offer Him such as we can procure; for He is indifferent, provided the heart which offers them be perfectly fixed in the resolution of loving Him. When the spring is fair the bees make more honey, and produce fewer young ones; for when the fine weather favors them, they are so busy in their harvest among the flowers that they forget the production of their young; but when the spring is sharp and cloudy they produce more young ones, and less honey; for, not being able to go abroad to gather honey, they employ themselves at home to increase and multiply their race. Thus it happens frequently, Philothea, that the soul finding herself in the fair spring of spiritual consolations, amuses herself so much in enjoying their sweetness, that in the abundance of these delights she produces fewer good works; whilst on the contrary, in the midst of spiritual dryness, the more destitute she finds herself of the consolations of devotion the more she multiplies her good works and abounds in the interior generation of the virtues of patience, humility, self-contempt, resignation, and renunciation of self-love."

"Many persons, especially women, falsely imagine that the spiritual exercises which they perform without relish, tenderness of heart, or sensible satisfaction, are less agreeable to the divine Majesty. Our actions are like roses, which when fresh have more beauty, yet when dry have more strength and sweetness. Our words performed with tenderness of heart are more agreeable to ourselves, who regard only our own satisfaction, yet when performed in the time of dryness they possess more sweetness, and become more precious in the sight of God. Yes, dear, Philothea, in the time of dryness our will forces us to the service of God, as it were, by violence; and, consequently, it must necessarily be more vigorous and content that in the time of consolation."

"It is not great merit to serve a prince in the time of peace, amongst the delights of the court; but to serve him amidst the hardships of war troubles and persecutions is a true mark of constancy and fidelity. The Blessed Angela de Fulgino says, that the prayer which is most acceptable to God is that which we make by force and constraint; the prayer to which we apply ourselves, not for the pleasure which we find in it, nor by inclination, but purely to please God; to which our will carries us, against our inclinations, violently forcing its way through the midst of those clouds of aridity which oppose it. I say the same of every kind of good works, whether interior or exterior; for the more repugnance we feel in performing them, the more agreeable they are in the sight of God. The less we consult our particular interest in the pursuit of virtues, the more brilliantly does the purity of divine love shine forth in them. A child easily is naturally affectionate to his mother when she gives him sugar; but it is a sign of a great love if he manifests the same affection after she has given him wormwood, or any other bitter potion."

"To illustrate the whole of this instruction I will here relate an excellent passage from the history of St. Bernard, as I found it in a learned and judicious writer. Almost all, says he, those who begin to serve God, and are not as yet experienced in the subtractions of grace, and in spiritual vicissitudes, finding themselves deprived of the sweetness of sensible devotion, and that agreeable light which invites them to run forward in the way of God, presently lose breath, and fall into pusillanimity and sadness. Persons of judgement account for this by saying that our rational nature cannot continue, for a long time, famished, as it were, and without some kind of delight, either heavenly or earthly. Now, as souls that are elevated above themselves, by the enjoyment of spiritual pleasures, easily renounce visible objects: so when, by the divine disposition, spiritual joy is withdrawn from them, finding themselves at the same time deprived of corporal consolations, and not being as yet accustomed to wait with patience for the return of the true sun, it seems to them as if they were neither in heaven nor on earth, and that they shall remain buried in a perpetual night. Thus, like little infants who have been weaned from the breast, they languish and moan, and become fretful and troublesome to every one, and especially to themselves. The following circumstance happened, in a journey mentioned in this history, to one of the company, named Geoffry of Peronne, who had lately dedicated himself to the service of God. Being suddenly deprived of consolation, and overwhelmed with interior disgust, he began to remember his worldly friends, his kindred, and the riches which he had lately forsaken; by which he was assaulted with so strong a temptation that, not being able to conceal it in his behavior, one of his greatest confidants perceived it, and, having taken an opportunity, accosted him with mildness, and said to him in private, 'What means this, Geoffry? Whence comes it, that, contrary to custom, thou art so pensive and melancholy?' – 'Ah, brother!' answered Geoffry, with a deep sigh, 'I shall never, never more be joyful whilst I live.' The other, moved to pity at these words, went immediately, with fraternal zeal, and told it to their common father, St. Bernard, who, perceiving the danger, went into the next church to pray to God for him; whilst Geoffry, in the meantime, being overwhelmed with sadness, and resting his head upon a stone, fell asleep. Shortly after both of them arose, the one from prayer, having obtained the favor he had asked for, and the other from a sleep, but with so pleasant and serene a countenance that his friend, surprised at so great and sudden a change, could not refrain from gently reproaching him with the answer he had a little before given him, to which Geoffry replied, 'If I told thee before, that I should never more be joyful, I now assure thee that I shall never more be sorrowful.'"

"Such was the issue of the temptation of this devout person. But observe, in this relation, dear Philothea."

1. "That God commonly grants some foretaste of heavenly delight to such as enter into His service, in order to withdraw them from earthly pleasures, and encourage them in the pursuit of divine love; as a mother who, to allure her little infant to her breasts, puts honey upon them."

2. "That, according to the secret designs of His providence, He is pleased to withhold from us the milk and honey of consolation, that, by weaning us in this manner, we may learn to feed on the more dry and solid bread of a vigorous devotion, exercised under the trials of disgust and spiritual dryness."

3. "That, as violent temptations frequently arise during this desolating aridity, we must resolutely fight against them, since they proceed not from God; but, nevertheless, we must patiently suffer the aridity itself, since God has ordained it for the exercise of our virtue."

4. "That we must never lose courage amidst those interior pains and conflicts, nor say with good Geoffry, 'I shall never more be joyful'; for in the midst of the darkness of the night we must look for the return of daylight; and, again, in the fairest spiritual weather we must not say, I shall never more be sorrowful; for, as the wise man says, 'In the day of good things be not unmindful of evils.' We must hope in the midst of affliction, and fear in the midst of prosperity; and on both occasions we must always humble ourselves."

5. "That it is a sovereign remedy to discover our evil to some spiritual friend, who may be able to give us comfort."

"I think it necessary to observe, Philothea, that in these conflicts God and our spiritual enemy have contrary designs. Our good God seeks to conduct us to perfect purity of heart, to an entire renunciation of self-interest in what relates to His service and to an absolute self-denial; whereas our internal foe endeavors, by these severe trials, to discourage us from the practice of prayer, and entice us back to sensual pleasures, that by thus making us troublesome to ourselves and to others he may discredit holy devotion. But, provided you observe the lessons I have given you, you will, amidst these interior afflictions, rapidly advance in the way of perfection. I cannot, however, dismiss this important subject without adding a few words more."

"It sometimes happens that spiritual dryness proceeds from an indisposition of body, as when, through an excess of watching, labor, or fasting, we find ourselves oppressed by fatigue, drowsiness, lassitude, and the like infirmities, which, though they depend on the body yet are calculated to incommode the spirit also, on account of the intimate connection that subsists between both. Now, on such occasions, we must never omit to perform several acts of virtue with the superior parts of our souls and the force of our will. For although our whole soul seems to be asleep, and overwhelmed with drowsiness and fatigue, yet the actions of the superior part cease not to be very acceptable to God; and we may say at the same time, with the sacred Spouse, 'I sleep, and my heart watcheth.' For, as I have observed before, though there is less satisfaction in this manner of performing our spiritual exercises, yet there is more merit and virtue. Now, the remedy on such occasion is to recruit the strength and vigor of our body by some kind of lawful recreation. So St. Francis ordained that his religious should use such moderation in their labors as not to oppress the fervor of their spirits."

"As I am speaking of this glorious father, I must not forget to tell you that he himself was once assaulted by so deep a melancholy of spirit that he could not help showing it in his behavior; for if he desired to converse with his religious he was unable; if he withdrew himself from them it was worse; abstinence and corporal mortification oppressed him, and prayer gave him no relief. He continued two years in this manner, so that he seemed to be quite abandoned by God; but at length, after he had humbly suffered this violent storm, our Saviour, in an instant restored him to a happy tranquillity. If therefore, the greatest servants of God are subject to these shocks, how can we be astonished if they sometimes happen to us?" (ST. FRANCIS DE SALES; pp. 332-333)

SPIRITUAL DIRECTION: Amusements, Potentially Harmful to the Soul

St. Francis of Sales states that innocent amusements can prove harmful to the soul if we develop an overly strong affection of fondness for them. Some amusements are harmful because of the vices they contain. Some may serve to inflame the passions, enervate the soul, and to dispose the soul to impure love. I quote him below as he speaks to a "soul desirous to love God" which he designates as Philothea:

"Play, dancing, feasting, dress, and theatrical shows, being things which, considered in their substance, are not evil, but indifferent, and such as may be used either well or ill; nevertheless, as all these things are dangerous, to bear an affection to them is still more dangerous. I say then, Philothea, that although it be lawful to play, to dance, to dress, to feast, or to be present at innocent comedies, yet to have an affection to such things is not only contrary to devotion, but also extremely hurtful and dangerous. The evil does not consist in doing such things, but in a fond attachment to them...As the stags, when grown too fat, retire into their thickets, because being encumbered with flesh, they know that they are not in a condition to run, should they be hunted so the heart of man, burdening itself with these unprofitable, superfluous, and dangerous affections, cannot certainly run after its God, the true point of devotion, readily , lightly, and easily."

(ST. FRANCIS DE SALES; pp 57-58)

SPIRITUAL DIRECTION: Human Relationships

"Dispose yourself carefully to avoid, resist, and overcome whatever may present itself that is prejudicial to your salvation and the glory of God. Now, it is not sufficient to make this resolution unless you also prepare the means of reducing it to practice. For example: if I foresee that I am to treat of any business with one that is passionate, and easily provoked to anger, I will not only resolve to refrain from giving him any offense, but will also prepare words of meekness to prevent his anger or use the assistance of some person that may keep him in temper. If I foresee that I shall have an opportunity of visiting some sick person, I will determine the hour of the visit, the comforts and assistances I may afford him: and so of the rest." (ST. FRANCIS DE SALES; p 80)

SPIRITUAL DIRECTION: Importance of Consultation

"....But before you consent to inspirations in things that are of great importance or that are out of the ordinary way always consult your spiritual guide, that he may examine whether the inspiration be true or false, lest you should be deceived; because the enemy seeing a soul ready to consent to inspirations, often proposes false ones to deceive her, which he can never do, so long as she with humility obeys her conductor."

"The consent being given, you must diligently procure the effects and hasten to put the inspiration into execution, which is the height of true virtue; for to have the consent within the heart without producing its effect would be like planting a vine and not intending it should bring forth fruit."

SPIRITUAL DIRECTION: One's State of Life Can Become a Prayer in Itself

This is in essence a summary of the thought of St. Francis of Sales regarding this point: Since one's duties in his state of life at work and while not working are both to be in conformity to the will of God, that is, we strive to do his will in all that we do throughout each day, then we must learn to make our actual life a prayer in itself, making the transition from our private prayer life to our public one with the same humility and devotion.

SPIRITUAL DIRECTION: Deceptive Desires Which Mislead

"Every one knows that we are obliged to refrain from the desire of vicious things, since even the desire of evil is of itself criminal; but I tell you, moreover, Philothea, you must not be anxious after balls, plays, or the like diversions, nor covet honors and offices, nor even vision and ecstasies; for there is a great deal of danger, deceit, and vanity in such things. Desire not that which is at a great distance, nor that which cannot happen for a long time, as many do, who, by this means, weary and distract their hearts unprofitably. If a young man earnestly desires to be settled in some office, before the proper time, what does all his anxiety avail him? If a married woman desires to be a nun, to what purpose? If I desire to buy my neighbor's goods before he is willing to sell them, is it not a loss of time to entertain this desire? If, whilst I am sick, I desire to preach, to celebrate Mass, to visit others that are sick, and perform the exercises of those who are in health, are not all these desires in vain, since it is out of my power to put them in execution? Yet in the meantime these unprofitable desires occupy the place of the virtues of patience, resignation, mortification, obedience, and meekness under sufferings, which is what God wishes me to practice at that time; but we are often in the condition of those who long for cherries in autumn, and grapes in the spring."

"I can by no means approve that persons should desire to amuse themselves in any other kind of life than that in which they are already engaged, nor in any exercises that are incompatible with their present condition; for this dissipates the heart, and makes it unfit for its necessary occupations. If I desire to practice the solitude of a Carthusian, I lose my time; and this desire occupies the place of that which I ought to have to employ myself well in my actual state. No, I would not that any one should even desire to have more talents or judgement than he is already possessed of; for these desires are not only useless, but moreover occupy the place of those which every one ought to have of cultivating the genius he inherits from nature; nor should any one desire those means to serve God which he has not, but rather diligently employ those which he has. Now, this is to be understood only of desires which totally occupy the heart; for, as to simple wishes, if they be not too frequent, they do no harm whatever."

"Desire not crosses but in proportion to the patience with which you have supported those which have been already sent you; for it is presumptuous to desire martyrdom and not have the courage to bear an injury. The enemy often suggests a great desire of things that are absent and which shall never occur so that he may divert our mind from present objects, from which, however trivial they may be, we might obtain considerable profit to ourselves. We fight with the monsters of Africa, in imagination; and, in the meantime, for want of attention, we suffer ourselves to be killed by every insignificant reptile that lies in our way. Desire not temptations, that would be rashness; but accustom your heart to expect them courageously, and to defend yourself against them when they shall come."

"A variety of food, taken in any considerable quantity, overloads the stomach, and if it be weak, destroys it; overcharge not then, your soul, either with a multitude of worldly desires, which may end in your ruin; or even with such as are spiritual, as they are apt to produce distractions. When the purified soul finds herself, freed from bad humors she feels a craving after spiritual things; and, as one famished, she longs after a variety of exercises of piety, mortification, penance, humility, charity, and prayer. Philothea, it is a sign of good health to have a keen appetite; but you must consider whether you can well digest all that you wish to eat. Amongst so many desires, choose, then, by the advice of your spiritual father, such as you can execute at present and turn them to the best advantage afterwards; God will send you others, which you may also practice in their proper season; and thus you will never lose your time in unprofitable desires, but bring them all forth in good order; but as to those which cannot be immediately executed, they should be reserved in some corner of the heart till their time come..." (ST. FRANCIS DE SALES; pp 256-258)

SPIRITUAL DIRECTION: Means of Attaining to Christian Perfection

(ST. FRANCIS DE SALES; pp. 365-368)

NOTE: A CONFERENCE BETWEEN AN EMINENT DIVINE OF THE FOURTEENTH CENTURY AND A POOR BEGGAR, ON THE MEANS OF ATTAINING TO CHRISTIAN PERFECTION. TRANSLATED FROM THE WORKS OF J. THAULERIUS, D.D., PRINTED AT PARIS, 1623, P 833.

There was a great divine who prayed, for the space of eight years, that God would vouchsafe to direct him to a man who might show him the way of truth. Now it happened, on a certain day, whilst he found his soul excited to offer this petition with a more than ordinary fervor, he heard a voice from Heaven, which said to him, "Go out to the church porch, and there thou shalt meet with a man who will teach thee the way of truth." On going thither he found a poor beggar, whose feet were covered with sores, dirt, and mire, and all the clothes on his back not worth three farthings. Having courteously saluted him, he wished him a good morning. To which the beggar replied, "I never remember to have had a bad morning."- "God prosper you," said the doctor. "What say you?" said the beggar; "I never was otherwise than prosperous." - "I wish you all happiness", replied the doctor; "but what do you mean by speaking in this manner?" -"Why", said the poor man, "I never was unhappy." - "God bless you," said the doctor; "explain yourself, for I cannot well understand your meaning." The poor man answered, "That I shall do very willingly. You wished me, master doctor, a good morning; and I answered that I never had a bad morning for if I am hungry I praise God; if I suffer cold I praise God; if it hail, snow, or rain, if the weather be fair or foul, I give praise to God; if I am miserable and despised by all the world, I still give praise to God; and therefore I never met with a bad morning. You also prayed that God would prosper me; to which I answered that I never was otherwise than prosperous; for having learned to live with God, I know for certain that all he does must necessarily be for the best; and therefore whatever happens to me by his will, or his permission, whether it be pleasant or disagreeable, sweet or bitter, I always receive with joy, as coming from his merciful hand for the best; and therefore I never was otherwise than prosperous. You wished me also all happiness; and I, in like manner, replied, that I had never been unhappy; for I have resolved to adhere to the divine will alone, and have so absolutely relinquished self-will as to will always whatever God wills, and therefore I was never unhappy; for I never desire to have any other will than his and there I resign my will entirely to him." "But what would you say", said the doctor, "if it should be the will of this Lord of majesty to cast you down into the bottomless pit?" - "How," said he, hastily, "cast me down into the bottomless pit! Why, if he should really do so, I have two arms, - the one of true humility, by which I am united to his most sacred humanity, which I place under him; the other, which is my right arm of love, by which I am united to his divinity; and with both I would embrace him so closely, and hold him so firmly, that he would be obliged to go down with me; and I would much rather choose to be, even in hell, with God, than in heaven without him." From this discourse the doctor learned that true resignation, accompanied with profound humility, is the shortest way to God. Having afterwards asked the beggar, whence he came, he answered, "From God." - "But where." said the doctor, "did you find God?" - "I found him" said he, "where I forsook all creatures." - "And where or with whom did you leave God?" said the doctor. "I left him," said he, "with the clean of heart, and amongst men of good will." - "but I pray thee tell me who, or what, art thou." - "I am a king," replied he. The doctor further asking him where his kingdom was, he replied, "My kingdom is in my soul; for I can govern both my exterior and interior senses so absolutely that all the affections and forces of my soul are in perfect subjection to me; which kingdom is doubtless more excellent than all the kingdoms of this world." The doctor asked him how he had attained to this perfection. He answered, "By silence, meditation, and by tending always to a union with God; for I could never rest," said he, "in anything less than God; and now, having found him, I enjoy peace and everlasting rest."

TEMPTATION: Nature of Temptations, How to Cope with Them

"Imagine to yourself, Philothea, a young princess, extremely beloved by her spouse, and that some wicked man, in order to defile her marriage bed, sends an infamous messenger to treat with her concerning his abominable design. First, the messenger proposes the intention of his master; secondly, the princess is pleased or displeased with the proposition; thirdly, she either consents or refuses. In the same manner, Satan, the world, and the flesh, seeing a soul espoused to the Son of God, send her temptations and suggestions, by which, 1. Sin is proposed to her; 2. She is either pleased or displeased with the proposal; 3. In fine, she either consents or refuses. Such are the three steps to ascent to iniquity: temptation, delectation, and consent. But though these three actions are not so manifest in all kinds of sins, yet are they palpably seen in those that are enormous."

"Though the temptation to any sin whatsoever should last during life it could never render us disagreeable to the divine Majesty, provided that we were not pleased with it, and did not give our consent to it: the reason is, because we do not act, but suffer in temptation; and as in this we take no pleasure, so we cannot incur any guilt. St. Paul suffered a long time the temptations of the flesh, and yet was so far from displeasing to God on that account, that, on the contrary, God was glorified by his patient suffering. The blessed Angela de Fulgina suffered such cruel temptation of the flesh that she moves to compassion when she relates them. St. Francis and St. Bennet also suffered such violent temptations that, in order to overcome them the one was obliged to cast himself naked on thorns, and the other into snow; yet they lost nothing of God's favor, but increased very much in grace."

"You must, then, be courageous, Philothea, amidst temptations, and never think yourself overcome as long as they displease you, observing well this difference between feeling and consenting, viz., we may feel temptations, though they displease us; but we can never consent to them unless they please us, since to be pleased with them ordinarily serves as a step towards our consent. Let, then, the enemies of our salvation lay as many baits and allurements in our way as they please, let them stay always at the door of our heart in order to gain admittance, let them make as many proposals as they can; still, as long as we remain steadfast in our resolution to take no pleasure in the temptation, it is utterly impossible that we should offend God, any more than the prince of whom I spoke could be displeased with his spouse for the infamous message sent to her, if she took no pleasure whatever in it. Yet, in this case, there is this difference between her and the soul, that the princess, having heard of the wicked proposition, may, if she please, drive away the messenger, and never suffer him to appear again in her presence; but is not always in the power of the soul not to feel the temptation, though it be always in her power not to consent to it; and therefore no matter how long the temptation may last it cannot hurt us as long as it is disagreeable to us."

"But, with respect to the delectation which may follow the temptation, it must be observed that, as there are two parts in the soul, the inferior and the superior, and that the inferior does not always follow the superior, but acts for itself apart, it frequently happens that the inferior part takes delight in the temptation without the consent, nay, against the will of the superior. That is that warefare which the Apostle describes when he says that the flesh lusts against the spirit, and that there is a law of the members and a law of the spirit."

"Have you never seen, Philothea, a large fire covered with ashes? should one come ten or twelve hours after in search of fire, he would find but little in the midst of the hearth, and even that would be found with difficulty; yet there it is, since there it is found, and with it he may kindle again the remainder of the coals that were dead. It is just so with charity, our spiritual life, in the midst of violent temptations; for the temptation, casting the delectation which accompanies it into the inferior part, covers the whole soul, as it were, with ashes, and reduces the love of God into a narrow compass; for it appears nowhere but in the midst of the heart, in the interior of the soul; and even there it scarcely seems perceptible, and with much difficulty we find it; yet there it is in reality, since, notwithstanding all the trouble and disorder we feel in our soul and our body, we still retain a resolution never to consent to the temptation; and the delectation, which pleases the outward man, displeases the inward, so that, although it surrounds the will, yet it is not within it; by which we that such delectation, being contrary to the will, can be no sin."

"As it is so important that you should understand this matter perfectly, I will explain it more at large. A young man, as St. Jerome, relates, being fastened down with bands of silk on a delicate, soft bed, was enticed by all sorts of filthy allurements by a lascivious woman, who was employed by the persecutors on purpose to stagger his constancy. Ah, must not his chaste soul have felt strange disorders? Must not his senses have been seized with delectation, and his imagination occupied by the presence of those voluptuous objects? Undoubtedly; yet among so many conflicts, in the midst of so terrible a storm of temptations and the many lustful pleasures that surrounded him, he sufficiently testified that his heart was not vanquished, and that his will gave no consent. Perceiving so general a rebellion against his will, and having now no part of his body at command but his tongue, he bit it off and spit it in the face of that filthy woman, who tormented his soul more cruelly by her lust than all the executioners could ever have done by the greatest torments; for the tyrant, despairing to conquer him by suffering, thought to overcome him by these pleasures."

"The history of the conflict of St. Catherine of Sienna, on the like occasion, is very admirable. The wicked spirit had permission from God to assault the purity of this holy virgin with the greatest fury, yet so as not to be allowed to touch her. He presented, then all kinds of impure suggestions to her heart; and, to move her the more, coming with his companions in form of men and women, he committed a thousand acts immodest in her presence adding most filthy words and invitations; and, although all these things were exterior, nevertheless, by means of the senses, they penetrated deep into the heart of the virgin, which, as she herself confessed, was even brimful of them; so that nothing remained in her except the pure, superior will, which was not shaken with this tempest of filthy carnal delectation. This temptation continued for a long time, till one day our Saviour, appearing to her, she said to Him: 'Where wert thou, my sweet Saviour, when my heart was full of so great darkness and uncleanness?' To which He answered: 'I was within thy heart, my daughter.' - 'But how,' replied she, 'could you dwell in my heart, where there was so much impurity? Is it possible that thou couldst dwell in so unclean a place?' To which our Lord replied: 'Tell me, did these filthy thoughts of thy heart give thee pleasure or sadness, bitterness or delight?' -'The most extreme bitterness and sadness', said she. 'Who was it, then,' replied our Saviour, 'That caused this great bitterness and sadness in thy heart but I, who remained concealed in the interior of thy soul? Believe me, daughter, had it not been for My presence these thoughts which surrounded thy will would have doubtless entered in, and with pleasure would have brought death to thy soul; but, being present, I infused this displeasure into thy heart, which enabled thee to reject the temptation as much as it could; but, not being able to do it as much as it desired, it conceived a greater displeasure and hatred both against the temptation and thyself; and thus these troubles have proved occasions of great merit to thee, and have served to increase thy strength and virtue.'"

"Behold, Philothea, how this fire was covered with ashes, and how the temptation had even entered the heart, and surrounded the will which, assisted by our Saviour, held out to the last, making resistance by her aversion, displeasure and detestation of the evil suggested, and constantly refusing her consent to the sin which besieged her on every side. Good God! how distressing must it be to a soul that loves God not to know whether He be within her or not, or whether the divine love, for which she fights, be altogether extinguished in her or not! But it is the perfection of heavenly love to make the lover suffer and fight for love for which, and by which, he fights."

"These violent assaults and extraordinary temptations, Philothea, are permitted by God against those souls only whom He desires to elevate to the highest degree of divine love, yet it does not follow that they shall afterwards attain it; for it has often happened that those who have been constant under these assaults have, for want of faithfully corresponding with the divine favor, been afterwards overcome by very small temptations. This I tell you, that, if you should happen hereafter to be assaulted by great temptations, you may know that God confers an extraordinary favor on you when He thus declares his will to make you great in His sight; and that, nevertheless, you must be always humble and fearful, not assuring yourself that you shall be able to overcome small temptations, after you have prevailed against great ones, by any other means than a constant fidelity to His divine Majesty."

"Whatever temptations, then, may hereafter befall you, or with whatever delectation they may be accompanied, so long as your will refuses her consent, not only to the temptation, but also to the delectation, give not yourself the least trouble, for God is not offended. As, when a man is so far gone in a fit as to show no sign of life, they lay their hand on his heart, and from the least palpitation they feel conclude that he is alive, and that by the application of some restorative he may again recover his strength and senses; so it sometimes happens that, through the violence of a temptation, our soul seems to have fallen into a fit, so as to have no longer any spiritual life or motion; but, if we desire to know how it is with her, let us lay our hand upon our heart, and consider whether our will still retains its spiritual motion, that is to say, whether it had done its duty in refusing to consent and to yield to the temptation and delectation; for so long as this motion of refusal remains, we may rest assured that charity, the life of our soul, remains in us, and that Jesus Christ, our Saviour, although concealed, is there present; so that by means of the continued exercise of prayer, the sacraments, and a confidence in God, we shall again return to a strong, sound, and healthful spiritual life."

"The princess, of whom we spoke before, could not prevent the dishonorable proposal which was made to her, because, as was presupposed it was made against her will; but had she, on the contrary, given it the least encouragement, or betrayed a willingness to give her affection to him that courted her, doubtless she would then have been guilty in the sight of God, and, however she might dissemble it, would certainly deserve both blame and punishment. Thus it sometimes happens that the temptation alone involves us in sin, because we ourselves are the cause of it. For example, I know that when I play, I fall easily into violent passions and blasphemy, and that gaming serves me as a temptation to those sins; I sin, therefore, as often as I play, and I am accountable for all the temptations which shall befall me. In like manner, if I know that certain conversations will expose me to the danger of falling into sin, and yet willingly expose myself to them, I am doubtless guilty of all the temptations I may meet on such occasions."

"When the delectation which proceeds from the temptation can be avoided, it is always a greater or less sin to admit it, in proportion as the pleasure we take, or the consent we give to it, is of a longer or shorter duration. The young princess before alluded to would be highly blamable, if, after having heard the filthy proposal, she should take pleasure in it, and entertain her heart with satisfaction on so improper a subject: for, although she does not consent to the real execution of what is proposed to her, she consents, nevertheless, to the spiritual application of her heart to the evil, by the pleasure she takes in it, because it is always criminal to apply either the heart or the body to anything that is immodest; but the sin depends so much on the consent of the heart, that without it even the application of the body could not be a sin."

"Wherefore, whenever you are tempted to any sin, consider whether you have not voluntarily given occasion to the temptation; for then the temptation itself puts you in the state of sin, on account of the danger to which you have exposed yourself; this is to be understood when you could conveniently have avoided the occasion, and foresaw, or ought to have foreseen, the approach of the temptation; but, if you have given no occasion to the temptation, it cannot by any means be imputed to you as a sin."

"When the delectation which follows temptation might have been avoided, and yet has not, there is always some kind of sin, more or less considerable, according to the time you have dwelt upon it, or the pleasure you have taken in it. A woman who has given no occasion to her being courted, and yet takes pleasure therein, is nevertheless, to be blamed, if the pleasure which she takes originate in no other cause than the courtship. But, for example, if the gallant who sues for love should play excellently well upon the lute, and she should take pleasure, not in his courtship, but in the harmony and sweetness of his lute, this would be no sin, though she ought not to indulge this pleasure long, for fear that she should pass thence to a desire of being courted. In like manner, if any one should propose to me some ingenious stratagem, to take revenge of my enemy, and I should neither delight in, nor consent to, the proposed revenge, but only be pleased with the subtlety of the artful invention; although it would be no sin, still I ought not to continue long amusing myself with this pleasure, for fear that by degrees I might be induced to take some delight in the revenge itself."

"We are sometimes surprised by certain symptoms of pleasure, which immediately follow the temptation, before we are well aware of it. This at most can only be a light venial sin; but it becomes greater, if, after we have perceived the evil which has befallen us, we stop some time, through negligence, to determine whether we shall admit or reject that delectation; and the sin becomes still greater, if, after being sensible of the delectation, we dwell upon it, through downright negligence, without being determined to reject it; but when we voluntarily, and with full deliberation, resolve to consent to the delectation, this of itself is a great sin, if the object in which we take delight be also a great sin....."

"As soon as you perceive yourself tempted, follow the example of children when they see a wolf or a bear in the country; for they immediately run into the arms of their father or mother, or at least they call out to them for help or assistance. It is the remedy which our Lord has taught: 'Pray that ye enter not into temptation.' If you find that the temptation, nevertheless, still continues, or even increases, run in spirit to embrace the holy cross, as if you saw our Saviour Jesus Christ crucified before you. Protest that you never will consent to the temptation, implore His assistance against it, and still refuse your consent as long as the temptation shall continue."

"But, in making these protestations and refusals on consent, look not the temptation in the face but look only on our Lord; for if you look at the temptation, especially while it is strong it may shake your courage. Divert your thought to some good and pious reflections, for, when good thoughts occupy your heart, they will drive away every temptation and suggestions."

"But the sovereign remedy against all temptations, whether great or small, is to lay open your heart, and communicate its suggestions, feelings, and affections to your director; for you must observe, that the first condition that the enemy of salvation makes with a soul which he desires to seduce is to keep silence; as those who intend to seduce maids, or married women, at the very first forbid them to communicate their proposals to their parents or husbands; whereas God, on the other hand, by his inspirations, requires that we should make them known to our superiors and directors."

"If, after all this, the temptation should still continue to harass and persecute us, we have nothing to do on our part but to continue as resolute in our protestations never to consent to it; for as maids can never be married as long as they answer no, so the soul, no matter how long the temptation may last, can never sin as long as she says no."

"Never dispute with your enemy, nor make him any reply but that with which our Saviour confounded him: 'Begone, Satan, for it is written the Lord thy God shall thou adore, and him only shalt thou serve.' For as a chaste wife would never answer the wicked wretch that makes her a dishonorable proposal, but quit him abruptly, and at the same instant turn her heart towards her husband, and renew the promise of fidelity which she has made to him: so the devout soul, that sees herself assaulted by temptation, ought by no means to lose time in disputing, but with all simplicity turn herself towards Jesus Christ her Spouse, and renew her protestation of fidelity to Him, and her resolution to remain solely and entirely His forever."

"Although we must oppose great temptations with an invincible courage, and the victory we gain over them is extremely advantageous, it may happen, nevertheless, that we may profit more in resisting small ones, for as great temptations exceed in quality, so small ones exceed in quantity; wherefore the victory of them may be comparable to that which is gained over the greatest. Wolves and bears are certainly more dangerous than flies; yet the former neither give us so much trouble, nor exercise our patience so much, as the latter. It is easy to abstain from murder, but is extremely difficult to restrain all the little sallies of passion the occasions of which present themselves every moment. It is very easy for a man or a woman to refrain from adultery, but is not as easy to refrain from glances of the eyes, from giving or receiving marks of love, or from uttering or listening to flattery. It is easy not to admit a rival with the husband or wife, as to the body, but not as to the heart; it is easy to refrain from everything that may be prejudicial to conjugal affection; it is easy not to steal other men's goods, but difficult not to covet them; it is easy not to bear false witness in judgement, but difficult to observe perfect sobriety; it is easy to refrain from wishing another man's death, but difficult to refrain from desiring what may be inconvenient to him; it is easy to abstain from defaming him, but it is sometimes difficult to refrain from despising him. In a word, these small temptations of anger, suspicion, jealousy, envy, fond love, levity, vanity, insincerity, affectation, craftiness, and impure thoughts are continually assaulting even those who are the most devout and resolute. We must, therefore, diligently prepare ourselves, my dear Philothea, for this warfare; and rest assured, that for as many victories as we shall gain over these trifling enemies, so many gems shall be added to the crown of glory which God is preparing for us in heaven. Wherefore I say, that being ever ready to fight courageously against great temptations we must in the meantime diligently defend ourselves against those that seem small and inconsiderable."

What Remedies We are to Apply to Small Temptations

"Now as to these smaller temptations of vanity, suspicion, impatience, jealousy, envy, fond love, and such like trash, which, like flies, and gnats, continually hover about us, and sometimes sting us on the legs, the hands, or the face; as it is impossible to be altogether freed from them, the best defense that we can make is not to give ourselves much trouble about them; for although they may tease us, yet they can never hurt us so long as we continue firmly resolved to dedicate ourselves in earnest to the service of God."

"Despise, then, these petty assaults, without so much as thinking of what they suggest. Let them buzz and hover here and there around you; pay no more attention to them than you would to flies; but when they offer to sting you, and you perceive them in the least to light upon your heart, content yourself with quietly removing them, not by contending or disputing with them, but by performing some actions of a contrary nature to the temptation, especially acts of the love of God. But you must not persevere, Philothea, in opposing to the temptation the act of the contrary virtue, for this would be to dispute with it but, after having performed a simple act of the contrary virtue, if you have leisure to observe the quality of the temptation, turn your heart gently towards Jesus Christ crucified, and by an act of love kiss His sacred feet. This is the best means to overcome the enemy, as well in small as in great temptations; for as the love of God contains within itself the perfection of all the virtues, and is even more excellent than the virtues themselves, so it is also the sovereign antidote against every kind of vice, and, by accustoming your mind on these occasions to have recourse to this remedy, you need not even examine by what kind of temptation it is troubled. Moreover, this grand remedy is so terrible to the enemy of our souls, that as soon as he perceives that his temptation incites us to form acts of divine love he ceases to tempt us. Let these general principles suffice with respect to small and ordinary temptation; he who would wish to contend with them in particular would give himself much trouble to little or no purpose.

How To Fortify Our Hearts Against Temptations

"Consider from time to time what passions are most predominant in your soul; and, having discovered them, adopt such a method of thinking, speaking, and acting, as may contradict them. If, for example, you find yourself inclined to vanity, think often on the miseries of human life; think of the inquietude which these vanities will raise in your conscience at the day of your death; how unworthy they are of a generous heart, and that they are nothing but empty toys, fit only for the amusement of children. Speak often against vanity, and, whatever repugnance you may feel, cease not to cry it down, for by this means you will engage yourself, even in honor, to the opposite side; for by declaiming against a thing we bring ourselves to hate it, though at first we might have had an affection for it. Exercise works of abjection and humility as much as possible, though with ever so great a reluctance; since by this means you accustom yourself to humility, and weaken your vanity; so that, when the temptation comes, you will have less inclination to consent to it, and more strength to resist it."

"If you are inclined to covetousness, think frequently on the folly of a sin which makes us slaves to that which was only made to serve us, and that with death we must part with all, and leave it in the hands of those who perhaps may squander it away, or to whom it may be a cause of damnation. Speak loud against avarice, and in praise of an utter contempt of the world. Force yourself to give frequent alms, and neglect to improve some opportunities of gain. Should you be inclined to give or receive fond love, often think how very dangerous this kind of amusement is, as well to yourself as others; how unworthy a thing it is, to employ in an idle pastime the noblest affection of our soul, and how worthy of censure is so extreme a levity of mind. Speak often in praise of purity and simplicity of heart, and let your actions, to the utmost of your power, be every comfortable to your words, by avoiding levity's and fond liberties. In short, in time of peace, that is, when temptations to the sin to which you are most inclined do not molest you, make several acts of the contrary virtue; and if occasions of practicing it do not present themselves; endeavor to seek them; for by this means you will strengthen your heart against future temptations."

Of Inquietude

"As inquietude is not only a temptation, but the source of many temptations, it is therefore necessary that I should say something concerning it. Inquietude, or sadness, then, is nothing else but that grief of mind which we conceive for some evil which we experience against our will, whether it be exterior, as poverty, sickness, contempt; or interior, as ignorance, avidity, repugnance, and temptation. When the soul, then, perceives that some evil has befallen her, she becomes sad, is displeased, and extremely anxious to rid herself of it; and thus far she is right, for every one naturally desires to embrace good, and fly from that which he apprehends to be evil. If the soul, for the love of God, wishes to be freed from her evil, she will seek the means of her deliverance with patience, meekness, humility, and tranquillity, expecting it more from the providence of God than from her own industry or diligence. But if she seeks her deliverance, from a motive of self-love then will she fatigue herself in quest of these means, as if the success depended more on herself that on God; I do not say that she thinks so, but that she acts as if she thought so. Now, if she succeeds not immediately according to her wishes, she falls into inquietude, which, instead of removing, aggravates the evil, and involves her in such anguish and distress. with so great loss of courage and strength, that she imagines her evil incurable. Thus, then, sadness, which in the beginning is just, produces inquietude, and inquietude produces an increase of sadness, which is extremely dangerous."

"Inquietude is the greatest evil that can befall the soul, sin only excepted. For, as the seditious and intestine commotions of any commonwealth prevent it from being able to resist a foreign invasion, so our heart, being troubled within itself, loses the strength necessary to maintain the virtue it had acquired, and the means to resist the temptations of the enemy, who then uses his utmost efforts to fish, as it is said, in troubled waters."

"Inquietude proceeds from an inordinate desire of being delivered from the evil which we feel, or of acquiring the good which we desire; and yet there is nothing which tends more to increase evil, and to prevent the enjoyment of good than an unquiet mind. Birds remain prisoners in the nets, because, when they find themselves caught, they eagerly flutter about to extricate themselves, and by that means entangle themselves the more. Whenever, then, you are pressed with a desire to be freed from some evil, or to obtain some good, be careful both to settle your mind in repose and tranquillity, and to compose your judgment and will; and then gently procure the accomplishment of your desire, taking in regular order the means which may be most convenient; when I say gently, I do not mean negligently, but without hurry, trouble, or inquietude, otherwise, instead of obtaining the effect of your desire. you will mar all, and embarrass yourself the more."

"'My soul is continually in my hands, O Lord, and I have not forgotten thy law,' said David. Examine frequently in the day or at least in the morning and evening, whether you have your soul in your hands, or whether some passion or inquietude has not robbed you of it. Consider whether you have your heart at command, or whether it has not escaped out of your hands, to engage itself in some disorderly affection of love, hatred, envy, covetousness, fear, uneasiness, or joy. If it should be gone astray, seek after it before you do anything else, and bring it back quietly to the presence of God, subjecting all your affections and desires to the obedience and directions of His divine will. For as they who are afraid of losing anything which is precious hold it fast in their hands; so, in imitation of this great king, we should always say, 'O my God! my soul is in danger, and therefore I carry it always in my hands; and in this manner I have not forgotten thy holy law.'"

"Permit not your desires, how trivial soever they may be, to disquiet you, lest afterwards those that are of greater importance should find your heart involved in trouble and disorder. When you perceive that inquietude begins to affect your mind recommend yourself to God, and resolve to do nothing until it is restored to tranquillity, unless it should be something that cannot be deferred; in that case, moderating the current of your desires as much as possible, perform the action, not according to your desire but your reason."

"If you can disclose the cause of your disquietude to your spiritual director, or at least to some faithful and devout friend, be assured that you will presently find ease; for communicating the grief of the heart produces the same effect on the soul as bleeding does in the body of him that is in a continual fever; it is the remedy of remedies. Accordingly the holy king St. Lewis gave this counsel to his son: 'If thou hast any uneasiness in thy heart, tell it immediately to thy confessor, or to some good person, and then thou shalt be enabled to bear thy evil very easily, by the comfort he will give thee.'" (ST. FRANCIS DE SALES; pp 288 - 209)

VIRTUES: General Observations and Precautions as Regards Their Practice

"....That low and servile fear which begets excessive scruples in the souls of new converts from a course of sin is commendable in beginners, and a certain foreboding of a future purity of conscience; but the same fear would be blamable in those who are far advanced, in whose heart love ought to reign which by imperceptible degrees chases away this kind of servile fear.

"St. Bernard, at the beginning, was full of rigor towards those that put themselves under his directions; he told them that they must leave the body behind, and come to him only with the spirit. When he heard their confessions he severely reprehended the most trivial faults, and urged them on to perfection, with such vehemence that, instead of making them advance forward, he drew them back; for they fell into despondency at seeing themselves so earnestly pressed up so steep and high an ascent. Observe, Philothea, it was an ardent zeal for perfect purity that induced this great saint to adopt this manner of proceeding. This zeal of the saint was a great virtue, but a virtue nevertheless reprehensible; of which God Himself, in a holy vision, made him sensible, infusing at the same time into his soul so meek, amiable, and tender a spirit, that, being totally changed, he repented of his former rigor and severity, and became so gracious and condescending to every one as to make himself all to all, that he might gain all. St. Jerome having related how his dear daughter, St. Paula, was not only excessive, but obstinate in the exercise of bodily mortification to such a degree that she would not yield to the contrary advice of Epiphanius, her bishop, and, moreover, that she suffered herself to be carried away with so excessive grief for the death of her friends as to be herself frequently in danger of death, concludes at length with these words: 'Some will say, that, instead of writing the praises of this holy woman, I write reprehensions and dispraises but I call Jesus to witness, whom she served, and whom I desire to serve, that I lie not either on the one side, or on the other, but set down sincerely what related to her, as one Christian should do of another; that is to say, I write her history, not her panegyric and that her vices are the virtues of others:' meaning that the failings and defects of St. Paula would have been esteemed virtue in a soul less perfect, and that there are actions esteemed imperfections in the perfect, which would be held great perfections in those who are imperfect."

"It is a good sign, when 'at the end of sickness' the legs of the sick person swell, for it shows that nature, now acquiring strength, expels her superfluous humors; but this would be a bad symptom in a healthy person; as it would show that nature has not sufficient strength to resolve and dissipate the humors. We must, my Philothea, have a good opinion of those who practice virtue, though imperfectly since we see the saints themselves have often practiced them in this manner. But, as to ourselves, we must be careful to exercise them, not only faithfully, but discreetly; and to this end we must strictly observe the advice of the wise man,'not to rely on our own prudence,' but on the judgement of those whom God has given us for conductors."

"There are certain things which many esteem as virtues, which in reality are not; I mean ecstasies, or raptures, insensibilities, impossibilities, deifical unions, elevations, transformations, and similar perfections, treated on in certain books, which promise to elevate the soul to a contemplation purely intellectual, to an essential application of the spirit, and a supernatural life. But observe well, Philothea, these perfections are not virtues, but rather the recompenses of virtues, or small specimens of the happiness of the life to come, which God sometimes presents to men, to make them enraptured with the whole piece, which is only to be found in heaven."

"But we must not aspire to their favors, since they are by no means necessary to the serving and loving of God, which should be our only pretension....neither are they such as can be obtained by labor and industry, since they are rather passions than actions, which we may indeed receive, but cannot produce in ourselves. I add that we have only undertaken, and must strenuously endeavor to render ourselves good, devout, and godly; but, if it should please God to elevate us to these angelical perfections, we, also, shall then be angels. In the meantime let us endeavor humbly and devoutly to acquire those simple virtues for which our Saviour has exhorted us to labor; such as patience, meekness, mortifications towards our neighbors, bearing with their imperfections, diligence, and holy fervor. Let us leave these supereminent favors to elevated souls; we merit not so high a rank in the service of God; we shall be too happy to serve Him in His kitchen or to be His domestics in much lower stations. If He should hereafter think proper to admit us into His cabinet, or privy council, it will be through the excess of His bountiful goodness. Yea, Philothea, the King of Glory, does not recompense His servants according to the dignity of the offices they hold but according to the measure of the love and humility with which they exercise them. Saul, seeking the asses of his father, found the kingdom of Israel. Rebecca, watering the camels of Abraham, became the spouse of his son. Ruth, gleaning after the reapers of Boaz, and laying down at this feet, was advanced to his side and made his wife. High and elevated pretensions to extraordinary favors are subject to illusion and deceit; and it sometimes happens that those who imagine themselves angels are not so much as good men, and that there is more sublimity in their words and expressions than in their manner of thinking and acting." (ST. FRANCIS DE SALES; pp. 123-127)

VIRTUES: Precautions on Their Use and General Observations

"As the queen of the bees never goes abroad into the fields without being surrounded by all her little subjects, so charity, the queen of virtues, never enters the heart without bringing all the other virtues in her train, exercising and disciplining them as a captain does his soldiers. But she neither employs them all at the same time, nor in the same manner, nor in all seasons, nor in every place; for as the just man, like a tree planted by the river side, brings forth fruit in due season, so charity, watering the soul, produces a variety of good works, each one in its proper time. 'Music, how agreeable soever in itself, is out of season in time of mourning,' says the proverb. It is a great fault in many who undertaking the practice of some particular virtue wish to exercise it on all occasions. Like some ancient philosophers, they either always weep or laugh; and what is yet worse, they censure those who do not always, like themselves, exercise the same virtues; whereas, we should 'rejoice with the joyful; and weep with them that weep,' says the Apostle; 'for charity is patient, kind, bountiful, discreet, and condescending.'

"There are, however, some virtues of so general utility as not only to require an exercise of themselves apart, but also communicate their qualities to the practice of other virtues. Occasions are seldom presented for the exercise of fortitude, magnanimity, and magnificence; but meekness, temperance, modesty, and humility are virtues wherewith all the actions of our life should be tempered. It is true, there are other virtues more agreeable but the use of these is more necessary. Sugar is more agreeable than salt; but the use of salt is more necessary and general. Therefore, we must constantly have a good store of these general virtues in readiness, since we stand in need of them almost continually."

"In the exercise of the virtues we should always prefer that which is most conformable to our duty, not that which is most agreeable to our imagination. St. Paula was prejudiced in favor of corporal austerities and mortifications, that she might more easily enjoy spiritual comfort; but she was under a greater obligation to obey her superiors, and therefore St. Jerome blamed her for using immoderate abstinences against her bishop's advice. The apostles, on the other hand, being commissioned to preach the gospel and distribute the bread of heaven, thought that they should act wrongly by interrupting these evangelical exercises for the relief of the poor, which, though, is in itself an excellent virtue. Every condition of life has its own peculiar virtue. The virtues of a prelate are different from those of a prince; those of a soldier from those of a married woman, or a widow, and so on through every class of society. Though all ought to possess all the virtues, yet all are not equally bound to exercise them, but each ought to practice, in a more particular manner, those virtues which are most requisite for the state of life to which he is called."

"Among the virtues unconnected with our particular duty we must prefer the excellent to the glittering and showy. Comets appear greater than stars, and apparently occupy a greater space; whereas, in reality, they can neither in magnitude nor equality be compared to the stars; for as they only seem great because they are nearer, and appear in a grosser manner than the stars, so there are certain virtues, which, on account of their proximity, become more sensible, or, to use the expression, more material, that are highly esteemed and always preferred by the vulgar. Hence, it is that so many prefer corporal alms before spiritual; the hair-shirt, fasting, going barefoot, using the discipline, and other such corporal mortifications, before meekness, mildness, modesty, and other mortifications of the heart; which are, nevertheless, more exalted. Choose, then, Philothea, the best virtues, not the most esteemed; the most noble, not the most apparent; those that are actually the best, not those that are the most ostensible or shining."

"It is profitable for every one to exercise some of them, and at the same time to advance in all virtues. Thus, if assaulted by pride or by anger, we must, in all our actions, practice humility and meekness; and make all our other exercises of prayer, and the sacraments of prudence, constancy, and sobriety, subservient to this end. For as the wild boar, to sharpen his tusks, wets and polishes them with his other teeth, and by this means sharpens all of them; so a virtuous man, having undertaken to perfect himself in that virtue of which he stands in most need for his defense, files and polishes it by the exercise of the other virtues, whilst they help to refine that one, make all of them become better polished. Thus it happened to Job, who, exercising himself particularly in patience, against the many temptations wherewith he was assaulted, became perfectly established and confirmed in all kinds of virtues. Nay, St. Gregory Nazianzen says, 'that by the perfect exercise of one only virtue a person may attain to the height of all the rest;' for which he alleges the example of Rehab, who, having exactly practiced the virtue of hospitality arrived at a great degree of Glory. But this is to be understood of a virtue which is practiced with great fervor and charity." (ST. FRANCIS DE SALES; pp. 117-122)

St. Teresa Of Avila

ST. TERESA OF AVILA

Spiritual Direction of St. Teresa of Avila

VOLUME ONE
The Book of Her Life
Spiritual Testimonies Soliloquies
Translated by
Kieran Kavanaugh, O.C.D.
and Otilio Rodriguea, O.C.D.
ICS Publications
Institute of Carmelite Studies
Washington, DC, 1976; pp. 1-406
Washington Province of Discalced Carmelites, Inc., 1976
ICS Publications
2131 Lincoln Road, NE
Washington, DC 20002

VOLUME TWO
The Way of Perfection
Meditations on the Song of Songs
The Interior Castle
Ibid, 1980; pp. 1-554
Volume Three
The Book of Her Foundations
Minor Works

The Constitutions - On Making the Visitation
A Satirical Critique - Response to a Spiritual Challenge - Poetry
Ibid, 1985; pp. 1-483

AUTHORITY: Preventing Excessive Attachments

"The Prioress should appoint as portress and sacristan persons whom she can trust. So as not to allow for any attachment to an office, she may remove them as she sees fit."

(ST. TERESA OF AVILA; Vol. III; p.330)

AUTHORITY: Firmness, with Charity in its Exercise

"It is very necessary that they understand there is some one in command, who is not tender hearted, when it comes to matters that would weaken the religious observance. The judge must be so upright in administering justice that they become convinced he will not turn aside from whatever might be more perfect and for the greater service of God even if the whole world crumbles." (ST. TERESA OF AVILA; Vol. III; p.337)

AUTHORITY: Pitfalls to be Avoided in its Exercise

"The one who is mortified thinks that anything she commands is easy to submit to, as it would be for her, but perhaps it would be very harmful for the nun to whom she gives the orders. We must be careful about this. If for ourselves something would be harsh, we must not order others to do it." (ST. TERESA OF AVILA, Vol. III; p.188)

BIBLE: Its Great Importance

"Teresa in her earlier life did not receive much exposure and very little training in Holy Scripture studies. In this observation of hers she reveals what her later acquired knowledge meant to her: 'But the fundamental problem of the world is ignorance of revelation of the word of God. All the harm that comes to the world come from its not knowing the truths of Scripture in clarity and truth.'" (ST. TERESA OF AVILA; Vol. III; p.37)

BIBLE: Humility in the Interpretation of Holy Scripture

Understanding the awesomeness of the task of interpreting the Scriptures, Teresa at one point exclaims:... "for one word of His will contain within itself a thousand mysteries, and thus our understanding is very elementary. The attitude, then, that must occupy anyone's approach to the Bible is humility." (ST. TERESA OF AVILA, Vol. II; p. 210).

BIBLE: Teresa's Interpretation of the "Song of Songs" of Solomon

NOTE: While admitting its perfect application to the Blessed Virgin Mary, to the Church, Teresa choose to concentrate in an interpretation that speaks of the love between Christ and the soul. (ST. TERESA OF AVILA, Vol II; p.211)

BIBLE: Interpretation of Holy Scripture, Avoid Fruitless Concern

"For one word of God's will contains a thousand mysteries, and thus our understanding is only elementary. When His Majesty desires to give us understanding of the words, without work or worry on our part, we shall surely find it." (ST. TERESA OF AVILA, Vol. II; p.217)

BIBLE: On Interpretation, on Not Understanding

"You should never dwell on what you do not understand in Holy Scripture or the mysteries of our faith, nor should you be startled by the lofty words that take place between God and the soul." (ST. TERESA OF AVILA, Vol. II; pp. 218-219)

BIBLE: God's Love and Holy Scripture

"God's love and His suffering can not be captured in Holy Scripture." (ST. TERESA OF AVILA, Vol. II; p 219)

BIBLE: Song of Songs, Interpretation of Passage

Teresa understood the words "sustain me with flowers" to mean that "the soul is asking to perform great works in the service of our Lord and of its neighbor". {NOTE: Great works could mean little or great acts of love}. (ST. TERESA OF AVILA, Vol. II; p.257)

BIBLE: Interpretation of The Gospel Narrative of Martha And Mary Hosting Jesus in Their Own Individual Way

Teresa offers another interpretation to the story of Martha and Mary, one that is often misinterpreted: "Believe me, Martha and Mary must join together in order to show hospitality to the Lord and have Him always present and not host Him badly by failing to give Him something to eat. How would Mary, always seated at His feet provide Him with food if her sister did not help her. His food is that in every way possible we draw souls that they may be saved and praise Him always. You will make two objections: One, that He said that Mary had chosen the better part. The answer is that she had already performed the task of Martha pleasing the Lord by washing His feet and drying them with her hair." {NOTE: The chiding of Martha by Jesus was a very gentle chiding merely calling attention to the fact that she was complaining too much about the little work there was to be done in the kitchen for the preparation of the food, for she was rendering a service to the Lord, but with a certain unbecoming reluctance}. (ST. TERESA OF AVILA; Vol. II, p.448)

BIBLE: An Awesome Reverence

Teresa: "Not one iota of Holy Scripture will fall short." (ST. TERESA OF AVILA; Vol. I: p.277)

BIBLE: Teresa's Knowledge of Holy Scripture

{NOTE: A study of Teresa's life as it is revealed in her *Collected Works,* and is so stated there reveals that Teresa's life clearly shows that she received no education in Sacred Scripture. Nonetheless one is amazed by her knowledge and use of Holy Scripture, despite this lack of formal training and the limited access she had to the contents of the Bible.}

BODY AND BLOOD OF CHRIST: Its Reception

Teresa approached its reception with awesome reverence. (ST. TERESA OF AVILA;

Vol. I; p.263)

BODY AND BLOOD OF CHRIST: Power of Divine Nourishment

Teresa makes a very penetrating observation from her life experiences on the unique power after receiving the BODY OR BLOOD OF CHRIST, namely: "Do you think this heavenly food fails to provide sustenance, even for those bodies, that it is not a great medicine even for bodily ills. This is a common experience, and the illnesses are very recognizable, for I don't think they could be feigned." (ST. TERESA OF AVILA, Vol. II; p.121)

BODY AND BLOOD OF CHRIST: True Presence

"In the Blessed Sacrament we have Him just as truly present as He was then. In Communion, the event is happening now, just as He walked on earth, and it is entirely true." (ST. TERESA OF AVILA, Vol. II, p.171)

BODY AND BLOOD OF CHRIST: After Receiving Him, a Choice Time for Contemplation

Teresa gives some exquisitely beautiful spiritual advice: "Be with Him willingly; don't lose so good an opportunity for conversing with Him as in the hour after receiving Communion. After having received the Lord, since you have the person Himself present, strive to close the eyes of the body and open those of the soul and look into your own heart. I can not repeat this too often, you should acquire the habit of doing this everytime you receive Communion. And you will desire to see Him so much that He will reveal Himself to you entirely." (ST. TERESA OF AVILA, Vol. II; p.173)

BODY AND BLOOD OF CHRIST: When One Cannot Receive Him, a Spiritual Communion Made at Intervals Throughout the Day is Beneficial

"A spiritual communion, that is one made without having received the Body or Blood of Christ is highly beneficial, through it you can recollect yourselves in the same way after Mass, for the love of this Lord is deeply impressed on the soul." (ST. TERESA OF AVILA, Vol. II; p.174)

BODY OR BLOOD OF CHRIST: Its Sincere Reception, It is to be Received with Great Reverence

"Certainly, I think that if we were to approach the most Blessed Sacrament with great faith and love, once would be enough to leave us rich. How much richer from approaching so many times as we do. The trouble is that we do it out of routine and it shows." (ST. TERESA OF AVILA, Vol. II, P 241)

CATHOLIC CHURCH: Beware of Deceptive Attacks Against the Faith

"The enemy will attempt to deceive the unwary by making them believe there are leaks in the 'Bark of Peter.'

CATHOLIC CHURCH: Teresa, Strong in the Faith

Teresa, ending her work on the "Interior Castle" of her *Collected Works* ends with a ringing affirmation of her Faith: "I submit in everything to what the Holy Roman Catholic Church holds, for in this Church I live, declare my faith, and promise to live and die." (ST. TERESA OF AVILA, Vol. II, p 452)

CATHOLIC CHURCH: Defenders of the Church

The ecclesiastical arm of preachers and theologians was in Teresa's time the defender of the Church. (ST. TERESA OF AVILA, Vol. I, p.22)

CATHOLIC CHURCH: True Faith, Loyalty, and Allegiance to It

Teresa gave us a model of allegiance when she said: "This can be held as certain, that through the goodness of God I always am, and will be, and have been subject to her." (ST. TERESA OF AVILA, Vol. II; p. 282 and p. 452)

CHRIST: Lack of Trust and a Betrayal of Christ

"How many must there be, like Judas, whom the Lord calls to the Apostolate by communing with them, and like Saul, whom He calls to be kings, who afterwards through their own fault go astray." (ST. TERESA OF AVILA; Vol. II; p. 348)

CHRIST: Jesus as our Best Companion and Friend

"No state is so sublime that a person must always be occupied with divinity and thus obliged to empty the mind of all reference to the human Christ. Life is long and there are in it many trials and we need to look at Christ our model, how He suffered them and also at His apostles and saints, so as to bear these trials with perfection, Jesus is too good a companion for us to turn away from Him. An effort to forget Christ and live in continual absorption in the Divinity will result in a failure of the spiritual development we aspire to." Teresa is most insistent on this. "The purification of the person is realized not merely through the sufferings inherent to the human condition, but especially through contact with the person of Christ in His humanity and divinity." (ST. TERESA OF AVILA, Vol. II; pp 275-276)

***CHRIST*:** Never Forgetting the Humanity of Christ Even in Contemplative Prayer

"The mere sight of the Lord fallen to the ground in the garden with that frightful sweat is enough to last the intellect not only an hour but many days, while it looks with a simple gaze at Who He is and how ungrateful we have been for so much suffering...It is good to strive to dwell on the mysteries of the suffering Christ in His humanity, for in doing so we will not impede the most sublime prayer in contemplation. In pure contemplative prayer the suffering of Christ may not be dwelled on actively, for God will suspend these operative faculties of the soul so that such sufferings take on no visionary form, imagery, thought, and so forth, in the soul, but the soul nevertheless always, literally, remembers the sufferings of Christ, our Saviour in the very depths of its soul." (ST. TERESA OF AVILA, Vol. II; p.402 and St. John of the Cross).

CONFESSION: A Prudent Approach

For some people as Teresa advises: "They should make their confession briefly and bring it to a conclusion." This advice is especially applicable to persons who have a tendency to scruples. (ST. TERESA OF AVILA, Vol. II; p.461)

CONFESSION: Selection of a Proper Confessor

Teresa placed great stress on "Not only the spiritual devotion of a confessor, but also upon his being learned as well." (ST. TERESA OF AVILA, Vol. II p. 461)

CONSCIENCE: Time for Examination of Conscience

In her Constitutions Teresa made provisions of " a quarter of an hour for the examination of consciences as to how they have spent the day." (ST. TERESA OF AVILA, Vol. III; p. 319)

DEVIL: Evolving Perspectives on the Devil Throughout Teresa's Life

Teresa early on in her spiritual development underwent a considerable transformation as regards the devils as enemies of the soul, for example:

In Her Early Life

"Those whom they fear - and it is right they fear and always ask the Lord to be freed from them - are the traitorous enemies, the devils who transfigure themselves into angels of light who are disguised. Not until they have done much harm to the soul do they allow themselves to be recognized. They suck our blood and destroy our virtues and we go about in the midst of the same temptation but do not know it." (ST. TERESA OF AVILA, Vol. II; p. 195)

Later in Her Life

"I'm sick and tired of those people who go about saying: 'The devil, the devil, the devil,' when instead they should be saying 'God, God, God'. I fear these kinds of persons more than the devil himself." (ST. TERESA OF AVILA, Vol. I; p.13 and p.170)

DEVIL: His Machinations as Regards Penance

"He tempts us in regard to excessive penances so that we might think we are more penitential than others and are doing something." (ST. TERESA OF AVILA, Vol. II; p. 190)

DEVIL: Bristle and Fine Thread of Lies Technique Which He Employs

"Beware, for the devil, through very small things drills holes through which very large things enter." (ST. TERESA OF AVILA, Vol. III; p. 279)

DEVIL: On a Leash Held Firmly Under the Control of the Hand of God

Teresa observed from her own spiritual life experience that "the Lord, it seems, gives the devil license so that the soul might be tried and even made to think that it is rejected by God." (ST. TERESA OF AVILA, Vol II; p. 364)

DEVIL: Characteristic of His Effect Upon the Soul

"The devil can give the savor and delight that seem to be spiritual, but he doesn't have the power to join pain - and so much of it - to the spiritual quiet and delight of the soul. For all of his powers are on the outside, and the pains he causes are never in my opinion, delightful or peaceful but disturbing and contentious. Thus, the devil has to get at the soul from outside of the soul since only God occupies the soul." (ST. TERESA OF AVILA, Vol. II p. 369)

DEVIL: His Shifting Tactics

"The devil has a good means of making us squander our thoughts on trifles. When he sees that one has no fear of him, he looks for other devices." (ST. TERESA OF AVILA, Vol. III; p. 194)

DEVIL: His Cunning in Exploiting Us

Teresa, while keeping the powers of the devil to attack the soul in clear perspective, cautions her nuns: "The devil needs nothing more than to see a little door open before playing a thousand tricks." (ST. TERESA OF AVILA, Vol. II; p. 416)

DEVIL: Serving God, the Soul Need Fear Neither Sin of Human Nature (From Our Own Soul), Nor That Temptation to Sin Offered to Us by the Devil.

When Teresa speaks so unsparingly of the devil, one thinks as one reads her remarks. Is there here nothing more than a popular personification of the forces of evil? The difficulty lies in discerning what precisely comes from the human realm and what from that superhuman realm of principalities and powers. The essential point is that through Jesus Christ she feels liberated, free of all worries about all interference coming from either human or demonic powers, and in her efforts to serve Jesus she discovers that in the end He is always victorious, never fails those who seek to serve Him. (ST. TERESA OF AVILA, Vol. III; p. 13)

DEVIL: A Healthy Perspective

Teresa developed a healthy perspective as regards the devil, although alert to his powers and potential to attack, she stressed instead concentrating on thinking of Jesus instead of an unhealthy, wasteful, concentration on the devil. She summed it up very aptly in saying: "I get sick and tired of those people who keep saying, 'the devil, the devil, the devil' when they could instead by saying 'God, God, God.' She also stated that she feared much more the people who talked too much about the devil, than the devil himself." (ST. TERESA OF AVILA, Vol. I; p.13 and p. 170.)

DEVIL: A Source of Some Bodily Disorders

Teresa indicated a number of times that "in her experience in the religious community and outside of it that certain bodily disorders were definitely caused by the devil." (ST. TERESA OF AVILA, Vol. I; p.213)

DEVIL: Recognition of His Attacks

"The onset of the attacks of the devil are clearly recognized by the agitating dryness, taking place throughout the attack." (ST. TERESA OF AVILA, Vol. I; p. 197)

DEVIL: Intensity of Some of His Attacks

"At times God permitted her soul to be kicked around by the devil as it is were a mere soccer ball. At such times the suffering then was indescribable." (ST. TERESA OF AVILA, Vol. I; p.198)

DEVIL: Attitude Toward Attacks

Teresa stated: "We should know that each time we pay no attention to them, they are weakened, and the soul gains much more mastery over them." (ST. TERESA OF AVILA, Vol. I; p. 206)

DEVIL: Deception by the Devil

"God will never let those who love Him to be deceived by the devil." (ST. TERESA OF AVILA, Vol. I; p. 157)

DEVIL: A Deadly Enemy to be Kept in Proper Perspective

"After self-love, he is the most deadly enemy who has no power but that which God permits him to have."

DEVIL: His Powers Kept in Perspective

Teresa: "Why shouldn't I have the fortitude to engage in combat with all of hell." I pay no more attention to devils than to flies. (ST. TERESA OF AVILA, Vol. I; p.12)

DEVIL: His Presence

"He very quickly shows who he is." (ST. TERESA OF AVILA, Vol. I; p. 186)

DEVIL: Department of Spiritual Red Tape and Dirty Tricks

Teresa: "He snarls up many an affair designed to do God's will." (ST. TERESA OF AVILA, Vol. I; p. 249)

DEVIL: Changing Tactics with the Passage of Time

"Over historical periods of time the devil sees that new weapons are needed in order to do harm." (ST. TERESA OF AVILA, Vol II; p.40)

DEVIL: Most Effective Weapon Against Him

"It is necessary to be careful and awake in everything for he does not sleep. There is no better remedy than prayer." (ST. TERESA OF AVILA, Vol II; p. 68)

DEVIL: Our Health, Fear can be Useless

"If the devil begins to frighten us about losing our health, we shall never do anything." (ST. TERESA OF AVILA, Vol. II; p. 79)

DEVIL: Physical Pain

"He can easily make one imagine non-existent pains." (ST. TERESA OF AVILA, Vol II; p.85)

DEVIL: Taking Revenge Upon Him

"If you wish to take revenge on the devil and free yourself from his wiles, double your willingness to do things contrary to your nature which inclines towards self-love." (ST. TERESA OF AVILA, Vol. II; p. 84)

DEVIL: Importance of Determination in Loving God

"He is extremely afraid of determined souls for he has experienced the great harm they can do. I know this well through experience." (ST. TERESA OF AVILA, Vol. II; pp. 126-127)

DEVIL: Example of His Wiles

"The way the devil can do a great deal of harm without our realizing it is to make us believe we have virtues when we do not." (ST. TERESA OF AVILA, Vol. II; p. 186)

DEVIL: His Deceptions

"The devil could deceive one with respect to the spiritual delights given by God if there were no temptations, and do much more harm than when temptations are felt."

DEVIL: Power to Produce a Vision

It is true that the devil can present a vision to the soul awake or asleep, but not with the truth and majesty of those produced by God. In other words, his are clearly counterfeits. If the vision is from the devil he will soon show a sign, and will be caught in a thousand lies. If the confessor has the ability to understand this he will give the proper spiritual direction accordingly." (ST. TERESA OF AVILA, Vol. II; p. 232)

DEVIL: His Mechinations Against the Soul

"The devil," Teresa points out, "gains much and is extremely pleased to see a soul afflicted and disquieted for he knows that disturbance impedes it from being totally occupied in loving and praising God." (ST. TERESA OF AVILA, Vol II; p. 418)

DEVIL: Real Adversary to Spiritual Growth

In Teresa's life another character playing a major role in her story and sharing center stage is the adversary, the devil, relentlessly plotting and struggling to spoil the Lord's work. In Teresa's life readers see him trying to impede her wary soul through the bad influences of the surrounding society, through inner cunning, deceptive suggestions, false visions, and even bodily attacks. Reflecting on the disturbances the devil brings upon the soul, she optimistically reflects: "When You Lord want to give courage how little do all contradictions matter. Rather, it seems I am encouraged by them, thinking that since the devil is beginning to be disturbed the Lord will be served in that monastery." (ST. TERESA OF AVILA, Vol. III; p. 11)

DEVIL: Keeping His Power in Reasonable Perspective

"The spiritual tradition deeply rooted among the people, particularly from the middle ages to the seventeenth century, told how the devil might act anywhere in the world among any persons at any hour of day or night, but always and only with the permission of God as St. Gregory affirmed in his commentary on Job." (ST. TERESA OF AVILA, Vol. III; p.12)

DEVIL: Spiritual Weapons Against

"St. Teresa's method of coping with the temptations of the devil were prayer which she called the place where the Lord gives light to understand truths, and the practice of Christian virtues like charity, humility, and obedience."

DEVIL: Not Necessary to Fear

"If we proceed with a pure conscience and obediently the Lord will never permit the devil to have enough influence to deceive harmfully our souls; on the contrary, the devil is the one who is left deceived." (ST. TERESA OF AVILA, Vol. III; pp. 113-114)

FEAR: An Ever-Present Holy Fear, a Healthy Condition of a Devout Soul

"Ultimately, people must always live with fear until You give them true peace and give them there where that peace will be unending. I say 'true peace' not because this peace is not true but because the first war could return if we were to withdraw from God. The more favored such devout souls are favored by God, His Majesty, the more they are afraid and fearful of themselves." (ST. TERESA OF AVILA, Vol. II; p. 443)

FEAR: Fear of Death

"In Teresa's later years little fear remained of death, a fear which she had greatly earlier in her life." (ST. TERESA OF AVILA, Vol. I; p. 258)

FEAR: The Holy Fear of God, an Observation

"Once the soul has reached contemplation, the fear of God also, as with love, becomes very manifest; it doesn't disguise itself even exteriorly. Despite the fact that you will watch these persons, contemplatives, carefully, you will not see them become careless." (ST. TERESA OF AVILA, Vol. II; p. 196)

FEAR: Coping with Temptations Prudently

"Let us beseech God always that the temptation may not be so strong as to offend Him, that its strength might not outweigh the fortitude He gives us to conquer it. This fear is what is important: it is what I desire may never be taken away from us, for it is what will help us." (ST. TERESA OF AVILA, Vol. II; p. 197)

FEAR: Blessings on Those Who Have a Holy Fear of God

"God will shower His blessings on those who have a holy fear of Him - not a cringing, frightful fear of a servile nature - but a fear of offending God through the slightest venial sin or in any way whatsoever. A fear which would rather face death if necessary out of love for Him rather than offending Him."

GOD: God's Will, Often Beyond Our Understanding

{NOTE: Teresa cites examples where God sometimes permits the mistake of putting unreasonable persons in office so as to perfect the virtue of obedience in those he loves. (ST. TERESA OF AVILA, Vol VIII. p. 220)

GOD: No Limits are to be Placed on God's Power

"God disdains the placing of any limits on the power of His works." (ST. TERESA OF AVILA, Vol II; p. 285)

GOD: Where His Love Is

Teresa, indicating that God is with those who suffer out of love for Him, cites the passage from the Old Testament: "David says that the Lord is with the afflicted." (ST. TERESA OF AVILA, Vol. II; p. 146)

GOD: Devotion and Knowing God

"But if we knew Him we would love in a way very different from that in which we do love Him." (ST. TERESA OF AVILA, Vol II; p. 151)

GOD: His Ever-Present Assistance to Those Who Trust in Him

Teresa equating strength of soul with a firm trust in God states: "God does not delay in doing His will in anyone He sees has strength." (ST. TERESA OF AVILA, Vol. II; p.162)

GOD: He Understands Our Problems and Human Frailties

"God knows our weakness, that we often show we do not understand what His will is." (ST. TERESA OF AVILA, Vol, II; p.165)

GOD: The Gift of the Father's Son

"Since by sharing in our nature He has become one with us here below - and as Lord of His own will - He reminds the Father that because He belongs to Him, the Father in turn can give Him to us." (ST. TERESA OF AVILA, Vol II; p. 168)

GOD: Teresa's Unique Observation on God, the Holy Spirit

Although we can pray individually to each Divine Person: The Father, The Son, or The Holy Spirit, or to the One God, Our Father, The Holy Trinity, all three Divine Persons hear and answer our prayers, in Their own time according to Their Will. Teresa offers a unique spiritual perspective as regards the Third Person, God the Holy Spirit in these words. "It seems to me the Holy Spirit must be a mediator between the soul and God, the One Who moves it with such ardent desires, for He enkindles it in a supreme fire, which is so near." (ST. TERESA OF AVILA, Vol II; p. 249)

GOD: Omnipotence of God and Trust in Him

"Teresa stresses again and again throughout her *Collected Works* that one must never put any limits on the power of God. God Himself through revelatory knowledge taught her several times not to limit His powers in any manner." (ST. TERESA OF AVILA, Vol II; p.255 and p. 285)

GOD: Omnipotence of God - What Folly it is to Place Limitations on God's Power

"What an amusing kind of progress in the love of God it is, to tie His hands by thinking that He cannot help us except by one path." (ST. TERESA OF AVILA, Vol III, p.118)

GOD: His Incomprehensibility and Our Limited Knowledge

"We go about here below like foolish little shepherds, for while it seems that we are getting some knowledge of You it must amount to more than nothing; for even in our own selves there are great secrets that we don't understand." (ST. TERESA OF AVILA, Vol II; p.234)

***GOD*:** God's Omnipresence

"You are with me and see me always." (ST. TERESA OF AVILA, Vol I; p.255)

GOD: His Power, Our Role

There is a recurrent theme running throughout Teresa's life of spiritual development, namely - and I paraphrase - God does it all but without us nothing is done if we don't cooperate with His love and grace.

GOD: His Omnipresence Within Our Soul Also

"Not only is God near, but He never takes his eyes off us." (ST. TERESA OF AVILA, Vol. II; p. 32 and p.134.)

"Consider what St. Augustine says that he sought Him in many places but found Him ultimately within himself. There is no need to go to heaven in order to speak with one's Eternal Father or to find delight in Him." (ST. TERESA OF AVILA, Vol I; p.140)

GOD: His Altar, Our Heart

Teresa uses a beautiful expression describing God's place in our soul: "In the soul when all self-love by the grace and love of God is removed from the soul, then God 'Our Father' rightfully takes His place upon His throne which is our heart. He never works in the soul as He does when it is totally His without any obstacle, nor do I see how He could. He is the friend of all good order." (ST. TERESA OF AVILA, pp. 143-145)

GOD: Our Absolute Dependence Upon God

"It must be understood that in whatever I say in spiritual direction, the underlying fact is that without God we can do nothing." {although in our self-love we may begin to think at times, more often than we realize, that we can."} (ST. TERESA OF AVILA, Vol II; p.317)

GOD: The Awesome Nature of God's Creative Powers

Teresa expresses her wonder at the awesome creative power of God and His creatures both great and small: "I believe that in each little thing created by God there is more than what is understood even if it is a little ant." (ST. TERESA OF AVILA, Vol. III; p.323)

GOD: The Profound Mystery of God's Omnipresence

"I knew a person who hadn't learned that God was in all things by presence, power, and essence, and through a favor of this kind that God granted her she came to believe it. After asking a half-learned man of the kind I mentioned earlier - he knew as little as she had known before God enlightened her - she was told that God was present only by grace. Such was her conviction that even after this she didn't believe him and asked others who told the truth, namely, that God was present in us not only by His grace, but also by His power and essence, with which she was greatly consoled." (ST. TERESA OF AVILA, Vol. II; p.340)

GOD: God's Manifestation of His Love for a Soul

"At a certain stage in the spiritual development of some souls it seems that our Lord wishes all to understand that the soul is now His, that no one should touch it. He will protect it from the whole world and even from hell." (ST. TERESA OF AVILA, Vol II; p 385.)

GOD: God's Tender Love for the Soul in Love with Him

God responds to souls in love with Him with a tender love and understanding. "Teresa recounts how when one person who before a crucifix was reflecting that she had never had anything to give to God, or anything to give up for Him, The Crucified Himself, in consoling her told her He had given all the sufferings and trials He had undergone in His Passion so that she could have them as her own to offer His Father. The comfort and enrichment was such that according to what I heard from her, she cannot forget the experience. Rather, every time she sees how miserable she is, she gets great encouragement and consolation from remembering these words." (ST. TERESA OF AVILA, Vol III; p. 388)

GOD: The Holy Spirit, His Effect Upon the Apostles

"It was only after the Holy Spirit descended upon the apostles at Pentecost that many truths of Jesus Christ and His meaning for each soul was revealed to the apostles. The apostles as Teresa points out, and as do many interpreters of Holy Scripture, were not as firm in the faith before the coming of the Holy Spirit but rather became strong in the faith and its truths after the Holy Spirit had descended upon them at Pentecost as reported about ten days after our Saviour Jesus Christ ascended into heaven." (ST. TERESA OF AVILA, Vol. II; p. 404)

GRACE: Profound Mystery of God's Amazing Grace

The spiritual directors cited throughout this work are in general in complete agreement that God's amazing grace does not follow our time schedule, in other words we have no control over its comings and goings, or knowledge as to whether we are truly in the state of His grace or not.

GRACE: The Ups and Downs of the Soul

Teresa exclaimed: "When grace was hidden from her, her soul seemed to amount to very little." {NOTE: All good spiritual directors, including the four cited in this book, explicitly point out that none of us in reality know what state of God's grace we are actually in, or if we are in His grace. Teresa states in her *Collected Works* which she was instructed to write by the Catholic Church ecclesiastical authorities, that none of us actually know how much we love God and how much He actually loves us - however - she states that there are some criteria or indicators for determining how much we truly love God. She mentions one specifically, and that is, how much we actually love our neighbor and show it in action. In her exclamation cited above, Teresa, in reference to this point, stated in another place in her *Collected Works* which I have cited elsewhere here in the words of spiritual guidance provided by Teresa that at times she "felt like a lion in the service of God, but when God appeared to leave her, as it seemed to her, she did not have the courage of an ant."} (ST. TERESA OF AVILA, Vol II; p.187)

GRACE: God's Amazing Grace, Its Mysterious Comings and Goings

Teresa in her marvelous, picturesque simplicity of expression makes this comment. "At other times I think I have great courage and that I wouldn't turn from anything of service to God; and when put to the test, I do have this courage for some things. Another day will come in which I won't find the courage in me to kill even an ant for God if in doing so I'd meet with any opposition." (ST. TERESA OF AVILA, Vol II; p. 187)

HEALTH: Worry Over It is Useless

"Worry over our health will not improve it." (ST. TERESA OF AVILA, Vol II; P. 312)

HEALTH: Bodily Pains

"Teresa who was full of an arsenal of ailments when she died, and some of which were extremely severe while she was living, definitely stated in her writing that she attributed some bodily pains to the work of the devil. The reference was not only to some of her specific bodily pains, but also some of those endured by some members of her religious community whose spiritual director she was." {NOTE: Teresa also suffered some physical ailments which were natural human health problems common to all our human nature.}

HELL: Fear of Hell

Teresa candidly stated: "I tell you truthfully that as wretched as I am I have never had fear of the torments of hell, for they would be nothing if compared to what I recall the condemned will experience upon seeing the anger in these eyes of the Lord, so beautiful, meek, and kind. It doesn't seem my soul could suffer such a sight. I've felt this all my life." (ST. TERESA OF AVILA, Vol II; p. 413)

HELL: God's Mercy in Sparing Us

Teresa: "Seldom is there anyone who hasn't done something by which they have merited hell." (ST. TERESA OF AVILA, Vol. II; p.86)

HUMAN NATURE: Opinions Often an Obstacle to Reason

Teresa found that contending with opinions became an obstacle: "O Jesus! What a trial it is to have to contend with many opinions." (ST. TERESA OF AVILA, Vol. III; p. 207)

HUMAN NATURE: More Orderly Inter-Action in Smaller Communities

"As foundress Madre Teresa discovered that fewer nuns meant greater harmony and quiet." (ST. TERESA OF AVILA, Vol III; p. 28)

HUMAN NATURE: Harmful Effects of Some Customs in a Religious Order

"In our human nature custom is a terrible thing, and little by little, through small things, irremediable harm is done to the Order." {NOTE: Teresa is speaking here of customs which have long outlived their usefulness not only in religious communities but in the secular communities of the world. This is a criticism directed towards those clinging to outmoded ways of doing things when new more effective and efficient ways have become available with the passage of time.) (ST. TERESA OF AVILA, Vol. III; p. 338)

HUMAN NATURE: Observation on Our Sinful Nature

"Our natural inclination or bent," Teresa states, "is more toward the worst than the best." (ST. TERESA OF AVILA, Vol I; p.36)

HUMAN NATURE: Teresa Makes Acute Observations of How Looks may be Deceiving Based on Her Own Personal Experiences

Teresa explains how subtly self-love will disguise itself: "There are some people who under general observations may appear to be good, they are peaceful as long as their self-interest is not involved; but when their self-interest is at stake their conscience is not so delicate, but actually easygoing. Some of these persons may be saints in their opinion. I recall that they caused me more fear after I spoke with them than all the sinners I have seen. I beg the Lord to give us light in this regard." (ST. TERESA OF AVILA, Vol II; p. 233)

HUMILITY: Acknowledgment of Our Weakness

"If His Majesty says that the divine and sinless flesh is weak, how is it we desire our flesh to be so strong that it doesn't feel the persecutions and the trials that come to it? And in these very trials the flesh will be as though subject to the spirit. When the soul's will is joined to the Will of God, the flesh does not complain." (ST. TERESA OF AVILA, Vol II; p. 240)

HUMILITY: Its Vital Importance

Teresa attached such great importance to this moral virtue that she stated: "While we are on this earth nothing is more important to us than humility." (ST. TERESA OF AVILA, Vol. II; p. 291)

NOTE: True humility helps us to recognize our sinful nature and its proclivity to sin, but also to acknowledge having a sinful nature before God Himself. Humility, the foundation of many other virtues, "brings us back into the light of communion between the Father and His Son Jesus Christ and with one another so that we receive from Him whatever we ask." (*Catechism of the Catholic Church*, para. 2731)

HUMILITY: A Virtue Constantly At Work

"Humility is like the bee making honey in the beehive always at work. Without it everything goes wrong." (ST. TERESA OF AVILA, Vol. II; p 291)

HUMILITY: ITS MANY ASPECTS

Teresa's many references to humility indicate clearly that her views regarding this very noble and important moral virtue are those shared by the other spiritual directors cited in this book.

HUMILITY: Self-Evaluation

"Who will say of himself that he is virtuous or rich? For at the very moment, when there is need of virtue one finds oneself poor. If we serve with humility, the Lord will succour us; but if this poverty of spirit is not genuinely present at every step, as they say, the Lord will abandon us." (ST. TERESA OF AVILA, Vol. II; p.187)

HUMILITY: One Good Indicator of Its Possible Presence

"The truly humble person walks in doubt about his own virtues and usually those he sees in his neighbors seem more certain and valuable." (ST. TERESA OF AVILA, Vol. II; p. 188)

HUMILITY: Some of Its Personal Manifestations

"Humility does not disquiet or agitate, however great it may be; it comes with peace, delight and calm. This humility expands the soul and enables it to serve God more." (ST. TERESA OF AVILA, Vol. II; p.189)

HUMILITY: A Multi-Faceted Virtue - One Facet

"It calls for great humility to be silent at seeing oneself condemned without fault."

HUMILITY: Doing God's Will in The Face of Adversities

Teresa offers a true guideline in such situation, I paraphrase her advice: "In striving to do the will of God one can not only accept adversities (persecution, condemnation, deprecation, contempt) without one's personal fault, but it is also noble to welcome it."

HUMILITY: A Multi-Faceted Virtue, One Aspect

"The just man falls seven times a day and knows it." (ST. TERESA OF AVILA, Vol II; p. 92)

HUMILITY: A Queen Among the Virtues

"There's no queen like humility to make the King surrender. The King does not give Himself but to those who give themselves entirely to Him." (ST. TERESA OF AVILA, Vol II; pp. 94-95)

HUMILITY: Trust and Growth in Humility

"For what always makes humility grow is to have a 'holy daring'", {that is, to place all our trust in God} (ST. TERESA OF AVILA; ,Vol I; p.98)

HUMILITY: Forgiveness, an Important Aspect

Teresa expresses her humility in a lovely simple phrase: "What will someone as poor as I do who has so little to pardon and so much to be pardoned for." (ST. TERESA OF AVILA, Vol II; p. 177)

HUMILITY: Our Unworthiness

Teresa advising her nuns: "Strive always Sister for humility and to see that you are unworthy of the favors you receive from God, do not seek favors from Him. I hold that the devil loses many souls who strive for this humility." (ST. TERESA OF AVILA, Vol II; p. 186)

HUMILITY: The Mother of God, Mary's Exquisitely Beautiful Trust in God

At the Annunciation: "She did not act as do some learned men (whom the Lord does not lead by this mode of prayer and who haven't begun a life of prayer), for they want to be so rational about things and so precise in their understanding that it doesn't seem anyone else but they with their learning can understand the grandeurs of God. If only they would learn something from the humility of the most Blessed Virgin. In spite of all her wisdom she asked the angel Gabriel: 'How can this be?' But after he answered, 'the Holy Spirit will come upon you, the power of the Most High will overshadow you,' she engaged in no further discussion. As one who had such great faith and wisdom, she understood at once that if those two intervened, there was nothing more to know or doubt." (ST. TERESA OF AVILA, Vol. II; p. 253)

HUMILITY: God's Gracious Love

God's greatest desire for us, for each soul, as St. John of the Cross expresses so eloquently, is to exalt it. Teresa in this regard comments: "that God in lowering Himself to commune with such miserable creatures as us, wants to show us the greatness of His love in desiring to exalt the soul." (ST. TERESA OF AVILA, Vol II; p. 418)

HUMILITY: Reflections on Humility

"Once I was pondering why our Lord was so fond of this virtue of humility, and this thought came to me - in my opinion not as a result of reflection but suddenly. It is because God is supreme Truth: and to be humble is to walk in truth, for it is a very deep truth; that of ourselves we have nothing good but - only misery and nothingness. Whoever does not understand this walks in falsehood. The more anyone understands it, the more he pleases the supreme Truth because he is walking in truth." (ST. TERESA OF AVILA, Vol II; p. 420)

HUMILITY: An Indication of a Lack of It

Teresa points out that "persons who by temperament like to be esteemed and honored and who look at the faults of others and never at their own and other similar things, that these traits arise from a lack of humility." (ST. TERESA OF AVILA, Vol II; p. 463)

HUMILITY: Avoiding the Temptation of False Humility

Teresa gives prudent words of caution to avoid false humility: "Well be on guard, daughters, against some humble thoughts, caused by the devil, with their great disquiet over the seriousness of past sins, about whether I deserve to approach Communion or whether I have prepared myself well or about my unworthiness to live with good people; things of this sort. When such thoughts come with quiet, calm, and delight, they should be esteemed because they bring self-knowledge. But if they come with agitation, disquiet, and oppression of soul, and if the mind cannot be quieted, believe that they are a temptation and don't consider yourselves humble, humility doesn't come in this way." (ST. TERESA OF AVILA, Vol II; p. 477)

HUMILITY: Teresa, Humble to the Very End Without Presumption

Teresa did not become presumptuous with God, ever considering herself a sinner. She says towards the end of her *Collected Works*: "I ask the reader to recite a Hail Mary out of love for Him that it may help me to leave Purgatory and reach the vision of Jesus Christ our Lord who lives and reigns with the Father and the Holy Spirit, forever and ever, Amen. (ST. TERESA OF AVILA, Vol III; p.97)

HUMILITY: Indicators of True Humility

"The first sign for seeing whether or not you have humility is that you do not think you deserve these favors and spiritual delights from the Lord or that you will receive them in your lifetime:" (ST. TERESA OF AVILA, Vol II; P. 326)

LOVE: It Should be All-Inclusive

"It is very important that love for another includes all and singles out no one in particular," (ST. TERESA OF AVILA, Vol. III; p.328)

LOVE: God's Longing for Us

"Our Lord desires intensely that we love Him and seek His company, so much so that from time to time He calls us to draw near Him. These calls may come to some persons in very extraordinary ways. However, most often they will come through ordinary occurrences, for example, through words spoken by other good people, or through sermons, or through the many things that are heard and by which God calls, or through illnesses and trials, or also through a truth that He teaches during the brief moments we spend in prayer; lukewarm they may be, God esteems them highly." (ST. TERESA OF AVILA, Vol. II; p.298)

LOVE: Expressing Our Personal Gratitude to God

"May it please His Majesty to give us understanding of how much we cost Him, of how the servant is no greater than his master, and that we must work in order to enjoy His glory." (ST. TERESA OF AVILA, Vol. II; p.303)

LOVE: Love for God Need not be Expressed in Great Deeds

Teresa, said in advising her nuns: "The smallest thing when done for the love of God is priceless; we should set our eyes, sisters, only on this goal of love and on pleasing Him." (ST. TERESA OF AVILA, Vol. III; p. 159)

LOVE: It will Never Fail Us If We Keep Our Trust in Jesus Christ

"Don't think that a soul that comes so close to God is allowed to lose Him so quickly, that the devil has an easy task. His Majesty would regret the loss of this soul so much that He gives it in many ways a thousand interior warnings, so that the harm will not be hidden from it." (ST. TERESA OF AVILA, Vol. II; p. 357)

LOVE: An Indicator of True Love for God

"The most certain sign, in my opinion, as to whether or not we are observing God's laws of loving Him and our neighbor as ourselves is whether we observe well the love of neighbor." (ST. TERESA OF AVILA, Vol. II; p.351)

LOVE: God's Grace and His Love are Our All

God does it all but without our cooperation with His grace and love nothing is done. As Teresa expressed it in her beautiful work on the "Interior Castle" section (of her *Collected Works* : "The journey in prayer through the interior castle to the center room is nothing else than the magnificent work of God's love." (ST. TERESA OF AVILA, Vol II; p.278)

LOVE: God's Great Desire for Us

"All that God wants is our will and that there be no impediment in the way of our giving it to Him completely and bringing it into perfect conformity with His will, for in this conformity is our good." (ST. TERESA OF AVILA, Vol. II; p.30)

LOVE: How Great is God's Love for Us

Teresa had in an extraordinary way received many revelations. In a personal dialogue of prayer, God alluded to His suffering for us. The response of Jesus coming spiritually into her soul was: "My great love and the desire I have that souls be saved are incomparably more important than these sufferings: and the very greatest sorrows that I have suffered and do suffer, after being in the world, are not enough to be considered anything at all in comparison with this love and desire to save souls." Teresa goes on to say: "This is true, for I have often reflected on the matter. I know the torment a certain soul of my acquaintance suffers and has suffered at seeing our Lord offended. The pain is so unbearable that she desires to die much more than to suffer it". (ST. TERESA OF AVILA, Vol II; p. 347)

LOVE: God's Great Love for Us Expressed in Jesus' Lifetime of Suffering for Our Salvation

"And what kind of life must He have suffered since all things were present to Him and He was always witnessing the serious offenses committed against His Father! I believe without a doubt that these sufferings were much greater than were those of His most sacred Passion. At the time of His Passion He already saw an end to these trials and with this awareness as well as the happiness of seeing a remedy for us in His death and of showing us the love He had for His Father in suffering so much for Him, His sorrows were tempered." (ST. TERESA OF AVILA, Vol II; p.3)

LOVE: The Great Generosity of God's Love

Teresa commenting upon God's generosity exclaimed: "That the

Lord who gave her the good desires also made it possible for her to exclaim: O greatness of God! How you manifest Your power in giving courage to an ant." (ST. TERESA OF AVILA, Vol III; p.11)

LOVE: Striving for a True Love in a True Friendship with Another

Teresa makes the profound observation concerning a true, strong love for another person: "In the case of perfect love, if a person loves there is a passion to make the other soul worthy of being loved, this person otherwise will not continue to love the other perfectly, it is always fearful less the soul it loves so much be lost and the two be separated forever." (ST. TERESA OF AVILA, Vol. II; pp.65-66)

LOVE: Powerful Division Which Exists in the Great Love Relationship of Friendship

Teresa explains this division thusly: "On the one hand they go about forgetful of the whole world, taking no account of whether others serve God or not only keeping account of themselves; on the other hand, with their friends they have no power to do this nor is anything covered over. They see the tiniest speck, I say that they bear a truly heavy cross." (ST. TERESA OF AVILA, Vol II p.67)

LOVE: For Christ

Teresa, "In comparison with one drop of blood the Lord shed for us everything is disgusting." (ST. TERESA OF AVILA, Vol. I; p. 273)

LOVE: A True Love of God

"It consists in the clear realization that everything displeasing to God is a lie. It is in understanding what a great blessing there is in not paying attention to what doesn't bring us closer to God." (ST. TERESA OF AVILA, Vol I; pp. 277-278)

LOVE: God's Love for Each Soul

Teresa: "I have seen it clearly and recall how much the Lord will suffer for only one soul." (ST. TERESA OF AVILA, Vol II; p.175)

LOVE: Teresa's Conception of It

"The important thing is not to think much but to love much. Perhaps we don't know what love it. It doesn't consist in great delight but in desiring with strong determination to please God in everything, in striving insofar as possible not to offend Him, and in asking Him for the advancement of the honor and glory of His Son" {and the increase of the Catholic Church} (ST. TERESA OF AVILA, p.272)

LOVE: Enkindling of Love in the Soul

St. Thomas Aquinas advises in the spiritual life it is not the repetitive nature of devotional practices, that is, of prayer, meditation, contemplation, and others, that is important, but that we make more rapid progress through an enkindling of this love, that is by intensifying these devotional practices constantly. Teresa points out that in such enkindling "the will often needs the help of the intellect so as to be enkindled." Teresa further elaborates on this point by indicating that we must not expect God to work miracles, but simply strive with all our heart to cooperate with God's love and grace which is always available to us for the asking. (ST. TERESA OF AVILA, Vol. II p. 400)

LOVE: Its Reward

"He who risks all out of love for God, loses and gains all." (ST. TERESA OF AVILA, Vol I; p.112)

LOVE: God's Love is Unfailing

"God never fails to help anyone who is determined to give up everything for Him. If it appears sometime that He will fail you, it will be for a greater good." (ST. TERESA OF AVILA, Vol II; p.41 and p.44)

LOVE: For Others

"An excessive love for others carries with it many evils and imperfections." (ST. TERESA OF AVILA, Vol II; p.54)

LOVE: The Nature Of Its Seeking

"When we desire love from some person, there is always a kind of seeking our own benefit or satisfaction." (ST. TERESA OF AVILA, Vol. II p.63)

LOVE: Importance of its Spiritual Benefit

"You shouldn't care whether you are loved or not, unless the love is for your spiritual benefit." (ST. TERESA OF AVILA, Vol II; p.64)

LOVE: Its True Intensity

"A soul truly in love with God strives with all its heart not to be outdone by God in generosity."

LOVE: A Truly Perfect Love for Another

"In the case of perfect love, if a person loves there is a passion to make the other soul worthy of being loved, this person otherwise will not continue to love the other perfectly, it is always fearful less the soul it loves so much be lost and the two be separated forever. (ST. TERESA OF AVILA, Vol II; p.65)

LOVE: Helping Each Other

"In a true love between persons, if they see them deviate from the path or commit some fault, they immediately prudently tell them about it." (ST. TERESA OF AVILA, Vol II; p.67)

LOVE: The Intention must be Right

"Everything done with a pure intention is perfect love." (ST. TERESA OF AVILA, Vol II; p.69)

LOVE: Solely for God

"We embrace the Creator but care not at all for the whole of His creation, meaning that His will is paramount." (ST. TERESA OF AVILA, Vol II; p.71)

LOVE: Its Exercise in Human Relationships

"Love must always prevail, but where a truly fraternal correction becomes necessary, it should be exercised with firmness accompanied by kindness and gentleness."

LOVE: Thirsting for God

"The more God slakes the thirst of the soul for Him, the more the soul thirsts for Him." (ST. TERESA OF AVILA, Vol II; p.107)

LOVE: Knowledge of God

"What son is there in the world who doesn't strive to learn who his father is when he has such a good One with so much majesty and power." (ST. TERESA OF AVILA, Vol II; p.139)

LOVE: God's Love

"Even in this life God begins to reward us. His Majesty never tires of giving." (ST. TERESA OF AVILA, Vol I; p151)

LOVE: God's Love, a very Intimate Friendship

"God begins to communicate with the soul in so intimate a friendship that He not only gives it back its own will but gives it His. For in so great a friendship The Lord takes joy in putting the soul in command, as they say, and He does what it asks since it does His Will." (ST. TERESA OF AVILA, Vol. II; p.164)

LOVE: The Immensity of God's Love

"Since He suffers and will suffer everything in order to find even one soul that will receive Him and lovingly keep Him within, let your desire be to do this." (ST. TERESA OF AVILA, Vol II; p.174)

LOVE: True Love

"Those who truly love God have no love for anything but truth and whatever is worthy of love. (ST. TERESA OF AVILA, Vol II; p.192)

LOVE: The Certainty of God's Love

"In loving God we are certain that He truly loves us." (ST. TERESA OF AVILA, Vol II; p.195)

LOVE: Honoring God

"I often praise the Lord thinking how it comes about that often a servant of God, without uttering a word, prevents things from being said against God." (ST. TERESA OF AVILA, Vol II; p. 198)

LOVE: God's Love Misunderstood

"Teresa felt that the Lord's love is so poorly understood that people refuse to think of the mysteries contained in these words spoken by the Holy Spirit." (ST. TERESA OF AVILA, Vol II; p. 207)

LOVE: In Small or Great Things

"Even though the things be very small do not fail to do what you can for love of Him. His Majesty will repay for them. He looks only at the love with which you do them." (ST. TERESA OF AVILA, Vol II;

p.218 and p.278)

LOVE: Active Love

"Love not put into action can be dead. Faith without works is dead. However, actions of love are not the only love, nor do works imply works of action; for actions of love and works of love can be considered to be also pure prayer from a sincere heart raised to God to be an action or work of the highest kind, especially when it is offered up out of pure love for God or on behalf of his neighbor in need."

LOVE: Signs of God's Favor

"One sign of contempt for all earthly things is the way in which they are judged to be as little as in fact they are. Another is not desiring one's own good because one's own vanity is already understood. A third not rejoicing except with those who love their Lord." (ST. TERESA OF AVILA, Vol II; p.237)

LOVE: Manifestations of Love According to the Mode of One's Soul and Its Receptivity to God's Love

"Love can be manifested in a variety of ways to God. It can be a love shown in both prayer and action. It can be a love of contemplatives, for example, in the religious life who pray not only themselves, but in actuality more for others. It can be a love of a very active spiritual nature in which the actions throughout each day can be offered up for the greater honor, glory, and love of God. This is especially true of people of various occupations of work, in which the very work they are doing can become a prayer. It can take the form of suffering in which the suffering persons offer up their suffering to God out of pure love for Him, for themselves and others throughout the world. The most vitally important thing about prayer is that it come from a pure heart - without distractions if possible, and be devoid of self-love, self-seeking, or self-interest."

LOVE: The Generosity of God

"God would never want to do anything less than give if He could find receivers." (ST. TERESA OF AVILA, Vol II; p.250)

LOVE: God's Inscrutable Way of Working with Each Soul

"So with the favors of the Lord; to one He gives a little wine of devotion, to another more, with another He increases it in such a way that the person begins to go out from himself, from his sensuality and from all earthly things; to some He gives great fervor in His service; to others, impulses of love; to others great charity towards their neighbors. These gifts are given in such a way that these persons go about so stupefied they do not feel the great trials that take place here." (ST. TERESA OF AVILA, Vol II p.251)

LOVE: Love of Neighbor

"If we fail in our love of our neighbor we are lost. Beg our Lord to give you this love of neighbor." (ST. TERESA OF AVILA, Vol II; p. 353)

LOVE: Teresa Expresses Her Humility and Abjection to Our God

"It doesn't do us any harm to see that it is possible in this exile for so great a God to commune with such foul-smelling worms; and, upon seeing this, come to love a goodness so perfect and a mercy so immeasurable." (ST. TERESA OF AVILA, Vol II. pp. 284-285)

LOVE: God's Tender Love

"God responds to souls in love with Him with a tender love and understanding. Teresa recounts how when one person who before a crucifix was reflecting that she had never had anything to give to God, or anything to give up for Him, The Crucified Himself, in consoling her told her He had given all the sufferings and trials He had undergone in His Passion so that she could have them as her own to offer His Father. The comfort and enrichment was such that according to what I have heard from her, she cannot forget that experience. Rather, every time she sees how miserable she is, she gets great encouragement and consolation from remembering these words." (ST. TERESA OF AVILA, Vol.II; p. 388)

LOVE: Intensity of Love for God

"Souls truly inflamed with a love for God would want the Lord to see that they do not serve Him for pay, but so to speak, desiring nothing in return only to love Him more and more. Their desire is to satisfy love, and it is love's nature to serve with deeds in a thousand ways." (ST. TERESA OF AVILA, Vol II; pp. 417-418)

LOVE: God's Love Rejected

"The greatest evil of the world is that God, our Creator, suffers so many evil things from His creatures within His very self, and that we sometimes resent a word said in our absence and perhaps with no evil intention." (ST. TERESA OF AVILA, Vol. II; p. 419)

LOVE: The Increase of Love for God

"Love increases in the measure that the soul discovers how much this great God and Lord deserves to be loved." (ST. TERESA OF AVILA; Vol II; p.421)

LOVE: The Inscrutability of God's Ways

Teresa in a strong aspiration of her love for God, once exclaimed: "Oh God, help me! Lord how you afflict your lovers! But everything is small in comparison with what you give them afterward." She goes on to say regarding the sufferings of this world: "And what can we do or suffer in so short a life that would amount to anything if we were thereby to free ourselves of those terrible and eternal torments." (ST. TERESA OF AVILA, Vol. II' p. 424)

LOVE: Observations of Teresa on the Love for God

"The important thing is not to think much but to love much; and so to do that best which stirs you to love." In Teresa's thinking love doesn't consist in great delight but in desiring with strong determination to please God in everything, in striving insofar as possible, not to offend Him, and in asking Him for the advancement of the honor and glory of His Son and the increase of the Catholic Church." (ST. TERESA OF AVILA, Vol II; p.274)

LOVE: No Limits to God's Love and Favors

"One must not place limits on a Lord so great and desirous to grant favors." Teresa observes in this regard: "Few are those to whom our Lord grants these favors without their having undergone many years of trials, and thus it may be understood that there are many exceptions." (ST. TERESA OF AVILA, Vol II; p.255)

LOVE: The Soul Truly in Love with God

"The soul truly in love with God looks only for the honor and glory of God in everything. It looks only at pleasing and serving the Lord." (ST. TERESA OF AVILA, Vol II; p. 258)

LOVE: God Rewards Love for Him Even Upon This Earth

"We strive to love a Lord who even here on earth gives us a reward, a foretaste of our eternal reward. When the Lord begins to grant greater favors here on earth, greater trials can be expected." (ST. TERESA OF AVILA, Vol. II; p. 163)

LOVE: The Working of God's Amazing Grace

Before the "Spiritual Marriage of Love" takes place, there occurs a stage of espousal or betrothal, however, as Teresa points out there is a price to pay: "The Spouse, God, does not look at the soul's great desires that the betrothal takes place, for He still wants it to desire this more, and He wants the betrothal to take place at a cost; it is the greatest of blessings." She goes on to emphasize this very strongly; stating; "Oh, God help me, what interior and exterior trials the soul suffers before entering the seventh dwelling place - that is the deepest heart of the soul where God occupies His most holy throne as King of the soul." Teresa goes on to describe the state of the soul and its tremendous courage and fortitude when it has arrived (by cooperating with the grace and love of God extended to it) at this seventh dwelling place before God's throne or holy altar of the soul in these words: "For once it has arrived there, the soul fears nothing and is absolutely determined to overcome every obstacle for God." (ST. TERESA OF AVILA, Vol. II; pp. 359-360)

LOVE: The Intensity of God's Love for Us

Teresa simply summed up God's gracious love, stating: "God wants no more than our determination so that He may do everything Himself." She points out that as regards the works of the devil against the person who loves Him, the devil can do no more than what the Lord allows for the sake of a greater good." She exclaims (speaking about the problems of one of her Foundations in Burgos, Spain), "But Oh Lord, how obvious it is that you are so powerful for the very scheme the devil used to prevent it, you used to do something better." (ST. TERESA OF AVILA, Vol. III; p. 13)

LOVE: God's Great Love

"I know persons who walk by the path of love as they ought to walk, that is only so as to serve their Christ crucified, not only do these person refuse to seek spiritual delights from Him or to desire them but they beseech Him not to give them these favors during their lifetime." (ST. TERESA OF AVILA, Vol II; p.326)

LOVE: God's Desire for Us

"The Lord desires that we beseech Him and call to mind that we are in His presence." (ST. TERESA OF AVILA, Vol. II; p.330)

LOVE: Spiritual Development

"When the soul has experienced spiritual delights from God, it sees that wordly delights are like filth. It finds itself withdrawing from them little by little, and it is more master of itself in so doing. At the same time there is an improvement in all the virtues." (ST. TERESA OF AVILA, Vol. II; p.382)

LOVE: Love for God, Its Rewards

"Teresa constantly stressed the theme that even in this life God gives the hundredfold," (ST. TERESA OF AVILA, Vol I; p.26)

LOVE: An Expression of Its Intensity

Teresa: "Either to die or to suffer, I don't ask anything else for myself." (ST. TERESA OF AVILA, Vol I; p.283)

LOVE: God's All-Giving Love

"God takes what we give Him; but He doesn't give Himself completely until we give ourselves completely." (ST. TERESA OF AVILA, Vol II; p.145)

LOVE: Should be All-Inclusive

"It is very important that love for one another includes all and singles out no one particular." (ST. TERESA OF AVILA, V.III; p. 328)

LOVE: The Soul as God's Dwelling Place

Teresa describes the intimate union of God with the soul in these words: "So in this temple of God, in this His dwelling place, He alone and the soul rejoice together in the deepest silence. There is no reason for the intellect to stir or seek anything, for the Lord who created it wishes to give it repose here and that through a small crevice it might observe what is taking place." (ST. TERESA OF AVILA, Vol II; p.442)

MARY, MOTHER OF GOD: A Model Exemplar

Mary "The Immaculate Conception" was Teresa's exemplar which she reiterates in her *Collected Works*."

MARY, MOTHER OF GOD: A Powerful Intercessor for Teresa's Carmelites

{NOTE: God's power was manifested greatly when Teresa had recourse to the Mother of God as the Mediatrix and Intercessor for her Order of Carmelite.)

MARY, MOTHER OF GOD: As a Patroness

"Imitate her and reflect that the grandeur of our Lady and the good of having her for your patroness must be indeed great, since my sins and being what I am have not been enough to tarnish in any way this sacred order of ours, that is, The Carmelites. One thing I advise you; not because you have such a Mother or Patroness should you feel secure for David was very holy, and you already know who Solomon was." (ST. TERESA OF AVILA, Vol II; p.305)

MYSTICAL THEOLOGY: Revelation to Teresa and the Meddling of Satan

"Satan, the devil, through his superior intellect informed others about Revelations received by Teresa." (ST. TERESA OF AVILA, Vol I: p.222)

MYSTICAL THEOLOGY: A Serious Barrier to Contemplation

"Teresa categorically denied that contemplation would ever be granted to someone in mortal sin." (ST. TERESA OF AVILA, Vol II; p.18)

MYSTICAL THEOLOGY: Insights of Teresa on Purgatory

Teresa reflected, in thinking of the sufferings here upon this earth, that such must be the nature of the sufferings of souls in Purgatory as she thought, that she concluded: "The fact that these souls have no body doesn't keep them from suffering much more than they do through all the bodily sufferings they endure here upon earth." (ST. TERESA OF AVILA, Vol. II; pp. 422-423)

MYSTICAL THEOLOGY: Courage Required in Receiving Mystical Graces

"The need for great courage in order to receive mystical graces is stressed a number of times by Teresa throughout her *Collected Works*."

MYSTICAL THEOLOGY: Contemplating Christ In His Humanity

Teresa recounts that: "Devotion to Christ in His humanity was never an obstacle to true contemplation. Christ suspended these thoughts (visions, forms, imaginations) of Him in His humanity during higher degrees of contemplative prayer. Christ in His humanity was a solace, like a forever faithful brother, a good friend who keeps us company.: (ST. TERESA OF AVILA, Vol. I; pp. 11-12)

MYSTICAL THEOLOGY: Being in a Profound State of Prayer

Teresa, spiritually in her prayer life, lived as if there was nobody else upon earth except her and God.

MYSTICAL THEOLOGY: Christ, the Importance of Never Forgetting His Humanity

"In prayer, never forgetting the humanity of Christ can lead to the most sublime contemplation." {NOTE: This does not mean to necessarily retain in one's mind forms, images, visions of Christ as He walked this earth as true God and true man, for God in true contemplative prayer may suspend the operative faculties of the soul so that these forms, visions, or images of His humanity may be erased (St. Teresa of Jesus of Avila and St. John of the Cross). (ST. TERESA OF AVILA, Vol. II; p. 397 and 399)

MYSTICAL THEOLOGY: Its Wild Movements

Teresa's imagination at times ran around, as she herself expressed it "like a madman." In studying intensively her *Collected Works* it becomes clear, and is so stated explicitly in the interpretive footnotes following at the end of each book of the three volumes of the *Collected Works* that Teresa for the longest time confused her imagination with her intellect. {NOTE: The imagination is considered to be an internal sense of the soul, while the intellect is an operative faculty of the superior part of the soul. (St. Thomas Aquinas and St. John of the Cross)

MYSTICAL THEOLOGY: Consolations (*Contentos*), Their Penetration Into the Soul

"Consolations it seems do not read the soul depth but only the senses and faculties," (ST. TERESA OF AVILA, Vol II; p.349

MYSTICAL THEOLOGY: God's Dwelling Place, the Seventh in the "Interior Castle."

Teresa, in discussing her explanation of the "Interior Castle" states: "When the soul is brought into the seventh dwelling place, the Most Blessed Trinity, all three Persons, through an intellectual vision, is revealed to it through a certain representation of the truth. First there comes an enkindling in the spirit in the manner of a cloud of magnificent splendor and these Persons are distinct, and through an admirable knowledge the soul understands as a most profound truth that all three Persons are one substance and one power and one knowledge and one God along. Each day this soul becomes more amazed, for these Persons never seem to leave it any more, but it clearly beholds that they are within it. In the extreme interior, in some place very deep within itself, the nature of which it doesn't know how to explain, because of a lack of learning, it perceives this divine company. Though the soul has this realization which is so amazing to it. The soul despite this awe of the presence of the Most Holy Trinity within its soul is much more occupied than before with everything pertaining to the service of God, and once its duties are over, it remains with that enjoyable company. It goes about with greater ease than ever not to displease the Most Holy Trinity, the one God, in anything." (ST. TERESA OF AVILA, Vol. II; pp 430-431.)

MYSTICAL THEOLOGY: Recognition of a "Substantial Locution"

St. John of the Cross instructs us in his *Collected Works* how to recognize it: "It is always said with a tender love, impossible for the devil to imitate. The words may be few, for example, 'Do Not Fear', 'Trust Me', 'I love you dear daughter or dear son', and so forth."

MYSTICAL THEOLOGY: Courage Needed in Spiritual Development

"With respect to the King of heaven, God, there is more need for courage than one would think. For if the soul were to see itself so near this great Majesty while in its senses, it would perhaps die." (ST. TERESA OF AVILA, Vol II; p. 379)

MYSTICAL THEOLOGY: God's Grace and Love Must Flow Freely through One's Soul, It cannot be Moved by Our Own Individual Desires.

Teresa, in a summary to her magnificent work on the "Interior Castle" in her *Collected Works* speaking about where God dwells on His throne in the very heart of the soul, cautions each soul as it progresses through the various dwelling places of the soul unto the very innermost dwelling place where God occupies His throne, stressing the importance of humility, and how without God we can do nothing, says: "True, you will not be able to enter all the dwelling places through your own efforts, even though these efforts may seem to you great, unless the Lord of the castle Himself bring you there. Hence I advise you to use no force if you meet with any resistance, for you will thereby anger Him in such a way that He will never allow you to enter them. He is very fond of humility. By considering that you do not deserve even to enter the third dwelling place you will more quickly win the favor to reach the fifth. And You will be able to serve Him from there in such a way continuing to walk through them often, that He will bring you into the very dwelling place He has for Himself." (ST. TERESA OF AVILA, Vol II; p. 451)

MYSTICAL THEOLOGY: Entryway to the Interior Castle

"The door to this castle is prayer" (which the soul enters through by the grace and love of God, with our cooperation the soul by the grace and love of God advances through prayer) (ST. TERESA OF AVILA, Vol II; p.286)

MYSTICAL THEOLOGY: The Spiritual Marriage of Love, a Distinction as Regards Spiritual Development.

"It seems that the prayer of union does not yet reach the stage of spiritual betrothal." {That is there may occur a spiritual union of prayer between the soul and God but not the "Spiritual Marriage or Union of Love" which St. Teresa of Jesus of Avila and St. John of the Cross entered into before departing from this earth.} (ST. TERESA OF AVILA, Vol II; p.355)

MYSTICAL THEOLOGY: The Spiritual Union of Love, Doing God's Will

"True union can very well be reached with God's help, if we can make the effort to obtain it by keeping our wills fixed only on that which is God's will. One cannot arrive at the delightful union if the union coming from being resigned to God's will is not very certain. Oh, how desirable is that union with God's will. Happy the soul that has reached it. Nothing in earthly events afflicts it unless it finds itself in some danger of losing God or sees that He is offended: neither sickness, nor poverty, nor death." (ST.TERESA OF AVILA,Vol II; p.349)

MYSTICAL THEOLOGY: Teresa's Great Desire in Life

"This union with God's will is the one I have desired all my life; it is the union I ask the Lord for always and the one that is clearest and safest." (ST. TERESA OF AVILA Vol II; p. 350)

MYSTICAL THEOLOGY: The Spiritual Union of Love, Incomprehensible to the Soul

"When God joins the soul to Himself, it doesn't understand anything of the kind of favor enjoyed. There occurs in this union an amazing intellectual vision of the Most Blessed Trinity." (ST. TERESA OF AVILA, Vol II; pp. 276-277)

MYSTICAL THEOLOGY: The Spiritual Union of Love, as Expressed by St. Paul

"He that is joined or united to the Lord becomes one spirit with Him and for me to live in Christ." (ST. TERESA OF AVILA, Vol II; p.277)

MYSTICAL THEOLOGY: The Fruits of The Spiritual Union of Love Must be Good

"The works of service may be outstanding ones as in Teresa's case but they need not be. One must concentrate on serving those who are in one's company. The Lord doesn't look so much at the greatness of our works as at the love with which they are done. His Majesty will join our sacrifice with that which He offered for us. Thus even though our works are small they will have the value our love for Him would have merited had they been great." (ST. TERESA OF AVILA, Vol II; p.278)

MYSTICAL THEOLOGY: Teresa's Interior Castle

One of Teresa's great special contributions to an "Apostolate of Spiritual Direction" is to be found in her *Collected Works* (Three Volumes), the full citation of which I give reference to in the bibliography of sources at the end of this work on *Spiritual Direction and Spiritual Directors* is her contribution entitled "The Interior Castle" Teresa states that this castle which she writes about is to be compared to our soul. Our soul is to be like a castle made entirely out of a diamond or of very clear crystal, in which there are many rooms, just as in heaven there are many dwelling places. (ST. TERESA OF AVILA, Vol II; p.283)

MYSTICAL THEOLOGY: A Substantial Locution, God's Form of Spiritual Direction

"At one time the Lord through a substantial locution conveyed to Teresa that she look after what is His and that He would look after what is hers. (ST. TERESA OF AVILA, Vol. II; p. 438)

MYSTICAL THEOLOGY: Teresa's Observation on the Spiritual Union of Love

"In my opinion, the union never lasts for as much as a half hour." (ST. TERESA OF AVILA, Vol II; p.343)

MYSTICAL THEOLOGY: God's Love, the Working of His Amazing Grace

Before the "Spiritual Union or Marriage of Love" takes place, there occurs a stage of espousal or betrothal, however, as Teresa points out there is a price to pay: "The Spouse, God, does not look at the soul's great desires that the betrothal takes place, for He still wants it to desire this more, and He wants the betrothal to take place at a cost; it is the greatest of blessings." She goes on to emphasize this very strongly, stating: "Oh, God help me, what interior and exterior trials the souls suffer before entering the seventh dwelling place - that is the deepest heart of the soul where God occupies His most holy throne as King of the soul." Teresa goes on to describe the state of the soul and its tremendous courage and fortitude when it has arrived (by cooperating with the grace and love of God extended to it) at this seventh dwelling place before God's throne or holy altar of the soul in these words: "For once it has arrived there, the soul fears nothing and is absolutely determined to overcome every obstacle for God."

MYSTICAL THEOLOGY: Locutions, Those Which Come from the Imagination

"When locutions come from the imagination there is no certitude, peace, or interior delight accompanying them." (ST. TERESA OF AVILA, Vol II; pp.359-360)

MYSTICAL THEOLOGY: Teresa Compares the Spiritual States of the Soul

"Between the spiritual betrothal and the spiritual marriage the difference is as great as that which exists between two who are betrothed and two who no longer can be separated." (ST. TERESA OF AVILA, Vol. II; p.433)

MYSTICAL THEOLOGY: Teresa's Profound Observations on the Soul

"The Lord," Teresa recounts from her spiritual experiences, "appears in the center of the soul, not in an imaginative vision but in an intellectual one, although very delicate, as He appeared to the apostle without entering through the door when He said to them, 'Peace Be With You!' (ST. TERESA OF AVILA, Vol II; p.433)

MYSTICAL THEOLOGY: Teresa Attempts to Capture the Nature of the Spiritual Unions of Love Through Analogies

"The union is like the joining of two wax candles to such an extent that the flame coming from them is but one, or that the wick, the flame, and the wax are all one. But afterward one candle can be easily separated from the other and there are two candles; the same holds for the wick. In the spiritual marriage the union is like what we have when rain falls from the sky into a river or fount; all is water, for the rain that fell from heaven cannot be divided or separated from the water or the river. Perhaps, apropos of what I have just said, this is what St. Paul means in saying: "He that is joined or united to the Lord becomes one spirit with him," and is referring to this sovereign marriage, presupposing that His Majesty has brought the soul to it through union. And he also says: "For me to live is Christ and to die is gain." (ST. TERESA OF AVILA, Vol II; p, 434)

MYSTICAL THEOLOGY: The Soul at an Advanced Stage of Spiritual Development

Teresa, speaking of the soul's state at this advanced stage of spiritual development, states: "The Lord puts the soul in this dwelling of His, which is the center of the soul itself." She acknowledges that this center of the soul or this spirit is something so difficult to explain and even believe in that she can not explain this center. For example, she says, there are trials and sufferings in the soul while at the same time the soul is at peace. Teresa continues to describe the mystical nature of the soul at this stage and adds words or caution. They say that the empyreal heaven where the Lord is does not move as do the other heavens, similarly, it seems, in the soul that enters here there are none of those movements that usually take place in the faculties and the imagination and do harm to the soul, nor do the stirrings take away its peace. It seems I'm saying that when the soul reaches this state in which God grants it this favor, it is sure of its salvation and safe from falling again. I do not say such a thing, and wherever I so speak that it seems the soul is secure, this should be taken to mean as long as the divine Majesty keeps it in His hand and it does not offend Him. The soul in this state goes about with much greater fear than before, guarding itself from any small offense against God and with the strongest desires to serve Him, and with habitual pain and confusion at seeing the little it can do and the great deal to which it is obliged. This pain is no small cross but a very great penance. For when this soul does penance, the delight will be greater in the measure the penance is greater. The true penance comes when God takes away the soul's health and strength for doing penance." (ST. TERESA OF AVILA, Vol II; p.p. 436-437)

MYSTICAL THEOLOGY: Spiritual Delights, Their Profound Mystery

"Spiritual delights (Gustos) are not something that can be imagined, because however diligent our efforts we cannot acquire them. The very experience of them makes us realize that they are not of the same metal as we ourselves but fashioned from the purest gold of the divine wisdom." (ST. TERESA OF AVILA, Vol II; p.325)

MYSTICAL THEOLOGY: Locutions, Their Origins and Some Observations of St. John of the Cross

According to Teresa: "Locutions - forms of supernatural communications through hearing while awake, or intellectual visions while asleep can be from God or from the devil, or from one's own imagination."

{Note: As St. John of the Cross rightly points out all locutions should be ignored by a person, except what he designates as a "Substantial Locution",This is a term of designation which I have explained the meaning of elsewhere at the very beginning of this work in the Introduction Chapter. A "Substantial Locution" coming from God effects what it says. For example, with one word (or phrase) alone of these locutions from the Lord (Don't Be Distressed) it is left calm and free from all distress with great light. With one word (or phrase) alone (It is I, Fear Not), the fear is taken away completely, and the soul is most comforted, thinking that nothing would be sufficient to make it believe anything else.} Teresa awed by the power of such a "Substantial Locution" gives praise to God in these words: "Oh Lord, if a word sent to be spoken through one of your attendants (For The Lord Himself Does Not Speak The Words) - at least not in this dwelling place - but an Angel has such power what will be the power You leave in the soul that is attached to You and You to it through Your love." (ST. TERESA OF AVILA, Vol II; pp. 372-373)

PRAYER: Being Truthful with God

"God likes us to be truthful with Him. If we speak clearly and plainly, so that we don't say one thing and act differently. He always gives more than we ask of Him." (ST. TERESA OF AVILA, Vol. II; p.184)

PRAYER: Security

"Souls who practice prayer walk so much more securely than those who take another road." (ST. TERESA OF AVILA, Vol. II; p.191)

PRAYER: Asking for Help

"In prayer you must ask help from the Lord for we ourselves can do little."(ST. TERESA OF AVILA, Vol II: p.230)

PRAYER: Its Power

"Prayer is a door that opens up into the mystery of God and at the same time a means of communing with Him. It actuates the personal relationship with the Lord present in the very depths of the spirituality. Prayer is the gate of entry to the center of the castle - God's dwelling place in the soul - where He sits upon His throne as King." (ST. TERESA OF AVILA, Vol I; p. 270)

PRAYER: A Useful Perspective

"Let your prayer always begin and end with self-knowledge." (ST. TERESA OF AVILA, Vol. II; p.190)

PRAYER: Temptation, an Observation

"What a strange thing! It's as though the devil tempts only those who take the path of prayer," (ST. TERESA OF AVILA, Vol. II; p.191)

PRAYER: Contemplative Prayer Life, a Changing State

"There are some souls - and there are many who have spoken about it to me - who brought by our Lord to perfect contemplation would like to be in that prayer always; but that is impossible." (ST. TERESA OF AVILA, Vol. II; p. 400)

PRAYER: It is Good to Pray for the Dead

{NOTE: Teresa carried on an apostolate to free souls from Purgatory.}

PRAYER: Teresa's Exhortation

"Whoever has not begun the practice of prayer, I beg for the love of the Lord not to go without so great a good." (ST. TERESA OF AVILA, Vol III' p.23)

PRAYER: Combining the Prayerful Life with an Active Life

Many good spiritual directors point out that one of the most difficult, but rewarding of spiritual lives to live is one where the prayerful (contemplative life) is combined with the active life. Teresa alludes to this, stating, "And let souls believe me that it is not the length of time spent in prayer that benefits one; when the time is spent as well in good works, it is a great help in preparing the soul for the enkindling of love." (ST. TERESA OF AVILA, Vol II; p.123)

PRAYER: Advancement

"To persevere in prayer and the struggle involved is to go forward." (ST. TERESA OF AVILA, Vol II; p. 271)

PRAYER: Praise

"Learning about God's work will lead a receptive person to the prayer of praise." (ST. TERESA OF AVILA, Vol. II; p.272)

PRAYER: Distractions are Inevitable

"Distraction, the wandering imagination, is a part of the human condition and can no more be avoided than eating and sleeping." (ST. TERESA OF AVILA, Vol II. p. 273)

PRAYER: Its Fruits

"The worth of one's prayer is not judged by its passive character; rather, it is in the effect and deeds following afterward that one discerns the true value of prayer." (ST. TERESA OF AVILA, Vol. II; p.273)

PRAYER: Contemplatives

"I notice in some persons - there are not many because of our sins- that the more they advance in this kind of prayer and the gifts of our Lord the more attention they pay to the needs of their neighbor, especially to the needs of their neighbor's souls." (ST. TERESA OF AVILA, Vol. II; p. 259)

***PRAYER*:** Disruptions

"For the most part all the trials and disturbances during prayer came from our not understanding ourselves." (ST. TERESA OF AVILA, Vol. II; p. 320)

PRAYER: In Prayer God Leads Souls by Many Paths

Teresa cautions prayerful people to keep in mind that God leads souls by many paths in prayer, she admonishes them thusly: "Let not those who can travel by the road of discursive thought, that is, meditation, condemn those who cannot, or judge them incapable of enjoying the sublime blessings that lie enclosed in the mysteries of our good Jesus Christ. Nor will anyone make me think, however, spiritual he may be, that he will advance by turning away from these mysteries." (ST. TERESA OF AVILA, Vol II; p.403)

PRAYER: God's Grace and Contemplative Prayer

Teresa realized at a certain point in her prayer life, that she was mistakenly not delighting in the thought of our Lord Jesus Christ as in contemplation, but that she was instead mistakenly becoming absorbed more in becoming absorbed in or waiting for the enjoyment of that delight, thus, trying, in essence, to anticipate the action of God's grace rather than allow it to flow freely and come and go at God's will, freely, like living waters. (ST. TERESA OF AVILA, Vol II; p. 404)

PRAYER: Types

Teresa, points out that both mental and vocal prayer is acceptable equally, depending on the nature of the person. As regards vocal prayer, of course, proper discretion need to be exercised as to the time and place. (ST. TERESA OF AVILA, Vol I; p.52)

PRAYER: God's Presence

Teresa advised prayerful persons to grow accustomed to recalling that the Lord is present within you and to speaking to Him often. (ST. TERESA OF AVILA, Vol II; p.32)

PRAYER: Presence of God

"It is good to be aware that one is in God's presence and of who God is." (ST. TERESA OF AVILA, Vol II;p.331)

PRAYER: Degrees of Prayer By Analogy

Teresa, in a uniquely, beautiful analogy with natural phenomena described four progressive degrees of prayer as follows:

"First Degree: Use of the water bucket, drawing water up from the well. (Meditation);

Second Degree: A water wheel dredging up water from its source (Recollection or Prayer of Quiet);

Third Degree: Diversion of a stream or a river (Sleep of the Faculties of the Soul);

Fourth Degree: Rain falling from Heaven (Prayer of Union)." (ST. TERESA OF AVILA, Vol I; p.23)

PRAYER: Some Descriptions of Prayer

Teresa viewed prayer as an actuation of the theological virtues. (Faith, Hope, and Love). Love or charity being a friendship with God. (ST. TERESA OF AVILA, Vol I; p.25)

PRAYER: Perseverance

"God favors those who use force to serve him, that is they persevere in working against their own will of self-love to do His will." (ST. TERESA OF AVILA, Vol I; p.41)

PRAYER: Its Essence
Persevering Prayer, Persevering Prayer, Persevering Prayer.

PRAYER: God's Gratitude Expressed
"The more a soul lowers itself humbly in prayer, the more God raises it up to Him." (ST. TERESA OF AVILA, Vol I; p.148)

PRAYER: The Spirit of True Prayer
"The words are meaningless if the desire and will are lacking." (ST. TERESA OF AVILA, Vol I.; p.230)

PRAYER: A Sustaining Power in Our Spiritual Life
Teresa constantly stressed the absolute necessity of unremitting, persevering prayer. (ST. TERESA OF AVILA Vol II; p53)

PRAYER: An Excellent Recommended Practice
"In prayer it is a good devout practice whenever or wherever to pray as if Christ were looking directly at us and we were looking directly at Him." (ST. TERESA OF AVILA, Vol I; p.12)

PRAYER: Mental or Vocal
"Mental or vocal prayer can all lead to perfect contemplation." (ST. TERESA OF AVILA, Vol II; p.152)

PRAYER: A Useful Friend
"Making solitude one's frequent friend is a great help for prayer." (ST. TERESA OF AVILA, Vol II; p.56)

PRAYER: Its Essence and Supports
"Unceasing prayer to God is a Carmelite Rule, combined with the practices of a love of neighbor, detachment, and humility." (ST. TERESA OF AVILA, Vol II p.28)

PRAYER: Types of Practice
Teresa favored spontaneity in prayer, did not believe in strict adherence to any one formula. (ST. TERESA OF AVILA, Vol II. p33)

PRAYER: As a Friendship with Jesus
Teresa, in regard to Jesus, our Saviour, valued variety, to be in trial

and sadness with Him in his passion, in joy with Him in His resurrection. (ST. TERESA OF AVILA, Vol. II; p.33)

PRAYER: Mystical Prayer-Aspects

"One's own efforts are to no avail in either producing or holding on to mystical prayer. Such prayer while satisfying the thirst of the soul for God at the same time increases it". (ST. TERESA OF AVILA, Vol II; p.34)

PRAYER: Let Prudence be Your Guide

"Prudence is to be used in prayer neglecting neither the body or intellect's energies." (ST. TERESA OF AVILA, Vol II; p.113)

PRAYER: Spirit of Prayer

Teresa: "It is always good to have your prayer or prayers coming from the mouth of the Lord. Much recollection is found there." (ST. TERESA OF AVILA, Vol. II; p.188)

PRAYER: Its Power

"Well believe me; and don't let anyone deceive you by showing you a road other than that of prayer." (ST. TERESA OF AVILA, Vol II; p.119)

PRAYER: Persevering Prayer

Teresa advised one of the Sisters under her spiritual direction to give this response to a person curious about their prayer life: "Tell him you have a rule that commands you to pray unceasingly for that is what our Rule commands us." There is a strong implication in Teresa's statement that every action of our daily life can become a prayer. (ST. TERESA OF AVILA, Vol II; p.121)

PRAYER: True Prayer Requires Full Attention

"It is impossible to be speaking to God while we are reciting the Our Father, and at the same time thinking of the world." (ST. TERESA OF AVILA, Vol. II; p.121)

PRAYER: Variety of Approaches

"Some persons are more adaptable to vocal prayer, some to mental prayer, some to mental/vocal prayer, all are beautiful and acceptable to

God when prayered from a sincere heart." (ST. TERESA OF AVILA, Vol.II; p. 122)

***PRAYER*:** Awesomeness of Our Indescribably Beautiful God

Teresa: "In a thousand lives we would never completely understand the way in which this Lord deserves that we speak with Him, for the Angels tremble before Him." (ST.TERESA OF AVILA,Vol. I; p.124)

***PRAYER*:** Vocal Prayers

"Vocal prayers should always be said in either a singular solitude or the unified solitude of a collective group; not in the presence of an assembly not unified in preparation for prayer." (ST. TERESA OF AVILA, Vol. I; p.129)

***PRAYER*:** Guiding Advice

"If there is difficulty in prayer, and there will be due to the imagination and other operative faculties of the soul, a person should pray as best they can; or even not pray, but like a sick person strive to bring some relief to their souls; let them occupy themselves in other works of virtue. This advice is not for persons who are careful and who have understood that they must not speak simultaneously to God and the world." (ST. TERESA OF AVILA, Vol. II; pp 129-130)

***PRAYER*:** An Understanding God

"If we abandon prayer for a day or two on account of some occupation or indisposition, God understands. Let the intention be firm; my God is not at all touchy; He doesn't bother about trifling things." (ST. TERESA OF AVILA, Vol. I. p.126)

***PRAYER*:** From the Heart

"God speaks well to the heart when we beseech Him from the heart. It is even an obligation that we strive to pray with attention. Center the mind upon the one to whom the words are addressed." (ST. TERESA OF AVILA, Vol I; p.130)

***PRAYER*:** The Our Father

"It is very possible that while you are reciting the 'Our Father' or some other vocal prayer, the Lord may raise you to perfect contemplation." (ST. TERESA OF AVILA, Vol II; p.131)

PRAYER: Contemplative

"This Divine Master in contemplative prayer is teaching it by suspending its faculties, for if they were to be at work they would harm rather than bring benefit. In pure contemplative prayer, we can do nothing. His Majesty is the Who does everything, for it is His work and above our nature. He will grant the gift of pure contemplative prayer to you, if you do not stop short on the road but try hard until you reach the end." (ST. TERESA OF AVILA, Vol II; pp 131-132)

PRAYER: Looking at God and Speaking to Him

Teresa, "I'm not asking you to do any more than look at Him, your Spouse never takes His eyes off you. God so esteems our turning to look at Him that no diligence will be lacking on His part. You will also delight in speaking to Him, not with ready-made prayers, but with those that come from the sorrow of your own heart, for He esteems them highly." (ST. TERESA OF AVILA, Vol III; pp. 134-135)

PRAYER: Guiding Advice

"Closing ones eyes while praying is a praiseworthy custom for many reasons. It is a striving so as not to look at things below." (ST. TERESA OF AVILA, Vol II; p. 142)

PRAYER: How Sweet It Is

"We will understand when beginning to pray, that the bees are approaching and entering the beehive to make honey." (ST. TERESA OF AVILA, Vol II; p. 142)

PRAYER: Meditative

Teresa makes a distinction as regards meditative and contemplative prayer. This recollection, meditative prayer, is not something supernatural, but it is something we can desire and achieve with the help of God, for without this help we can do nothing, not even have a good thought. This recollection is not a silence of the faculties; it is an enclosure of the faculties within the soul." (ST. TERESA OF AVILA, Vol. II; p. 147)

PRAYER: God's Omniscience

"If we are about to say 'Our Father' many times, He will understand us after the first." (ST. TERESA OF AVILA, Vol. I; p. 148)

***PRAYER*:** God Within Our Soul

"If you speak strive to remember that the One with Whom you are speaking is present within." (ST. TERESA OF AVILA, Vol I; p.148)

***PRAYER*:** Vocal and Mental

"It may seem to anyone who doesn't know about the matter that vocal prayer doesn't go with contemplation; but I know that it does. Some persons can best pray vocally, some mentally, and some best mentally and vocally." (ST. TERESA OF AVILA, Vol II; p. 152)

***PRAYER*:** The "Our Father", an Exquisitely Beautiful Prayer

"We ought to give great praise to the Lord for the sublime perfection of this evangelical prayer. I marvel to see that in so few words everything about contemplation and perfection is included; it seems we need to study no other book than this one."

***PRAYER*:** Detachment from Earthly Things

"Contemplatives and persons already very much committed to God, who no longer desire earthly things, ask for heavenly favors that can. through God's goodness, be given on earth." (ST. TERESA OF AVILA, Vol II; p.183)

***PRAYER*:** The "Our Father"

"Contemplatives and persons already very much committed to God, both should consider that two of the things mentioned pertain to all; giving Him our will and forgiving others. The perfect will give their will in the way perfect souls do and forgive with that perfection that was mentioned." (ST. TERESA OF AVILA, Vol II; p.183)

***PRAYER*:** The "Our Father" Reminds Us Also to Keep Our Enemies in Mind.

"The words: 'And lead us not Lord, into temptation; but deliver us from evil,' are a constant reminder that we have enemies, and that it is very dangerous to be negligent with regard to these enemies."

***PRAYER*:** Security

"Souls who practice prayer walk so much more securely than those who take another road."

PRAYER: Asking for Help

"In prayer you must ask help from the Lord for we ourselves can do little."

PRAYER: Its Power

"Prayer is a door that opens up into the mystery of God and at the same time a means of communing with Him. It actuates the personal relationship with the Lord present in the very depths of the spirit. Prayer is the gate of entry to the center of the castle - God's dwelling place in the soul - where He sits upon His throne as King." (ST.TERESA OF AVILA, Vol. II ;p.270)

PURGATORY: Insight of Teresa

Teresa reflected, in thinking of the sufferings here upon this earth, that such must be the nature of the sufferings of souls in purgatory she concluded: "The fact that these souls have no body doesn't keep them from suffering much more than they do through all the bodily sufferings they endure here upon the earth." (ST. TERESA OF AVILA, Vol II; pp. 422-423)

PURGATORY: It is Good to Pray for the Dead

Theresa carried on an Apostolate to free souls from Purgatory.

RELIGIOUS: Some Authorities in The Religious Community at Times may have Their Priorities Askew

Teresa observed at times throughout her life in the religious community "that the 'Business' of religious institutions may take priority to that of saving souls." She elaborates briefly: "The prelate who is the superior may not be concerned for what benefits the soul but concerned only that the business he thinks is fitting for the community be attended to." (ST. TERESA OF AVILA, Vol. III; p.119)

RELIGIOUS: Dealing With Others In The Religious Community of the Catholic Church, Considerable Prudence was a Requisite

Teresa had to learn flawless tact in dealing with Bishops and others in authority. (ST. TERESA OF AVILA, Vol. III; p.10)

SAINTS: Our Models

Teresa, referring to adopt as models the saints: "Behold the saints who have entered this chamber of our King, our Lord and Majesty and you will see the difference between them and us." (ST. TERESA OF AVILA, Vol. II; p.307)

SAINTS: St. Mary Magdalene, A Good Model for Imitation

"Let the soul imitate Mary Magdalene, for if it is strong God will lead it into the desert." (NOTE: Various historical accounts indicate that St. Mary Magdalene spent the last thirty years of her life praying in the desert. Despite the fact that these accounts report that she herself was an eloquent preacher. She found, reportedly, that God's will for her would be best accomplished through a life of prayer in the solitude of the desert). (ST. TERESA OF AVILA, Vol. I; p.149)

SAINTS: Our Friends

Teresa made many friends among the saints and angels, to name but a few from her writings: St. Clair, St. Joseph, St. Mary Magdalene, St. Michael, the Archangel.

SAINTS: Intercessors in the Spiritual Life

Teresa disclosed throughout her *Collected Works* that Saints Peter, Paul, Augustine, and Mary Magdalene were some of her favorite intercessors.

SCRUPLES: A Source of Great Trials for the Soul

"Terrible trials are suffered because we don't understand ourselves and that which isn't bad at all but good we think is a serious fault." (ST. TERESA OF AVILA, Vol. II; p.320)

SCRUPLES: A Weapon of the Devil

Teresa points out with regard to scruples that "as regards one's confessor, persons who practice prayer when they observe the holiness of a confessor and that he understands their mode of procedure will get to love him deeply. In such a situation the devil batters one with scruples which is what the devil wants to do." (ST. TERESA OF AVILA, Vol II; p. 260)

SCRUPLES: Attacks by Trivia

Teresa's imagination was seized suddenly by trivia which at other times she would simply, easily laugh off. (ST. TERESA OF AVILA, Vol. I: p.198)

SELF-LOVE: Importance of Complete Detachment

Teresa expresses the danger of self-love in the spiritual life: "It is not enough to be detached from everything, we must be detached from ourselves, that is, from all self-love. There is no worse thief than ourselves." {We steal the love that belongs to God to satisfy our self - love} (ST. TERESA OF AVILA, Vol II; p. 76)

SELF-LOVE: All That is Good in Us is God's Gift, All Else is Self-Love

"You already know my God that if I have some good, it is a gift from no one else's hands but yours." (ST. TERESA OF AVILA, Vol. II: p.42)

SELF-LOVE: All Self-Love Given up for the Love of God

"A person's greatest good is within and is won by giving up everything for the love of God." (ST. TERESA OF AVILA, Vol. I; p.1)

SELF-LOVE: Checking its Growth, a Healthy Perspective

Teresa did not call anything of herself good. As she expressed: "I knew that I had no good in me but what the Lord gave me without my meriting it."

SELF-LOVE: A Good Antidote to Self-Love

"They like others to know about their sins and like to tell about them when they see themselves esteemed." (ST. TERESA OF AVILA, Vol II; p. 181)

SELF-LOVE: A Subtle Spiritual Phenomenon

"People living in their own homes at times cannot know their own faults, even though they want to because they want to please the Lord. For, in the end, what they want to do is their will." (ST. TERESA OF AVILA, Vol II; p.234)

SELF-LOVE: How It Deceives Us

Teresa makes a cogent observation about her religious community which, though it has an exaggerated emphasis, indicates how pride inflated the self-love of her Sisters at times: "Since our human nature doesn't allow us to recognize ourselves for what we are each of the nuns thinks she's an expert." (ST. TERESA OF AVILA, Vol III; p.343)

SIN: Venial, a Spiritual Perspective

Teresa: "One venial sin can cause us more damage than all the devils in hell." (ST. TERESA OF AVILA, Vol I; p. 169)

SIN: The Prayer for the Gift of Tears, That is, a True Compunction for One's Own Sins, is a Very Laudable Prayer

Teresa prayed for and received the gift of tears in which she had a deep, sorrowful compunction for her sinfulness which was deep in her heart, but at the same time was a non-agitating compunction which prevented her from having wasteful scruples and anxieties.

SIN: True Contrition

"Always fear when some fault you commit does not grieve you. For in regard to sin, even venial, you already know that the soul must feel deep sorrow and glory to God...".(ST. TERESA OF AVILA, Vol. II; p.22)

SIN: Venial Sin

"For love of God take great care never to grow careless about venial sin, however small." (ST. TERESA OF AVILA, Vol II; p. 231)

SIN: Venial Sins, the Harmful Effects of Ignoring Them

Teresa recounted how in her spiritual life she for a long time at one stage in her life ignored venial sins and thereby did considerable harm to her soul. (ST. TERESA OF AVILA, Vol. I; p.43)

SIN: Advertence to Sin

"There is an advertence to venial sin that is deliberate; another that comes so quickly that committing the venial sin and adverting to it happen almost together in such a way that we don't realize what we are doing. But from any deliberate sin, however small it may be, God deliver us." (ST. TERESA OF AVILA, Vol II; p.197)

SIN: Importance of Avoiding Occasions Of Sin

"The failure to avoid occasions of sin, that is, situations in life where sin can ensnare us or the chances of falling into sin, can prove to be quite dangerous to the soul aspiring to love God with its whole heart." (ST. TERESA OF AVILA, Vol. II; p. 190)

SOUL: Teresa's Admiration for Its Potential

One of Teresa's main themes was the beauty and astounding capacity of the human person made in the image and likeness of God. (ST. TERESA OF AVILA, Vol I; p.35)

SOUL: The Soul in Love with God

"The soul in love with God thinks that it is obligated to Him more than anyone and any fault it commits pierces it to the core of its being and rightly so. However, at such times, while the conscience should always be so acutely sensitive, the love, mercy, goodness and kindness of God should not be forgotten, lest we fall into too rash and harsh a disposition towards our soul, and thereby fall into a state of wasteful, harmful scruples, anxieties, worries, and so forth." Teresa goes on to say, "God is so faithful that He will not allow the devil much leeway with a soul that doesn't aim for anything else than to please His Majesty and spend its life for His honor and glory; He will at once ordain how it may be undeceived. And if He sometimes permits the devil to tempt the soul, He will so ordain that the evil one will be defeated. However, the soul must exercise great caution, for when the soul is so favored by God, it could grow more careless. Throughout these travails of the spiritual life the person should, whenever possible, have recourse to a confessor who is both learned and devout." (ST. TERESA OF AVILA, Vol. II; pp. 408-409)

SOUL: Teresa's Vision of It

"The soul is like a castle made entirely out of a diamond or of very clear crystal in which there are many rooms, just as in heaven there are many dwelling places. (ST. TERESA OF AVILA, Vol II; p.283)

SOUL: Its Comprehension

"The soul, just as God, cannot be comprehended by the intellect, for as God Himself has stated, He Himself created the soul in His own image and likeness." Teresa goes on to say: "Well, if this is true, as it is, there is no reason to tire ourselves in trying to comprehend the beauty of this castle." (ST. TERESA OF AVILA, Vol. II; p.283)

SOUL: It Does not Receive Its Proper Consideration and Care

"Because we have heard and because faith tells us so, we know we have souls. But we seldom consider the precious thing that can be found in this soul, or who dwells within it, or its high value. Consequently, little effort is made to preserve its beauty." (ST. TERESA OF AVILA, Vol. II; p.284)

SOUL: God's Workings in the Soul

"The Lord often desires that dryness and bad thoughts afflict and pursue us without our being able to get rid of them." (ST. TERESA OF AVILA, Vol. II; p.301)

SOUL: The Soul Surrendered to God

"When the devil sees the soul entirely surrendered to its Spouse, God, he doesn't dare do so much because he fears it. He has experienced that if sometimes he tries he is left with a great loss; and the soul with further gain. And yet a word of caution: I tell you that I have known persons who had ascended high and had reached a certain spiritual union with God who were turned back, and won over by the devil with his deep cunning and deceit." (ST. TERESA OF AVILA, Vol. II; pp. 355-356)

SOUL: Its Pain of Love

"The soul's pain lies in seeing that what it can now do by its own efforts amounts to nothing. (ST. TERESA OF AVILA, Vol. II; p.438)

SOUL: Stages of Spiritual Development

"The soul at a certain stage of its spiritual development has a great desire to suffer, but not the kind of desire that disturbed it at an earlier stage of its spiritual development. The soul assumes the attitude that if God desires the soul to suffer, well and good; if not, it doesn't kill itself as it used to. These souls also have a deep interior joy when they are persecuted, with much more peace than mentioned, and without any hostile feelings towards those who do, or desire to do, them evil." (ST. TERESA OF AVILA, Vol. II; p. 439)

SOUL: At an Advanced Stage of Development

"Souls who have already seen the trials and afflictions which they experienced of wanting to die so as to enjoy the Lord become transformed, they now have just as great a desire to serve Him and through them that He be praised and that they may benefit some soul if they could. For not only do they now not have the desire to die, but they desire to have many years suffering the greatest trials if through those they can help that the Lord be praised, even though in something very small. If, they knew for certain that in leaving the body the soul would enjoy God, they wouldn't pay attention to that; nor do they think of the glory of the saints. They do not desire at that time to be in glory. Their glory lies in being able some way to help the Crucified, especially when they see He is so offended and that few there are who, detached from everything else, really look after His honor." (ST. TERESA OF AVILA, Vol. II; p.439)

SOUL: Will and Love, Teresa's Perspective

"I was wondering whether there is some difference between will and love. And it seems to me there is. I don't know whether or not I am speaking foolishly. But it seems to me that love is like an arrow sent forth by the will. If it travels with all the force that the will has freed from all earthly things, and directed to God alone it truly must wound His Majesty. Thus, fixed in God Himself, Who is love, it is brought back from there with the greatest gain, as I shall say, I have seen performed by some persons who our Lord has brought to this great favor in prayer that He brings them to this holy inebriation with a suspension, and that even exteriorly one can see they are not in themselves." (ST. TERESA OF AVILA, Vol I; p.252)

SOUL: Knowing One's Self

"Teresa stated that in her opinion we shall never completely know ourselves if we don't strive to know God. By gazing at His grandeur we get in touch with our own lowliness; by looking at His purity we shall see our own filth, by pondering His humility we shall see how far we are from being humble." (ST. TERESA OF AVILA, Vol. II; p. 292)

SOUL: Teresa's Visualization of It

"Let us consider that this castle has as I said, many dwelling places; some up above, others down below, others to the sides; and in the center and middle is the main dwelling place where the very secret exchanges between God and the soul takes place." (ST. TERESA OF AVILA, Vol. II; p.284)

SOUL: Inner Reflection

"You have already heard in some books on prayer that the soul is advised to enter within itself, well that's the very thing I'm advising."

SOUL: Teresa's Vivid Imagery of God Occupying the Soul

"It should be kept in mind that the fount, the shining sun that is in the center of the soul does not lose its beauty and splendor; it is always present in the soul, and nothing can take away its loveliness. But if a black cloth is placed over a crystal that is in the sun, obviously the sun's brilliance will have no effect on the crystal even though the sun is shining on it." (ST. TERESA OF AVILA, Vol. II; p.289)

SOUL: Teresa's Interior Castle

"One of Teresa's great special contributions to an Apostolate of Spiritual Direction is to be found in her *Collected Works* (Three Volumes) the full citation of which I give reference to in the bibliography of sources at the end of this work on *Spiritual Direction and Spiritual Directors* in her contribution entitled: "The Interior Castle." Teresa states that this castle which she writes about is to be compared to our soul. Our soul is to be like a castle made entirely out of a diamond or of very clear crystal, in which there are many rooms, just as in heaven there are many dwelling places." (ST. TERESA OF AVILA, Vol II; p.382)

SOUL: Teresa's Revelatory Vision of the Soul

"There was a most beautiful crystal globe like a castle in which she saw seven dwelling places, and in the seventh, which was in the center, The King of Glory dwelt in the greatest splendor. From there He beautified and illumined all those dwelling places to the outer wall. The inhabitants received more light the nearer they were to the center." Teresa (speaking of the soul in sin) compared the Divinity to a very clear diamond in which everything is visible including sin with all its ugliness. (ST. TERESA OF AVILA, Vol. II; pp. 268-269)

SOUL: Its Pleasure in Imitation of Christ

"Its pleasure is in somehow imitating the laborious life that Christ lived. A soul that is surrounded by crosses, trials, and persecutions has a powerful remedy against often continuing in the delight of contemplation. It finds great delight in suffering; but suffering doesn't consume it and waste its strength, as would this suspension, if very frequent, of the faculties in contemplation." (ST. TERESA OF AVILA, Vol. II; p.259)

SOUL: Operative Faculties of the Soul

Teresa for many years found that the faculties of her soul were occupied and recollected in God while her mind, on the other hand, was distracted. This distraction puzzled her until a learned man whom she consulted informed her that the imagination was not the intellect to which she had been attributing the distractions during prayer. Having learned this she was quite relieved and became aware that the imagination (an internal sense strongly weakened through original sin) could prove very troublesome in prayer throughout ones lifetime.

SOUL: Understanding the Soul

"Let's not blame the soul for what a weak imagination, human nature, and the devil cause." (A clearer understanding of some of these enemies of the soul reveals to us how easily we can fall into sin and self-love). (ST. TERESA OF AVILA, Vol. II; p.322)

SOUL: The Perplexities Which Confront It and Confuse It

"At times the soul doubts whether a certain experience it went through was given by God; or whether the devil transformed himself into an angel of light. It is left with a thousand suspicions. That it has them is good, for as I have said, even our own nature can sometimes deceive us at a very advanced stage of spiritual development." Teresa goes on to say: "The devil will set a thousand fears before you and strive that others do so." (ST. TERESA OF AVILA, Vol II; p.193)

SOUL: God's Amazing Grace

God so places Himself in the interior of the soul [though God never actually moves in the soul (St. John of The Cross)] that when it returns to itself it can in no way doubt that it was in God and God was in it." (ST. TERESA OF AVILA, Vol. II; p.339)

SOUL: Its Spiritual Appreciation by the Individual

Teresa points out that: "Each one of us has a soul, but since we do not prize souls as is deserved by creatures made in the image of God, we do not understand the deep secrets that lie in them. Consequently

little effort is made to preserve the souls beauty."
(ST. TERESA OF AVILA, Vol II; pp. 282-283)

SOUL: Profound Mysteries of the Soul

It seemed to Teresa that the soul and its faculties are not one but different. There are so many and such delicate things in the interior of the soul, Teresa says, that it would be boldness on her part to explain them. (ST. TERESA OF AVILA, Vol II; p.427)

SOUL: Influence of the Body Upon the Soul

Teresa, acknowledged the deep effects which bodily ills can exert upon the soul, she says: "If her trials could affect her physical state, her bodily illnesses by the same token could affect her psyche." She confesses: "Often I complain to our Lord about how much the poor soul shares in the illness of the body. It seems the soul can do nothing but abide by the laws of the body and all its needs and changes." (ST. TERESA OF AVILA, Vol. III; p.268)

SOUL: Some Cogent Observations

"The soul is not the mind, nor is the will directed by thinking, for this would be very unfortunate. Hence, the soul's progress does not lie in thinking much but in loving much." (ST. TERESA OF AVILA, Vol. III; p. 117)

SOUL: Trust in God

"Leave the soul in God's hands, let Him do whatever He wants with it with the greatest disinterest about your own benefit as is possible and the greatest resignation to the will of God. The soul truly in love with God gives Him all of its freedom, memory, intellect, and will." (ST. TERESA OF AVILA, Vol. II; p. 336)

SOUL: Effects of Mortal Sin

"Mortal sin clouds the soul like a mist clouds a mirror and leaves it black. Thus the Lord in such a soul can not be seen or revealed." (ST. TERESA OF AVILA, Vol. II; p.279)

SOUL: Where to Look for God

"There is where one must look for God, must see Him, deep within one's soul. He is there but He is hidden, one must continue to search for Him there." (ST. TERESA OF AVILA, Vol. I; p. 279)

SOUL: Teresa's Observations

"The soul is capable of much more than we can imagine, and the sun that is in this royal chamber shines in all parts of it." (ST. TERESA OF AVILA. Vol II; p.291)

SOUL: Characteristics of the Soul Devoutly Advanced in Its Love for God

"There is a great detachment in such a soul from everything and a desire to be always either alone or occupied in something that will benefit some soul."

SOUL: Truly in Love with God

"At a certain stage of its spiritual development in its love for God the soul has so little esteem for all earthly things in comparison to the things it has seen that the former seem like dung. From then on its life on earth is very painful, and it doesn't see anything good in those things that used to seem good in it." Teresa goes on to further describe the soul's state in eloquent terms with a pointed reference to poor confessors: "As a result of these wonderful favors the soul is left so full of longings to enjoy completely the One who grants them that it lives in a great though delightful torment. With the strongest yearnings to die, and thus usually with tears, it begs God to take it from this exile. Everything it sees wearies it. When it is alone it finds some relief, but soon this torment returns; yet when the soul does not experience this pain, something is felt to be missing. In sum, this little butterfly is unable to find a lasting place of rest; rather, since the soul goes about with such tender love, any occasion that enkindles this fire more makes the soul fly aloft. As a result, in this dwelling place the raptures are very common and there is no means to avoid them even though they may take place in public. Hence, persecutions and criticism. Even though the soul may want to be free from fears, others do not allow this freedom. For there are many persons who cause these fears, especially confessors... ". "Thus, in its opinion, it would not commit knowingly a venial sin even were others to crush it to pieces. It is intensely afflicted upon seeing that it cannot free itself from unknowingly committing many venial sins. God gives these souls the strongest desire not to displease Him in anything, however small, and the desire to avoid if possible every imperfection. For this reason alone, if for no other the soul wants to flee people, and it has great envy of those who have lived in deserts. On the other hand, it would want to enter into the midst of the world to try to play a part in getting even one soul to praise God more."

SOUL: A Soul in Love with God

"A soul truly in love with God can do a great deal of harm to the devil by getting others to follow it, and it could be of great benefit to God's Church. Such a soul suffers much combat, and if it goes astray, it strays much more than do other souls. As regards the warfare of such a soul, when the devil observes such a soul in love with God this knowledge is sufficient for him to wear himself out trying to lead the soul to perdition." (ST. TERESA OF AVILA, Vol II; p.333)

SOUL: The Strength of the Soul is Most Critical

"Bodily strength is not necessary for those to whom God does not give it." (ST. TERESA OF AVILA, Vol. II; p.336)

SOUL: The Intellect and the Imagination

In her prayer life St. Teresa of Jesus of Avila was for a long time confused between what was her intellect at work [The Intellect: An Operative Faculty of the Superior Part of the Soul (St. John of the Cross)] and what was her imagination [The Imagination: An Internal Sense of the Soul (St. Thomas Aquinas).]

SOUL: Give Your Soul to God

"Give your soul to God like a little ball, He loves to play with it," as Teresa lovingly spoke of God's love for the soul. (ST. TERESA OF AVILA, Vol. I; p.112)

SOUL: Effects of Original Sin (St. Thomas Aquinas)

"With original sin a great disharmony appeared in the soul. It became like a perfectly musically coordinated, directed symphony orchestra in which suddenly the various players of the orchestra began to play off-key, out of tune, playing the wrong notes at various times, with the instruments of the players improperly tuned, and so forth. The orchestra was still there complete with all the players, but the music they were now playing was full of dissonance, disharmony, and without direction." St. Teresa of Jesus of Avila very specifically and pointedly refers to these various effects of original sin throughout her *Collected Works*.

SPIRITUAL DIRECTION: Trust, Its Importance

Teresa in a prudent admonition to her nuns advises prudently: "Believe me, the safest way is to want only what God wants. He knows more than we ourselves do, and He loves us. Let us place ourselves in His hands so that His will may be done in us, and we cannot err if with a determined will we will always maintain this attitude." (ST. TERESA OF AVILA, Vol II; p.417)

SPIRITUAL DIRECTION: Worldly Weariness

"From the very unhappiness caused by worldly things arises the ever so painful desire to leave this world" [NOTE: According to St. John of the Cross the desire to die is in spiritual terms considered to be an imperfection of the soul.]. "In some way perhaps the sorrow proceeds from the deep pain it feels at seeing that God is offended and little esteemed in this world, and that many souls are lost, heretics as well as others; although those that grieve it most are Christians." (ST. TERESA OF AVILA, Vol. II: p.345)

SPIRITUAL DIRECTION: Perfection Lies in a Perfect Conformity of Our Will with God's Will.

Teresa in an often quoted passage regarding perfection stated: "The highest perfection obviously does not consist in interior delights or in great raptures or visions or in the spirit of prophecy, but in having our will so much in conformity with God's will that there is nothing we know He wills that we do not want with all our desire, and in accepting the bitter as happily as we do the delightful when we know that His Majesty desires it." (ST. TERESA OF AVILA, Vol III; pp.32-33)

SPIRITUAL DIRECTION: Consultation with Others

Consultation with the devout and learned was one of Teresa's spiritual trademarks, a great strength of her, by the grace and love of Jesus Christ. (ST. TERESA OF AVILA, Vol II; P.57)

SPIRITUAL DIRECTION: A Cogent Observation on Friendship

"What friendship there would be among all if there were no self-interest about honor and money! I think this absence of self-interest would solve all problems. The quest for prestige and money puts one in opposition to God's work." (ST. TERESA OF AVILA, Vol. III; p.37)

***SPIRITUAL DIRECTION*:** Perseverance, Greatly Admired by God

"God greatly admires determination to do His will, a determination accompanied by humility and without self-trust." (ST. TERESA OF AVILA, Vol. I; p.89)

SPIRITUAL DIRECTION: Short-Cuts are to be used in the Spiritual Life when the Occasion Presents Itself

"In the spiritual life look for short-cuts to God, He will give them to you by His grace and Love." (ST. TERESA OF AVILA, Vol. I; p.90)

SPIRITUAL DIRECTION: As Regards Health and Other Persons

"Avoid excessive imprudent attention to health of mind and body. Avoid excessive care and anxiety about sins and failings of others, pay closer attention to your own soul and pleasing God. Observe their good deeds and virtues, cover their defects with thoughts of your own sins, considering others better than ourselves." (ST. TERESA OF AVILA, Vol. II; p.92)

SPIRITUAL DIRECTION: To Distrust Oneself and Place All Trust In God

Teresa learned to lose all trust in herself and to place all her trust in her Majesty, the loving term of endearment (one of her favorites) for God - expressed in another way she always strove to find God's will, to do God's will, and avoid doing her own will out of self-love.

SPIRITUAL DIRECTION: Desire for Consolation, a Fault

Teresa considered desire for God's consolation a fault. [Her reasoning being that we were always to accept both prosperity and adversity from God with gratitude, but with indifference as to whether we should receive consolation from God in certain situations, merely maintaining our trust in Him] (ST. TERESA OF AVILA, Vol. I p.84)

SPIRITUAL DIRECTION: Fear of Carrying the Cross

"Do not be afraid to carry the Cross, the Lord will help you carry it with profit." (ST. TERESA OF AVILA, Vol. I; p.85)

SPIRITUAL DIRECTION: Moderation in Penance, Avoiding Extremes

"Penance can do harm to one's health if done without discretion." (ST. TERESA OF AVILA, Vol II; p.91)

SPIRITUAL DIRECTION: An Expression of Gratitude to God

Teresa: "If I have some good it is a gift from no one else' hands but you dear Lord." (ST. TERESA OF AVILA, Vol. II; p.92)

SPIRITUAL DIRECTION: God Remedies Injustices

"When you are wronged or unjustly accused, His Majesty will inspire someone to defend you, and when He doesn't, the defense won't be necessary." (ST. TERESA OF AVILA, Vol. II; p.93)

SPIRITUAL DIRECTION: Devotion to God with Determination

"When we do not give ourselves to His Majesty with the determination with which He gives Himself to us, He does a good deal by leaving us in mental prayer, and visiting us from time to time like servants in His vineyard. Oh Lord, how true it is that all harm comes to us from not keeping the eyes of our soul upon you. " (ST. TERESA OF AVILA, Vol. II; p.97);

SPIRITUAL DIRECTION: The Contemplative Life and Sanctity

"Not all souls are suited for contemplation and some reach it late. The truly humble person must be content with the path along which God leads him. To be a contemplative is a gift from God, and since being one is not necessary for salvation, nor does God demand this, a person should not think it will be demanded of them. St. Martha was a saint even though they say she was not a contemplative." (ST. TERESA OF AVILA, Vol II. pp.98-100)

SPIRITUAL DIRECTION: Diverse Prayer Lives

"Those who are led by the active life should not be complaining about those who are very much absorbed in contemplation.

Contemplatives do not have a lighter cross." (ST. TERESA OF AVILA, Vol II; pp.100-102)

SPIRITUAL DIRECTION: Carrying the Flag of Devotion

Teresa uses a beautiful metaphor to explain intense devotion: "Since he carries the flag he cannot defend himself, and even though they cut him to pieces he must not let it out of his hands. The contemplative must be careful about what he is doing, for if he lets go of the flag the battle will be lost." (ST. TERESA OF AVILA, Vol. II; p.104)

SPIRITUAL DIRECTION: Moderation in Penance

"Indiscreet penances are to be avoided." (ST. TERESA OF AVILA, Vol. III; p.31)

SPIRITUAL DIRECTION: Diverse Paths in Spiritual Development

"The Lord had different paths by which to go to Him, just as there are many dwelling places. But He did not say some come by this path and other by another." (ST. TERESA OF AVILA, Vol II; p.114)

SPIRITUAL DIRECTION: Unyielding, Unrelenting, Perseverance and Determination

"You must always proceed with this determination to die rather than fail to reach the end of the journey." (ST. TERESA OF AVILA, Vol II; p.114)

SPIRITUAL DIRECTION: Conversation, an Action to Bring Good

Teresa: "I beg you that your conversation always be directed toward bringing some good to the one with whom you are speaking, for your prayer must be for the benefit of souls. (ST. TERESA OF AVILA, Vol. II; p.114)

SPIRITUAL DIRECTION: Perseverance with Resolute Determination in the Love for God

"You must have a very resolute determination to persevere until reaching the end, come what may happen, whatever work is involved, whatever criticism arises, or if the world collapses." (ST. TERESA OF AVILA, Vol. II; p. 34)

SPIRITUAL DIRECTION: Giving Our Will Entirely to God

"Unless we give our wills entirely to the Lord so that in everything pertaining to us He might do what conforms with His will, we will never be able to drink from the fountain of His Divine love." (ST. TERESA OF AVILA, Vol II; p163)

SPIRITUAL DIRECTION: Giving God Our Will in Gratitude

"What can those of us repay who as I say, don't have anything save what we have received? All we can do is know ourselves and what we are capable of, which is to give our will and give it completely." (ST. TERESA OF AVILA, Vol. II; pp. 164-166)

SPIRITUAL DIRECTION: Omnipotent Power of God

Paraphrasing Teresa's stress on God's Omnipotent Power: "Without God we can do nothing but with Him all things are possible. God does it all but without us cooperating with His grace nothing is done."

SPIRITUAL DIRECTION: Inadequate Spiritual Direction

"What we ourselves can do in prayer is explained to us by spiritual directors, but little is explained about what the Lord does in a soul, I mean about the supernatural." (ST. TERESA OF AVILA, Vol. II; p.290)

SPIRITUAL DIRECTION: A Variety of Ways in Serving God and Doing His Will

[NOTE: The works of service for God may be outstanding ones as in Teresa's case but they are not a necessity. One must concentrate on serving those who are in one's company] Teresa stated "The Lord doesn't look so much at the greatness of our works as at the love with which they are done. His Majesty will join our sacrifice with that which He offered for us. Thus, even though our works are small they will have the value our love for Him would have merited had they been great." (ST. TERESA OF AVILA, Vol II; p.278)

SPIRITUAL DIRECTION: Obedience, Its Rewards

"The strength given by obedience usually lessens the difficulty of things that seem impossible." (ST. TERESA OF AVILA, Vol. II; p.281)

SPIRITUAL DIRECTION: A Very Resolute Determination to do God's Will

"And thus I beg you with St. Augustine, and will full determination that you 'give me what you command and command what you will'. Never, with your favor and help, will I turn my back on you." [NOTE: This spiritual theme of St. Augustine quoted by Teresa can be more explicitly interpreted as asking God to take all of our freedom, all of our memory, all of our intellect, and all of our will, and all of our heart (soul) and give us His heart in return. St. Augustine desires, in essence, to be not only a good true servant of God, a true good friend, but also God's loving slave, that is, he does not wish his heart to retain any self-love, but to give all of his love, all of his soul (heart) to God.] (ST. TERESA OF AVILA, Vol. II; p.246)

SPIRITUAL DIRECTION: Penance in This Life

"Let us praise God; let us force ourselves to do penance in this life. How sweet will be the death of one who has done penance for all of his sins, of one who won't have to go to Purgatory. Even from here below you can begin to enjoy glory." (ST. TERESA OF AVILA, Vol. II; p.195)

SPIRITUAL DIRECTION: Trust, Confidence in God

"When we are determined we are less confident of ourselves for confidence must be placed in God." (ST. TERESA OF AVILA, Vol. II; p.198)

SPIRITUAL DIRECTION: Spiritual Guidelines as to Judging

In a paraphrase of the thinking of Teresa and the other spiritual directors cited in this book on this subject of judging the following observations have been made by them: "Judging should be done only under extraordinarily special conditions, and only the action can be judged but not the person as regards the slightest degree of sinfulness to be attributed to the person - this is God's province only - however, judges, spiritual directors, and parents have the right and responsibility to judge human actions quite often, and to take the necessary corrective action so that faulty actions not be repeated again and again. However, this right must be exercised with great prudence."

SPIRITUAL DIRECTION: The Rewards for Loving God and Doing His Will may be Given in This Life

"Oh, Christians and my daughters! Let us now for love of the Lord, awake from this sleep and behold that He does not keep the reward of loving Him for the next life alone. The pay begins in this life." (ST. TERESA OF AVILA, Vol. II; p.246)

SPIRITUAL DIRECTION: Fortified Spiritual Castles

"Love and fear of God: what more could you ask for. They are like two fortified castles from which one can wage war on the world and the devils." (ST. TERESA OF AVILA, Vol. I; p. 192)

SPIRITUAL DIRECTION: The Finding of Virtue

Teresa quotes an old Spanish proverb regarding the finding of virtue: "Look for virtue not in corners away from the din but right amidst the occasions of sin." (ST. TERESA OF AVILA, Vol. II; p.498)

SPIRITUAL DIRECTION: Evangelization, a Great Service for God

Teresa thought that the greatest service one could render the Lord was to bring souls to Him." (ST. TERESA OF AVILA, Vol. III; p.4)

SPIRITUAL DIRECTION: Contemplative Life or the Contemplative-Active Life

[NOTE: There is a general consensus of agreement among the spiritual directors cited throughout this book that the contemplative life, depending upon one's state of life has to be intermittently set aside for the active service for good. For some souls the purely contemplative life may be suitable, but for others the contemplative-active life (which is one of the hardest to live) may be the path along which God guides many souls who respond to His call. To live the contemplative-active life is very difficult for many persons during this spiritual warfare of life. Also, contemplative life lived in utter isolation can be exceedingly dangerous to one not strongly fortified by the grace and love of God to endure it.]

SPIRITUAL DIRECTION: The Enkindling of Love

Teresa had an important spiritual lesson for all who must live the active life, namely: "It is not the length of time spent in prayer that benefits one, when the time is spent as well in good works, it is a great help for the enkindling of love." (ST. TERESA OF AVILA, Vol. III; p.10)

SPIRITUAL DIRECTION: Seeking God

Teresa advised that in one's search for God:"Find God in all things, in troublesome clashes as well as in the hermitage" - or, in her proverbial statement, "even among the pots and pans." (ST. TERESA OF AVILA,Vol III; pp.10-11)

SPIRITUAL DIRECTION: A Prudent Spiritual Guide for Those Seeking to Find and Do God's Will

Teresa states that "Sometimes the devil gives us great desires so that we will avoid setting ourselves to the task at hand, serving our Lord in possible things and instead be content with having desired the impossible. Apart from the fact that by prayer you will be helping greatly you need not be desiring to benefit the whole world but must concentrate on those who are in your company, and thus your deed will be greater since you are more obliged toward them.. In sum my sister, what I conclude is that we shouldn't build castles in the air. The Lord doesn't look so much at the greatness of our works as at the love with which they are done...Thus, even though our works are small they will have the value our love for Him would have merited had they been great." (ST. TERESA OF AVILA, Vol. II; pp. 449-450)

SPIRITUAL DIRECTION: The "Our Father" Prayer, Its Consolations

Teresa gives one example of the solicitude and consolation of God's love for us found in the "Our Father" prayer: "Here you see how with these two virtues - love and fear of God - you can advance on this road with calm and not think that at every step you see a ditch you can fall into; that way you would never arrive. But since we cannot even know with certitude that we in truth have these virtues that are necessary, the Lord taking pity on us because we live in so uncertain a life and among so many temptation and dangers, teaching us to ask - and asking for us - says with good reason: But deliver us from evil. Amen." (ST. TERESA OF AVILA, Vol II; p.478)

SPIRITUAL DIRECTION: The Impact of Original Sin Upon the Imagination

Teresa points out that the "instability and rebellion of the imagination is a consequence of the disorder produced in us through original sin." (ST. TERESA OF AVILA, Vol. II; p. 488)

SPIRITUAL DIRECTION: Power of Trust in and Love of God

"Oh, strong love of God! And how true it is that nothing (p311) seems impossible to the one who loves. Don't fail to go on fighting with faith for God can do all." [NOTE: This is reminiscent of the beloved Archbishop Fulton Sheen's spiritual dictum: "God does it all but without us nothing is done. All He asks is that we cooperate with His love and grace which He is always generously waiting to give us."] (ST. TERESA OF AVILA, Vol. II p.238)

SPIRITUAL DIRECTION: Value of Good Works

"And when you have to suffer something for our Lord or for your neighbor, do not be afraid of your sins. You could perform one of these works with so much charity that all your sins would be pardoned." (ST. TERESA OF AVILA, Vol. II; p.239)

SPIRITUAL DIRECTION: Sins of the Past, Kept in Perspective

"If the Lord should grant you the favor of offering you something to be done for Him, pay no attention to the fact that you have been sinners." (ST. TERESA OF AVILA, Vol II; p.240)

SPIRITUAL DIRECTION: When Human Consolation can be a Solace

"It is a consolation to air out our complaints to those who we know feel our trials and love us more." (ST. TERESA OF AVILA, Vol. II; p.241)

SPIRITUAL DIRECTION: Mortification, Accompanied by Trials

"Let us observe that when the soul begins to mortify itself, everything is painful to it. If it begins to give up comforts, it grieves; if it must give up honor, it feels torment, and if it suffers an offensive word, the hurt becomes intolerable to it." (ST. TERESA OF AVILA, Vol II; p.241)

SPIRITUAL DIRECTION: Control of the Imagination During Prayer

"The imagination is like a grinding mill, often during prayer. The best way to cope with its interruptions is to ignore it." [NOTE: The Imagination, an internal sense, was one of the senses most strongly affected by original sin (St.Thomas Aquinas)] (ST.TERESA OF AVILA, Vol I; p.293)

SPIRITUAL DIRECTION: Do not be Concerned About Eating

"Without worry we eat what the Lord sends since His Majesty takes care that we lack nothing." (ST. TERESA OF AVILA, Vol . II; p.170)

SPIRITUAL DIRECTION: Poverty, a Spiritual Perspective

Teresa speaks on poverty: "What is necessary, daughters, is that we be content with little. As for you daughters, look always for the poorest things which will be enough to get by on: in clothing as well as in food." (ST. TERESA OF AVILA, Vol. II; p.226)

SPIRITUAL DIRECTION: Vanity, Beware of Certain Praises

"What can do you great harm is praise - for once it starts it never ends - if you are not careful so as to humble yourselves more afterwards. The most common way is by telling you you are saints in such exaggerated terms that it seems the devil teaches these words. And indeed he does sometimes." (ST. TERESA OF AVILA, Vol II; p. 227)

SPIRITUAL DIRECTION: Be Wary of Praise

"You should never let a word of praise pass by without it moving you to wage war interiorly, for this is easily done if you acquire the habit. Praise from others if one is not extremely careful can easily draw one into the sin of pride." (ST. TERESA OF AVILA, Vol II; p.227)

SPIRITUAL DIRECTION: How to Manage Praise

"Remember your sins, and if in some matters people speak the truth in praising you, note that the virtue is not yours and that you are obliged to do more. Although you think the praise does you no harm, do not trust it." (ST. TERESA OF AVILA, Vol. II; p.227)

SPIRITUAL DIRECTION: Precautions Regarding Praise

"Always wage an interior war against praises, for thus you will come away from them with the gain of humility, and the devil and the world who are on the lookout for you will be abashed." (ST. TERESA OF AVILA, Vol. II; p.227)

SPIRITUAL DIRECTION: Weakness of the Flesh

"The flesh is very fond of comfort, a comfort which should always be subject to reasonable control." (ST. TERESA OF AVILA, Vol II; p.80)

SPIRITUAL DIRECTION: Wisdom of Consulting with Others

In the lives of the spiritual directors cited in this book, the importance of consulting with others was stressed. I paraphrase here the teachings of St. John of the Cross on this point, which St. Teresa of Jesus of Avila also shared to a very large extent, however, St. John of the Cross in his *Collected Works* elaborated upon this need for consultation more extensively; St. John of the Cross: "God prefers that the person always consult with others, and yet as with Moses, when consultation is not available or proves unreliable, God is always there to be spoken to in prayer as an ever-present recourse. At one point in his life Moses was sent by God to his brother Aaron for consultation when he wavered in whether an action was in accordance with God's will or not. His brother Aaron fortified Moses after the consultation and dispelled the particular fear which caused Moses to balk in doing what God wanted him to do.

SPIRITUAL DIRECTION: Religious Positions or Posts, Proper Attitude Towards Them

"Anyone who is about to receive a Prelacy must be far from desiring it, or at least from striving after it." (ST. TERESA OF AVILA, Vol I; p. 282)

SPIRITUAL DIRECTION: The Soul Follows the Will

"Give your will to God and the soul will follow directly after it." (NOTE: St. John of the Cross)

SPIRITUAL DIRECTION: Angels, Their Consideration by Us

"To desire to be like them while on earth is foolishness." (ST. TERESA OF AVILA, Vol I; p.148)

SPIRITUAL DIRECTION: Christ, a Growing Intimacy with Him

"When we embrace Him with our heart, He becomes more and more our best friend, sharing our burdens." (ST. TERESA OF AVILA, Vol. I; pp. 11-12)

SPIRITUAL DIRECTION: Bearing the Cross, No Matter How Heavy

[Embracing the Cross is most important, Jesus, our Saviour drank the cup of suffering to its dregs] Teresa advises the soul accordingly: "Embrace the cross your Spouse has carried and understand that this must be your task." (ST. TERESA OF AVILA, Vol. II; p.301)

SPIRITUAL DIRECTION: Disciplining the Will

"Even in little things which draw us away from God, the body must be trained to submit completely to the spirit." (ST. TERESA OF AVILA, Vol. II; p. 82)

SPIRITUAL DIRECTION: Honor and Serving God

Teresa gives this admonition: "God deliver us from persons who are concerned about honor while trying to serve Him." (ST. TERESA OF AVILA, Vol. II; p.85)

SPIRITUAL DIRECTION: Proper Spirit in Suffering Wrongs

"Wrongs suffered should often be carried in the spirit of Christ carrying His cross without expressions of complaint.: (ST. TERESA OF AVILA, Vol II. P.85)

SPIRITUAL DIRECTION: Interior and Exterior Expression

"Although interiorly it takes time to become totally detached and mortified, exteriorly it must be done immediately," (ST. TERESA OF AVILA, Vol. II; p.88)

SPIRITUAL DIRECTION: Determination in Loving God

Teresa: "I truly believe that the Lord highly favors the one who has real determination in loving God." (ST. TERESA OF AVILA, Vol II; p.88)

SPIRITUAL DIRECTION: An Admirable Simplicity

"There is a holy simplicity that knows little about the affairs of the world but a lot about dealing with God." (ST. TERESA OF AVILA, Vol. II; p. 89)

SPIRITUAL DIRECTION: A Healthy Spiritual Attitude Towards Censure or Blame Received

Teresa gives some excellent advice on this subject which reflects also the spiritual advice of the other spiritual directors cited in this book. I paraphrase her advice: There lies a great good in not excusing oneself even when blamed without fault. However, it is very prudent to speak out in reply when, if we were not to do so, we were to cause scandal or anger among those present, or in the instance when a injustice was being done to a person; young or old, unable to protect or defend themselves. In general, not making excuses is very meritorious and gives great edification. (ST. TERESA OF AVILA. Vol. II; pp. 90-91)

SPIRITUAL DIRECTION: Regarding Suffering Resulting from Sins

"...Suffering over one's sins increases the more one receives from our God. And, for my part, I hold that until we are there where nothing can cause pain this suffering will not be taken away. True, sometimes there is greater affliction than at other times; and the affliction is also of a different kind, for the soul doesn't think about the suffering it will undergo on account of its sins but of how ungrateful it has been to One to whom it owes so much and who deserves so much to be served."... "...the memory these souls have of their sins cling like thick mire, it always seems that these sins are alive in the memory, and this is a heavy cross."

"I know a person who, apart from wanting to die in order to see God, wanted to die so as not to feel the continual pain of how ungrateful she had been to One to whom she ever owed so much and would owe." "As for the fear of hell, such persons don't have any. That they might lose God at times - though seldom - distresses them very much. All their fear is that God might allow them out of His hand to offend Him, and they find themselves in as miserable a state as they were once before. In regard to their own suffering or glory, they don't care. If they don't want to stay long in purgatory, the reason comes from the fact of their not wanting to be away from God - as are those who are in purgatory - rather than from the sufferings undergone there."

"... No relief is afforded this suffering by the thought that our Lord has already pardoned and forgotten the sins. Rather, it adds to the suffering to see so much goodness and realize that favors are granted to one who deserves nothing but hell. I think such a realization was a great martyrdom for St. Peter and the Magdalene." (ST. TERESA OF AVILA, Vol. II; pp. 397-398)

SPIRITUAL DIRECTION: Always Keeping in Our Hearts the Humanity of our Lord Jesus Christ, Even in Deep Contemplation

"It will also seem to some souls that they cannot think about the Passion, or still less about the Blessed Virgin and the lives of the saints; the remembrance of both of these latter is so very helpful and encouraging. I cannot imagine what such souls are thinking of. To be always withdrawn from corporal things and enkindled in love is the trait of angelic spirits not of those who live in mortal bodies. It's necessary that we speak to, think about, and become the companions of those who having had a mortal body accomplished such great feats for God. How much more is it necessary not to withdraw through one's own efforts from all our good and help which is the most sacred humanity of our Lord Jesus Christ." (ST. TERESA OF AVILA; Vol. II; p. 399)

SPIRITUAL DIRECTION: An Enkindling of the Love for God

"And note this point, Sister; it is important, and so I want to explain it further: the soul desires to be completely occupied in love and does not want to be taken up with anything else, but to be so occupied is impossible for it even though it may want to; for although the will is not dead, the fire that usually makes it burn is dying out, and someone must necessarily blow on the fire, so that heat will be given off. Would it be good for a soul with this dryness to wait for fire to come down from heaven to burn this sacrifice that it is making of itself to God, as did our Father Elijah? No, certainly not, nor is it right to expect miracles. The Lord works them for this soul when He pleases, as was said and will be said further on. But His Majesty wants us to consider ourselves undeserving of them because of our wretchedness, and desires that we help ourselves in every way possible. I hold for myself that until we die such an attitude is necessary however sublime the prayer may be."

"At the beginning of the life of prayer it may be that the Lord will not give this fire in a year or even in many years. His Majesty knows why; we must not desire to know nor is there any reason why we should."

SPIRITUAL DIRECTION: Faith, a Spiritual Perspective

Teresa: "For me faith is what the Church holds, the truths of Holy Scripture." (ST. TERESA OF AVILA, Vol. II; p.21)

SPIRITUAL DIRECTION: Importance of Consultation

"I have always consulted others even though I find it difficult." (ST. TERESA OF AVILA, Vol II; p.21)

SPIRITUAL DIRECTION: Catholic Church, Christ's Church

Teresa: "What was done against the Catholic Church was done against Christ." (ST. TERESA OF AVILA, Vol II; p.22)

SPIRITUAL DIRECTION: Gentleness Draws People to God

"Too much restraint and harshness drives people away from God." (ST. TERESA OF AVILA, Vol. II; p.24)

SPIRITUAL DIRECTION: Indomitable Resolution, Determination a Great Theme of Teresa's Love for God

The Spanish expression used with regard to Teresa sums up the central theme of Teresa's life, namely: *MUY DETERMINADA DETERMINACION,* that is, "A VERY RESOLUTE DETERMINATION to love God." Thus one could say, if I may paraphrase Teresa's expression of this quality of determination, that by the grace and love of God, come hell or high water Teresa would never lose this spirit of great determination in her love for God. (ST. TERESA OF AVILA, Vol. I; p.83)

SPIRITUAL DIRECTION: Friendship with God Paramount

"It is certain that having need of no one a person has many friends." [NOTE: This is Teresa's way of expressing the spiritual advice that by not attaching ourselves to anyone or anything in a way that would hinder our carrying out God's will is highly advisable. The great, true and resolute, unbreakable attachment to God should always be paramount throughout our lives.] (ST. TERESA OF AVILA, Vol II; p.45)

SPIRITUAL DIRECTION: The Ruse, to be Used Prudently, Rarely, and with Caution When Necessary

Teresa's writings indicate examples that she was not averse to using a ruse prudently, resorting to deep secrecy if necessary, however, she tried to be charitable at the same time."

SPIRITUAL DIRECTION: Sociability, an admirable Trait to Cultivate, but Under Control

"So, Sisters, strive as much as you can without offense to God to be affable and understanding in such a way that everyone you talk to will love your conversation and desire your manner of acting and living, and not be frightened and intimidated by virtue; the holier they are the more sociable they are with their Sister. We must strive earnestly to be affable, agreeable, and pleasing to persons with whom we deal." (ST. TERESA OF AVILA, Vol II; p.199)

SPIRITUAL DIRECTION: Love and Fear of God, Guidelines

"Here you see how with these two virtues - love and fear of God - you can advance on this road calmly and quietly for fear of offending God must always take the lead. As long as we live we will never have complete security; that would be a great danger. And this is what our Teacher understood when at the end of the prayer, the "Our Father", He spoke these words to His Father as one Who well understood they were necessary. (ST. TERESA OF AVILA, Vol II; p.200)

SPIRITUAL DIRECTION: Practice of Casuistry, of a Clever Honest Ruse

[NOTE: Teresa was very adept in the art of casuistry, that is, the use of a clever, honest ruse to deceive any of the enemies of our soul. She employed this art of honest deception with considerable skill on rare occasions when it became necessary to do so. She used it sparingly, but cautiously and effectively.]

SPIRITUAL DIRECTION: Caution to be Observed in Consulting with Others

Peter of Alcantara, a saint for whom Teresa had a great admiration, remarked, with a slight wink of his eye, that: "In the spiritual life one should consult with those who are living this life, and not jurists or theologians." Others of his time held to the same view inferring that not all jurists were just and not all "theologians" were theologians. (ST. TERESA OF AVILA, Vol I. p.292)

SPIRITUAL DIRECTION: Using Time Prudently Throughout Life

Teresa gives very succinctly good advice on conserving precious time in this short phrase: "Life lasts but a couple of hours." (ST. TERESA OF AVILA. Vol. II; p.46)

SPIRITUAL DIRECTION: The Sole Owner of Our Will

"Let our will be slaves to no one except Him Who bought our salvation with His Blood." (ST. TERESA OF AVILA, Vol II; p.55)

SPIRITUAL DIRECTION: The Wisdom of Seeking Counsel

"Many mistakes have been made without counsel on matters that could be harmful to someone." (ST. TERESA OF AVILA, Vol II; p.57)

SPIRITUAL DIRECTION: On Spiritual Directors

Teresa, speaking about spiritual directors, states: "There are different paths along which God will lead souls, and one director will not, perhaps, know them all." (ST. TERESA OF AVILA, Vol II; p.60)

SPIRITUAL DIRECTION: Cultivating God's Friends

"A good means to having God is to speak with His friends, for one always gains very much from this. (ST. TERESA OF AVILA, Vol II; p.67)

SPIRITUAL DIRECTION: Compassion is Needed When Working with Persons of a Sensitive Nature

"Little things can bring much distress to persons with sensitive natures. If you are not like them do not fail to be compassionate." (ST. TERESA OF AVILA, Vol II; p30)

SPIRITUAL DIRECTION: Opposing Our Own Will

Teresa provides a guideline: "A great aid in going against your will is to bear in mind continually how all is vanity and how quickly everything comes to an end." (ST. TERESA OF AVILA, Vol II; p.76)

SPIRITUAL DIRECTION: Humility and Its Twin-Like Sister

"Humility and the virtue of detachment from all things not of God seem to go together. They are like two inseparable sisters." (ST. TERESA OF AVILA, Vol II. p.31)

SPIRITUAL DIRECTION: A Healthy Perspective Concerning the Flesh

"We must strive to rid ourselves of love for our bodies. However, we must always take care of our health as a God-given gift." (ST. TERESA OF AVILA, Vol II. p.77)

SPIRITUAL DIRECTION: Life, a Warfare

"There must be war in this life. In the face of so many enemies it is not possible for us to sit with our hands folded; there must always be this care about how we are proceeding interiorly and exteriorly." (ST. TERESA OF AVILA, Vol II; p.223)

SPIRITUAL DIRECTION: Temptation Often a Good Sign

"In fact a soul doesn't disturb me when I see it with great temptations. If love and fear of our Lord are present the soul will always gain very much." (ST. TERESA OF AVILA; Vol. II; p.223)

SPIRITUAL DIRECTION: Continuous War is to be Expected, but There may Come a Cessation

"To be without war is impossible once the Lord has brought the soul to an abundance of contemplation. For some the war may indeed continue to their dying breath."

SPIRITUAL DIRECTION: Charity and Giving an Accounting

"As God's stewards we share our wealth among the poor and must give a strict account for the time we keep a surplus in our coffers, while delaying and putting off the poor who are suffering." (ST. TERESA OF AVILA, Vol.II; p.225)

SPIRITUAL DIRECTION: When You Suffer Poverty

"Praise His Majesty because He has made you poor, and that you accept poverty as a particular favor from Him." (ST. TERESA OF AVILA, Vol. II; p.225)

SPIRITUAL DIRECTION: Mysteries of Faith Need not be Proved

Teresa offered this admonition regarding the penetration of profound mysteries: "Do not waste your thought in subtle reasoning about what you cannot understand. We should accept with simplicity what the Lord gives us, that is, what He may enlighten us about, and what He doesn't we shouldn't tire ourselves over." (ST. TERESA OF AVILA, Vol II p.216)

SPIRITUAL DIRECTION: Jesus, Two Friends

"Jesus as a human being was Teresa's friend, as God He was also a friend she could speak to." [NOTE: As a Divine Person, Jesus Christ had a divine nature and a human nature (St. Thomas Aquinas)] (ST. TERESA OF AVILA, Vol. I; p.253)

SPIRITUAL DIRECTION: Alertness During This Spiritual Warfare

"We cannot be careless in either small things or great." (ST. TERESA OF AVILA, Vol II p.336)

SPIRITUAL DIRECTION: The Crucified Christ Our Model

Teresa offers the crucified Christ as our model: "Fix your eyes on the Crucified and everything will become small for you. If His Majesty showed us His love be means of such works and frightful torments, how is it you want to please Him only with words? Do you know what it means to be truly spiritual? It means becoming the slaves of God... And if souls aren't determined about becoming His slaves, let them be convinced that they are not making much progress, for this whole building, as I have said, has humility as its foundation... Thus, Sisters, that you might build on good foundations, strive to be the least and the slaves of all, looking at how or where you can please and serve them." [NOTE: Teresa's use of the word "slave" is used here explicitly in the sense of a complete submission to always striving to do God's will with a pure heart of love for Him responding to every beat of His most Sacred Heart of Love for us] (ST. TERESA OF AVILA, Vol II; p.447)

SPIRITUAL DIRECTION: God Will Provide the Necessary Fortitude

Teresa, speaking of fortitude makes this observation: "If here below, as David says, in the company of the saints we will become saints, there is not reason to doubt that being united with the Strong One through so sovereign a union of spirit with spirit, fortitude will cling to such a soul; and so we shall understand what fortitude the saints had for suffering and dying." (ST. TERESA OF AVILA, Vol II; pp. 447-448)

SPIRITUAL DIRECTION: God and the World

"One should continually cultivate a continual solicitude for pleasing God and despising the world." Teresa, it can be clearly seen from her writings, had cultivated this ability over the years, and it was not easy for her to have this disdain for the world and its false superfluous rules of etiquette, she calls it all "dung" (ST. TERESA OF AVILA, Vol I. p.256)

SPIRITUAL DIRECTION: The Prudent Use of Conversation

Teresa, while, of course, observing the social amenities in conversation, advised very prudent use of conversation, saying: "I would advise not to desire to have conversation with anyone unless it be about God's great favors and delights." We must remember that such remarks of Teresa were directed to those in the religious community where as she expressed it: "We must desire solitude even when involved in the things I am speaking about (that is, activities of the religious community), this desire is continually present in souls that truly love God." (ST. TERESA OF AVILA, Vol II; p.122)

SPIRITUAL DIRECTION: Observations on Trust in God

In speaking about the vital importance of trust in God, Teresa, cites the example of St. Peter, saying: "How could it be known whether a man were valiant if he were not seen in battle? St. Peter thought he was very courageous, see how he acted when the action presented itself. But he came through that experience not trusting at all in himself, and as a result he trusted in God and subsequently suffered the martyrdom about which we know." (ST. TERESA OF AVILA, Vol III; p. 10 and p. 123)

SPIRITUAL DIRECTION: Reason and Being Spiritually Alert

Teresa warns regarding reason: "that anything that so controls us that we know our reason is not free should be held as suspect. Know that the liberty of spirit will never be gained in this way. For one of the traits reason has is that it can find God in all things and be able to think about them." (ST. TERESA OF AVILA, Vol III; p.130)

SPIRITUAL DIRECTION: Consolations are Secondary or of Little Importance

"Teresa offers the advice that souls mortify themselves and be brought to understanding that refraining from doing one's own will is more fitting than the experience of consolation, temporary, which may thereby be derived." (ST. TERESA OF AVILA, Vol. III; p.131)

SPIRITUAL DIRECTION: Reverence for the Holy Eucharist

"The soul should rejoice that it is offered an occasion to please the

Lord in something so costly as receiving the privilege of receiving its Lord and Saviour, Jesus Christ, True-God and True-Man, and it will humble itself and be just as satisfied by making a spiritual communion."

SPIRITUAL DIRECTION: Teresa on Human Relations in a Mood of Frustration

"To have to consider someone a rational person and to deal with them as such even though they aren't is an intolerable burden." (ST. TERESA OF AVILA, Vol. III; p.134)

SPIRITUAL DIRECTION: Indiscreet Pieties

"There are some people who are deceived with indiscreet pieties and end up disturbing all with their confusion." (ST. TERESA OF AVILA, Vol. III; p.136)

SPIRITUAL DIRECTION: Depression Among Members of Religious Communities

Teresa encountered this serious problem among members of her religious community. Her approach to depression is quite revealing of her observations made over 400 years ago, she says: "Nowadays the term is used more than usual and it happened that all self-will and freedom go by the name of melancholy. Thus I have thought that in these houses and all religious houses, this term should be uttered. For the term seems to bring along with it freedom from any control. Rather the condition should be called a serious illness- and how truly it is one - and be cared for as such." (ST. TERESA OF AVILA, Vol III; p.137)

SPIRITUAL DIRECTION: Reverence to Mary, The Mother of God, Valued by Our Lord.

"It is important to know that our Lord is pleased with any service rendered to His Mother and great is His mercy." (ST. TERESA OF AVILA, Vol III; p.147)

SPIRITUAL DIRECTION: A Caution as Regards Self-Love

"It is a dangerous thing to be satisfied with ourselves." (ST. TERESA OF AVILA, Vol I: p.216)

SPIRITUAL DIRECTION: Holy Fear

"We should always walk in Holy Fear, that is, the fear only of offending God, as long as we are in this exile." (ST. TERESA OF AVILA, Vol. II; p.445)

SPIRITUAL DIRECTION: The Direction of Souls

Teresa offers this profound advice to those in positions of spiritual authority: "Some Prioresses, who are very spiritual, would like to reduce everything to prayer; in sum, the Lord leads souls by different paths. But the Prioresses must remember that they are not there for the purpose of choosing a path for others according to their own liking but so as to lead subjects by the path of the rule and constitutions even though they themselves might desire and feel urged to do something else. Once I was living in one of these houses with a Prioress who was fond of penance; she led all the others along this path. For the love of our Lord, The Prioresses should be attentive to this, for discretion and knowledge of each one's talents are very important in these matters. If the Prioresses are not carefully attentive, they will do much harm and leave them disturbed instead of helping them. The Prioress must not think that she knows a soul at once. Let her leave this to God, for it is He alone Who can understand it." (ST. TERESA OF AVILA, Vol. III; pp.188-189)

SPIRITUAL DIRECTION: The Imagination, an Internal Sense of the Soul

"It is in the imagination that the devil produces his wiles and deceits." (ST. TERESA OF AVILA, Vol. II; p.352)

SPIRITUAL DIRECTION: Works, or Love in Action

"Works are what the Lord wants. Works need not be comprised only of active works of love in action, but also of "prayer works" themselves of diverse forms of prayer. {NOTE: The scene in the Holy Gospel of Jesus - Martha and Mary - bring this out quite eloquently.} (ST. TERESA OF AVILA, Vol. II; p.352)

SPIRITUAL DIRECTION: Praise, Its Implications as Regards Humility

"If you see a person praised, the Lord wants you to be much happier than if you yourself were being praised. This indeed is easy, for if you have humility you will feel sorry to see yourself praised. Praise, as such, is a worthy act, however, receiving too much of it may plunge us into pride and self-love." (ST. TERESA OF AVILA, Vol II; p.352)

SPIRITUAL DIRECTION: Pride as Regards Lineage and Social Status

Teresa makes the point that she had always esteemed virtue above lineage. She explicitly states in strong affirmation of this observation "that God at one time in a locution to her insisted that lineage and social status mattered not all in the judgements of God. (ST. TERESA OF AVILA, Vol. III; p. 38)

SPIRITUAL DIRECTION: The Best Guide in All Matters

"When immersed in controversy and doubt, her one desire was always to do the will of God. Teresa goes on to say that "if we begin discussing opinions, the devil disturbs everything." (ST. TERESA OF AVILA, Vol III; p.46)

SPIRITUAL DIRECTION: Trust in God, a Great Fortifier

"Teresa showed throughout her life as recounted in the *Collected Works* that trusting in God's grace and love, even as regards serious problems of health such as she long experienced throughout her life, never interfered substantially with her capacity for intellectual and organizational work or for full spiritual growth." (ST. TERESA OF AVILA, Vol III; p.52)

SPIRITUAL DIRECTION: Having Understanding for Others

Teresa, writing to her ecclesiastical superiors stressed the virtue of forgiveness, saying: "But let your Reverence consider that it is characteristic of children to err, and of parents to pardon and not look at faults. (ST. TERESA OF AVILA, Vol III; p.68)

SPIRITUAL DIRECTION: God's Will, He Has Laid Out Its Path for Us

"If like the young man in the Gospel, we turn our backs and go away sad when the Lord tells us what we must do to be perfect what do you want His Majesty to do?" (ST. TERESA OF AVILA, Vol II; p.308)

SPIRITUAL DIRECTION: Placing Greater Trust in God's Grace and Love

"In this work of the spirit the one who thinks less and has less desire to act does more. It would not be wrong to avoid working with the intellect." (ST. TERESA OF AVILA, Vol II; p.329)

SPIRITUAL DIRECTION: Avoid Preoccupation with Eating

Teresa cautions: "Carefully avoid wasting your thought at any time on what you will eat." (ST. TERESA OF AVILA, Vol II; p.170)

SPIRITUAL DIRECTION: Honor, Its Superficiality in the Worldly Sense

"The soul's profit and what the world calls honor can never go together. It's a frightful thing the world moves in the opposite direction. For when truly the Lord has given His Kingdom below, the soul no longer loves honor." (ST. TERESA OF AVILA, Vol II; p.178)

SPIRITUAL DIRECTION: Forgiveness, a Great Virtue

"To be forgiving is a virtue difficult for us to attain by ourselves but most pleasing to the Son's Father." (ST. TERESA OF AVILA, Vol II; p.180)

SPIRITUAL DIRECTION: Contemplatives Suffer Great Trials

"The trials of contemplatives are great, and so the Lord looks for contemplatives among people who have been tested. The joy of the contemplatives comes from their seeing that the Lord has placed in their hands something by which they will gain more graces and perpetual favors from His Majesty than they would in ten years through trials they might wish to undertake on their own." (ST. TERESA OF AVILA, Vol II; p.181)

SPIRITUAL DIRECTION: Remembering the Mercy Shown to Us in the Past by God

"I cannot believe that a person who comes so close to mercy itself where he realizes what He is and the great deal God has pardoned him of, would fail to pardon his offender immediately." (ST. TERESA OF AVILA, Vol II; p.182)

SPIRITUAL DIRECTION: Joy in the Achievement of God's Will

Teresa explains this joy in her own inimitable way: "I am certain that those who reach perfection do not ask the Lord to free them from trials, or temptations, or persecutions, or struggles. On the contrary these persons desire, ask for and love trials. They are like soldiers fighting the good fight joyfully to do God's will always, the more wars there are to be fought in this glorious cause, the more hope they have of winning the ultimate victory: God Himself. They are eager to fight such wars." (ST. TERESA OF AVILA, Vol II; p.185)

SPIRITUAL DIRECTION: The Spiritual Pace in Serving God

"I should like us to use our reason to make ourselves dissatisfied with this way of serving God, always going step by step, for we'll never finish this journey." (ST. TERESA OF AVILA, Vol II; p.312)

SPIRITUAL DIRECTION: Obedience, Ultimately Always To God

"And in matters touching on obedience He doesn't want the soul who truly loves Him to take any other path than the one He did: *obedien usque ad mortem* [obedient unto death]." (ST. TERESA OF AVILA, Vol. III; p.117)

SPIRITUAL DIRECTION: God's Will Carried Out with Prayer or with Deeds

"When the soul cannot help with deeds, it will do so with prayer, begging the Lord for the many souls that is sad to see being lost." (ST. TERESA OF AVILA, Vol III; p.118)

SPIRITUAL DIRECTION: Don't be Discouraged

If you at times fall don't become discouraged and stop trying to advance. Remember the Biblical injunction: "The just man falls seven times a day but rises seven times." (ST. TERESA OF AVILA, Vol IV; p.92)

SPIRITUAL DIRECTION: God is Always Our Available Guide

"Provided that we don't give up, the Lord will guide everything for our benefit, even though we may not find someone to teach us." (ST. TERESA OF AVILA, Vol II; p.303)

SPIRITUAL DIRECTION: Where to Begin to Look for Peace

"Believe me, if we don't obtain and have peace in our own house we'll not find it outside." (ST. TERESA OF AVILA, Vol II; p.302)

SPIRITUAL DIRECTION: Praise and Dispraise, How the Soul Turns Them Into an Asset

"When the soul reaches the stage at which it pays little attention to praise it pays much less to disapproval; on the contrary it rejoices in this and finds it a very sweet music. This is an amazing truth. Blame does not intimidate the soul but strengthens it. Experience has already taught it the wonderful gain that comes through this path. It feels that those who persecute it do not offend God; rather that His Majesty permits persecution for the benefit of the soul." (ST. TERESA OF AVILA, Vol II; pp. 361-362)

SPIRITUAL DIRECTION: Perfection in Spiritual Development, Its Nature

"Perfection as well as its reward does not consist in spiritual delights but in greater love and in deeds done with greater justice and truth." (ST. TERESA OF AVILA, Vol. II; p.313)

SPIRITUAL DIRECTION: Prudence Must be Exercised in Selecting Spiritual Directors

"I have had a great deal of experience with learned men and have also had experience with half-learned, fearful ones: these latter cost me dearly." (ST. TERESA OF AVILA, Vol II; p.339

SPIRITUAL DIRECTION: Weariness in Spiritual Development

As the soul grow spiritually, Teresa points out: "Everything wearies it, for it has learned through experience that creatures can not give it true rest." (ST. TERESA OF AVILA, Vol.II; p.344)

SPIRITUAL DIRECTION: A Prudent Attitude Towards Praise

"Praise from others," as Teresa elaborates upon in great detail, "while being charitably appreciated, generally is ignored, lest it leads one into pride. All credit for any gifts possessed by the person is to be given to God Who is the giver of any and all gifts we receive, whatever form they may take: health, wealth, talents for performing any professional, cultural, artistic, or other tasks and occupations throughout our life." (ST. TERESA OF AVILA, Vol. II; P.361)

SPIRITUAL DIRECTION: A Prudent Attitude Towards Praise Received

Teresa was tormented upon seeing that she was esteemed, especially by eminent persons, for she realized that Christ and the saints didn't advance except through contempt and insults.

SPIRITUAL DIRECTION: Trust, Where to Always Place It

"We must always be mistrustful of ourselves, placing our complete trust in God." (ST. TERESA OF AVILA, Vol. II; p.357)

SPIRITUAL DIRECTION: Prudence During This Warfare Upon This Earth

Teresa stressed that it is well during this warfare here upon this earth to be ever on one's guard, in these words: "There must be war in this life. In the face of so many enemies it's not possible for us to sit with our hands folded; there must always be this case of how we are proceeding interiorly and exteriorly." (ST. TERESA OF AVILA, Vol. II; p.223)

SPIRITUAL DIRECTION: The Truth and Us

"We should walk in truth before God and people in as many ways as possible. Especially there should be no desire that others consider us better than we are. And in our work we should attribute to God what is His and to ourselves what is ours and strive to draw out the truth in everything." (ST. TERESA OF AVILA, Vol. II; p.420)

SPIRITUAL DIRECTION: Obedience, the Great Good It Bring To A Soul

Throughout Teresa's works, she, just as St. John of the Cross, reflected the truth that obedience is a virtue which should be exercised prudently depending upon a given situation. However, at the same time we see that she placed great value on the virtue of obedience, for example: " I have seen through experience the great good that comes to a soul when it does not turn aside from obedience. It is through this practice that I think one advances in virtue and gains humility... Those who practice obedience remember that they resolutely surrendered their own will to God's will using submission to the one who stands in God's place as a means to this surrender." (ST. TERESA OF AVILA, Vol. III; p.95)

SPIRITUAL DIRECTION: Gaining Souls for Christ a Great Gift to God

Teresa placed great value on winning souls to Christ, saying: "It seems to me that the Lord prizes a soul that through our diligence and prayers we gain for Him, through His mercy, more than all the services we can render Him." (ST. TERESA OF AVILA, Vol. III; p.102)

SPIRITUAL DIRECTION: Works for the Glory of God, Why We Fail in Doing Them

Teresa exclaims with great spiritual vigor: "Oh greatness of God! How you manifest your power in giving courage to an ant! How true my Lord, that it is not because ofYou that those who love you fail to do great works, but because of our own cowardice and pusallinimity." (ST. TERESA OF AVILA, Vol. III; p.105)

SPIRITUAL DIRECTION: A Guide To Doing God's Will

"The person who knows God better does God's work more easily." (ST. TERESA OF AVILA, Vol. III; p.108)

SPIRITUAL DIRECTION: Obedience, and the Liberty to Speak Out According to Reason

While Teresa stressed the considerable importance of the virtue of obedience, she placed this virtue in a balanced perspective lest she be misinterpreted, thusly: "There are some nuns with such great simplicity that they think it a serious fault on their part to tell the visitor about the faults of the prioresses in matters that have to be corrected. These nuns must be told that even though they may think this an unworthy action they are obliged to do so, and also that they should beforehand humbly tell the prioress when they see that she is at fault in observing the constitutions or in matters of importance, for it could be that she doesn't realize this." (ST. TERESA OF AVILA, Vol. III; p.349)

SPIRITUAL DIRECTION: Arriving at the Truth, Haste Should be Avoided

Teresa advises prudence in getting at the truth of a situation, she states: "It is now my practice not to believe anyone until I have gathered all the information so that I can make the one who is deceived understand that she has been." (ST. TERESA OF AVILA, Vol. III; p.350)

SPIRITUAL DIRECTION: Crosses, Particularly Painful Ones

"A particularly heavy cross to bear is one in which you have a good person think ill of something innocent that you do." (ST.TERESA OF AVILA,Vol. I; p.196)

SPIRITUAL DIRECTION: False, Deceptive Joy

"I am convinced that one who looks for joy in earthly things, or in words or praise from other human beings is very much mistaken, without mentioning the little advantage there is in them." (ST. TERESA OF AVILA,Vol. III; p.249)

SPIRITUAL DIRECTION: The Importance of Seeking Counsel from Others

{NOTE: It was Teresa's custom never to do anything on her own but rather to seek the opinions of learned and virtuous persons}

SPIRITUAL DIRECTION: Fasting as a Spiritual Weapon

"At a time you will think you are so weak that you'll be unable to go without eating meat, but by fasting for one day you will overcome this weakness." (ST. TERESA OF AVILA,Vol II; p.229)

SPIRITUAL DIRECTION: Exercise of Discipline

"We must not rest in being lax, but must test ourselves sometimes." (ST. TERESA OF AVILA,Vol. II; p.229)

SPIRITUAL DIRECTION: Maintain Your Fortitude, God Will Always Help You as You Strive to do so in Doing His Will

"Always have courageous thoughts. As a result of them the Lord will give you grace for courageous deeds." (ST. TERESA OF AVILA, Vol. II; p.230

SPIRITUAL DIRECTION: Advice for a Good Confession

"Always strive so that you don't go to the confessor each time to confess the same fault. It is true that we cannot live without faults, but at least there should be some change so they don't take root." (ST. TERESA OF AVILA,Vol II; p.230)

SPIRITUAL DIRECTION: Purity of Conscience

"It is very important always to have a good conscience so pure that nothing hinders you from asking our Lord for the friendship the bride asks for." (ST. TERESA OF AVILA, Vol. II; p.231)

SPIRITUAL DIRECTION: Carrying the Cross with the Holy Spirit

"Some people do not embrace the Cross but drag it along, and so it hurts and wearies them and breaks them to pieces. However, if the Cross is loved it is easy to bear, [it becomes lighter and does not drag one down as much. It can be used as a crutch, a friend, a support, or as a weapon also] (ST. TERESA OF AVILA, Vol II; p.234)

SPIRITUAL DIRECTION: Fear, Prudently Exercised

"A soul fearful of anything other than offending God is at a serious disadvantage." (ST. TERESA OF AVILA, Vol. I; p.170)

SPIRITUAL DIRECTION: Caution Against Probing the Mind of God

Teresa cautions her nuns in her spiritual direction: "Sisters, we don't have to look for reasons to understand the hidden things of God. Since we believe He is powerful, clearly we must believe that a worm with as limited a power as ours will not understand His grandeurs." (ST. TERESA OF AVILA, Vol II; p.381)

SPIRITUAL DIRECTION: God's Guidance

Because each soul is so different one from another, at times radically different in its spiritual nature or make-up, Teresa points out that the Lord leads each soul as He sees necessary. St. John of the Cross whom Teresa chose as spiritual director for herself and her Camelite nuns points out that the Lord in leading each soul leads it in: 1) an orderly way; 2) kindly and gently; and 3) according to the particular mode or receptivity, responsiveness of the soul.

SPIRITUAL DIRECTION: Uncertainty of God's Grace and Love in Each Individual Soul

Teresa points out in considering spiritual development that "one should consider the virtues and who it is who serves our Lord with greater mortification, humility, and purity of conscience; this is the one who will be the holiest. Yet, little can be know here below with certitude. In heaven we will be surprised to see how different God's judgement is from what we can understand here below." (ST. TERESA OF AVILA, Vol II; p.410)

SPIRITUAL DIRECTION: Forgiveness, a Virtue for All to Aspire to

Speaking about the virtue of forgiveness Teresa states "that the Lord is right in wanting all to pardon the wrongs done them." (ST. TERESA OF AVILA, Vol II; p.420)

SPIRITUAL DIRECTION: Knowledge Can Be a Great Help in Everything

"Providing that what knowledge God gives you is used solely for His honor and glory and praise and love above all, and there is always a true awareness and acknowledgment with that gratitude that it comes from God." (ST. TERESA OF AVILA, Vol II; p. 318)

SPIRITUAL DIRECTION: Don't Be Shocked by Others Faults

"Let us look at our own faults and leave aside those of others, for it is very characteristic of persons with such well-ordered lives to be shocked by everything." [NOTE: Those persons with a definite responsibility for the spiritual direction of others are obliged to develop an acute perception of the faults of others, without in any way judging the degree of sin involved, it is only in this way that they can be truly helpful in providing effective spiritual direction.] (ST. TERESA OF AVILA, Vol II; p.315)

SPIRITUAL DIRECTION: Imagination, Difficult to Discipline

"Just as we cannot stop the movement of the heavens, but they proceed in rapid motion, so neither can we stop the imagination- although we can with perseverance and determination bring it under a tight discipline." (ST. TERESA OF AVILA, Vol. II; p.320)

SPIRITUAL DIRECTION: A Healthy Attitude Regarding Thoughts

"It isn't good for us to be disturbed by our thoughts as troublesome as they may be - as long as we do not advert to them, desire them, or accept them as they come."

SPIRITUAL DIRECTION: Teresa Comments Upon the Troublesome Nature of the Imagination

The imagination was so troublesome throughout her life, especially during prayer that she said at one point: "We must let the mill clapper go clacking on, and must continue grinding our flour and not fail to work with the will and the intellect." (ST. TERESA OF AVILA, Vol II; p.322)

SPIRITUAL DIRECTION: Critical Observation Regarding Prayer

Teresa complains that: "While we are admonished to pray, only what we can do ourselves is explained and little is said of what the Lord does. I mean about the supernatural." It is in response to this need souls have of knowing about passive prayer that Teresa felt she could contribute. (ST. TERESA OF AVILA, Vol. II; pp. 271-272)

SPIRITUAL DIRECTION: Obstacles on the Road to the Spiritual Union of Love

Teresa asserts strongly: "I tell you there is need for more courage than you think. Without the courage, which must be given by God, such a union would be impossible. This fortitude comes through many trials both exterior and interior; opposition from others, praise (itself becoming a trial) severe illnesses, inner sufferings, fears, and misunderstanding on the part of the confessor and the consequent anxiety that God will allow one to be deceived and a feeling of unbearable oppression; and even of being rejected by God." (ST. TERESA OF AVILA, Vol II; p.274)

SPIRITUAL DIRECTION: A Great Consolation Here Upon This Earth

"One of the greatest consolations a person can have on earth must be to see other souls helped through his own efforts." (ST. TERESA OF AVILA, Vol II; p.258)

SPIRITUAL DIRECTION: The Value of Obedience

"Obedience usually lessens the difficulty of things that seem impossible." {NOTE: As soon as one recognizes the gifts given by God to others he should be happy to be subject to them if they are using them according to God's will and not out of self-love.} (ST. TERESA OF AVILA, Vol II; p.266)

SPIRITUAL DIRECTION: Consolations, Their Origins

"Consolations (Contentos) in prayer have their beginning in our own human nature and end in God. Spiritual delights (gustos), however, begin in God, and human nature feels and enjoys them passively much more than consolations (contentos). (ST. TERESA OF AVILA, Vol II; p. 272)

SPIRITUAL DIRECTION: Perseverance in the Faith, be Wary and Alert

"But when I see, as I have said, that Judas was in the company of the Apostles and always conversing with God himself and listening to His words, I understand that it is dangerous and there is no security in being lulled into over-confidence in the warfare against the world, the flesh, and the devil. The best spiritual antidote against this false complacency is not to trust in ourselves - for it would be foolish to do so - but to trust in God." (ST. TERESA OF AVILA, Vol. II; p.356)

SPIRITUAL DIRECTION: Progress in the Spirit

"In the spiritual life the soul never is at a standstill, it is always either falling back or advancing." As Teresa advised her Sisters in giving them spiritual direction at some length, she said: "Let this in sum be the conclusion that we strive always to advance. Love is never idle, and a failure to grow would be a very bad sign." (ST. TERESA OF AVILA, Vol. II; pp. 357-358)

SPIRITUAL DIRECTION: Joy in Love of God, a Great Inspiration

"Joy will reach such an excess that the soul will want to be a herald to the entire world that all might help it praise the Lord." (ST. TERESA OF AVILA, Vol. III; p.275)

SPIRITUAL DIRECTION: A Tribute to the Confessors

"God is very fond of our speaking as truthfully and clearly to the one who stands in His place, as we would to Him, and of our desiring that the confessor understand all our thoughts and even more our deeds however small they may be."

SPIRITUAL DIRECTION: Spiritual Objects, Reverence for Them

Teresa in speaking of spiritual objects points out that we must have great respect for any crucifix or portrait we see of our Emperor. As St. John of the Cross, one of her spiritual directors of whom she was especially fond pointed out, all spiritual objects can serve to enkindle a greater love of God in the soul, however, he advises that upon seeing the spiritual object we should always attempt to raise our souls immediately from the spiritual object observed to the ineffable, incomprehensible God in our soul and in heaven."

SPIRITUAL DIRECTION: God Does It All Through Our Cooperation with His Grace and Love

"The soul by cooperating with God's grace and love wins the victory, and like one who has escaped from a dangerous battle and been victorious, it comes out praising our Lord; for it was He who fought the victory. It knows very clearly that it did not fight, for all the weapons with which it could have defended itself are seen to be, it seems, in the hands of its enemies." (ST. TERESA OF AVILA, Vol. II; p.364)

SPIRITUAL DIRECTION: Melancholy (Depression), Its Origins as Regards the Soul

"Melancholy does not produce or fabricate its fancies except in the imagination." The imagination: (St. Thomas Aquinas) An internal sense of the soul, and an operative faculty of the soul which was most strongly affected or weakened as a result of original sin. (ST. TERESA OF AVILA, Vol. II: p.369)

SPIRITUAL DIRECTION: False Consolation of Love

"Teresa said it would be a cross for her to find consolation in anything that was not God." (ST. TERESA OF AVILA, Vol. III; p.159)

SPIRITUAL DIRECTION: Trust, How God Overcomes All Obstacles

Teresa, affirming her trust in God in many of the problem situations facing her exclaimed: "Oh, God help me, how many obstacles I have seen in these business matters that seemed impossible to overcome, and how easy it was for His Majesty to remove them." (ST. TERESA OF AVILA, Vol. III; p.163)

SPIRITUAL DIRECTION: Ruse, a Strategy to Defeat the Enemy be it Sin, Satan, or Ignorance

"The ruse, used by many saints, was an act designed to deceive the enemy (sin, Satan, or ignorance) without resorting to immoral acts of guile, deceit, or deception. The ruse, however must be used rarely and sparingly, for it must be used without the slightest taint of immorality."

SPIRITUAL DIRECTION: Afflictions at Time of Death

Teresa stressed the gratuity of God in granting us a happy death, she pointed out that, "many suffer affliction at the hour of death and encounter cunning deceit whereby the devil tempts them. [Teresa emphasized that such temptations need not be feared as long as we are being protected by God, she so advised the nuns of the monasteries] (ST. TERESA OF AVILA, Vol. III; pp. 177-178)

SPIRITUAL DIRECTION: Intercessors, Their Importance

Teresa stressing the importance of intercessors between our soul and God recommended that: "We must take the Blessed Mother of Jesus and His saints as intercessors so that these intercessors may fight for us, for the soul' faculties (she refers to them as vassals) have little strength to defend themselves." (ST. TERESA OF AVILA, Vol. II; p.293)

SPIRITUAL DIRECTION: The Quest to Achieve Perfection of the Soul

Teresa advised her sisters throughout the Carmelite Foundations: "Let us understand my daughters that true perfection consists in love of God and love of neighbor as ourselves, the more perfectly we keep these two Commandments the more perfect we will be." (ST. TERESA OF AVILA, Vol. II; pp. 295-296)

SPIRITUAL DIRECTION: Expressions of Gratitude to God

{NOTE: Teresa cultivated the admirable habit of expressing gratitude to God quickly upon receiving any gifts from God}

SPIRITUAL DIRECTION: Its Our Will That God Seeks

"Don't think He needs our works; He needs the determination of our wills." (ST. TERESA OF AVILA, Vol. II; p.308)

SPIRITUAL DIRECTION: Expressing Our Gratitude to God

"What can we do for a God so generous that He died for us, created us, and gives us being? Shouldn't we consider ourselves lucky to be able to repay something of what we owe Him for His service toward us? I say these words: 'His service toward us' unwillingly: but the fact is that He did nothing else but serve us all the time He lived in this world. And yet we ask Him again for favors and gifts." (ST. TERESA OF AVILA, Vol. II; p.308)

SPIRITUAL DIRECTION: True Security, not in This Life

"There is no true security in this life as long as we live. It is a great misery to have to live a life in which we must always walk like those whose enemies are at their doorstep; they can neither sleep nor eat without weapons and without being always frightened lest somewhere these enemies might be able to break through this fortress. I say that the blessedness we must ask for is that of already being secure with the blessed." (ST. TERESA OF AVILA, Vol. II; pp. 304-305)

SUFFERING: The Value of Suffering

"God is powerful enough to make the weak strong and the sick healthy. And when our Lord does not do this, suffering will be the best for our souls; and fixing our eyes on His honor and glory, we should forget ourselves. What is the purpose of life and health save that they be lost for so great a King and Lord? Believe me Sisters, you will never go astray in following this path." (ST. TERESA OF AVILA, Vol. III; p.257)

SUFFERING: Its Severe Duration in Some Lives

"I know a person who cannot truthfully say that from the time the Lord began forty years ago to grant the favor that was mentioned she spent one day without pains and other kinds of suffering (from lack of bodily health I mean) and other great trials." (ST. TERESA OF AVILA, Vol. II; p.362)

SUFFERING: A Safe Path to Choose

Teresa places the value of enduring suffering in a clear perspective when she explicitly stated: "I would always choose the path of suffering, if only to imitate our Lord Jesus Christ if there were no other gain;

especially since there are always so many other benefits." (ST. TERESA OF AVILA, Vol. II; p.362)

SUFFERING: A Soul in Torment

Teresa offers advice regarding a soul in torment from various sufferings from which it does not appear to find consolation. "The best remedy (I don't mean for getting rid of such sufferings, because I don't find any, but so that they may be endured) is to engage in external works of charity and to hope in the mercy of God who never fails those who hope in Him. May He be forever blessed. Amen. In sum, there's reason for thinking that they can do more than what the Lord allows them to do; and provided that one doesn't lose ones mind, everything is small in comparison with what was mentioned...For even though some favors cause still more severe suffering than those mentioned, as will be seen from the condition in which the body is left after such suffering, they do not deserve to be called trials." (ST. TERESA OF AVILA, Vol. II; pp. 365-366)

SUFFERING: Teresa Speaks Admiringly of Another Religious - Beatriz de la Encarnacion

"As for her trials which were very severe, there were terrible illnesses, with intense pain, and she suffered them with the greatest willingness and happiness, as if they were choice favors and delights." (ST. TERESA OF AVILA, Vol. III; p.157)

SUFFERING: A Perspective

"It is very common for souls who practice prayer to desire trials when they do not have any." (ST. TERESA OF AVILA, Vol III; p.158)

SUFFERING: Severe Physical Suffering not an Insurmountable Obstacle to Sanctity

"St. Teresa of Jesus of Avila during the course of her life suffered tremendous spiritual, physical, and psychological trials. Upon her death her body was a whole arsenal of ailments as reported by the findings of the medical doctors." (ST. TERESA OF AVILA, Vol. I; p.5)

SUFFERING: Its Intensity

"Some of the most severe sufferings occur when bodily illnesses are combined with spiritual sufferings of the soul simultaneously and for protracted periods of time." (ST. TERESA OF AVILA, Vol. I; p.197)

SUFFERING: Coping with Unbearable Suffering

"When the suffering in Teresa's life became excruciating, she cultivated the habit of praying in supplication to God that he might give here the patience to remain in this state until the end of the world," (ST. TERESA OF AVILA, Vol. I; p.204)

SUFFERING: Secret of Its Endurance

"In fixing our eyes upon how Jesus, Our Saviour, our Redeemer suffered all becomes easy." (ST. TERESA OF AVILA, Vol. I; p.172)

SUFFERING: Its Positive Value

Sickness itself, if not treatable can be a great gift from God, as it proved to be in Teresa's life.

SUFFERING: A Light-Hearted Perspective

"If our body has mocked us so often, shouldn't we mock it at least once." (ST. TERESA OF AVILA, Vol II: p.81)

SUFFERING: In Love for God

"God will see that whoever loves Him much will be able to suffer much for Him; whoever loves Him little will be capable of little suffering. I myself hold that the measure for being able to bear a large or small cross is love." (ST. TERESA OF AVILA, Vol. II; p.162)

SUFFERING: Can be a Precious Gift

"Just as others prize gold and jewels, they prize trials and desire them; they know that these latter are what will make them rich." (ST. TERESA OF AVILA, Vol. II; p.121)

SUFFERING: Patience in Trials

"The resolve to suffer wrongs and suffer them even though they may be painful is itself a great gift." (ST. TERESA OF AVILA, Vol II; p.182)

SUFFERING: Endurance in Fortitude

"When you suffer often, praise God that He is teaching you the virtue of patience and strive to endure for the suffering is a sign that in this way He wants you to pay for the virtue." (ST.TERESA OF AVILA, Vol II; p.188)

SUFFERING: A Healthy Perspective

"When you find yourself afflicted, stop thinking of your misery, insofar as possible, and turn your thoughts to the mercy of God, to how He loves us and suffered for us." (ST.TERESA OF AVILA,Vol. II; p.190)

SUFFERING: Spiritual Direction

Teresa: "Sisters, let us beseech God that if therefore we are to receive suffering that they will be received here below." (ST. TERESA OF AVILA,Vol. II; p.195)

SUFFERING: Of Our Saviour Jesus Christ

"What was His whole life but a continuous death in which He always saw beforehand that cruel death they were going to inflict upon Him." (ST.TERESA OF AVILA,Vol. II; p.200)

SUFFERING: A Perspective

"If we consider bodily ailments and hardships, who is without very many and in many ways. Nor is it good that we ask to be without them." (ST.TERESA OF AVILA,Vol. II; p.201)

SUFFERING: A Very Painful Type of Suffering

"And what is unendurable Lord, is not to know for certain that I love you or that my desires are acceptable to you." (ST.TERESA OF AVILA,Vol. II; p.202)

SUFFERING: Merit of Trials

"St. Paul says all the trials of the world are not worthy to be compared with the glory we await. (ST.TERESA OF AVILA,Vol. II; p.245)

SUFFERING: God's Inscrutable Ways

Teresa makes this profound observation as regards suffering: "The Lord is never content with giving us as little as we desire. I have seen it here. He grants the soul in answer to some of its petitions an opportunity to merit and suffer something for Him, whereas the soul's intention was to suffer only what its strength could bear. Since His Majesty can make one's strength increase in payment for the little that one determines to do for Him. He will give so many trials and persecutions and illnesses that a poor man won't show himself." (ST. TERESA OF AVILA, Vol II; p.251)

SUFFERING: The Intensity of the Sufferings of Teresa

She says she was left with so powerful a desire to suffer that she begged God earnestly to exercise her in suffering in every way. His Majesty did not fail to fulfill this desire. During these eight years they bled her more than five hundred times, without counting the many cuppings; the body shows them clearly. (ST. TERESA OF AVILA, Vol. III; p.213)

SUFFERING: Teresa, Aided in Her Suffering by a Substantial Locution

"Believe Me and hope for I am He who can do all things; you will be healthy for He who had the power to prevent so many illnesses, each deadly in itself from bringing about their effect will more easily take them away." (ST. TERESA OF AVILA, Vol III; p.216)

SUFFERING: Imitation of Christ, Fervor in Gratitude for His Love

"There are some souls in their love for God who complain to His Majesty when no opportunity for suffering presents itself." (ST. TERESA OF AVILA, Vol II; p.384)

SUFFERING: Compassion for the Sufferings of Others

Teresa, speaking of how a soul can have no better sustenance than trials, makes it clear that this conviction does not remove the pain of seeing others suffer. I mean there must be a whole world of difference between sufferings oneself and seeing one's neighbor suffer. (ST. TERESA OF AVILA, Vol. III; p. 53)

SUFFERING: Penances of the Saints

Teresa, speaking of the interior strength of the soul, which she terms here the center, states: "The great penances that many saints - especially the glorious Magdalene who had always been surrounded by so much luxury - performed must have come from this center. Also that hunger which our Father Elijah had for the honor of his God and which St. Dominic and St. Francis had so as to draw souls to praise

God, I tell you though they were forgetful of themselves, their sufferings must have been great." (ST. TERESA OF AVILA, Vol. II; p.448)

SUFFERING: Interpretation of Holy Scripture

Teresa makes a very enlightening remark for those persons who misinterpret the gospel as regard the Martha and Mary narrative in which our Saviour gently chides Martha for being unduly concerned needlessly. Teresa points out as regards, Mary Magdalene, the suffering she endured in this words: "Moreover, the many trials that afterward she suffered at the death of the Lord and in the years she subsequently lived in His absence must have been a terrible torment. You see she wasn't always in the delight of contemplation at the feet of the Lord." (ST. TERESA OF AVILA, Vol. II; p.449)

SUFFERING: An Example of God's Inscrutable Ways in Permitting Suffering

"...The bishop never loses a day or an hour without working; although his health was not good, for he had lost his vision in one eye. This was my affliction in Soria, for it saddened me that the vision that was so beneficial in the service of the Lord should be lost. These are God's judgments. He must have allowed this so that His servant might gain, for the bishop did not work any less than before, and so as to test His servant's conformity with His will. The bishop told me it caused him no more distress than if it had happened to his neighbor and that sometimes he reflected that it would not grieve him if he lost sight in the other eye as well because this would allow him to live in a hermitage serving God without any other obligation." [NOTE: This could have been a mere rationalization on the bishop's part to assuage the pain of his suffering, for it does not appear to be a constructive thought. Teresa, herself, always advised taking care of your health, but do not fret over it when you can do nothing about improving it with all the means at hand.] (ST. TERESA OF AVILA, Vol. III; p.283)

SUFFERING: The Body and Soul in Anguish

"...Often I complain to our Lord about how much the poor soul shares in the illness of the body. It seems the soul can do nothing but abide by the laws of the body and all its needs and changes..."One of the great trials and miseries of life, I think, is this helplessness experienced when there is no strong spirit to bring the body into submission.

For if the soul is alert, I don't consider the suffering of illness and pain a problem, even though this may be a trial, for the soul is praising God and accepting this as coming from His hand. "It has no other remedy here than patience, knowledge of its misery, and abandonment of itself to the will of God who makes use of it for what He wants and in the way He wants. This is the condition I was in then, although I was already convalescing. But, nonetheless, the weakness was so great that I lost even the confidence God usually gives me when I begin one of these foundations. Everything looked impossible to me. If I had met some person at the time to encourage me, this would have been a great help. But some only added to my fear; others, even though they gave me some hope did not encourage me enough to help me overcome my faintheartedness." (ST. TERESA OF AVILA, Vol. III; pp.268 - 269)

SUFFERING: Carrying the Cross with Grace

"There are no better weapons than those of the cross. We can use it not only as a support to lean upon, but also as a comfort to embrace. It can also be used as a weapon to wield." Teresa used it in a variety of ways. She suggested clearly: "Embrace the cross your Spouse has carried and understand that this must be your task." (ST. TERESA OF AVILA, Vol. II; p.301)

SUFFERING: God's Great Purifier

"The Lord is wont also to send the soul severe illnesses. This is a much greater trial especially when the pains are acute. For in some way if these pains are severe, the trial is, it seems to me the greatest on earth. I say 'if the pains are severe' because then they afflict the soul interiorly and exteriorly in such a way that it doesn't know what to do with itself...After all God gives no more than what can be endured and His Majesty gives patience first. But other great sufferings and illnesses of many kinds are the usual thing." (ST. TERESA OF AVILA, Vol II; p.362)

SUFFERING: A Severe Type of Trial

"One of the worst types of trials was that resulting from various contradictions of good men." (ST. TERESA OF AVILA, Vol. I; p.196)

TRUST: God, a Friend Always Available

Teresa, when in the direst of straits, as she expressed it "always raised the eye of her heart to God." (ST. TERESA OF AVILA, Vol I; p.188)

TRUST: Place not Limits on God's Power

[Everything Is Possible With The Lord] "God does not like us to place limits on his power."

TRUST: The Confidence That a Firm Trust in God Gives

Teresa, fearless in the Holy Spirit, did not hesitate to firmly tell off some theologians who advised her like pedants." (ST. TERESA OF AVILA, Vol. I; p.236)

TRUST: Its Essence

Teresa: "I placed myself completely in the hand of God so that He could carry out His will completely in me."

VIRTUE: The Virtue of Prudence is to be Exercised in Correction

Teresa instructed her Sisters: " No nun should reprove another for the faults she sees her commit. If they are serious, she should admonish her in a charitable way. And if the nun after being told three times does not amend, the Mother prioress should be told but no other Sister." (ST. TERESA OF AVILA, Vol. III; p.32)

VIRTUES: A Pictorial Foundation as Expressed in Teresa's Collected Works

POVERTY
CHASTITY OBEDIENCE
HUMILITY

VIRTUES: God's Gifts

"When they are from God the virtues grow so strong and love becomes so enkindled that there's no concealing the two. Even without any specific desire on the part of the soul, they always bring profit to other souls." (ST. TERESA OF AVILA, Vol. II; p.255)

VIRTUES: The Virtue of Fortitude

"Fortitude is founded on solid ground, as is the case with those who are tried in suffering, for these latter know about the storms of the world and what little reason there is to fear them or desire the world's consolations."

VIRTUES: The Harmful Effects of Vices

"If one caterpillar of a vice remains, all the virtues will become worm-eaten." (ST. TERESA OF AVILA, Vol. I; p.211)

VIRTUES: The Necessity for a Constant Striving for and Practice of Virtues

"I repeat it is necessary that your foundation consist of more than prayers and contemplation. If you do not strive for the virtues and practice them you will always be dwarfs. And please God it will only be a matter of not growing, for you already know that whoever does not increase, decreases. I hold that love where present cannot possibly be content with remaining always the same." (ST. TERESA OF AVILA, Vol. II p.447)

VIRTUES: Obedience, as Regards the Religious Community

"Teresa points out that in the religious community obedience is highly important, even in situations where the superiors may not be exercising their authority prudently with wisdom. She indicates that obedience under such circumstances needs to be given and its carrying out being considered like another cross in imitation of Christ." [NOTE: Since, laypersons do not take vows of obedience, they need not follow the disorderly or imprudent exercise of another layperson appointed over them. Thus, in any matter of sufficiently serious consequence or import, they have the prerogative of exercising their own reasoning powers if they believe they are doing God's will, and so they have the right in such instance to not only refuse obedience, but also appeal to a higher level of religious jurisdiction freely, immediately if necessary. In some instances where the matter in dispute is not of a serious nature it is more humble to simply submit to the will of another rather than become contentious and disturb the peace of all parties involved in such a situation. (St. Thomas Aquinas, St. Teresa of Jesus of Avila, St. John of the Cross, and Thomas a Kempis).

VIRTUE: Compassion, an Admirable Virtue Should be Exercised Prudently Depending Upon the Circumstances

"When dealing with persons who are in need of spiritual direction, especially in serious moral situations, compassion and love should always be exercised, but a certain firmness and application of discipline becomes absolutely necessary when working with either irrational, temperamental, immature or sick persons, also rational and well persons. In other words, there are definite situations where a firm hand of control needs to be applied also in the exercise of this virtue."

VIRTUE: Perseverance, Its Value

"One always gains much through perseverance, especially perseverance in prayer. (ST. TERESA OF AVILA, Vol. II; p.298)

VIRTUE: Being Rooted in Virtue

Teresa spoke of one person she observed who was rooted in virtue: "He was so rooted in virtue that it doesn't seem to me I ever say him angry, which amazed me very much and made me praise our Lord, for when one is rooted in virtue, the occasions of sin are of little consequence." (ST. TERESA OF AVILA, Vol. III; p.285)

VIRTUE: Simplicity Was a Virtue for Which Teresa had Great Admiration

Teresa loved simplicity. The text of her Constitutions is simple and sparse, indicating that she who when speaking of prayer was often extravagant with words was frugal with them when writing laws. As for her own method of governing and the spirit in which she wrote her laws: "These things should be done with a mother's love." Teresa detested superfluous complexities, saying: "It is a strange thing that visitators do not think they have accomplished their task unless they make regulations. And as for Padre Roca's regulations, just reading them tired me out, what would I do if I had to follow them." (ST. TERESA OF AVILA, Vol. III; p.312, p.315, and p.316)

VIRTUE: Obedience, an Admirable Virtue

Obedience is a virtue stressed again and again by Teresa. "It is better to go to excess in obedience by mistake than to be willfully disobedient (especially among religious)" [NOTE: Because of the increasingly pronounced role which the Laity in the Catholic Church is playing today it is important that lay people do not confuse the spiritual practices of the religious community with those of the Laity. This a very fertile area for spiritual direction which needs much more to be written on in order to eliminate the wasteful tensions, confusion, lines of authority, reverence, service, and so forth.] (ST. TERESA OF AVILA, Vol. III; p.191)

VIRTUE: Obedience, Its Rewards

"The strength given by obedience usually lessens the difficulty of things that seem impossible." (ST. TERESA OF AVILA, Vol II; p.266)

WILL: Conformity with God's Will, a Cardinal Principle

Teresa elaborates on a very important fundamental principle in spiritual development, namely: "The whole aim of any person who is beginning prayer - and don't forget this, because it is very important - should be that he work and prepare himself with determination and every possible effort to bring his will into conformity with God's will. Be certain that the greatest perfection along the spiritual path lies in this conformity as to who will receive more from the Lord and be more advanced on this road. Don't think that in what concerns perfection there is some mystery or things unknown or still to be understood, for in perfect conformity to God's will lies all our good." (ST. TERESA OF AVILA, Vol. II; p.301)

WORLD: Avoiding Superfluous Conversations of the World

Teresa provided in her Constitutions a safeguard against worldly affairs for her nuns, namely: "As much as they can, the Sisters should avoid a great deal of conversation with relatives. Let the Sisters be very careful in speaking with outsiders, even though these may be close relatives. If these persons are not the kind who find their satisfaction in speaking about the things of God, they should be seen seldom and the visits kept short." (ST. TERESA OF AVILA, Vol. III; p.324)

Thomas a Kempis

Source: *My Imitation of Christ,* Revised Translation
Illustrated. Confraternity of the Precious Blood.
Rt. Rev. Msgr. Joseph B. Frey, Director
5300 Ft. Hamilton Parkway,
Brooklyn, 19, NY;

pp.1-474 [NIHIL OBSTAT: Martin J. Healy, S.T.D.]
Censor Librerum

Imprimatur:
Thomas Edmundus Mulloy, S.T.D.
Archrepiscopus - Episcopus
Brooklyniensis
Brooklyn, XVII, Man. 1954

BIBLE: Main Objective in Reading Holy Scripture

"Truth is to be sought for in Holy Scripture not eloquence." (Thomas a Kempis; p. 18)

BIBLE: Reading Holy Scripture with Wisdom

"Our curiosity often is an obstacle to many of us in reading Holy Scripture when we attempt to understand something which should really be passed over. We should read with simplicity and humility of heart and with Faith." (Thomas a Kempis; p. 18)

CONSCIENCE: Its Great Value

"A pure conscience gives one a great confidence in God." (Thomas a Kempis; p. 88)

CONSCIENCE: A Source of Rejoicing

"No man is secure in rejoicing unless he has within him the testimony of a good conscience. Yet the same security of the saints was always full of a holy fear of God." [NOTE: That is, the fear of offending God, not a cringing fear of unnecessary guilt or scruples over trivia] (Thomas a Kempis; p. 66)

CONSCIENCE: A Good One Is A Source Of Joy

"There is no true liberty, nor solid joy, but in the holy fear of God with a good conscience." (Thomas a Kempis; p 71)

CONSCIENCE: The Glory of It

"The glory of a good man is the testimony of a good conscience. Keep a good conscience and you shall always have joy. (Thomas a Kempis; p. 121)

DEVOTION: To God in Prayer

"Give me, O most sweet and loving Jesus, to repose in You above all things created: above all health and beauty, above all glory and honor, above all power and dignity, above all knowledge and subtlety, above all riches and arts, above all joy and gladness, above all fame and praise, above all sweetness and consolation, above all hope and promise, above all merit and desire. In essence, above angels and archangels, and all the hosts of heaven, above all things visible and invisible, and above all that which is less than You, my God. For you, O Lord, my God! are the best above all things. You alone are most high. You alone most powerful. You along most sufficient and most full. You alone are most sweet and comforting. You alone most beautiful and most loving. You alone are most noble and most glorious above all things." (Thomas a Kempis; p. 230)

DEVOTION: A Prayer for God's Grace

"Give me grace, dear Jesus, to call to mind all your benefits, so that I may worthily give thee thanks. All that I have in soul and body, all that I possess outwardly or inwardly, by nature or grace, are thy benefits and give testimony of your generosity, mercy, and goodness, from Whom we have received all good. For he who esteems himself the vilest of men and judges himself the most unworthy, is fittest to receive the greatest blessings." (Thomas a Kempis; p. 236)

GOD: Turning to God

"As iron put into the fire loses the rust and becomes all glowing, so a person who turns himself wholly to God puts off his sluggishness and is changed into a new man." (Thomas a Kempis; p. 116)

GOD: His Gifts

"If one considers the dignity of the giver, God, no gift will seem to thee too small which is given by so great a God. Yes, although He gives punishment and stripes it ought to be acceptable; for whatever He permits to happen to us, He always does it for our salvation." (Thomas a Kempis; p. 139)

GOD: His Visitations

"I am accustomed to visit My elect in two ways, by trial and by comfort. I read them daily two lessons, one to rebuke their vices, and the other to exhort them to the increase in virtues."

GOD: Unrelenting Trust in God, He is Our Fortress, He Fortifies

"Is anything difficult to Me? Or shall I be like one that promises and does not perform? Where is thy faith? Stand firmly and with perseverance. Have patience and be of good courage, comfort will come to you in its proper season. Wait for Me, wait, I will come and cure thee." (Thomas a Kempis; p. 262)

GOD: With Him is the Greatest Friendship

"Without Me no friendship is of any strength, nor will it be durable; nor is that love true and pure of which I am not the bond." (Thomas a Kempis; p.301)

GOD: The Most Faithful Friend

"A faithful friend is rarely to be found who perseveres in all the distresses of his friend. You alone Lord are most faithful in all things, and besides Thee, there is no other to be compared to as a true friend. Oh, how wise is that soul that says my friendship and mind is strongly settled and grounded upon Christ." (Thomas a Kempis; p.309-310)

GOD: Do not be Disheartened in Doing God's Will

"Be not dismayed with the labors which you undertake in carrying out God's will, neither let the trials you encounter in doing so cast you down into discouragement, but let My promise strengthen you and comfort you in every event. I, your God, is all you need to reward you beyond all measure." (Thomas a Kempis; p. 318)

GOD: Keeping God's Will Alway Before One as the Goal for Every Action

"Blessed is he Oh Lord, who for thee, O Lord lets go all things created; who offers violence to his nature, and through fervor of spirit crucifies the lusts of the flesh; that so his conscience being cleared up, he may offer to thee pure prayer, and may be worthy to be admitted among the choirs of angels, having excluded all things from the earth, both from without and from within."

GOD: Total Renunciation to His Will

"Lord, I will suffer willingly for thee whatsoever you are pleased should befall me. I will receive with indifference from thy hand good and evil, sweet and bitter, joy and sorrow, and will give you thanks for all that happens to me. Keep me only from sin and I will fear neither death nor hell. (Thomas a Kempis; p. 217)

GRACE: Its Comings and Goings

"When the grace of God comes to one then he is strong and powerful for all things; and when it departs then he is poor and weak, left as it were only to scourging. He rides at ease who is carried by the grace of God." (Thomas a Kempis; p.132)

GRACE: Its Comings and Goings Among Great Saints

"One person said, at the time when grace was with him: 'In my abundance I said I shall never be moved.' But when grace was withdrawn he immediately tells us what he experienced in himself: 'You, dear Lord, turned you face from me and I became troubled.' If it has been thus with great saints, we that are weak and poor must not be discouraged if we are sometimes fervent, sometimes cold, because the Spirit comes and goes according to His own good pleasure. When we appear to be forsaken by God's grace, at such a time there is no better remedy than patience and denial under the will of God. (Thomas a Kempis; p. 134-135)

GRACE: Gratitude to God in Prosperity and Adversity

"He that desires to retain the grace of God, let him be thankful for grace when it is given, and patience when it is withdrawn; let him pray that it may return; let him be cautious and humble, lest he lose it." (Thomas a Kempis; p. 139)

GRACE: A Foretaste of the Heavenly Country

"That good and delightful affection, which you sometimes perceive, is the effect of present grace and a certain foretaste of thy heavenly country, but you must not rely too much upon it, because it comes and goes. Neither is it an illusion that sometimes you are rapt in ecstasy and soon again return to the accustomed weakness of your heart." (Thomas a Kempis; p. 177-178)

GRACE: The Promise of Jesus Christ

"They who freely and willingly serve Me shall receive grace for grace." (Thomas a Kempis; p. 189)

GRACE: Its Mysterious Presence

"When you think I am far from you my dear one, says the Lord, I am often nearest to you." (Thomas a Kempis; p. 53)

GRACE: The Power of Grace

"How exceedingly necessary is your grace for me O Lord, to begin that which is good, to go forward with it, and to accomplish it. For without it I can do nothing; but I can do all things in You, when your grace strengthen me."

GRACE: A Mighty Source of Our Strength, a Meditation

"If I be tempted and afflicted with many tribulations I will fear no evil while your grace is with me. She is my strength; she gives counsel and help. She is mightier than all my enemies, and wiser than all the wise. She is the mistress of truth, the teacher of discipline, the light of the heart, the comforter in affliction, the banisher of sorrow, the expeller of fears, the nurse of devotion, the producer of tears. What am I without her but a piece of dry wood, and an unprofitable stump, fit for nothing but to be cast away. Let thy grace, therefore, O Lord, always go both before me and follow me, and make me ever intent on good works, through Jesus Christ Thy Son. Amen." (Thomas a Kempis; p. 357-358)

GRACE: Discerning the Different Motions of Grace and Nature (Op. Cit., pp. 349-353)

CHRIST:

1."Son, observe diligently the motions of nature and grace; for they move in very opposite and subtle ways, and can hardly be distinguished but by a spiritual man, and one that is internally illuminated.

All men indeed aim at good, and pretend to do something good in what they do and say: therefore, under the appearance of good, many are deceived.

2."Nature is crafty and draws away many; she ensnares and deceives them and always has self for her end.

But grace walks with simplicity, turns aside from all appearance of evil, offers no deceits, and does all things purely for God, in whom also she rests as in her last end.

3."Nature is not willing to be mortified, or to be restrained, or to be overcome, or to be subject; neither will she of her own accord be brought under.

But grace studies the mortification of her own self, resists sensuality, seeks to be subject, covets to be overcome, aims not at enjoying her own liberty, loves to be kept under discipline and desires not to have the command over any one; but under God ever to live, stand, and be, and for God's sake is ever ready humbly to bow down to all human creatures.

4."Nature labors for her own interest, and considers what gain she may reap from another.

But grace considers not what may be advantageous and profitable to herself, but rather what may be profitable to many.

5."Nature willingly received honor and respect; But grace faithfully attributes all honor and glory to God.

6."Nature is afraid of being put to shame and despised; But grace is glad to suffer reproach for the name of Jesus.

7."Nature loves idleness and bodily rest; But grace cannot be idle and willingly embraces labor.

8."Nature seeks to have things that are curious and fine, and does not care for things that are cheap and coarse: But grace is pleased with that which is plain and humble, rejects not coarse things, nor refuses to be clad in old clothes.

9."Nature has regard to temporal things, rejoices at earthly gain, is troubled at losses, and is provoked at every slight injurious word: But grace attends to things eternal, and cleaves not to those which pass with time; neither is she disturbed at the loss of things, nor exasperated with hard words, for she places her treasure and her joy in heaven, where nothing is lost.

10."Nature is covetous, and is more willing to take than to give, and loves to have things to herself: But grace is bountiful and open-hearted, avoids selfishness, is contented with little, and judges it a more blessed thing to give rather than to receive.

11."Nature inclines to creatures, to her own flesh, to vanities, and to gadding abroad: But grace draws to God and to virtue, renounces creatures, flies the world, hates the desires of the flesh, restrains wandering about, and is ashamed to appear in public.

12."Nature willingly received exterior comfort, in which she may be sensibly delighted: But grace seeks to be comforted in God alone, and beyond all things visible to be delighted in the Sovereign Good.

13."Nature doth all for her own gain and interest; she can do nothing gratis, but hopes to gain something equal, or better, or praise, or favor for her good deeds; and covets to have her actions and gifts much valued: But grace seeks nothing temporal, nor requires any other recompense but God alone for her reward, nor desires anything more of the necessaries of this life than may be serviceable in attaining a happy eternity.

14."Nature rejoices in a multitude of friends and kindred; she glories in the nobility of her stock and descent; she fawns on them that are in power, flatters the rich, and applauds such as are like herself: But grace loves even her enemies, and is not puffed up with having a great many friends, nor esteems family or birth, unless when joined with greater virtue. She rather favors the poor than the rich; she has more compassion for the innocent than the powerful; she rejoices with him that loves the truth, and not with the deceitful. She ever exhorts the good to be zealous for better gifts, and to become like unto the Son of God by the exercise of virtues.

15."Nature easily complains of want and of trouble; But grace bears poverty with constancy.

16."Nature turns all things to herself, and for herself she labors and disputes: But grace refers all things to God, from whom all originally proceed; she attributes no good to herself, nor does she arrogantly presume of herself; she does not contend, nor prefer her own opinion to others, but in every feeling and thought she submits herself to the eternal wisdom, and to the divine examination.

17."Nature covets to know secrets, and to hear news; is willing to appear abroad, and to have experience of many things by the senses; desires to be taken notice of, and to do such things as may procure praise and admiration; but grace cares not for the hearing of new and curious things, because all this springs from the old corruption, since nothing is new or lasting upon earth. She teaches, therefore, to retrain the senses, to avoid vain complacency and ostentation, humbly to hide those thing which are worthy of praise and admiration; and from everything, and in every knowledge, to seek the fruit of spiritual profit, and the praise and honor of God. She desires not to have herself or what belong to her extolled; but wishes that God may be blessed in His gifts, who bestows all through mere love.

18."This grace is a supernatural light and a certain special gift of God, and the proper mark of the elect, and pledge of eternal salvation, which elevates a man from the things of the earth to the love of heavenly things, and from carnal makes him spiritual. Wherefore the more nature is kept down and subdued, the greater abundance of grace is infused; and the inward man, by new visitations, is daily more reformed according to the image of God." (Thomas a Kempis; p. 349-353)

KNOWLEDGE: Limitation on Its Value

"There are many things the knowledge of which is of little or no profit to the soul." (Thomas a Kempis; p. 8)

KNOWLEDGE: As Related to Holiness

"The more knowledge one acquires the more serious the judgment of one's soul unless one's life also increase in holiness with the increase of knowledge. Do not become proud as your knowledge increases but rather be fearful as to how you use this knowledge in carrying out God's will." (Thomas a Kempis; p.9)

KNOWLEDGE: Beware of Pride

"Regardless of how much knowledge you may possess, never forget the infinity of the things you may be ignorant of."

KNOWLEDGE: A True Knowledge of Self, the Highest Science

"To truly know ourselves and have a true realization of the lowliness, the baseness, the meanness that we are potentially capable of is a high science of the soul." (Thomas a Kempis; p. 9)

KNOWLEDGE: Learning, Cautions

"Never read anything that you may appear more learned or more wise. Study rather to mortify your vices, for this will be more profitable to you than knowing about many profound questions of knowledge. Woe to them that inquire of many people after many curious things, and are but little curious of finding out ways in which they can serve Me." (Thomas a Kempis; p. 304)

KNOWLEDGE: Our Best Teacher

"The Lord says: 'I am He that in an instant elevates a humble mind to comprehend more reasons of the eternal truth than could be acquired by ten years' study in schools. I teach without noise of words, without confusion of opinions, without ambition of honor, without contention of arguments. I teach to despise earthly things, to loathe things present, to seek and relish things eternal, to fly honors, to endure scandals, to repose all hope in me, to desire nothing out of Me, and above all things, ardently to love Me. If one loves Me entirely, I will teach him divine things and he will speak wondrously.'" (Thomas a Kempis; p. 305)

KNOWLEDGE: Avoidance of Excessive Curiosity

"It is not prudent to dispute of mysteriously profound questions of life, nor of the hidden judgments of God; why this man is left thus, and this other is raised to so great a grace, or why this person is so much afflicted and that other so highly exalted. These questions are above the reach of man's reasoning powers, nor can any reason or discourse penetrate into the judgments of God. When, therefore, the enemy suggests to you such things as these, or you hear of curious persons inquiring into them, answer with the prophet: 'You are just, O Lord, and your judgment is right. Your judgments are to be feared Lord, not to be searched into; for they are incomprehensible to human understanding.' In like manner, do not inquire nor dispute concerning the merits of the saints, which of them is more holy than the other, or which is greater in the Kingdom of Heaven." (Thomas a Kempis; p. 368)

KNOWLEDGE: A Healthy Perspective

"Learning in and of itself is a worthy thing ordained by God, but a good conscience and a virtuous life are always to be preferred before it." (Thomas a Kempis; p.13)

KNOWLEDGE: A Perspective

"One's life should be a living book of love, not a display of books one has read. He is very learned indeed who does the will of God and renounces his own will, who looks upon all earthly things as nothing that he may gain Christ."

KNOWLEDGE: Through Reading

"Let not the authority of the writer influence you regardless of his prestige, great or small, but let the love of pure truth lead you to read." (Thomas a Kempis; p. 18)

HUMILITY: Virtue is to be Preferred Over Excessive Learning

"It means very little if one can discourse extensively of the Holy Trinity but be lacking in humility, for sublime use of words do not make a person holy but a virtuous life makes one dear to God. Thus, it is better to show compunction, that is, sorrow for the sufferings and weaknesses of others, than to be able to define the word compunction." (Thomas a Kempis; p. 5)

HUMILITY: Perspectives in Life

"A humble farmer who loves God is better than a proud philosopher who neglecting his soul intently studies the universe." (Thomas a Kempis; p. 8)

HUMILITY: A Healthy Perspective

"If you have any good that is within you, believe better things of others that you may preserve humility."

HUMILITY: In God's Eyes

"The saints that are highest in the sight of God are the least in their own eyes; and the more glorious they are the more humble they are in themselves. They being full of the truth and heavenly glory are not desirous of vainglory or self-love." (Thomas a Kempis; p. 138)

HUMILITY: Self-Love, a Barrier

"If you are not willing to be humbled and confounded for your defects, it is then plain that you are not truly humble, nor truly dead to the world, nor the world crucified to you." (Thomas a Kempis; p. 138)

HUMILITY: We, in God's Eyes

"For as much as one is in thy eyes, dear Lord, so much is he and not more, says the humble, St. Francis of Assisi." (Thomas a Kempis; p. 337)

HUMILITY: Contrition

"Humble contrition for sins is an acceptable sacrifice to you, O Lord."

HUMILITY: One Important Spiritual Perspective

"Never think that you have made any progress until you look upon yourself as spiritually inferior to all." (Thomas a Kempis; p. 110)

HUMILITY: Danger of Excessive Knowledge

"It is better to have little knowledge with humility and a weak understanding, than greater treasures of learning with self-conceit."

JESUS CHRIST: Our Light in the Darkness

"He that follows Me walks not in darkness says our Lord Jesus Christ. He is our enlightenment, delivering us from all blindness of heart." (Thomas a Kempis; p. 5)

JESUS CHRIST: Understanding His Words

"He who would fully understand the words of Christ must make his life conform to that of Christ." (Thomas a Kempis; p.5)

JESUS CHRIST: In His Service

"Be not ashamed to serve others and to appear poor in this world for the love of Jesus Christ."

JESUS CHRIST: Always Faithful

"Men quickly change and soon fail, but Christ remains forever, and stands by us firmly to the end. Great confidence should not be placed in frail mortal man, though he will prove useful and beloved, nor must one grieve if sometimes he be against thee and cross thee. For human beings that are with you today may be against you tomorrow; and on the other hand often changed like the wind. Place thy entire confidence in God and let Him be thy fear and thy love; He will support you and do what is best for you." (Thomas a Kempis; p. 104)

JESUS CHRIST: Our Model in Adversity

"Christ was also in this world despised by men, and in His time of greatest need forsaken by His acquaintances and friends in the midst of reproaches."

JESUS CHRIST: The Mind of Christ, the Truth

"He to whom all things are known as they are, not as they are esteemed to be or said to be, is wise indeed, and taught rather by God than by men."

JESUS CHRIST: Seek and You Shall Find

"If in all things you seek Jesus without doubt you will find him." (Thomas a Kempis; p. 124)

JESUS CHRIST: He is Our All

"What can the world profit you without Jesus? To be without Jesus is a grievous hell and to be with Jesus a sweet paradise. If Jesus be with thee no enemy can hurt thee."

JESUS CHRIST: Offending God

"We ought rather choose to have the whole world against us than offend Jesus." (Thomas a Kempis; p. 124)

JESUS CHRIST: Faithful to His Promise

"What I have promised I will give, what I have said I will make good provided a man continue to the end faithful in My love." (Thomas a Kempis; p. 164)

JESUS CHRIST: His Suffering

"I came down from heaven for your salvation. From the hour of My Incarnation till My expiring on the cross, I was never without suffering." (Thomas a Kempis; p. 219)

JESUS CHRIST: The Supreme Loving Gift of God Himself, the Body and Blood of Christ.

"The angels and the archangels stand with a reverential awe; the saints and the just are afraid; and You say, Come you all to Me: Unless You, O Lord, did say it who could believe it to be true? And unless you did command it who would dare to approach? How great ought to be the reverence and devotion which I and all Christian people should have in the presence of this sacrament, and in receiving the most excellent Body of Christ. If this most holy sacrament were only celebrated in one place, and consecrated by only one priest in the world, how great a desire would men have to go to that place, and to such a priest of God; that they might see the divine mysteries celebrated." (Thomas a Kempis; pp 384-389)

JESUS CHRIST: Assault by the Devil During the Reception of the Body and Blood of Christ.

"When some are preparing themselves to receive the sacred Communion they suffer the greater assaults of Satan. This wicked spirit, as it is written in Job, comes among the sons of God, to trouble them with his accustomed malice, or to make them overfearful and perplexed, so that he may diminish their devotion, or, by his assaults, take away their faith; so that perhaps, they may altogether omit Communion, or at least approach it with tepidity. No regard should be paid to his wiles and suggestions, be they ever so filthy and abominable; but all his attempts are to be turned back upon his own head. He is to be condemned and scorned, nor is the Holy Communion to be omitted for his assaults, and the commotions which he causes." (Thomas a Kempis; p. 422-423)

JUDGMENT: Judging Others

"To know our true self and to think well and highly of others is great wisdom and a high perfection of soul. If you see another openly sin or commit some heinous crime do not ever esteem thyself better. We are all weak, but always remember to think no one more weak than thyself in the tendency to sin."

JUDGMENT: Of Other Persons

"In judging others a man labors in vain, often errs, and easily sins; but in judging and looking into himself he always profits {NOTE: We can with reason judge the actions of others sometimes but never the degree of sinfulness attached to them, this is particularly true of judges, spiritual directors, fathers and mothers} (Thomas a Kempis; p. 44)

JUDGMENT: Our Weakness in Judging

This is a summary of what Thomas a Kempis had observed as regards judging others: "Our weakness in judging is that frequently we judge actions of others through what we have in our own heart. Thus self-love blinds us to make a true judgment of an action. (Thomas a Kempis; p. 115)

JUDGMENT: Preparing for It Personally

"In all your actions keep your end in sight, and how you will stand before your judge, your God, from whom nothing is hidden."

JUDGMENT: Of Being Judged by Others

"Although Paul endeavored to please all in the Lord and made himself all unto all, he became all things to all in Christ, yet he made little account of his being judged by the judgment of men. He labored for the edification and salvation of others as much as he could and as was possible to him, but he could not prevent his being sometimes judged or despised by others. Therefore, he committed all to God, Who knows all and defended himself, by patience and humility, against the tongues of those that spoke evil, or thought vain and false things and said whatever they pleased about him. However, he answered them sometimes, lest his silence might give occasion to the weak. (Thomas a Kempis; p. 284)

LOVE: Preferable Always to Vast Learning

"If you knew the Bible by heart and all the sayings of the philosophers of what profit would it be without the love of God and His Grace." (Thomas a Kempis; p.p 5-6)

LOVE: Pure Love of God, Its Rewards

"He that loves God with his whole heart neither fears death, nor punishment, nor judgement, nor hell; because perfect love gives secure access to God." (Thomas a Kempis; p. 89)

LOVE: Love for God, Accompanied Always by a Holy Fear

"He that does not always retain a holy fear of God (that is the fear of offending God) will not be able to continue long in doing good, but will quickly fall into the snares of the devil." (Thomas a Kempis; p. 90)

LOVE: The Soul's Sole Affection

"A soul that truly loves God despises all things that are less than God, that is, it does not hate them but is completely detached from them in its complete, true attachment to God alone in love. For none but God alone, eternal and incomprehensible, can give true comfort to the soul and true joy to the heart.: (Thomas a Kempis; p. 119)

LOVE: The True Lover of Jesus

"The person who gives up all things for the love of Jesus is a lover of Jesus. But who is truly a great lover of Jesus? It is he who leaving all things for Jesus also leaves himself and wholly leaving even himself retains nothing of self love. And when he has done all of this thinks to himself that he has done nothing, he says after all this, I am an unprofitable servant, I am, he says with the prophet: alone and poor. Yet no one is indeed richer than such a person, none more powerful, none more free, who knows how to leave himself and all things, and place himself in the very lowest place."

LOVE: The Richest Love Comes from the Heart

"Some only carry their devotion in their books, some in pictures and outward signs and figures. Some have Me in their mouths, but little in their hearts." (Thomas a Kempis; p. 170)

LOVE: Its Excellence

"Love is an excellent thing which alone makes all that is burdensome light, and is not to be detained by things beneath. For it carries a burden without being burdened and makes all that is bitter sweet and savory. Nothing is sweeter than love; nothing stronger, nothing higher, nothing more generous, nothing more pleasant, nothing fuller or better on heaven or on earth; for love proceeds from God and cannot rest but in God above all, from whom all good flows and proceeds." (Thomas a Kempis; p. 172-173)

LOVE: Its Excellence

"Love watches, and sleeping, slumbers not. When weary is not tired; when straitened is not constrained; when frightened is not disturbed, but like a living flame and a torch all on fire it mounts upward and securely passes through all opposition. Love is swift, sincere, pious, pleasant, and delightful; strong, patient, faithful, prudent, long-suffering, courageous, and never seeking itself. For where a man seeks himself there he falls from love." (Thomas a Kempis; p. 174-175)

LOVE: Trusting, Obedient, and Thankful

"Love is submissive and obedient to superiors, in its own eyes mean and contemptible, devout and thankful to God, always trusting and hoping in Him, even when it tastes not the relish of God's sweetness, for there is no living in love without some pain and sorrow." (Thomas a Kempis; p. 175)

LOVE: A Valiant Lover of God

"He is pleased with God in prosperity and does not become displeased with Him in adversity." (Thomas a Kempis; p. 177)

LOVE: Gratitude to God

"In this, dear God, have you most of all shown me the sweetness of your love, that when I had no being you created me, and when I strayed far from you, you have brought me back again, that I might serve thee, and you have commanded me to love thee." (Thomas a Kempis; p. 192)

PRAISE: A Healthy Attitude Towards It

"He who knows himself well is mean in his own eyes and does not take delight in the praise of others." {NOTE: This does not refer to honest, healthy praise now and then} (Thomas a Kempis; p. 8)

PRAISE: A Healthy Attitude Towards It

"It is better to ignore words of praise, but to pay serious attention to words of dispraise, and immediately to correct oneself as soon as possible if they are true or have reasonable merit." (Thomas a Kempis; p. 122)

PRAISE: Beware of Pride

"It has been very hurtful to many a soul to have its virtue known and over-hastily praised." (Thomas a Kempis; p. 312)

PRAYER: Omissions Need not be of Concern

"If for spiritual reasons, or because of the necessity of performing an act of charity for our neighbor we omit our regular prayer we can then readily resume our prayer exercise without qualms or scruples about it. But if through a loathing of mind or negligence we lightly omit our regular prayer exercises this may prove very hurtful to us."

***PRAYER*:** Diversity is the Norm of Human Nature

"All cannot practice the same prayer exercises, one may be more proper, suitable or appropriate for one person but not for another. We stand in need of one kind of prayer during temptation and of another type during peace and rest. " (Thomas a Kempis; p. 62)

***PRAYER*:** Go to Your Heart for Divine Assistance

"Moses always had recourse to the tabernacle for the deciding of all doubts and questions, and fled to the help of prayer against the dangers and wickedness of men. So must you in like manner fly to the innermost depths of your heart and there most earnestly implore the divine assistance." (Thomas a Kempis; p. 291)

***PRAYER*:** Be Alert in Turning to Divine Assistance

"Watch and pray says the Lord that you enter not into temptation. The old enemy, who opposes all that is good, fails not to tempt; but day and night lays his dangerous plots to draw the unwary into his deceitful snares."

***PRAYER*:** Fortitude, a Prayer to God for Strength

"Give me dear Lord the power to be strengthened in the inward man and to cast out of my heart all profitable care and trouble; let me not be drawn away with various desires of anything whatsoever, whether it be of little or great value; but teach me to look upon all things as passing away and myself as passing along with them."

REASON: The Interior War of the Soul

"Our natural reason is surrounded by a great mist, having yet the judgment of good and evil, and the discernment of truth and falsehood, though it be unable to fulfill all that is approves; neither does it now enjoy the full light of truth, nor the former purity of its affections. Hence it is, Oh my God, that according to the inward man, I am delighted with thy law, knowing Thy command to be good, just, and holy, and reproving all evil and sin, as what ought to be shunned. And yet in the flesh I serve the law of sin, whilst I rather obey sensuality than reason. Hence it is, that to will is present with me, but to accomplish that which is good I find not." (Thomas a Kempis; p. 355-356)

SELF-LOVE: A Great Troubler of the Soul

"What is a greater hindrance and trouble to the soul than uncontrolled self-love."

SELF-LOVE: In Our Actions

Thomas a Kempis, and I summarize a series of his views on this subject: Many unknowingly to themselves, act out of motives of self-love. They are at peace when things are done according to their will and judgment, but if not they become frustrated.

SELF-LOVE: Manifested Towards All God's Creations

"Nothing so defiles and entangles the heart of a man as impure love towards all things of God's creations, which of themselves are good." (Thomas a Kempis; p. 107)

SELF-LOVE: Personal Blindness as Regards Others

"Some persons know well how to excuse or paint their actions in good colors, but they will not excuse the actions of others. It would be a greater justice on their part if at times they would accuse themselves and excuse the actions of others."

SELF-LOVE: Extremely Hurtful to the Soul

I summarize the observations of Thomas a Kempis here on this point: The selfish self-love of oneself is very hurtful to the spiritual health of the soul. (Thomas a Kempis; p. 253)

SELF-LOVE: Forsaking All for God

"Forsake all and you find The All. Give up all self-love and have the working towards loving God with all your heart, mind, and soul as a goal. You cannot possess perfect liberty unless you wholly deny yourself. All self-lovers and self-seekers are as if in chains, full of desires, full of cares, unsettled, and seeking always their own ease, and not the things of Jesus Christ, but oftentimes devising and framing that which will not stand. For all shall come to nothing that proceeds not from God. Forsake all and you shall find The All, leave all of your useless desires and you will find rest."

SELF-LOVE: A Constant Enemy to Doing God's Will

"The fire often burns, but the flame ascends not without smoke. So also some people's desires are on fire after heavenly things, and yet they are not free from the temptation of carnal affection. And therefore it is not altogether purely for God's honor that they act when they so earnestly petition him. For that is not pure and perfect which is infected with self-interest." (Thomas a Kempis; p. 327)

SELF-LOVE: The Perfect Victory Over Self-Love

"The perfect victory comes when in striving to do God's will we triumph over all self-love. This vice, self-love, the breeding ground for all vices, by which a man inordinately loves himself, is at the bottom of all that which is to be rooted out and overcome in one's soul; which evil, that of self-love being once conquered and brought under control, there then comes a great peace and tranquillity in the soul." (Thomas a Kempis; p. 347)

SELF-LOVE: Beseeching God for Protection Against Self-Love

"Grant dear Lord that I may prudently avoid him that flatters me." (Thomas a Kempis; p. 252)

SOUL: Encouraging Interior Sorrow

"It is good to ask God for the gift of tears whereby we weep silently within the interior of our soul praying thus: 'Feed me, O Lord, with the bread of tears and give me drink of tears in good measure.'" (Thomas a Kempis; p. 73)

SOUL: Power of a Pure Heart

"A pure heart has the power to understand many of the mysteries of heaven and hell." (Thomas a Kempis; p. 115)

SOUL: Watch Your Own Soul Above All

"A person interiorly truly recollected in heart prefers looking at himself before all else as regards his sinful nature, and when he does so remains easily silent as regards the faults of others. If one concentrates on wholly doing God's will he will preoccupy himself very little with what goes on in the affairs of others.

SOUL: Its Various Manifestations in Our Daily Life

"As long as you live you are subject to change, even against your will; sometimes you will be joyful, at other times sad; now relaxed and carefree, then troubled; now devout, at another time dry; sometimes fervent, at other times sluggish; one day heavy, another light." (Thomas a Kempis; p. 274)

SOUL: Greed, a Great Enemy

" For a small wordly gain man will labor and toil, but the loss of the soul is little thought of. (Thomas a Kempis; p. 306)

SOUL: Its Nourishment, Food and Light

"While I am kept in the prison of this body I acknowledge myself to need two things, namely, food and light. You have therefore given to me, weak as I am, your Sacred Body, for the nourishment of my soul and body, and you have set your word as a lamp to my feet. Without these two I could not well live, for the word of God is the light of my soul and your Sacrament is the bread of life." (Thomas a Kempis; p. 428)

SPIRITUAL DIRECTION: Death and the Brevity of Life

"Act as if one were to die immediately. Thus, we should some mornings imagine that we shall not live till night; and when evening comes we should not presume that we will arise in the morning. Let death never find me unprepared in not a morbid state of mind but a healthy attitude of preparation." (Thomas a Kempis; p. 79-81)

SPIRITUAL DIRECTION: Making Saints, Friends in This Life

"Honor the saints in this life by imitating their actions prudently according to one's state in life, that even though you may seem to have failed in this life, they will welcome you into their eternal dwelling." (Thomas a Kempis; p. 83-84)

SPIRITUAL DIRECTION: Patience, a Great Virtue

"A patient man receiving injuries is more concerned at the person's sins than the wrong done to him; he willingly prays for his adversaries and from his heart forgives offenses; he delays not to ask forgiveness of others; who is easier moved to compassion than to anger, he frequently strongly disciplines his soul, and labors to bring the flesh wholly subject to the spirit." (Thomas a Kempis; p. 86)

SPIRITUAL DIRECTION: Mortification, Relishing God

"When one arrives at the stage of spiritual development that he seeks comfort from nothing created by God, but only from God, then he will begin to perfectly relish or taste God."

SPIRITUAL DIRECTION: Trust, Mainly In God

"We cannot trust too much in ourselves, because we often want grace and understanding." (Thomas a Kempis; p. 117)

SPIRITUAL DIRECTION: Glorying In Tribulation

"To glory in tribulation is not hard to him that loves for so to glory is to glory in the Cross of our Lord." (Thomas a Kempis; p.121)

SPIRITUAL DIRECTION: Sin, A Wholesome Fear

"Fear nothing so much, blame nothing so much as thy vices and sins, which ought to displease thee more than any losses whatsoever." (Thomas a Kempis; p. 169)

SPIRITUAL DIRECTION: Seeking an Excessive Knowledge of God

"Some persons walk not sincerely before me; but being led by a certain curiosity and pride, desire to know the hidden things of My providence and to understand the high things of God, neglecting themselves and their own salvation. These often fall into great temptations and sins through their pride and curiosity, because I stand against them. Presume not to examine the works of the Most High, but search into thine own sinfulness of soul." (Thomas a Kempis; p. 169)

SPIRITUAL DIRECTION: Perseverance Throughout Life

" Fight like a good soldier, and if sometimes you fall through frailty rise up again with greater strength than before, confiding in My more abundant grace, take great care you do not yield to any vain complacency and pride." (Thomas a Kempis; p. 182)

SPIRITUAL DIRECTION: Devotion, Imprudence to be Avoided

"Some, wanting discretion, have ruined themselves by reason of the grace of devotion, because they were more desirous of doing more than they could, not weighing well the measure of their own weakness, but following rather the inclinations of the emotions of their heart than of reason." (Thomas a Kempis; p. 182)

SPIRITUAL DIRECTION: Prudence, Evaluation of Choices of Action

"Every inclination which appears good should not be immediately taken nor is every contrary inclination to a course of action to be immediately rejected." (Thomas a Kempis; p. 196)

SPIRITUAL DIRECTION: Devil, Prayer the Best Weapon Against His Attacks

"The old serpent will tempt thee and give you trouble, but by prayer he shall be put to flight; moreover, by keeping yourself always employed in useful labor his access to you shall be in great measure impeded." (Thomas a Kempis; p. 201)

SPIRITUAL DIRECTION: Peace, Achieving a Tranquillity of Heart

"That person has great tranquillity of heart who cares neither for praise or criticism except in so far as it instills greater humility in him. You are what you are nor can you be greater than God sees you to be.

Man behold the face, but God looks upon the heart. Man considers the actions, but God weighs the intentions." (Thomas a Kempis; p. 122)

SPIRITUAL DIRECTION: Detachment from All Other Loves

"We must become detached from all that we love, including our most loved ones, prudently, for our Beloved, Jesus will be loved alone above everything. He that remains attached to creatures imprudently shall fall with them, but he that wholly with all his heart embraces Jesus shall stand firm forever. Jesus is of such a divine nature that He will admit of no other love to compete with love for Him, but will have thy heart to Himself, and sit there like a King upon his throne." (Thomas a Kempis; p. 125)

SPIRITUAL DIRECTION: Patience and the Cross

"Dispose yourself to patience rather than consolation, and to bear the cross rather than to rejoice." (Thomas a Kempis; p. 136)

SPIRITUAL DIRECTION: Divine Consolations

"No person can enjoy divine consolations as they would wish, because the time of temptation is not long absent. What very much opposes these heavenly visits, consolations, is a false liberty of mind and a great confidence in one's self. In a number of instances the reason why the gifts of grace cannot flow in us, is because we are ungrateful to the giver, nor do we return all to the fountainhead of these gifts, these living waters, God. For grace will always be given to one who duly returns thanks to God, and what is given to the humble will be taken away from the proud."

SPIRITUAL DIRECTION: Warfare of Life

"Who wages a greater warfare in life than he who by the grace and love of God strives to overcome himself. This warfare should be our daily business." (Thomas a Kempis; p. 12)

SPIRITUAL DIRECTION: Trust in God

"Do not place your trust in yourself but in God alone."

SPIRITUAL DIRECTION: God Our Foundation, Our Rock

"A person should be so grounded in Jesus Christ that he have no need of seeking many comforts from men."

SPIRITUAL DIRECTION: Why We are Disturbed When Our Opinions are Resisted

"Because God is not always the object of our desire we at times are disturbed at resistance to our opinions."

SPIRITUAL DIRECTION: God's Will is Paramount

"God will have us to be perfectly subject to Himself and to transcend all reason by inflamed love for Him." (Thomas a Kempis; p.45)

SPIRITUAL DIRECTION: Admonition, Correcting Others

"If anyone being admonished once or twice does not comply do not become contentious but leave the matter in God's Hand for His will to work out." (Thomas a Kempis; p. 50)

SPIRITUAL DIRECTION: Leading a Spiritual Life

"Quite often we must become ready to be made a fool for Christ in striving to do His will." (Thomas a Kempis; p. 53)

SPIRITUAL DIRECTION: Controlling Carnal Desires of the Flesh

"Place a bridle on the wild horse of gluttony and you will thereby restrain all carnal inclinations." (Thomas a Kempis; p.61)

SPIRITUAL DIRECTION: An Idle Mind is the Devil's Storehouse

"It is wisdom to not be altogether idle, but either reading or writing, praying, meditating, or contemplating, or laboring for something that may be for the common good." (Thomas a Kempis; p. 62)

SPIRITUAL DIRECTION: Be Always Watchful and Alert

"Blessed is that servant, says the Evangelist whom, when his Lord shall come He shall find watching. Amen, I say to you He shall set him over all his possessions." (Thomas a Kempis; p. 63)

SPIRITUAL DIRECTION: Personal Obstacles

"There is one thing which keeps many back from spiritual progress and fervent amendment of life; and that is, dread of difficulty, or the labor which must be gone through in the conflict." (Thomas a Kempis; p. 93)

SPIRITUAL DIRECTION: Spiritual Warfare, Perseverance

"He that is persevering, diligent and zealous in warring against his vices, although he may have more of them to contend with, will be able to make more rapid progress in his spiritual development than another person who has fewer vices to contend with but is less persevering, diligent and zealous in the pursuit of virtue. In this warfare victory is won by withdrawing from that vice(s) which one's human nature is viciously inclined to, and to earnestly labor for that virtue(s) which one wants most. It is prudent to concentrate within one's own soul on those faults which one finds displeasing in others."

SPIRITUAL DIRECTION: Spiritual Wisdom

"It is a greater task to resist vices and discipline the passions than to toil at bodily labors. He that does not eliminate small defects little by little begins to acquire great defects." (Thomas a Kempis; p. 97)

SPIRITUAL DIRECTION: Attainment of Peace

"To be a good peacemaker one must be at peace in his own soul." (Thomas a Kempis; p. 111)

SPIRITUAL DIRECTION: Warfare of Life

"A person must go through a long and great conflict in himself before he can learn fully to overcome himself, and to draw his whole affection to God."

SPIRITUAL DIRECTION: Fear, a Waste of Time

"What does solicitude about the future accidents bring you but only sorrow upon sorrow. Sufficient to the day is the evil thereof." (Thomas a Kempis; p.263)

SPIRITUAL DIRECTION: God Speaks to the Soul

"You are never secure in this life; but as long as you live you always have need of spiritual arms. You are in the midst of enemies and being assaulted on the right hand and on the left. If you do not fix your heart on Me with a sincere will of suffering all things for the love of Me you will not be able to support the heat of this warfare, and you will not be able to attain to the victory of the saints. I advise you therefore to strive to go through all courageously, with fortitude and determination, and to use a strong hand against all that wages warfare upon your soul. If you seek rest in this warfare of life, how then will you come to rest in the eternal life. Seek true rest and peace, not upon earth, but in heaven; not in men, nor in other things created, but in God alone. Learn then, My dear one, to suffer all things, namely: labors and sorrows, temptations and vexations, anxieties, necessities, sickness, injuries, detractions, reprehensions, humiliations, confusion, correction, and contempt. I will reward you most abundantly, and will be with you in all your tribulations and trials." (Thomas a Kempis; pp. 281-282)

SPIRITUAL DIRECTION: Fear, Its Elimination

"He that trusts in Me will be free from the fear of men." (Thomas a Kempis; p. 313)

SPIRITUAL DIRECTION: Repentance Brings Pardon and Grace

"If a man does his best, and is truly penitent, as often as he shall come to Me for pardon and grace, as I live says the Lord, I desire not the death of the sinner, but that he should be converted from his way and live." (Thomas a Kempis; p. 413)

SPIRITUAL DIRECTION: Daily Life's Imperfections

Thomas a Kempis observes, and I summarize a number of his thoughts, that: All of our ostensibly perfect daily actions are often accompanied by some element of imperfection.

SPIRITUAL DIRECTION: Warfare in Disciplining Our Passions

"It is by disciplining our passions (joy, hope, sorrow, fear, and so forth) that we find a true peace of heart." (Thomas a Kempis; p.34)

SPIRITUAL DIRECTION: Talents, Avoidance of False Pride in Them

"Do not take pride in your ability or talent, lest you displease God who is the giver of abilities and talents." (Thomas a Kempis; p. 22)

SPIRITUAL DIRECTION: Prudence to be Exercised in Confiding to Others

" Do not open your heart's secrets to every one but only to a person who is wise and has a holy fear of God." (Thomas a Kempis; p.25)

SPIRITUAL DIRECTION: Socializing

"Do not socialize too much with young people or with strangers." {NOTE: Because of the wisdom which many young people lack; and the fact that unless you know a person well enough he may easily draw you into sin, or his unknown imperfections and weaknesses will leave a mark upon your soul} (Thomas a Kempis; p.8)

SPIRITUAL DIRECTION: Speaking with a Purpose

"If it be appropriate and necessary to speak, speak those words which will be enlightening."

SPIRITUAL DIRECTION: Vices, Struggle Against

"If every year we rooted out one vice we should soon become perfect men." (Thomas a Kempis; p. 34)

SPIRITUAL DIRECTION: Adversity in This World

"Perfect security and full peace cannot be found in this world." (Thomas a Kempis; p. 36)

SPIRITUAL DIRECTION: Trials, to be Expected Throughout Life

"All the saints have passed through many tribulations and temptations and have profited by them. As long as we live in this world we cannot be without tribulation and temptation. The life of man upon this earth is a temptation. (Thomas a Kempis; p.39)

SPIRITUAL DIRECTION: Habits, not Easily Broken

"Old habits which are spiritually harmful or potentially harmful are discarded or modified with difficulty; good habits have no problem."

SPIRITUAL DIRECTION: Resolutions to Do Good

"The resolutions of the just depend on the grace of God, rather than on their own wisdom; they place all of their trust in God in whatever they apply their hands and will to."

SPIRITUAL DIRECTION: Recollection, Withdrawing Daily Into the Interior of Our Heart.

"It is good to recollect ourselves at the least once a day, morning or evening. In the morning make your resolution and in the evening examine how you have fulfilled it." (Thomas a Kempis; p. 61)

SPIRITUAL DIRECTION: Socializing, One Spiritual Perspective

"The greatest saints avoided socializing excessively, when necessary out of expedience and charity in doing God's will they socialized as necessary. Whoever desires to arrive at interior, spiritual purity of heart must in imitation of Jesus go aside from the crowd prudently at appropriate times." (Thomas a Kempis; p.65)

SPIRITUAL DIRECTION: Solitude, Benefits of Prudent Relationships

"God with his holy angels will draw near to those who withdraw themselves from excessive, waste of time with acquaintances and friends." (Thomas a Kempis; p.67)

SPIRITUAL DIRECTION: Caution Against Excessive Unnecessary Travel

"It often happens that a joyful going abroad often brings forth a sorrowful coming home, or as the expression has it a merry evening makes a sad morning. The heavens and the earth and all the elements are the same wherever we go. However, an occasional prudent change of scenery, vacation or recreation is good for the soul." (Thomas a Kempis; p. 68)

SPIRITUAL DIRECTION: Eliminating Bad Habits

"Bad habits are best overcome by replacing them with good habits." (Thomas a Kempis; p. 71)

SPIRITUAL DIRECTION: Priorities

"If human beings would exert as much effort in rooting out vices and planting virtues as they do in the pursuit of knowledge there would not be so much evil in this world." (Thomas a Kempis; p.13)

SPIRITUAL DIRECTION: Human Relations, and Charity and Tensions

"It is no great thing to be able to converse with them that are good and meek, for this is naturally pleasing to all. But to live peacefully with those that are harsh and perverse, or disorderly, or such as oppose us, is a great grace, and highly commendable and manly." (Thomas a Kempis; p.113)

SPIRITUAL DIRECTION: Compassion, Forbearance Towards Others

"We must support one another, comfort one another, assist, instruct and admonish one another." (Thomas a Kempis; p. 49)

SPIRITUAL DIRECTION: Amending One's Life to the Good

"What we cannot amend for the good in ourselves or others we must bear with patience until God ordains otherwise. In the meantime pray to God perseveringly." (Thomas a Kempis; p. 50)

SPIRITUAL DIRECTION: Compassion, Patience is Crucial

"Be patient in supporting the defects and infirmities of others, always remember how others must exercise patience as regards your own weaknesses. We would have others perfect but do not correct our own defects. We would have others strictly corrected but are not willing to have ourselves collected. It is evident how seldom many of us apply the same standards of good conduct to ourselves that we apply to others." (Thomas a Kempis; p. 56)

SPIRITUAL DIRECTION: Adversity, Its Value

"Adversity shows us how great our virtues are, they do not weaken us but show us what we may be lacking in virtue in doing the will of God at all times." (Thomas a Kempis; p. 16)

SPIRITUAL DIRECTION: Virtues, Interior and Exterior

"The life of a good spiritual man ought to be strong in all the virtues, he should be such interiorly in his soul as he appears to others exteriorly." (Thomas a Kempis; p.60)

SPIRITUAL DIRECTION: A Healthy Attitude Towards Death

"It is better to think prudently about death than a long life, for in doing so we more fervently amend our lives for the good. Thoughts at appropriate times on hell and purgatory will make us more willingly endure labor and pain and fear no kind of austerity."

SPIRITUAL DIRECTION: Vice, Overcoming It

"Unless one wages a violent war against one's vices they will not be eliminated." (Thomas a Kempis; p. 97)

SPIRITUAL DIRECTION: A Warfare, a Spiritual Perspective

" One must always preserve a good and firm hope of winning the victory; but must not think oneself secure lest one becomes negligent or proud during this warfare of life." (Thomas a Kempis; p. 92)

SPIRITUAL DIRECTION: Prudence, Sage Advice

"Always remember your end and that time once lost never returns." (Thomas a Kempis; p.103)

SPIRITUAL DIRECTION: The Presence of God

"All the glory and beauty of God is in the interior of the soul and there is where He is most pleased to reign." (Thomas a Kempis; p.103)

SPIRITUAL DIRECTION: God's Will is Paramount

"Be not much concerned who is for thee or against thee, but let it be thy concern only that God may be with thee in everything you do. Have a good conscience, and God will sufficiently defend thee. For He whom God will help no man's malice can hurt." (Thomas a Kempis; p.109)

SPIRITUAL DIRECTION: Creatures, Beauty of God's Creation

"If your heart is right, then every creature would be to you a mirror of life and a book of holy doctrine. There is no creature so little and contemptible as not to manifest the will of God." (Thomas a Kempis; p. 115)

SPIRITUAL DIRECTION: Peace, Interior Liberty

"If you seek nothing but the will of God and the love of your neighbor, you shall enjoy interior liberty." (Thomas a Kempis; p. 115)

SPIRITUAL DIRECTION: Obedience, a Challenge to Our Virtues

"It is a great achievement to be subject to obedience to a superior authority and a challenge to our virtues. In such situations of obedience if God is with us we must sometimes give up our own opinion to find peace. Although our opinion be good, yet if for God's sake we withhold it to follow that of another it will be more profit to our soul. Refusing to yield to others, even though one's opinion may be just as good can be a sign of pride and unyielding will." (Thomas a Kempis; pp 27-28)

SPIRITUAL DIRECTION: Speech, Avoiding Contentious Discourses

"It is more profitable to turn your eyes away from such things as displease thee, and to leave everyone his own way of thinking, than to give way to contentious discourses." (Thomas a Kempis; p.307)

SPIRITUAL DIRECTION: Criticism, a Healthy Perspective

"Stand firm and trust in Me says the Lord; for what are words; they fly through the air but hurt not a stone. If you are guilty, think that you will willingly amend yourself. If your conscience accuse you not, think that you will willingly suffer this for God's sake." (Thomas a Kempis; p. 314)

SPIRITUAL DIRECTION: Criticism, a Healthy Perspective

"If all should be said against you which the malice of man can invent what hurt could it do thee if you let it pass and ignore it, and take no account of it. Could it even so much as pluck one hair from your head. The just man will not care if anything is wrongfully pronounced against him, for he knows that it is I, the Lord, who sees into the innermost depths of each heart." (Thomas a Kempis; 307)

SPIRITUAL DIRECTION: The Saints, Our Models

"If we could see the everlasting crown of the saints in heaven, we would be glad to suffer tribulations for God's sake." (Thomas a Kempis; p. 317)

SPIRITUAL DIRECTION: Commandments, Loving God

"He that has My commandments, and obeys them, he it is that loves Me; and I will love him and manifest Myself to him, and I will make him sit with Me in the Kingdom of My Father." (Thomas a Kempis; p.361)

SPIRITUAL DIRECTION: The Holy Sacrifice of the Mass, Our Personal Offering of Our Hearts Also

"As I willingly offered myself to God, My Father for your sins, with My hand stretched out upon the cross, so you too must willingly offer yourself daily to Me in the Mass, for a pure and holy oblation, together with all your powers and affections, as intimately as you are able to offer yourself to Me, and give your whole self to Me and your offering will be accepted." (Thomas a Kempis; p.415)

SPIRITUAL DIRECTION: Peace of Heart, How to Achieve It

"Endeavor to do the will of another than your own. Choose always to have less than more. Always seek the lowest place and to be inferior to everyone. Always wish and pray that the will of God may be entirely fulfilled in you."

SPIRITUAL DIRECTION: Honor, Avoiding Vanity

"Be not solicitous for the shadow of a great name. Neither seek to be familiarly acquainted with many, nor to be particularly loved by men. For these things lead one astray and to a great darkness in the heart." (Thomas a Kempis; p.243)

SPIRITUAL DIRECTION: World, a Constant Warfare

"To never feel any trouble, nor to suffer any grief of heart or pain of body, is not the state of this present life, but of everlasting rest." (Thomas a Kempis; p.246)

SPIRITUAL DIRECTION: Flesh, Its Burdens

"Eating, drinking, clothing, and other necessaries which pertain to the support of a body are burdensome to a fervent spirit. Grant that I may use such things with moderation, and not be entangled with any inordinate affection. It is not lawful to cast them all away, for nature must be supported. But to luxuriate foolishly in anything beyond these basic needs is not spiritually prudent, for then the flesh would rebel against the spirit." (Thomas a Kempis; p. 251)

SPIRITUAL DIRECTION: The Devil, His Wiles

"He cares not whether it be with things true or false that he abuses and deceives you, whether he overthrow you with the love of things present or the fear of things to come." (Thomas a Kempis; p. 263)

SPIRITUAL DIRECTION: God's Will Should be Paramount In

Dealings With Others

"He who seeks not to please men, nor fear their displeasure, shall enjoy much peace." (Thomas a Kempis; p. 257)

SUFFERING: The Cross, Carriers of the Cross

"The higher a person is advanced in spirit, the heavier crosses shall he often meet with, because the pain of his banishment increases in proportion to his love. When you have arrived so far spiritually in soul that tribulation becomes sweet and savory to you for the love of Christ, then think that it is well with you, for you have found a paradise on earth. If indeed, there had been anything better and more beneficial to man's salvation than suffering, Christ certainly would have showed it by word and example. Jesus, Himself, shows us the way of the cross, saying: 'If any one will come after Me, let him deny himself and take up his cross and follow Me.'" (Thomas a Kempis; p. 152)

SUFFERING: Patience, the Truly Patient Man

"The truly patient man minds not by whom it is he is exercised, whether by his superior, or by one of his equals, or by an inferior; whether by a good and holy man, or by one that is perverse and unworthy. Nothing, how little soever it may be, that is suffered for God's sake, does not pass without merit in the sight of God."

SUFFERING: The Cross, Bearing It with Fortitude

"Lord, I have received the cross, I have received if from Thy hand; I will bear it, yes, I will bear it until death, as you have laid it upon me. Indeed the life of a good religious man is a cross, but it is a cross that conducts him to paradise. We have now begun the warfare of carrying the cross, it is not prudent to turn away from carrying it, nor is it wisdom to stop carrying it. Therefore, take courage and let us go forward together carrying the cross. Behold our King, Jesus, marches before us Who is our captain and leader, He will fight for us. Let us follow Him manfully; let no one shrink through fear; let us be ready to die valiantly in battle, and not stain our glory by flying from the standard of the cross." (Thomas a Kempis; p. 362)

SUFFERING: Peace, Where to Find It

"All our peace in this miserable life is rather to be placed in humble sufferings than in not feeling adversities. He who knows how to suffer will enjoy much peace. Such a one is a conqueror of himself and lord of the world, a friend of Christ and an heir of heaven." (Thomas a Kempis; p.113)

SUFFERING: The Cross, Love for Jesus

"Jesus has many lovers of his heavenly Kingdom but few that are willing to bear His cross. Many love Jesus as long as they meet with no adversity. Many praise Him and bless Him as long as they receive consolation from Him. But if Jesus hides Himself, and leaves them for a little while, they either fall into complaints or excessive dejection. There are some lovers of Jesus who, if He should never give them consolation, they would still always praise Him and always give Him thanks. It is not easy to find a person who would serve God gratis." (Thomas a Kempis; p.141-142)

SUFFERING: The Cross, Following Jesus Christ

"Take up thy cross and follow Jesus. In the cross is salvation, in the cross is life; in the cross is protection from thy enemies. In the cross is infusion of heavenly sweetness; in the cross is strength of mind; in the cross is joy of spirit. In the cross is the height of virtue; in the cross is the perfection of sanctity. There is no health of soul nor hope of eternal life but in the cross. If you carry the cross willingly, it will carry thee and bring thee to thy desired end; namely, to that place where there will be an end of suffering, though here there will be no end. If you carry it unwillingly you make it a burden for yourself and thus make it heavier, but still you will have to carry it. If you fling away one cross, without doubt you will find another and perhaps a heavier one. Do not think that you can escape that which no mortal could ever avoid." (Thomas a Kempis; pp 145, 146, 147)

SUFFERING: State of All Human Nature

"There is no person on this earth without some trouble or affliction. Who is it then who is most at ease in the midst of suffering? He who is willing to suffer some affliction for God's sake." (Thomas a Kempis; p. 22)

SUFFERING: Take Advantage of Healthy Times

"When one is well many good things can be accomplished, but when one is sick many activities must be curtailed, for human nature is such that few persons are improved by sickness." (Thomas a Kempis; p. 82)

TEMPTATION: Positive Aspects

"Temptations are often very profitable to a man although they be troublesome and grievous; for in them a man is humbled, purified, and instructed. A person is never entirely secure from temptation as long as he lives; because we have within us the source of temptation, having been born in sin." (Thomas a Kempis; p.39)

TEMPTATION: Coping with It

"In temptation often take counsel. Deal not roughly with one who is tempted; but comfort him as you would desire to be comforted when temptation assails you." (Thomas a Kempis; p. 40)

TEMPTATION: Alertness at Its Beginning

"We must be especially alert at the beginning of a temptation, because then the enemy is easily overcome if he is not permitted to enter the door of the soul but is kept out and resisted at the first knock." (Thomas a Kempis; p. 40-41)

TEMPTATION: Its Progressive Nature

"In temptation first a thought comes to the mind; then a strong imagination; afterwards delight in the temptation, an evil motion towards it and finally consent to it." (Thomas a Kempis; p.41)

TEMPTATION: Its Variation

"Some suffer temptations early in life, some towards the end of their life, and some person are much troubled by temptations in varied ways all of their lifetimes." (Thomas a Kempis; p. 41)

TEMPTATION: Prayer, a Powerful Weapon Against It

"We must not despair when tempted but pray to God with so much more fervor. God will dispose of the temptation that we may be able readily to cope with it." (Thomas a Kempis; p. 41)

TEMPTATION: Great and Small

"Some persons are protected by God from great temptations and are often overcome by little ones; thus, being humbled, they do not become presumptuous as regards great temptations who find themselves weak as regards little temptations." (Thomas a Kempis; p. 42)

TEMPTATION: Casting Off Despondency

"All is not lost if you feel yourself often afflicted, or grievously tempted. You are a man and not a god; you are flesh, and not an angel. How can you think that you can continue always in the same state of virtue, when this was not found in the angels of heaven, nor in the first man in paradise." (Thomas a Kempis; p. 365)

TEMPTATION: Its Benefits

"Heavenly comfort is promised to such as have been proved by temptation. To him that overcomes, says the Lord, I will give of the tree of life. Divine consolation is given that a man may be better able to support adversities, and temptation follows that he may not be proud of it." (Thomas a Kempis; p.135)

TRUTH: Elimination of Confusion

"He to whom the Eternal Word, Jesus Christ speaks is freed from a multitude of opinions." (THOMAS a KEMPIS; p.10)

TRUTH: Elusive Without Christ

"Our reasoning and our senses often deceive us without Christ's enlightenment." (THOMAS a KEMPIS; p.11)

TRUTH: A Guiding Prayer

"O Truth, my God, make me one with thee in eternal love." (THOMAS a KEMPIS; p.11)

VANITY: Of Life

"Vanity of vanities and all is vanity except to love God and serve Him alone." (THOMAS a KEMPIS;p.6)

VANITY: The True Objective of Life

"It is vanity to seek riches, honors, lusts of the flesh, to wish for a long life, to excessively concentrate on this present life. The true objective of life is to concentrate on the heavenly kingdom, God and His love for us and our love for Him." (THOMAS a KEMPIS ; p. 6)

VANITY: Without God All in This World is Nothing

"All then is vanity but to love God and to serve Him alone." (THOMAS a KEMPIS; p.4)

WISDOM: The Highest Wisdom

"The highest wisdom is to despise the world and to concentrate on heavenly kingdoms." (THOMAS a KEMPIS; p.6)

WISDOM: Jesus Christ, the Perfect Truth

"I counsel you to buy of Me gold fire-tried, that you may be made rich, that is heavenly wisdom, which treads under foot all things below. Set aside earthly wisdom, all human and self-love satisfactions, and you will find Me the perfect wisdom, the perfect truth, the supreme perfect love." (THOMAS a KEMPIS; p.272)

WORLD: A Realistic Perspective

"He that seeks in this world any other thing than purely God and the salvation of his soul will find nothing but trouble and sorrow. Here it is that men are tried, as gold in the furnace." (THOMAS a KEMPIS; pp 53-54)

WORLD: A Spiritual Perspective of Saints

"The saints hated their lives in this world that they might possess them for eternity. They labored all the day and in the night they gave themselves to prayer. They were strangers to the world, but near and familiar friends to God." (THOMAS a KEMPIS; pp.56, 55)

WORLD: Spiritual Development

"The more one desires to grow spiritually the more this world becomes distasteful to him; for he then better understands the defects of human corruption. For the inward spiritual man is much burdened with the necessities of the body in this world. The saints of God, their hopes and actions in this world were an aspiration of eternal goods." (THOMAS a KEMPIS; pp.75-76)

***WORLD*:** Followers of the World

"The greater number listen more to the world than to God, and more readily follow the desires of the flesh that the will of God. Who is it that serves and obeys God in all things with that great care which the the world and its lords are served? For small living men run a great way, for eternal life many will scarce move a single foot from the ground." (THOMAS a KEMPIS; pp163-164)

***WORLD*:** Its False Attraction

"If you desire too inordinately these present things you will lose those that are heavenly and everlasting. You cannot be satisfied with any temporal good, because you were not created for the enjoyment of such things. Although you should have all created goods, yet this could not make you happy and blessed; but in God, who created all things your blessings and happiness consist."

St. John of the Cross

Source:
The Collected Works
of
St. John of The Cross
Translated by
Kieran Kavanaugh, O.C.D.
and
Otilio Rodriguez, O.C.D.
ICS Publications
Institute of Carmelite Studies
Washington, D.C.
1979; pp 1 - 774

Imprimi Potest: Christopher Latimer, O.C.D.
Provincial

Nihil Obstat: Kevin Culligan, O.C.D. and Jerome Flynn, O.C.D.
Censores Deputati

Imprimatur: Patrick A. O'Boyle, Archbishop of Washington
October 23, 1963

ISBN 0 -9600876 - 5 - 6
Library of Congress Catalog Card Number 78 - 65789

St. John of the Cross

Second Edition 1979 by ICS Publications
Institute of Carmelite Studies
2131 Lincoln Road, Northeast
Washington, D.C. 20002

General Survey of His Life and Works

The spiritual direction of St. John of the Cross, the "Sanjuanist Spirituality" is so unique and so systematically presented, with its wealth of specific detailed explanation of each fundamental principle of spiritual direction in his one-volume *Collected Works*, that it would be impractical to present his spiritual direction in this chapter as I have presented that of St. Francis of Sales, ST. TERESA OF AVILA, and Thomas a Kempis. Instead, I enthusiastically recommend that the reader procure this volume. He will find there rich treasures of spiritual direction, beautifully presented and superbly translated from the original writings of St. John of the Cross by the good Rev. Fathers Otilio Rodriguez, O.C.D. and Kieran Kavanaugh, O.C.D.

After about seven years of prayerful reading and study of these *Works*, and with an intensive analysis of their practical application in one's daily life, I decided to undertake a personal "apostolate" of my own. Its objective was to bring to a broader readership the rich treasures of spiritual wisdom of this very beautiful saint and brilliantly learned spiritual director, so gifted by the grace and love of God. In undertaking this apostolate I was exceedingly fortunate to have the Rev. Fathers of the Carmelite Order, San Jose, CA and the daughters of St. Paul, Boston, MA publish two of my articles on St. John of the Cross. I cite this fact, because the first article "A Spiritual Director for All Time for All" (*Carmelite Digest*, Autumn 1989; pp. 19 - 32) is, in essence, a detailed summary of the main spiritual principles underlying the "Sanjuanist Spirituality" as described throughout the entire one volume. My objective was to delineate the "skeletal structure" of this unique spirituality, and thereby to serve as an introductory piece for the reader who had not as yet started to read the entire *Collected Works*. It was an attempt to literally build a good foundation for the reader, thereby removing many of the analytical, technical difficulties confronting the reader at his first exposure to the *Works* of St. John of the Cross. The other article "Spiritual Development of St. John of the Cross" (*Inner Horizons* - a magazine of spirituality, Fall 1989; pp. 42 - 44) was a continuation of that effort, containing St. John of the Cross' classic explanation of the true nature of contemplative prayer.

Not For Those With "A Spiritual Sweet Tooth"

St. John of the Cross frankly stated that his spiritual direction was not designed to satisfy those who had a mere "spiritual sweet tooth". He meant that the prayerful reading, study, absorption, and actually putting into daily practice the fundamental principles of his spiritual direction would not come easy. Diligent prayerful reading, rereading and perseverance would be required throughout the reading. Despite this admonition he did provide encouragement and inspiration by stating that if the readers of his works would persevere through a number of readings, they would be well rewarded. He emphasized very strongly that although not everything found in his works would be applicable to all of its readers, there would be something of considerable value found there for all who would prayerfully apply themselves to their study. It is in this sense that he is truly "A Spiritual Director for All Time for All."

It is very important to know that St. John of the Cross had brought together his *Collected Works* in their written form after he, by the grace and love of God, had attained to the highest spiritual state of perfection possible here on earth, referred to variously as: "The Spiritual Marriage of Love", "The Spiritual Union of Love", or the spiritual state of "A Likeness to God" (Participatory)[1] . In his works we encounter much of Mystical Theology (Secret Wisdom, Secret Understanding, or Secret Knowledge of God). It is termed "Secret" because it is experienced without knowing it. St. John of the Cross affirmed that if anyone were to go through this experience, and were asked to describe it, such a person would be compelled to say as he did, "I don't know what it is."

Catholic Church and St. John of the Cross

St. John of the Cross was declared a Doctor of Mystical Theology by the Catholic Church in 1926 by Pope Pius XI. He had earlier been beatified by Pope Clement X in 1675, and canonized by Pope Benedict XIII in 1726. Because both, his prose and poetry soared in to the realm

1 Participatory, because it will forever be impossible for even God's highest Angels to become like him. However, in a participatory way, by virtue of His grace and love, God allows them to "participate" or to actually share in the possessions of His Divine attributes, for example, goodness, truth, mercy, love, power, and so forth.

of Mystical Theology, he suffered greatly throughout his life because of a lack of understanding of his works in this subject field, and his detailed explanations of the principles of spiritual direction which they contained. His sufferings were very severe not only at the hands of some of the laity of his time, but more importantly so by the clergy within his own Carmelite Order.

Prose and Poetry Examples of His Mystical Theology

I can cite below three passages (two prose , one poetry) reflecting his thinking in Mystical Theology to give the reader a clearer awareness of the profundity

of his thought. In the times in which he lived his brilliance as a spiritual director, and his expressions of it at times in profound Mystical Theology terms very new and unique to many of the readers of his works, confused as well as frightened many upon their first exposure to them. In fact, as the reader of his works will find out, a considerable number of his writings were tragically burned because of the general atmosphere of fear prevalent during his times. The first passage I cite is one in prose in which God (The Bridegroom) is speaking to the soul (His bride) of their espousal (*Collected Works*, pp. 500 - 502):

"This espousal we are dealing with is that which God makes known through Ezechiel by saying to the soul: 'You were cast out upon the earth in contempt of your soul on the day you were born. And passing by you I saw you trodden under foot in your blood. And I said to you as you were in your blood: live and be as multiplied as the grass of the field. Increase and grow great and enter and reach the stature of womanhood, and your breasts grew and your hair increased, and you were naked and full of confusion. And I passed by you and looked at you and saw that your time was the time of lovers, and I held my mantle over you and covered your ignominy. And I swore to you and entered into a pact with you and made you mine. And I washed you with water and cleansed the blood from you and anointed you with oil; and I clothed you in color and shod you with violet shoes, girded you with fine linen and clothed you with fine woven garments. And I adorned you with ornaments, put bracelets on your hands and a chain on your neck. And above your mouth I placed a ring, and I put earrings in your ears and a beautiful crown upon your head. And you were adorned with gold and silver and clothed in fine linen and embroidered silk and many colors. You ate very choice bread and honey and oil, and you became exceedingly beautiful and advanced to rule and be queen. And your name was spread among the people because of your beauty' (1 EZ. 16:5-14). These are the words of Ezechiel. And so it happens with the soul of which we are speaking."

The second prose quotation (*Collected Works*, p. 547) speaks of the soul (the bride) immersed in the ineffable, incomprehensible loving beauty of God (The Bridegroom):

"And let us go forth to behold ourselves in Your beauty, This means: Let us so act that by means of this loving activity we may attain to the vision of ourselves in Your beauty in eternal life. That is: That I be so transformed in Your beauty that we may be alike in beauty, and both behold ourselves in Your beauty, possessing now Your very beauty; this, in such a way that each looking at the other may see in the other his own beauty, since both are Your beauty alone, I being absorbed in Your beauty; hence, I shall see You in Your beauty, and You shall see me in your beauty, and I shall see myself in You in Your beauty, and You will see Yourself in me in Your beauty; that I may resemble You in Your beauty and Your beauty be my beauty; wherefore I shall be You in your beauty, and You will be me in Your beauty, because Your very beauty will be be my beauty; and therefore we shall behold each other in Your beauty."

The third quotation, a poetic example of Mystical Theology, describes the soul (the bride) during its highest stage of a burning love for its God (The Bridegroom). In this state the burning, living hot flames of love for God in the soul leap or fly out upwards from the fire of love for God in the soul as flying sparks or living flames of fire as if they wish to be completely engulfed in the higher burning fire of God's love, as God draws the soul into His most Sacred Heart of Love (*Collected Works*; pp. 717 - 718):

LLAMA DE AMOR VIVA	THE LIVING FLAME OF LOVE
Canciones del alma en la intima communicacion de union de amor de Dios.	Songs of the soul in the intimate communication of loving union with God.
1. !Oh llama de amor viva que tiernamente hieres de mi alma en el mas profundo	1. O living flame of love that tenderly wounds my soul in its deepest center! Since

centro!
Pues ya no eres esquiva,
acaba ya, si quieres:
!rompe la tela de este dulce
encuentro!

now you are not oppresive,
now consummate! if it be your
will:
tear through the veil of this
sweet encounter.

2. !Oh cauterio suave!
!Oh regalada llaga!
!Oh mano blanda! !Oh toque
delicado,
que a vida eterna sabe,
y toda deuda paga!
Matando, muerte en vida la has
trocado.

2. O sweet cautery,
O delightful wound!
O gentle hand! O delicate touch
that tastes of eternal life
and pays every debt!
In killing you changed death to
life.

3. !Oh lamparas de fuego,
en cuyos resplandores
las profundas cavernas del
sentido,
que estaba oscuro y ciego,
con extranos primores
calor y luz dan junto a su
Querido!

3. O lamps of fire!
in whose splendors
the deep caverns of feeling,
once obscure and blind,
now give forth, so rarely, so
exquisitely,
both warmth and light to their
Beloved.

4. !Cuan manso y amoroso
recuerdas en mi seno,
donde secretamente solo moras,
y en tu aspirar sabroso,
de bien y gloria lleno,
cuan delicadamente me
enamoras!

4. How gently and lovingly
you wake in my heart,
where in secret you dwell alone:
and in your sweet breathing,
filled with good and glory, how
tenderly you swell in my heart
with love.

A Spiritual Director For All Time For All

In my article on St. John of the Cross contained at the end of this Chapter (Appendix A), entitled: "St. John of the Cross, A Spiritual Director For All Time for All" I have attempted to explain why he is truly a spiritual director for all. He himself indicated that there would be something valuable to be found in his spiritual direction for all. However, at the same time, he emphasized repeatedly that not everything in his spiritual direction would be applicable to each soul. It is for this reason that persons prayerfully studying his *COLLECTED WORKS* should do so, preferably, under the guidance of competent persons thoroughly knowledgeable as regards the meanings of the principles of spiritual direction of this wonderful saint. This is especially important during the early stages of their spiritual development. St. John of the Cross himself acknowledged, and cautioned the readers of his works of spiritual direction to not get discouraged as they proceed to study them, but to persevere until such time as he stresses, gradually, these principle begin to be clearly understood. Thus, competent spiritual directors will have to be consulted to guide many persons early on as they are exposed to his unique and very enriching principles. Such competence will be especially required to guide persons in the application of these principles to their daily life. This in turn will be contingent on professions in life, their vocations and avocations, their state of life (religious or laity in all faiths), and so forth. Ultimately, St. John of the Cross points out, that by the grace and love of God, many persons hopefully may perhaps reach a stage in their spiritual development when they will no longer have a need to consult so often with their spiritual directors. For, as he clearly indicates that at some point in time, with patience, God, the Holy Spirit, will then become one's spiritual guide. Competent spiritual directors are a must for all during the early stages of their progress.

Sanjuanist Spirituality

The underlying main theme throughout the spiritual direction of St. John of the Cross is that it is not the external actions of the person which will lead him into a true contemplative life described variously as the "Spiritual Union of Love", the "Spiritual Marriage of Love", a transformation into a "State of Likeness" (participatory) with God. It is rather the total destruction of all the self-love of the appetites which exist in the soul for anything that is not God himself. The appetites referred to here are for all those things of the world and flesh, which in anyway whatsoever exclude the love of God. The reference is also to those appetites which become satisfied or satiated with the satanic temptations offered to us in the diabolical manipulations of the world and the flesh offered to us by Satan and his cohorts of devils. Thus, the greatest dangers to the soul come mainly from the self-love from within our own very soul. This self-love is comprised of vices which originate from within our soul's fallen sinful state; a state of proclivity or tendency to sin transmitted from our ancestors through our own human nature. A transmission which passes on original sin with its potentially, devastating effects for the future life.

Obstacles To Spiritual Development

St. John of the Cross states candidly that God would desire that more of His children, His people would arrive at the advanced stages of spiritual development cited above while here on earth. However, he states that it is because they refuse to accept the cross which Jesus Christ offers them, and embrace it wholeheartedly, that they do not arrive at this stage of spiritual development during their lifetime here upon earth. He stresses the importance of accepting the cross of suffering, and actually using it as a support or as a "spiritual crutch" to lean upon in times of great adversity especially. The more the cross is embraced, heavy as it may seem to be, the lighter, paradoxically, it actually will become. By the grace and love of God it will become easier to carry.

Key Aspects of Spiritual Direction

It is impossible to discuss the spiritual direction of St. John of the Cross without an explicit explanation of certain of its salient points. Thus it is necessary to understand his profound exposition of the soul's war against the world, the flesh, and the devil or devils, for there are diverse types of evil spirits which attack the soul. It is also absolutely necessary to clearly understand his differentiation between the involuntary and voluntary appetites of the soul, and their significance as regards the selfish love of the soul as contrasted to a true, pure love of the soul for God alone exclusively. A clear understanding is necessary of his very lucid and simple explanation of the role which meditation and contemplation play in the prayer life of the soul, and of when the true contemplative state of prayer has been achieved (by the grace and love of God), as opposed to the earlier state of meditation. Other aspects of his spiritual direction which are highly significant are his descriptions of the state of meditative-contemplative prayer life whereby the soul moves back and forth between the two states until it arrives at the final state of a true, pure contemplative prayer life. Of paramount importance also throughout his spiritual direction is the role of suffering in imitation of our Lord and Saviour Jesus Christ and of persevering prayer. St. John of the Cross strongly emphasizes that although all sufferings, trials and tribulations of our life have their particular importance in God's eyes, that it is not by them that we are saved but by the blood and suffering of Jesus Christ Himself in dying for us after a lifetime of suffering of His own upon this earth. What God values most is a pure heart reaching out to Him, always seeking out His will and doing it, searching Him out, the incomprehensible God in the very heart of our soul in an ever-growing love. The author's of the *Collected Works* explain thusly:

"St. John of the Cross often urges his readers not to think that his descriptions of God's graces are incredible or sheer exaggerations, for, he insists, 'God diffuses Himself abundantly wherever there is room, and He gladly shows Himself "along the highways and byways", and does not hesitate to share His delights with the children of men.' (F1, 15). He has only one desire for a soul: and that is to exalt it (C28,1). The Saint's descriptions in fact fall far short of the reality. 'Who can express how much God exalts the soul that pleases Him? It is impossible to do so, nor can this even be imagined, for, after all, He does this as God, to show who He is' (C33 8). Why is it then, that so few reach this high state of perfect union with God? St. John of the Cross answers that it is not because God wishes that there be few - He would rather want all to be perfect - but because there are few willing to make room for Him and to bear the trials necessary to reach this state. (F2,27). But neither should one think these trials in themselves are worth anything in God's eyes:'...all our works and all our trials, even though they are the greatest possible, are nothing in the sight of God...through them we cannot give Him anything or fulfill His only will, which is the exaltation of the soul.' (C28.1). If they have value, it is because through them the soul is purified of its evil and imperfect habits and becomes perfect in love, and this love is the means by which God can most exalt it. Since there is no way by which He can exalt her more than by making her equal to Himself, He is pleased only with her love. For the property of love is to make the lover equal to the object loved" (*Collected Works*, pp. 575-576).

St. John of the Cross points out and emphasizes that those who pray to God to raise them to the states of holiness mentioned above must not expect to acheive this having what he terms a "spiritual sweet tooth." He cautions persons such as these that the quest for God means the undertaking of what appear to be impossible human tasks of life. In conjunction with this point, he explains in considerable detail how the soul progresses through a "dark night of the soul" which he discusses as three phases through which the soul must pass in its severe trials, tribulations, and horrible spiritual and other sufferings. These three phases of the "dark night of the soul" are: 1) The Mortification of the Appetites (the twilight phase of the night); 2) The Journey in Faith (the midnight phase of the night); and 3) The Communion of God to the soul (the dawn phase of the night) in a secret, hidden profoundly mystical way of the infusion of His love to the soul.

There are many other aspects of his spiritual direction which I will treat of later throughout this presentation, however, those I have cited above constitute most of the essential ones. I respectfully suggest to the reader that he prayerfully study, meditate, and contemplate what I am describing here, but above all, to himself prayerfully study the actual *Collected Works* of St. John of the Cross - with this very important consideration - namely, that because one soul is so different from another, as he expresses it, sometimes by as much one half, each soul will find something in his spiritual direction which will prove to be of great value to it. However, because as stated earlier not everything in his work of spiritual direction is applicable to each soul, it would be prudent to undertake the prayerful study of his *Works* under the guidance of devout and learned, competent spiritual directors whenever possible.

Sources of His Spiritual Direction Knowledge

One of the best ways to facilitate in the reading of and the profiteering from the spiritual direction of St. John of the Cross is to have a solid grasp of Holy Scripture. In a number of examples throughout his work he explains why this is so, stating that many people often either do not know where to look for the spiritual meanings with which Holy Scripture is replete, but they frequently understand it in its literal sense instead of in its spiritual sense, the more important one. He drew from three different sources in formulating the "Sanjuanist Spirituality:" 1) Holy Scripture; 2) His life experiences; and 3) His knowledge based upon the natural sciences. He makes it quite clear that it was Holy Scripture from which he drew upon most heavily in his chosen apostolate. He had a tremendous love for the Word of God, Holy Scripture. There is a story recounted that while visiting a certain region in

Spain he was invited to go to a certain village to meet a highly respected holy man with prophetic powers. John responded that he would prefer to spend his time in the study of Holy Scripture that day. He was indeed very richly endowed, by the grace and love of God, to interpret what the Holy Spirit is telling us, distilling for us into mere human words of expression the most profound mysteries of the One God, The Holy Trinity. He cites many examples of how the not truly, spiritually developed person will misinterpret Holy Scripture, and give it a literal interpretation instead of the spiritual interpretation. Citing for us many examples, he stresses over and over again how it is the spiritual interpretation of Holy Scripture that is of paramount importance, otherwise the truly devout, prayerful scholar of Holy Scripture will easily fall into the serious error of interpreting what God is telling us, and thereby will spread this error to those he may be teaching the interpretation of Holy Scripture. St. John acknowledges that our knowledge of Holy Scripture as with our knowledge of our own faith will remain an imperfect knowledge. He states candidly that we should not seek precision in matters of faith as we would in our approach to many of the sciences. However, having been a very keen scholar of the works of St. Thomas Aquinas, he has a clear realization that as our faith grows stronger the insights of knowledge that we receive into the divine wisdom of God Himself far surpass the wisdom that we can collect through the study of the natural sciences themselves. Such insights derived from a very strong faith take a quantum leap over the actually very small knowledge which we derive from a study of the natural sciences during a lifetime, no matter how studiously and diligently we may have worked in such studies. However, he drew many spiritual lessons from the other two sources which provided him with valuable insights, and which enabled him to impart very valuable spiritual lessons to others. The quotation below is somewhat indicative of how he draws from nature the materials for his spiritual direction:

"He was willing to give the simple and unlearned as much time as he gave to others. The ease which the humble lay sister, Catalina de la Cruz felt in his presence is evident in the kind of candid questions she asked the holy doctor. Once she inquired why when she went near the pond in the garden the frogs that were on the brink leapt into the water, almost before they could hear the sound of her footsteps and hid themselves in the depths of the pool. Fray John, a master of the spiritual application answered that it was because they felt safe in the depth of the pool and 'that is what you must do-flee from creatures and hide yourself in God.' (pp. 28 - 29, *Collected Works)*

Aspects of the Soul

In his *WORKS* he humbly acknowledges the profound mystery of the soul created in the image of God, when he rhetorically asks: "Who can understand the profound mystery of the soul and its true operations." The soul is pure spirit. It would appear that the soul does not reside in the body, but rather should be considered as being diffused throughout the entire body, so to speak, from head to toe. Having no other choice, it becomes necessary to use worldly terms as instruments for conveying profound thoughts.

Thus, the soul is described by St. John of the Cross as an entity possessed of a superior or upper part, and a lower, or inferior part. In the superior or spiritual part, the occupants or operative faculties would be the memory, the intellect, and the will. The inferior or lower part would be the animal or sensory part of the soul. The inferior part would be the place of entry for all knowledge which comes through the five senses into the soul: touch, taste, smell, hearing , and seeing. The soul from the very time of its conception when the body and soul are fused together by God's Hand is a *tabula rasa*, that is, a clean slate, meaning that there is no natural knowledge which enters the soul which does not come through the senses. Because St. John of the Cross was a keen student of the works of St. Thomas Aquinas, there is implicit in his works of spiritual direction the information, that in addition to the five senses, which are the port of entry for all natural knowledge, there are four internal senses: the imagination, the memory, common sense, and the evaluative sense. The evaluative sense is the sense which enables us to pass judgment upon the goodness or the evil of a course of action presented to us. The imagination, as a result of the first fall into sin of our ancestors Adam and Eve, was one of the internal senses of the soul most damagingly affected. This point is a very critical one, because the angelic spirits, the good spirits, or the evil angelic spirits who fell completely from God's love and grace (the devils) work very considerably through the imagination or the senses, that is the lower or animal operative sensory faculties of the soul.

The intellect and will are inviolate to their attacks, that is those coming from the evil spirits, although they coax and cajole these faculties from outside the soul through the senses and the imagination. Thus, the intellect which is considered to be the noblest operative faculty of the soul - it is called the eye of the soul with its pupil being Faith - and the will are sacrosanct as regards the influence of angelic spirits (good and evil ones) within the soul itself. The will nurtured by the understanding transmitted to it is completely free as to its selection of a course of action towards committing a good or evil act. It is a profound mystery, that although the human soul has free will, yet in a way unknown to us God does move the will (always to the good) without violating the freedom of the will to act.

Who Occupies the Soul

The soul is occupied solely by God. God does not move within the soul, although it would seem to the person that He does so. God, according to St. John of the Cross, occupies the soul in three ways: 1) by His essence; 2) by His grace; and 3) by His spiritual affection for the soul. He remains always in the soul, no matter how hardened it may become in sin. All of these operative faculties cited above in the soul, in both its spiritual (superior) and animal (inferior) nature, interact so profoundly, mysteriously in the soul that it requires the divinely inspired brilliance of a spiritual director such as St. John of the Cross to understand them in order to provide the spiritual direction needed by each individual soul. He, himself, in certain passages of his *Collected Works* prays to God, the Holy Spirit to guide his hand as he writes and explains, lest he not present the profound truths of mystical theology correctly. In the explanations relating to God Himself, he stresses throughout his spiritual direction that we should not take pride in what little we know about God through our Faith, but instead take a true, very humble pride in the profoundly infinite knowledge of God which we do not comprehend or understand and never will. The profundity of this statement can be appreciated in the observation of St. John of the Cross, concerning His absolute supreme perfection (Ens a se). He describes how even the highest of God's angels, those closest to Him around His throne, have a greater knowledge of how much more there is for them to understand about the true nature or essence of God, than those angels further from His celestial throne of glorious majesty. This would also be true of the Blessed Mother of God, Mary, The Immaculate Conception herself, whom Catholics believe was given by God the glorious title of queen of all God's saints and angels. In other words, it is only God Who among His many attributes is also omniscient, omnipotent, omnipresent, is the only One Who knows Himself perfectly in His absolute supreme perfection, has and will throughout all eternity. St. John of the Cross brings out this truth very eloquently in his spiritual direction, when he advises us to constantly strive to contemplate or meditate on the God Who is totally incomprehensible to us, rather that the One of Whom we know so very little indeed as regards His attributes.

Appetites of the Soul - Their Crucial Role in Spiritual Development

There exists involuntary and voluntary appetites which originate from within the soul itself. The involuntary appetites are those which are absolutely necessary to carry on our daily life activities, such as eating, drinking, sleeping, procreation, and so forth. We simply can not dispense with these altogether, although we may attenuate them, for example, by fasting we could firmly discipline the involuntary appetites of eating and drinking. By abstinence or continence we could attenuate or completely discipline the appetite involved in the powerful drive to procreation. The involuntary appetite of drinking can become the voluntary appetite of excessive drinking or intemperance. Within the morally licit state of marriage, or outside of it, the involuntary sexual appetites of healthy God - ordained acts of the procreative drive or instinct can degenerate into the voluntary appetite of using God's gift of sex desires for lustful, immoral purposes, and so forth. He states in his spiritual direction that we must wage a constant war for the health of the soul to prevent the involuntary appetites from evolving into voluntary appetites which then result in sinful acts of conduct, or bad human actions which are contrary to reason and harmful to the soul. Thus, we can readily see the recurrent theme or essence of St. John of the Cross' spiritual direction, namely, that it is not the external things of this world, in whatever form, which do serious damage to the soul, but it is rather the very appetites for them from within the soul that do great harm to the soul. The expression often heard "we are our own worst enemies" contains much truth. Our own worst enemies are the appetites of a self - love in the soul. These enemies go out to devour God's very gifts themselves in sinful conduct while turning away from God Who is the Giver of the gifts. These appetites, sometimes ravenous, sometimes very mild, are not only the result of bad human actions, that is, mortal sin or venial sin, but also of imperfections and weaknesses of our soul inherent in our own fallen human nature. Some examples of such imperfections would be: loquacity of speech, an excessive attachment to some object or place. It could be an excessive preoccupation with spiritual or sacred objects themselves whereby they become little idols in themselves. A condition identified by St. John of the Cross in the Latin phrase *hebetudo mentis* [2] would constitute such a weakness.

Suffering and Prayer - Their Vital Roles

The important value of suffering is stressed in his spiritual direction, that is, the wilful embrace of whatever misfortune may befall us, accepting it from God's hands as a purifier of the soul. He did not believe in suffering for sufferings sake in a stoical fashion. In fact, throughout his life whenever he saw the sufferings of others, he made quick efforts to either alleviate them or to relieve them. He did not believe in harsh or severe penances, self-inflicted ones which he considered could degenerate into a penance of beasts. He stressed the constant reception of the Holy Eucharist as a source of strength accompanied by regular confession as required. He emphasized again and again the power of persevering prayer. Considerable attention in his spiritual direction was given to the principles or modes of prayer, and the vital importance of prudently, cautiously choosing devout and learned spiritual directors. He was especially firmly critical of spiritual directors who undertook to give spiritual advice to persons, but who lacked the necessary abilities and competence to do so.

He emphasized the important distinctions between the prayer of meditation, the prayer of meditation-contemplation, and pure contemplative prayer. He was firmly critical of spiritual directors who, lacking the necessary competence, misguided many souls in their progress through these various stages of prayer. He described very simply and clearly how the soul in its prayer life will engage in meditative prayer and then alternate between meditative and contemplative prayer;

---

2 A natural dullness transmitted through human nature as a result of original sin. It engenders, among other things, a spiritual type of laziness when prayer or the worship and adoration of God is to be undertaken. Those persons striving to improve their prayer life will find this to be a common obstacle to overcome.

and then finally, by the grace and love of God, enter into the stage of purely contemplative prayer. During these alternations in prayer, if the soul does not have good spiritual guidance, or can not guide itself personally, it will not be able to recognize these various stages of prayer. He describes how the soul will know that it is in the stage of pure contemplative prayer, thusly: Three conditions must exist simultaneously: 1) The soul no longer can pray with thoughts of forms, visions, figures or images; 2) The imagination which always wanders often uncontrollably during prayer, although it still continues to wander somewhat, becomes subject to a more firm control by the will. It is, so to speak, reigned in and does not wander so freely; and 3) The prayerful soul in pure contemplative prayer seeks as complete a solitude as it can while praying. Until this stage of pure contemplative prayer is reached, the soul will at times meditate or meditate-contemplate, or move back and forth in these stages until it reaches the final stage of pure contemplative prayer. He points out that under the guidance of incompetent or unqualified spiritual directors, the prayerful soul will frequently be kept in the meditative or meditative-contemplative state of prayer too long, when it should already have arrived at the stage of pure contemplative prayer. He illustrates this by using the analogy of an orange, stating that such souls have already completed the process of peeling the rind or skin from the orange, and are now ready to bite into and taste the succulent fruit itself in pure contemplative prayer. However, they unfortunately will come under the guidance of an unqualified spiritual director who will ask them to peel away again the skin of the orange which has already been peeled away. He thereby keeps them from tasting the sweetness of the fruit in pure contemplative prayer. In other words, such spiritual directors delay or frustrate their tasting of the sweet fruit of the prayer of pure contemplation, which they are already well prepared to do, and thereby they confuse such poor souls in their prayer life, and they regress instead of progressing in their spiritual developments.

Prayer and the Use of Sacred Objects

St. John of the Cross points out that sacred objects (sacramentals) such as statues, religious articles, spiritual relics, crucifixes, rosaries, holy water, and so forth, can play an important role in the spiritual life. However, some people in their prayer life become so attached to these sacred objects that they begin to lose the spiritual benefits they bring.

He explains it thus. In the early stages of the spiritual life - he identifies the stages as beginners, advanced, and proficients - God does lead people to him through such sacred objects. However, as they advance in their prayer life from meditative prayer to meditative-contemplative, and finally into pure contemplative prayer, he emphasizes very strongly that they, upon seeing any of these sacred objects, should immediately raise their hearts (souls) to the hidden, incomprehensible God in heaven Who resides within our own very souls. For He is closer to us than we are to ourselves, but still remains always a hidden God for Whom we should continually search for in our soul. A God Whom we must constantly search out through our prayer life, and through the carrying of our crosses in imitation of Jesus Christ our Saviour. He points out very clearly that when persons sincerely strive for spiritual development and a greater love for God, for holiness, they should avoid the habits of preferring this crucifix to that one because of the quality of wood or metal; or to accumulate rosaries of various types, preferring one to the other because of its colour, metal, size, form and so forth. They begin to accumulate all kinds of statues one after another. In contrast St. John of the Cross affirms that one of the most devout persons he knew had made for himself a rosary of fish bones. Another carried all of his life a simple crucifix made of a palm fastened with a pin.

In following these practices of a habitual attachment to sacred objects considered by them to be more valuable they cease to derive as much spiritual benefit from these sacred objects, than if they had fewer of them. He recommends that they should instead discipline themselves to prayerfully raise their hearts from these sacred objects to the hidden, incomprehensible God. For he cautions, that as such persons excessively attach themselves to sacred objects they are in actuality detaching themselves from a more true, pure love of the hidden God in their hearts and in heaven. He emphasizes, however, lest there be a misinterpretation of what he is advising, that sacred objects are always an aid to raising one's heart closer to God; providing that at a certain stage in one's prayer life, upon seeing these sacred objects, they immediately make a very determined effort to raise their hearts to the ineffable, incomprehensible God.

Enemies of the Soul - World, Flesh, and Devil

St. John of the Cross discusses at great length the many obstacles or pitfalls confronting persons striving for a greater, deeper devotion to

God. Thus, he identifies the three great enemies of the soul as being the world, the flesh, and the devil. He considers the world the most easily of the enemies to overcome through the practise of the supernatural or Godly virtue of hope. He considers the devil to be the most difficult to conquer, because he is the most difficult of these three enemies to understand. He stresses that the greatest enemy of satan or the devil is a pure, strong faith, pointing out that the devil has a terrible fear of a soul truly in love with God. The flesh, he considers to be the most tenacious of the enemies to overcome, emphasizing that it is overcome by the greatest virtue of them all: the Godly or supernatural virtue of love. Within these three principal categories of enemies of the soul he discusses a very large variety of specific other enemies, for example, unqualified or incompetent spiritual directors as mentioned earlier. Such directors he emphasizes can do a person's soul considerable harm, warning that we must always be very prudent in our selection of spiritual directors. Later in this presentation I will elaborate more on these enemies of the soul when I describe the "Dark Night of the Soul" (the twilight, midnight, and dawn phases referred to above).

STAGES OF THE DARK NIGHT OF THE SOUL

Introductions

The reader should bear in mind that St. John of the Cross describes all of these spiritual phenomena after he had gone through the entire three stages of the "The Dark Night of the Soul", and had - by the grace and love of God - attained the "Spiritual Union of Love" or the "Spiritual Marriage of Love"' or to a "Transformation into a Likeness (participatory) with God." He had climbed from the base foothills of the spiritual mountain to its highest pinnacle on top. This is the highest stage of spiritual development possible to any soul before it departs from this earth. It is from the top of this spiritual mountain, therefore, that he is describing in his *Collected Works* the spiritual direction every soul hungers for or seeks. Some saintly souls in this world achieve this "marriage" or "union", or "transformation" by climbing a higher mountain while others have a smaller mountain to climb. It is God, with us cooperating with his grace and love, Who leads the soul gently, in an orderly way, and according to the particular mode or receptivity of the soul. There is, however, much excruciating suffering along the way in the imitation of our Saviour Jesus Christ. We carry a mere sliver of the most Holy Cross which He, in essence, carried throughout His entire life. St. John of the Cross personally suffered very intensely throughout his life. However, with his impending death, when someone commented upon the sufferings he had undergone, he simply exclaimed, I paraphrase "it is nothing, for it is by His blood, suffering, and dying for us that we are saved, the love for us of our Creator, our Saviour and Redeemer Jesus Christ."

In the progression of the soul to as full a love of God as (by the grace and love of God) is possible for it to achieve here upon this earth, the soul passes through three spiritual stages of development. Such development, hopefully, will culminate here upon this earth - as it did for St. John of the Cross and his compatriot sister St. Teresa of Jesus of Avila in the "Spiritual Union or Marriage of Love", or to a "Transformation to the State of Likeness (participatory) with God" before they depart from this earth. These three stages are: 1) The Mortification of the Appetites (Twilight Stage); 2) The Journey in Faith (Midnight Stage) ; and 3) The Communication with God (Dawn Stage). The result of the soul's passing through these stages is that the soul acquires while still here upon earth that lustrous beauty of soul (in Latin, nitor, a word difficult to render in translation) which God so loves. Its beauty can be compared to a brilliant facet of loveliness in an incomprehensibly, ineffably lovely large diamond of unsurpassing beauty, that is God. Thus, in worldly terms of expression it achieves a "Likeness (participatory) with God", otherwise referred to also as "The Spiritual Union of Love" or "The Spiritual Marriage of Love." Not all persons who are fortunate enough to (by the grace and love of God) have reached this stage of spiritual love or development achieve the same degree of this spiritual stage of development here upon this earth. Wherefore, as in heaven, each will enjoy a participatory joy in the glory of love as each soul is capable of. If by analogy, we were to compare the soul of each person to an ordinary drinking glass, one would say that some of the souls are smaller glasses, some are medium size, and some are larger. Each, however, is full of the joy and glory of God graciously given to it. Each soul is fully, spiritually content in the glory (participatory) of God allotted to it by Him. One soul will enjoy a lesser amount of this glory, another more; neither soul knowing the difference, for its glass (soul) will be filled to the brim with the glory of God. While still upon this earth this

"Spiritual Union of Love" for the soul will be of a transient nature. It will come and go, however, upon leaving the earth it will become a permanent union in the enjoyment of God's glory as described. For some saints these transient unions of a "Spiritual Marriage of Love" are very powerful and incomprehensibly profound. The fire of love for God generated within them becomes so intense that it actually may become clearly manifested in their external body in the form of a stigmata. As it did, for example, for St. Francis of Assisi, and so many other saints. For some other souls, such as that of St. John of the Cross and ST. TERESA OF AVILA, their soul with the body will actually be raised to an ecstasy of love for God which is indescribable to all human beings.

In the spiritual development stage of "The Mortification of the Appetites" the soul is constantly (by the grace and love of God) being purified of the appetites for ungodly things originating from selfish self-love. Thus, all of of the voluntary appetites are brought under control, and the appetites of the soul are always being directed to God alone. Until these voluntary appetites are made subject completely to reason, and the reason is made completely subject to God, the "Spiritual Union of Love" cannot be achieved upon this earth. During such time as this spiritual renewal or transformation is taking place, there is a constant warfare being waged. It is waged against all mortal and venial sins, and against the imperfections and natural weaknesses of the soul which are not necessarily sinful actions, but which are an inherent part of our fallen human nature. Examples of such weakness and imperfections would be, an unusual attachment to an object, place, or to something which has nothing to do with giving greater glory to God. A tendency to a loquacity of speech would be another example to such imperfections. Another one would be that so well expressed in Latin phrase *hebetudo mentis*, that is the natural dullness which came to our human nature through original sin. An example of such dullness would be the lethargy or sloth we may encounter in our various devotions or prayer life. Thus, it may manifest itself in a reluctance to pray, perform devotional acts, to worship God regularly and give Him the adoration due Him; or to receive the sacraments such as that of confession regularly, and so forth. One of the more damaging manifestations of this *hebetudo mentis* would be an excessive wandering of the imagination during devotions, prayers and worship.

The Imagination

The imagination, an interior sense, was especially hard hit through the effects of original sin and its transmission through human nature. It plays a great role in the spiritual development of the soul. It is a powerful disruptive force if left undisciplined. In the very intimate relationship which exists between the memory, the intellect, and will, it will become very disruptive indeed, if not controlled.[3]

During the deepest meditation or contemplation the imagination will tend to wander, more or less. However, as stated above earlier, during pure contemplative prayer it will wander but not without restraint. For in the state of pure contemplation, although it may wander somewhat it will be held in check or reigned in like a wild horse under the firm control of the will. The imagination will always wander some until death, but as long as it is controlled by the will it is harmless.

Mortification of the Appetites

During the spiritual stage of "The Mortification of the Appetites" (the twilight phase of the "Dark Night of the Soul"), there takes place a continuing detachment from everything which would not give glory to God. All the senses, external and internal, are employed in the pursuit of the hidden, incomprehensible God, Who although hidden and ineffable is within our soul closer to us than we are to ourselves. However, as St. John of the Cross explains, God remains a hidden God for which the soul constantly searches. Thus, in his spiritual direction he advises that the soul not seek Him in the heavens but within the soul itself. The soul that truly seeks Him out will find that if she is seeking Him devoutly with all of its heart, mind and soul, and with all of its strength; God Himself is even seeking it much more so as to draw it to Himself into the loving embrace of His most Sacred Heart of Love. This spiritual stage of development of the soul, that is, that of "The Mortification of the Appetites" is an absolutely necessary preparation for the second stage of spiritual development leading to the "Spiritual

3 St. Teresa of Avila confessed to having a very wild, almost uncontrollable imagination as she progressed in her spiritual development; she compared it to that of a wild stallion. She, for the longest time in her life, confused her intellect with her imagination as is brought out clearly in a reading of the three-volume *Collected Works of St. Teresa of Avila.*

Marriage" or "Union of Love", namely "THE JOURNEY IN FAITH" (the midnight phase of the "Dark Night of the Soul."

THE SECOND STAGE OF THE DARK NIGHT OF THE SOUL

"THE JOURNEY IN FAITH"

The second stage is the most frightening of all the three stages. The soul (ANIMA) animates the body through this second stage in pure faith alone, as if in a complete void or spiritual vacuum. It journeys towards an incomprehensible, ineffable God, Who can not be envisioned in any way by any of the operative faculties of the soul described above. God occupying the soul remains a hidden God. He is to be searched for with an imperfect faith, for if it were perfect where would be the hope of faith in a living God.

In beautiful imagery St. John of the Cross describes in mystical terms the God we seek in faith as having a silvered-over face. A face which our faith presents to us while on earth, but underneath the face that faith gazes at is God's golden face which we will see upon departing this earth and if we enter into His glory. He warns in his spiritual direction that we should not seek precision in our faith, as a scientist would in conducting his experiments, for he stresses that our faith will remain an imperfect one here on this earth in the sense that we know all that there is to know, for example, in correctly interpreting Holy Scripture. He states that the intellect is the noblest part of the soul, comparing it to a candle holder upon which sits the unlit candle of faith showing a light ray of complete darkness to the soul. And yet it is faith which takes us as if in a quantum leap and carries the soul far beyond any human intellectual powers. He incisively points out that these powers are puny as regards capturing the essence of the truths of either natural knowledge or supernatural knowledge. He uses the analogy of faith as being the feet while love is its guide. As regards the soul itself, it is the will which the soul follows.

In this stage there are all kinds of violent attacks against the soul originating from within our own sinful nature, as well as attacks from the devils. There are also attacks made upon the soul originating from the world itself, and from the flesh. While many of the temptations which our soul is subjected to have nothing to do with devils, nevertheless there are a number of occasions in which the devils manipulate the world and the flesh in their war against the soul which seeks to love its God with all the strength of its soul.

Evil Spirits Encountered

Diabolic attacks may come from various types of evil spirits or demons. Thus, St. John of the Cross explains that there will be the attacks coming from spirits which he identifies as "Blasphemous Spirits". These are evil spirits which may attack the soul with the most sordid, ugly, horrible thoughts - especially at the very time when one is actually worshipping and adoring God. This may occur during the most sacred moments of the most Holy Sacrifice of the Mass. There will be attacks from what he terms the "Spirit of Fornication". This is an evil spirit which attempts to fill our soul with the most ugly, vulgar, impure thoughts during the day, or especially during the time of prayer, devotion, or worship. There is also an evil spirit which he identifies as the "Loathsome Spirit". This spirit attempts to confound the soul with literally thousands of anxieties, perplexities, worries, confused thoughts, and scruples. Thus, for example, we may go over in our mind, literally, thousands of times thinking and wondering whether we have offended God in anyway through some action of ours.

Mystical Theology - Some Profound Aspects

It was his faith that revealed to St. John of the Cross the indescribable beauty and incomprehensible aspects of the Holy Trinity, the three Divine Persons in one God. Thus, although he does not discuss what faith revealed to him of the Holy Trinity, the one God, he explains that such a spiritual experience could not be conveyed except in terms of the expression of profound amazement: "I don't know what it is and yet it is". He gives some very small indication of this profoundly moving mystical experience when he states that it was indescribably beautiful, seeing the soul in the state of God's image. At one point in his *Collected Works* in a discussion of the purification of the soul, he states how the Holy Trinity purifies the soul. Thus, he states that the Hand that is laid upon the soul in purification is that of God the Father and that it is a very gentle Hand. The touch of the finger upon the soul is that of God the Son, and His finger is very light upon the soul. While the cautery being applied by the hand of God is that of the Holy Spirit. The cautery applied by God the Holy Spirit is a healing cautery, although the effect upon the soul is a very painful, burning and excruciating experience. This is because it is a healing not a destructive cautery, purifying the soul of all its impurities, weaknesses and imperfections.

Some of the experiences which St. John of the Cross explained above were lived prior to his having entered into the last stage of the "Dark Night" (the dawn):"The Communication of God to the Soul". This third stage is completely incomprehensible, even to the person experiencing it. The second stage, "The Journey in Faith" (the midnight stage) is the one most full of indescribable horrors. In this stage the world, the flesh and devil wage a horrendous warfare against the soul - a warfare beyond human description - with the devil and various evil spirits manipulating the world and the flesh in indescribable, almost insufferable ways against the soul itself. I cite as an example of these horrors the spiritual communications which the soul may be especially exposed to during this second stage of "The Dark Night of the Soul". He spends considerable time in his spiritual direction stressing the vital importance of ignoring all supernatural communication which may come to us in a variety of forms, awake or asleep during our life of spiritual development. He points out that many of them, such as visions, forms, images, voices, locutions, and so forth, come from the devil himself. Some of them may actually come from God Himself for reasons best known to Him; some perhaps to test the soul or to strengthen it in a number of ways in its very weaknesses. He points out that all such supernatural communication should be ignored, and also never desired. In following this advice which he offers, he points out that the soul will thereby avoid all unnecessary confusion, anxiety and spiritual perplexity. He, however, makes one exception to this very strict admonition or warning in his spiritual direction. The exception is what he terms as a "Substantial Locution". This, he explicitly states, is not to be ignored. He explains what he means in this way. The soul at certain times of its spiritual development, perhaps during times of severe crisis, may without knowing how or where the words come from, hear such words as; I paraphrase, "You are precious to me dear child, I love you dear son." Or, "Stand fast daughter, do not fear, I am with you." He points out that these substantial locutions are precious to the soul and are to be treasured. They are indelibly impressed upon the soul and are of great comfort and strength to it. He further elaborates that the soul will know that these substantial locutions actually come from God, because they are spoken with an indescribably tender, deep loving affection for the soul, an expression of such love which is impossible for the devil to deceptively imitate.

Before I now very briefly refer to the third stage of spiritual development, that is, "The Communication of God to the Soul" (the dawn stage), I wish again to emphasize to the reader that in this presentation I am concentrating only on the main themes and structure of St. John of the Cross' spiritual direction. I therefore refer the reader to his *Collected Works* themselves for the very detailed specific explanations which he provides there at considerable length of his main principles of spiritual direction.

THE THIRD STAGE OF "THE DARK NIGHT OF THE SOUL"

"THE COMMUNICATION OF GOD TO THE SOUL"

In the stage of "The Communication of God to the Soul" (the dawn stage) there takes place a secret infusion of God's love incomprehensible to the soul and indescribable. If the person who has entered this stage of spiritual development were to be asked to describe this infusion of God's love, he would reply as St. John of the Cross did: "I don't know what it is, but it is there." And yet despite it being a very profound, secret infusion of God's love, the soul in some mystical way unbeknown to itself knows of its presence. During this stage of spiritual development the soul may be still engaged in meditative prayer, or meditative-contemplative prayer, alternately going back and forth from one to the other. However, when the soul finally arrives at pure contemplative prayer it assumes such a prayerful mode that it becomes receptive to God's secret, mystical infusions of His love. It is at this very time that the soul (by the grace and love of God) is brought into the "Spiritual Union" or "Spiritual Marriage of Love" with God. The union or marriage which is attained, however, is a transient one, that is, it comes and goes. For were it to become a permanent union then the soul would have departed from this earth. Because of the very profundity of this stage which is indescribable; "The Communication of God to the Soul" (the dawn), it is impossible to provide my own personal description of it here. I will, however, attempt to describe it instead by providing excerpts from St. John of the Cross' attempts at description of this mystical "I don't know what it is" spiritual stage of development. In attempting to do so he, himself, said "May God be pleased to help me here, for I certainly need His help to explain the deep meaning of this stanza", or of this passage. These direct quotations cited below will provide the reader, I believe, with a deep sense of the profound mystical theology which permeates the spiritual direction of St. John of the Cross as he (by the grace and love of God) guides souls towards the spiritual unions and marriages of love briefly described above.

"In heaven the union will be a most intense, continuous, and permanent act. Here on earth the acts of intense living union cannot be permanent: they come and go and are more or less prolonged, deep in quality and frequent according to God's will for the soul".

At its highest point of intensity the "spiritual union of love" becomes what St. John of the Cross describes as an "actual union", he describes it thus:

"...the soul is so inwardly transformed in the fire of love, and has received such quality from it that it is not merely united to this fire but produces within a living flame..." (*Collected Works of St. John of the Cross*; p. 572).

"This flaring of the flame" as described in the *Collected Works of St. John of the Cross* (p. 573) "amounts to an actual union, very intense and deep in quality; the habitual state of this transformation resembles that of 'glowing embers' and when the union becomes actual, the embers not merely glow but shoot forth a living flame."

ACADEMIC, PROFESSIONAL, AND PERSONAL LIFE OF ST. JOHN OF THE CROSS

Academic

Because the academic background provides us with valuable insights into the spiritual development of his life as it evolved from an early age, I have cited below, verbatim, from his *Collected Works* the nature of his academic background:

"John began to attend the Catechism School, an institution resembling an orphanage in which the children of the poor were fed and clothed and given an elementary education. While at this school he was chosen to serve as an acolyte at the Convent of the Augustinian

Nuns; this meant duties in the sacristy for four hours in the morning, and in the afternoons whenever the Superior, the Chaplain, or the Sacristan needed him. In addition to his elementary studies, he also received the opportunity to learn something of carpentry, tailoring, sculpturing, and painting through apprenticeships to local craftsmen. When he was about seventeen years of age, he began to work at the Plague Hospital de la Concepcion, and the founder of the hospital, Don Alonso Alvarez, allowed him to enroll in the recently established Jesuit College in Medina del Campo, provided of course that he also fulfill his duties at the hospital.

"John attended the Jesuit College during the years 1559-63, and there received a solid formation in the humanities. Six hours a day, three in the morning and three in the afternoon, were devoted to classes in grammar, rhetoric, Greek, Latin, and religion. The grammar and rhetoric courses in both Latin and Spanish were taught by the great humanist Padre Juan Bonifacio, S.J. In his Spanish course, this renowned Jesuit followed the text of Nebrija, who was the foremost Spanish grammarian of the times, and supplemented the text with readings from the classics. He required his students to write compositions in prose and verse, in both Latin and native Castilian. In Padre Bonifacio's own words about his teaching we have an enlightening report concerning the extent of the humanistic training he gave to his students: 'I lecture without any difficulty on Valerius Maximianus, Suetonius, Aliciatus; I explain some passages from Ammianus Marcelinus, Pliny, and Pomponius Mela; I translate some difficult passages from the Breviary including some of the hymns, also the Catechism, the letters of St. Jerome, and the proceedings of the Council of Trent. To my non-clerical pupils I lecture on Cicero, Virgil, and sometimes Seneca's tragedies, Horace and Martial expurgated. Caesar, Sallust, Livy, and Curtius, that they might have examples of everything: speeches, poetry, and history.'

"John's professors of the Greek language and culture were Fathers Juan Guerra and Miguel de Anda. Although we do not know the methods used, we can surmise that they were not much different from those used by Father Juan Bonifacio. John's professor in religion was Padre Gaspar Astete, who later became famous for his Catechism, one of the most popular in the Spanish language. It is uncertain whether or not John studied philosophy while he was at this college, but we can affirm with certainty that he left the Jesuit College 'well trained in Latin and rhetoric,' and that 'he learned to read and write very well,' and that 'to these years must be assigned his first contact with the Latin and Spanish classics and the beginning of his love for humanism...on the basis of an abundance of exercises, reading, and composition.'

"After John had completed his four years of study in the humanities, Don Alonso offered to defray the cost of his education for the priesthood, if John so desired. In this way, too, once ordained, John could become Chaplain to the hospital, a post which would have provided him with the means to assist his mother and eldest brother in their material needs (his other brother had died early in life). But John believed that God was calling him to a Religious Order. In 1563, at the age of twenty, he entered the Carmelite Order at the Monastery of Santa Ana in Medina del Campo; he received the habit of Our Lady of Mount Carmel February 24, 1563, changing his name to Juan de Santo Matia.

"Little is known about his life in the Novitiate, but after his profession of vows he was sent for studies to his Order's College of San Andres at Salamanca, a journey of fifty miles. Besides attending classes at the Carmelite College, he studied at the University of Salamanca, which at the time ranked with the great universities of Bologna, Paris, and Oxford. The name of Fray Juan de Santo Matia appears on the matriculation record for the first time during the school year of 1564-65. His name is found again on the records of the School of Arts for the years 1565-66, and 1566-67. We do not know exactly which courses he followed as an Arts student, but we do know the courses that were taught and the names of the eminent men who held professorships. Master Enrique Hernandez, the author of a treatise on Philosophy, taught the classes in Natural Philosophy; Francisco Navarro held the Chair of Ethics; Hernando de Aguilera, who had worked out an astrolabe, held the Chair of Astronomy; Francisco Sanchez, known as El Brocense, taught grammar and even today is considered an authority on the subject; Master Martin de Peralta explained the Summulas (an introduction to Logic), and Juan de Ubredo held the Chair of Music. The statutes of the University prescribed the works of Aristotle for the Arts course, but this merely meant that a prescribed text from the philosopher was to be read at the beginning of the lecture; the professor could then go on to interpret it with full liberty, if not leave it aside entirely.

"Fray John registered in the theology course at the University of Salamanca only during the school year of 1567-68. It seems that he did most of his theological studies at the College of San Andres and complemented these with some courses taken at the University. Again, we posses no record of which classes in theology he attended. Probably he assisted at the Prime Lecture, which lasted an hour and a half and began at eight o'clock in the morning in the winter and at seven in the morning from Easter until the end of term. This Chair of Theology, the most important one at the University, was held by a Dominican Father, Mancio de Corpus Christi, who explained the *Summa Theologica* of St. Thomas Aquinas. In addition, Juan probably attended the lectures in Sacred Scripture given by Gaspar Grajal. At this particular time the University was troubled by a lively struggle of ideas concerning the interpretation of Sacred Scripture. The "scholastics," tenacious partisans of fidelity to the biblical tradition of the preceding centuries, opposed the "scripturists," who sought the literal sense of Scripture through a development of scientific methods and the study of languages. Grajal, Fray John's probable teacher, was a prominent figure among the "scripturists," and was later on account of his ideas imprisoned for for a time by the Inquisition.

"While still a student, John was appointed Prefect of Studies. This office, conferred only on the most outstanding students, obliged him to teach class daily, defend public theses, and assist the Regent Master in resolving those objections which were raised."

Professional Life

St. John of the Cross, in addition to being an excellent spiritual director, was also a very competent administrator. He held very important positions within the Catholic Church of a very diversified nature. This quotation from his Collected Works very succinctly summarizes the range of positions he held:

"..Fray John of the the Cross was Rector of the Carmelite College in Baeza...

At Alcaia, in March, 1581, the first Chapter of the Reform, which he attended in his capacity as Rector of Baeza, he was elected Third Definitor. One year later, the Fathers of Granada elected him Prior. At the Chapter of Lisbon, March 1585, he was elected Vicar Provincial of Andalusia, a position which made him responsible for the monasteries of the friars in Granada, El Calvario, La Penuela, Malaga, Caravaca, Seville, and Guadalcazar. He also had in his charge all the houses of nuns in that part of Spain, for they were under the direct and total jurisdiction of the Order. At the Chapter of Vallodolid, April 1587, he was elected again Prior of Granada. In June, 1588, at the Chapter of Madrid, he was elected Major Definitor and Third Counselor; it was thus his duty likewise to act as Prior of Segovia. Besides his work in administration, he gave much time to prayer. We can surmise the high character of his contemplation and absorption in God from a perusal of his writings on the state of perfect union with God. It was, in fact, during these years that he also did most of his writing. Furthermore, as always throughout his priestly life, he was much sought out as a spiritual director, and was liberal with his time in guiding his own friars, the nuns, and the many lay persons who came to him.

But toward the end of Fray John of the Cross' life, the outward calm was disturbed by a new clash, one this time within the reform. Father Nicolas Doria, Vicar General of the Discalced, called an extraordinary Chapter in June, 1590 for the purpose of undertaking two controvertible moves. First he desired to abandon jurisdiction over the nuns".(p.24)

Personal Life

St. John of the Cross was a very self-sacrificing person who always tried whenever possible to come to the aid of those in need, those suffering or in a state of melancholy or depression. Thus, when St. Teresa of Jesus of Avila asked him to assist her in her own religious community, he, despite his considerable responsibilities at the time decided to come to her assistance. She had selected him to be her own spiritual director when he was but a mere young man of twenty-five and she fifty-two years of age. She had quickly recognized in him the brilliant qualities of an excellent spiritual director, and recommended him strongly to other members of her religious community for this reason, as well as his great devotion to God, and for other outstanding technical qualifications. His especially strong compassion for persons suffering manifested itself in his periodic visits to various religious communities. Upon his visitations he would go to the Blessed Sacrament to pray and then immediately go to visit the sick. Persons in a depressed state for whatever reason always found him a good advisor and an inspiration in drawing them out of their states of depression. It saddened him to see them in such a state. When certain religious became ill and did not have the proper needed medication, he would make a personal sacrifice of his time and money to see to it that they were provided with the required medication. He was quick to turn his hand to physical labour and when the necessity arose he assisted those doing manual labour. His greatest strength to carry his Apostolate of Spiritual Direction which was his life's main chosen vocation was derived from his nourishment with the Body of Christ; while the most Holy Sacrifice of the Mass was his life's greatest joy.

Sufferings

Throughout his life St. John of the Cross suffered considerably not only through the spiritual horrors, trials, and severe tests and tribulations brought upon his soul as he went through the "Dark Night of the Soul". For according to the information found by others relating to this aspect of his life and recounted in his *Collected Works*, he was subjected to harsh abuse and severe cruelty from members within his own religious community. Thus, for example, because of the unwarranted persecution directed at him by religious members of his own religious community he endured considerable hardships as described below:

"In September of 1576, the Discalced friars convened at Almodovar in a Chapter presided over by Fray Jeronimo Gracian, the Provincial designated by Ormaneto. Among other things it was decided that Fray John of the Cross relinquish his office at the Incarnation and return it to the Calced, who coveted the position. For he had not gone unharassed while there, and the Calced at the beginning of 1576 had already, a first time, carried him off by force to Medina. Only through the intervention of Ormaneto did they restore him to his post at Incarnation, but the situation was obviously strained, and the frail young confessor had suffered much. However, the nuns at the Incarnation, regardless of the decision of the Chapter, wanted Fray John, and at their request the Nuncio ordered that he stay in that office.

"In June of 1577, Ormaneto, the Nuncio who had been so friendly toward the Discalced, died. His death, together with the disturbing news that the Discalced had convened the Chapter at Almodovar, prompted the Calced to execute the resolutions of Piacenza. Thus during the night of December 2, 1577 a group of Calced Fathers, men-at-arms, and some seculars, seized Fray Juan and his companion to bring them to a Calced monastery. Fray John of the Cross was taken to Toledo where the acts of the Chapter of Piacenza were read to him and a complete renunciation of the Reform was demanded. If he refused to renounce the Reform, he would be declared a rebel. But Fray John of the Cross did not renounce it. He was keen-minded enough to distinguish properly in this maze of conflicting jurisdiction and concluded that the proscriptions of the Chapter were directed against the Friars of Granada, Seville, and Penuela, and not against him, and that he had been at his post at the Incarnation by orders of the Nuncio, which were still in effect. However, the tribunal called him both rebellious and contumacious and prescribed imprisonment.

"Fray John was led to his prison cell, a little room originally intended as a closet, six feet wide and ten feet long. It had no window; the only opening was a slit high up in the wall. It was frightfully cold there in winter, and suffocating in summer. They deprived him of his hood and scapular as a token of punishment for his rebellion. His food was bread, sardines, and water. Three evenings a week he had to eat kneeling on the floor in the middle of the refectory. Then when the friars were finished their supper, his shoulders were bared and each member of the community struck him with a lash, some very vigorously, for the wounds he received would not heal properly for years. This scourging lasted for the time it takes to recite the Psalm Miserere. Since he continued in his refusal to renounce the Reform, they would then conduct him back to his bleak prison. No compassion could be shown him, for the Constitutions under the most severe penalties forbade one to show favor to a prisoner. After six months of prison life, the Saint was assigned a new warder. This one did manifest some elements of compassion; for instance, he gave him a change of clothes, and also furnished him with paper and ink, thus enabling him in these sad surroundings to write down the great lyric poems which, as a means of passing the time, he had been composing in his mind.

"Taking advantage of the leniency of his new jailer. Fray John familiarized himself with every aspect of the monastery during his daily reprieves from the prison cell. On the night of August 16, 1578, in a manner some declare was miraculous, he managed to escape and find his way to the Discalced nuns in Toledo, who hid him from the search party. Eventually he was able to journey to El Calvario in the south of Spain, where he was safer and had the opportunity to restore his health."

(C.W.; pp. 16-22)

This pattern of suffering at different intervals throughout his life continued on even until the time of his approaching death which he was clearly aware was impending sometime before his actual death, as indicated below:

"Father John of the Cross was sent to the solitude of La Penuela in Andalusia and arrived there with a joyful heart, August 10, 1591. Yet the awesome silence of Penuela was soon shattered by incredible and shocking news. Efforts were being made to expel Fray John of the Cross from the Reform. Fray Diego, a former but resentful subject of Fray John, was seeking to gather information against him by means of intrigue and defamation of character. This hateful process was never completed, however, for Fray John died in the meantime.

"In mid-September he noticed a slight fever which was caused by an inflammation of the leg. At first he thought it was nothing serious, but since it persisted he was ordered by his Superior to seek further medical attention, which was not available at La Penuela. He was given the choice of one of two places, Baeza or Ubeda. 'I will go to Ubeda, for at Baeza they know me very well and in Ubeda, nobody knows me.' He left Penuela on September 28, 1591; this was to be his last journey in life. The Prior of Ubeda, Fray Francisco Crisostomo, did not welcome the sick man. Even though learned and a famous preacher, Fray Crisostomo possessed a mean and rigid temperament and completely lacked the qualities of a good superior. He was unfriendly toward Fray John. His cold lack of consideration was evident in the fact that he assigned him the worst cell in the monastery and voiced his vexation at the expenses incurred by him. He felt a particular aversion to Fray John precisely because of his reputation for holiness.

Fray John's sickness grew worse; his legs were already ulcerated, and the disease spread to his back where a new tumor appeared, larger than the size of a fist. On December 13, realizing that time was running out, he called for the Prior and begged his pardon for all of the trouble and expenses he had caused him. Fray Crisostomo, in turn, begged for forgiveness and left the cell in tears. This circumstance profoundly changed him, for he was later to die in the odor of sanctity. That same night, without agony, without struggle, at the age of forty-nine, Fray John of the Cross died, repeating the words of the Psalmist: 'Into your hands, O Lord, I commend my spirit.' The favors he had asked for in his declining years he had now received: Not to die as a superior; to die in a place where he was unknown; and to die after having suffered much.

"St. John of the Cross was beatified by Clement X in 1675, canonized by Benedict XIII in 1726, and declared a Doctor of the Church by Pius XI in 1926."

(C.W.; pp. 25-26)

SUMMARY

I wish now to summarize what I believe to be most of the important points of the spiritual direction of St. John of the Cross. I respectfully beg the readers pardon for any repetition or redundancy throughout this summary of material presented earlier. However, it is necessary for me to stress and emphasize these points once again, perhaps from somewhat different perspectives in order to place them into a sharper focus for the reader. Having said this, I again urge the reader to go to the original *Collected Works of St. John of the Cross* prepared by the good Fathers mentioned above. This should be done, preferably, if possible, with the guidance of someone who is already quite familiar with these works. This is extremely important especially at the beginning of such study. What I have done, hopefully, in this presentation is to introduce the reader who has a strong desire to follow in the footsteps and to imitate the Master Spiritual Director, our Saviour Jesus Christ, to a remarkable spiritual director so richly gifted by the grace and love of God for the Apostolate of Spiritual Direction.

The profundity of the mystical meaning of St. John of the Cross' poetry matches the exquisitely beautiful reasoning of his spiritual direction in its simplicity and clarity. As stated earlier, it was somewhat marred by his ponderous writing style. When he first wrote his works of spiritual direction, and they were brought to the attention of various persons in the religious community of his native land, their very profound mystical import was lost upon many persons in the religious communities and among laity. Because their mystical meaning was difficult to understand by many persons, they actually looked upon his work with fear, confusion, and bewilderment. Some persons judged them with serious suspicion, as if he were presenting something heretical.

In St. John of the Cross' spiritual direction it is the internal purity of the soul — the destruction of all self-love for the love of God above all — rather than the externals of life's action that are of paramount importance. For, he stresses repeatedly, that unless the soul is purified of all self-love and loses its attachment to everything which does not give glory to God, then the soul is in a constant state of conflict or tension, and not at peace. It will continuously be filled with all kinds of useless concerns, anxieties, lack of tranquility, and so forth. For God, although he resides in the soul as a hidden God, cannot fully occupy the soul with the lustrous radiance of His love when there remains in it anything of a selfish self-love; a self-love or attachment to anything even to the slightest degree, which excludes love for Him and for His greater glory. In His tremendous love for the soul, God desires to sit on His rightful throne in the soul reigning as its King. His greatest desire for the soul is to exalt it, and to draw it more closely into the loving embrace of His most Sacred Heart of Love. This can be summed up briefly in the spiritual precept which embodies the entire teachings of Holy Scripture: "Thou shall love the Lord, thy God, with all thy mind, with all thy heart, with all thy soul, and with all thy strength — and thy neighbor as thyself." St. John of the Cross stresses this point throughout his spiritual direction.

Once all of the appetites and faculties of the soul are focussed upon God like a powerful spiritual laser beam, and upon Him alone - completely detached from all else in this world (ordinary life activities being carried on concurrently) - then the soul can be truly said to have achieved a "Spiritual Union of Love" or a "Spiritual Marriage of Love" with God. Thus, in St. John of the Cross' spiritual direction, when there is a complete internal purification of the soul, the external actions will follow and flow freely. He indicates very explicitly that many persons, unfortunately, attach such excessive importance to external actions that they do not (by the grace and love of God) tear out at the very roots of their soul all of the sinful tendencies or proclivities to sin lying there like a coiled snake always ready to strike.

He stresses the vital importance of being prudent in the selection of good spiritual directors. He has some very strong words for those persons responsible for the spiritual direction of souls who are not competent to do so. He states simply, but very firmly, that they will be held accountable to God for having misled souls entrusted to their spiritual guidance. In this connection he points out that each soul is often very different from one another, as he expresses it, for example, by as much as one-half. He offers to spiritual directors the best "Guide Model" when he states that God guides and draws the soul to Himself in: 1) an orderly way; 2) gently and kindly; and 3) according to the mode or receptivity of the particular soul He is guiding, drawing to Himself. He provides us with the beautiful analogy that the virtues in the soul are like plants planted there by God's grace. These plants are brought to full bloom by God's continuous love at work in the soul. These virtues (plants) however, are not brought to full fruit here on this earth. This takes place when the soul joins God in His glory.

St. John of the Cross strongly affirms that no soul was ever directed to God through harshness, severity, and unkindness. This statement refers considerably to incompetent spiritual directors. This avoidance of harshness, cruelty in spiritual direction is a hallmark of his approach to all persons seeking spiritual guidance.

The Memory - Its Vital Importance

In his spiritual direction he stresses the vital importance of locking out from the memory all things not of God. Throughout his "Works" he strongly emphasizes the role of the memory in spiritual development. He states explicitly and in considerable detail that Satan has a powerful weapon against souls who do not lock out completely from their memory all that it not of God - that is, all that does not give glory to God above all. He acknowledges that this control of the memory is very difficult to achieve, but that with persevering prayer God will bring about this control of the memory so highly to be desired by those who truly love Him. Because the memory works intimately with the intellect and the will, these two operative faculties, similarly have to be detached from all that is not God, and the imagination (an internal sense) must be reigned in and completely disciplined.

Meditative and Contemplative Prayer - Their Distinction

St. John of the Cross explains that for pure contemplative prayer to exist three conditions must be, simultaneously, present: 1) The soul no longer can pray while thinking in forms, images, and so forth; 2) The soul seeks and desires complete solitude in prayer whenever possible; and 3) The imagination although it wanders, even during pure contemplative prayer, is quite firmly reigned in, and is disciplined and under the control of the will. Its wanderings are restricted or curtailed under the power of will. In spiritual development the soul follows the will, and when its will is in conformity with God's will it moves towards its creator on the feet of faith alone with love being its guide. The wanderings of the imagination as regards the prayer life may continue until our death here upon earth. With the fall of our human nature through original sin - transmitted on from generation through our human nature - the imagination was one of the operative faculties of the soul which was most adversely affected. This very fundamental, grave weakness of the imagination is a theme which runs like a constant thread throughout St. John of the Cross' spiritual direction. It is by our constant cooperation with God's love and grace and persevering prayer, with the *muy determinado determinacion* (a very resolute determination) of St. Teresa of Jesus of Avila. This, combined with a willingness to carry our crosses uncomplainingly in imitation of our Saviour Jesus Christ, advances the soul as a bride to meet its bridegroom, The Most Holy Trinity, its God and Father.

GRATITUDE TO FRS. OTILIO RODRIGUEZ AND KIERAN KAVANAUGH, O.C.D.

The *Collected Works* which St. John of the Cross left behind in a variety of letters, notes, writings, instructions, and so forth, represent only a part of his prolific writings as regards spiritual direction. This is so because at one point in his life when his writings were unjustly judged by others, the nuns of his religious community, in great fear of reprisals from their religious superiors, burned sacks of his writings and correspondence. In speaking of his writings, it must be pointed out that it is now very obvious why the works of his spiritual direction have not become as well known as they deserve to be. It was because his style of writing which, paradoxically, although very clear in its thought and reasoning was at the same time, unfortunately, very ponderous or heavy. For example, we find this "heaviness" of his style of writing summarized very well in the quotation cited below:

"In the field of Spanish literature, St. John of the Cross has won a prominent place, particularly for his poetry. As a poet he is ranked among the greatest in the history of Spain. Such eminent critics as Menendez Pelayo and Damaso Alonso have confessed to a religious terror they felt before the beauty and the burning passion of his verses.

"His prose style, on the other hand, has not gained such certain praise. It is in the main didactic and often discursive, especially in the *Ascent*. Concerned with the practical goals of teaching, of pointing out the way that leads to perfection, St. John obviously made no particular effort to phrase his ideas in graceful, stylish, and impeccable prose. We find it quite unpolished (he himself complained of his style), cluttered with repetitions, redundancies, ambiguities, split constructions that are often complicated and obscure, Latinisms, and so on. His long, labyrinthine sentences have not infrequently proved a challenge to his editors seeking clear punctuation. We have the fantastic examples in a recent Spanish edition of his works in which one sentence has been buttressed with fifty commas, four semicolons, two uses of parentheses, and a use of the dash. In spite of all, however, there are not lacking prose passages in which the Mystical Doctor shows plainly his literary genius for expressing a thought in phrases of beauty, originality, and power."

The enormously difficult and very meticulous work of translation done by the good Fathers Otilio Roderiquez and Kiernan Kavanaugh, O.C.D., have brought out the true clarity of the thoughts and writing of St. John of the Cross without marring any of the spiritual direction meanings so well presented there, but suffering somwhat from the ponderous style of writing described above. Many owe and will owe an immense gratitude to these priests for the excellent translations which they have made available to us.

A PERSONAL NOTE

As I was preparing this work, I happened to see a picture of a person who undoubtedly is a living saint. I have never met her. I actually know nothing about her except through a picture of her which I had seen. The picture speaks volumes, eloquently and vividly for itself. The person is Esperanza Guevara. She is sitting in an invalid's chair made for her in her very simply furnished room. The chair is beside her bed. Her body is half-wasted away in leprosy. There is a simple crucifix of our Saviour and Redeemer Jesus Christ behind her on the wall over her bed. It is so small, it is barely noticeable. A little child's teddy bear is sitting astride her bed, leaning his head against her pillow. A gentle light is streaming in from the window lighting up the small room. Esperanza. The picture's caption tells a great story of courage and fortitude in a few words. Eperanza Guevara is now seventy-one years old. She had been committed to a special institution for lepers fifty-six years ago when she was a mere young girl of fifteen. The caption relates to a viewer a heartbreakingly tragic, yet hauntingly beautiful picture, with the light streaming into the window making Esperanza actually glow. It eloquently tells the story of her indescribable suffering during so long a time; a suffering endured with a truly amazing indomitable spirit, and a resolute trust in and love for her God. The caption above the picture states in words of undying love: "I carry Hansen's (leprosy) disease as my cross, the way Jesus did." St. John of the Cross in his recounting of the suffering encountered in the purification undergone during the three stages of the "Dark Night of the Soul" could not have expressed it more succinctly, poignantly and beautifully.

I now end this Chapter V with my two articles (published). The first (Appendix A) entitled "A Spiritual Director for All Time for All," represents my attempt to encapsulate in summary form the essential spiritual principles of spiritual direction contained in the entire *Collected Works of St. John of the Cross* (one volume) cited in the bibliographic reference. It is my fervent hope that it will facilitate and make for easier prayerful reading, study and understanding of this 773 - page work so full of rich treasures of spiritual direction. The article "St. John of the Cross and Spiritual Development" which follows it provides the classic description of St. John of the Cross of the differences between the prayer of Meditation and the prayer of Pure Contemplation — one of the most succinct explanations to be found on these stages of prayer.

May God bless all you readers of this book on these four brilliant spiritual directors and holy men and women.

APPENDICES TO CHAPTER V

APPENDIX A: "A Spiritual Director for All Time for All" in *Carmelite Digest*, Autumn 1989; pp.19-32.

APPENDIX B: "Spiritual Development and St. John of the Cross" in *Inner Horizons - A Magazine of Spirituality*; pp. 42-44.

CARMELITE DIGEST Volume 4 Number 4 Autumn 1989

CONTENTS

Editor: Fr. Pascal Pierini, OCD
Editorial Consultants: Fr. Patrick Sugrue, OCD
Fr. John Melka, OCD
Peter Torreano
Circulation Director: Fr. Gerald Werner, OCD

CARMELITE DIGEST is a Catholic Quarterly published in Winter, Spring, Summer and Autumn by the California-Arizona Province of Discalced Carmelites. Subscription rates: USA $12.00 per year. Additional subscriptions by the same subscriber may be purchased at $10.00 per year. Outside USA, $14.00 US per year. All communication should be addressed to CARMELITE DIGEST, P.O. BOX 3180, SAN JOSE, CA 95156.

Contributors of original articles on Carmelite or Carmelite related subjects are welcomed. The manuscript submitted should be typed double-spaced. Should the contributor wish the return of his or her manuscript a suitable envelope and sufficient postage must be supplied by the contributor.

A SPIRITUAL DIRECTOR FOR ALL TIME FOR ALL
by Joseph Kozlowski, Rockville, MD

In these days of severe trials and tribulations in our national life, throughout the world, and within our own Catholic Faith, there is a serious need within our own Catholic Faith for competent spiritual directors. This statement refers not just to the clergy within the Catholic Church hierarchy at various levels, but also to outstanding Catholic laymen who have the potential to act as or to become good spiritual directors. Ideally a competent spiritual director should be both a devout and a learned man. That is, above all, he should be both a prayerful man, and one learned or trained and educated in such a way that he can guide and competently advise in today's exceedingly complex world - which is living at such a frenetic pace - persons who come to him to seek solutions for either spiritual or other problems. It is difficult to find many spiritual directors who are both very devout and very learned at the same time. There is much more assurance of receiving competent spiritual direction from a person who, although he may not be so learned, is devout or prayerful and therefore has the humility to answer those questions which he has competence in, and to refer a person seeking spiritual advice to one more learned than he when he realizes he simply cannot help certain persons as regards specific concrete problems relating to the hard realities encountered in striving to lead a good spiritual life.

Because of the serious lack of clergy and the very pressing need for their services, the finding of spiritual directors to whom one can go to for competent guidance is a difficult task in the Catholic Church today. To meet this serious problem, I would suggest that we have at our disposal for guidance within the Catholic Church some of the most excellent spiritual directors one could wish for oneself personally. Because of the excellent translations available to us, we now have at our fingertips materials of excellent spiritual direction which are very pertinent to the problems confronting persons in our fast paced scientific and technological age of today, despite the fact that they were written many centuries ago.

Overview

St. John of the Cross drew essentially from three sources: science, life experience, and above all the most holy Word of God, Holy Scripture, the Bible. He makes it clear that Holy Scripture, whose author is Almighty God Himself, was the principle source of his inspiration together with persevering prayer, the Holy Sacrifice of the Mass, and the Most Blessed Sacrament of the Body of Christ, all of which were the very heart of his prayer life. At the outset it can be said that three controlling themes are stressed again and again throughout his works. These are: 1) The achievement through the grace and love of God of the highest stage of spiritual development humanly possible of attainment in the world, that is, a "spiritual union of marriage" between the human soul and God, or as he refers to them the bride and the Bridegroom. 2) In this journey to the apex of spiritual life in this world there are three dangerous enemies encountered which have to be destroyed before such a spiritual marriage can take place. These are: the world, the flesh, and the devil. The world he states is the most easily overcome. The flesh is the most tenacious of the enemies because it fights against the soul until death. The devil is the most difficult enemy to defeat because he is the most difficult to understand. 3) The journey to the spiritual apex of life, that is, to the" spiritual marriage" en route to destroying the enemies barring the way to the spiritual marriage or union of love with God progresses in three principle stages summarized briefly as: a) the mortification of the appetites; b) the journey through Faith; and c) the communication of God to the soul, or of the love of God (the Bridegroom) to the soul (the bride). St. John of the Cross in his brilliant exposition of these themes uses poetic imagery to provide greater clarity in the presentation of such richly, divinely inspired themes. Because his poetry ranks him among the greatest of the Castillian Spanish poets, the poetic imagery he employs soars breathtakingly in elevating the spirit as it strives to raise its soul closer and closer to God. However, St. John of the Cross makes it abundantly clear that the soul cannot arrive at the apex summit of the spiritual life by its own natural powers, that is, "the spiritual marriage" or "spiritual union of love with God." To express it another way, it cannot do so under the volition of its own natural powers or natural reasoning. It is only by the aid of the supernatural powers of God that it arrives there. Expressed simply, God does it all, and yet without the soul's cooperation with His love and grace nothing is done or achieved. The key element of the achievement therefore is cooperation with God's love and grace in the fulfilment of God's Will accompanied by intense suffering of a kind which St. John of the Cross candidly states is formidable and painful to behold and endure. Thus, as the soul (the bride) advances toward God (the Bridegroom) guided by the Divine Hands of love and grace it goes through a dark night of spiritual trials which can be considered as, in actuality, three nights of varying darkness of suffering and spiritual trials. Viz. 1) the mortification of the senses - the twilight of the soul, that phase in the time of day when the light of the spiritual day is beginning to disappear and the darkness of the night is descending; 2) the journey in Faith - the midnight of the soul when the light has all faded away and darkness has completely descended; 3) the communication of God (the Bridegroom) to the soul (the bride). That is the phase or time of day when the darkness of midnight is beginning to dissipate and the light of day comes on, and the break of day begins. St. John of the Cross indicates clearly that God desires that more souls would enter this spiritual union of love in this "spiritual marriage" with Him, but that many whom He does invite do not wish to endure the severe suffering of all types through which it is necessary to pass before they depart from this earth when the soul leaves the body.

Having now summed up the main themes of the *Collected Works of St. John of the Cross,* I will now proceed to explain, to the best of my ability, the specific details of the main themes stressed throughout his masterful work of spiritual direction.

The Twilight Period

In the first part of the dark night, that is, the mortification of the appetites, the twilight period, the soul begins the process of being stripped of all its appetites, that is, of all the animal appetites which originate in the senses and the imagination, and of all the spiritual appetites which originate in the will, thereby giving all of the strength of the heart, mind, body, and the entire soul to God alone above all. The appetites referred to here are the voluntary appetites and not the involuntary appetites of the soul. The distinction between these appetites is critical, for the involuntary appetites of the soul are those which are used and necessary in our daily living, such as the animal appetites of eating, drinking, and so forth, absolutely necessary to sustain our daily lives. St. John of the Cross indicates explicitly that the involuntary appetites need not necessarily be a barrier to entering the spiritual union of love with God. The voluntary appetites are those we voluntarily exercise, but are not at all essential to our daily existence. Thus, for example, an involuntary appetite such as the act of eating, which is normal, can become a voluntary appetite when we become gluttonous in our eating, drinking actions, and so forth. These voluntary and involuntary appetites originate in the soul. Thus, for example, they originate in the will of the soul. At this point it becomes necessary to explain the make-up of the human soul as described by St. John of the Cross in his magnificent exposition. This knowledge of St. John's understanding of the human soul which is a pure spirit is absolutely essential to an intelligent grasp of his spiritual direction.

The human soul, the incomprehensibly profound animating force or life principle of our human existence, is known perfectly only to God. It is a pure spirit with no parts, and nobody occupies it except God. Under extremely extraordinary conditions, and very rarely, God permits angelic spirits to enter the human soul for reasons known only to Him, as has occurred, for example, with certain great Saints so graced by God. Although the soul has no parts, it is in a mystical, profound way endowed by God with what I will term here faculties of operation. These faculties are found in the superior nature of the soul and are termed the intellect, the memory, and the will. This superior nature of the soul is the spiritual nature, as opposed to the inferior nature of the soul which we have in common with the animals, and where the sense appetites are operative through the five senses of seeing, hearing, smelling, touching, and tasting. These five senses are considered as external senses since they are exposed to the external reality of the world. It may be said that they are the windows of the soul to the external reality of the world. There are also four internal senses which supplement these external senses. These are the memory (also a part of the superior nature of the soul), common sense, the imagination, and the evaluative sense which enables us to pass judgment upon the goodness or the evil course of action presented to us. With the first fall of our ancestors Adam and Eve, imagination was one of the internal senses of the soul most damagingly affected. This point is critical, for the angelic spirits, the good spirits, or the evil angelic spirits who fell completely from God's love and grace work through the imagination or the sense, the animal or lower, sensory faculties of the soul. The intellect and will are inviolate to their attacks, although they do coax and cajole them to sin from outside the soul through the senses and the imagination. Thus, the intellect (which is considered to be the noblest operative faculty of the soul — it is called the eye of the soul with its pupil being Faith) and the will are sacrosanct as regards the influence of angelic spirits (that is good or evil ones) within the soul itself. The will nurtured by the understanding transmitted to it is completely free as to its selection of a course of action towards committing a good or evil act. It is a most profound mystery, that although the human soul has free will, yet in a way unknown to us, God does ~~not~~ move the will (always to the good) without violating the freedom of the will to act.

Thus, in the biblical injunction of God, thou shalt love the Lord thy God with all thy heart, with all thy mind, with all thy soul, and with all thy strength, and thy neighbor as thyself, the entire soul is emptied of all that is not God, and the soul's full strength is directed to the love of God above all. Thus, all of the senses of the animal nature of the soul are detached from all that is not God, or work for the glory of God solely; and all the lower senses, and the operative faculties of the superior nature of the soul are emptied of all that is not God, and are directed solely to the love, honor, and greater glory of God. Thus, the memory is emptied of all that is not God, the intellect also, and the will, while at the same time all these faculties are responsive to carrying out the daily life activities required for normal living. I refer the reader of this article at this point to the actual *Collected Works of St. John of the Cross* where he provides very detailed specific explanations of how all the appetites and all the operative faculties of the soul are completely detached from all that is not God, and the soul (the bride) begins the journey towards the Bridegroom, its God, in joy, hope, sorrow, and holy fear (relating to God alone), to give herself to her Bridegroom, God ultimately, hopefully in a "spiritual marriage" or "union of love" — as St. John of the Cross expresses it so beautifully in both prose and poetry.

A Caution

Before I proceed to discuss the second phase of the "dark night of the soul," "The Journey of Faith," a few words of St. John of the Cross are pertinent here. St. John of the Cross points out that the "dark night of the soul" is indeed filled with trials through which the soul must pass for its purification, so that before it meets its God, it has what St. Thomas Aquinas describes in Latin as *nitor* — a word not easily translated into English — which among other possible translations means: a shining, lustrous splendor of purity, beauty, and love which God would desire to see in the soul as it appears before Him when it departs from the body through death in this earthly life. St. John of the Cross stresses that his spiritual direction, although containing something valuable for spiritual advice for all souls *is not for those who have merely a spiritual sweet tooth.* He indicates in many places the horrors of the sufferings the soul must endure throughout this spiritual trial and testing encountered in the "dark night," in order to enter a spiritual union of love with God or the state of "spiritual marriage" with God - the highest state or degree of love for God which is possible for any person to achieve by the love and grace of God before departing this earthly existence.

This brilliant spiritual director so beautifully graced by God's love points out that the soul cannot arrive at the spiritual marriage state of love with God of its own volition, or efforts, and natural knowledge and spiritual striving, no matter how hard it may attempt to do so, or how hard it may work and pray at the effort, but that it is only through the supernatural uplifting powers of God's love and grace that this spiritual marriage or union of love is achieved. He states candidly that God would desire to bring more souls to the "spiritual marriage" between God (the bridegroom) and the soul (the bride), but that many souls that he does invite do not accept the invitation because of their spiritual disinclination to endure the suffering necessary to achieve a pure heart filled with God's love and grace - which as David, the great prophet-king of God, states that a pure heart is - thus, loving God with the full force of all its heart, mind (intellect), and the full strength of the soul. He indicates, therefore, that more souls who would be willing to carry but a sliver of the Cross which our Saviour Jesus Christ carried in suffering (throughout His entire Life) could conquer the world (the easiest to conquer through hope in Him); the devil (the hardest to understand and therefore the most formidable enemy conquered through unquestioning, unflagging, unflinching Faith in God); and the flesh (the most tenacious of the enemies of the soul for it wars relentlessly against the spirit until our earthly death).[4] St. John of the Cross explicitly states that since souls differ from each other, the prayerful reader and serious student, must exercise a prudent selection in adapting to his own soul various forms of spiritual direction explained and elaborated in great detail by this eminently outstanding and remarkable Saint of God who was also an excellent and superb spiritual director. He states explicitly that there is something good as regards spiritual direction in his works for all, but frankly acknowledges that not everything in his work of spiritual direction is applicable to all.

Midnight

I shall now proceed to a very brief discussion of the midnight phase of the "dark night of the soul," the "Journey of Faith," with the caution to the reader that in this article I am merely focusing a spotlight upon the highlights of the work of this remarkable spiritual director.

---

[5] Flesh: Overcome by the virtue of love.

The "Journey of Faith" of the soul, that is the midnight phase of the entire spiritual dark night of the soul, is one of complete darkness, and yet it is termed mystically by St. John of the Cross to be a "Light Ray of Complete Darkness." The soul in this stage becomes detached from all things and progresses through pure Faith, that is, all its appetites (except the involuntary normal appetites necessary for daily living) are employed only for God and His glory. The full strength of the very heart of the soul is focused upon the invisible God, a hidden God, hidden somewhere within the very deep recesses of the very heart of the soul. He is hidden because there is nothing that comes, or has come through our senses that tells us what God is like. All that we observe throughout the universe are mere traces which remind us of Him, mere faint footprints left behind as evidence of His almighty creative powers. Thus whatever we have perceived through our senses, or will perceive, tells us only that God is their Creator. Thus, our Faith tells us that He is our Creator, but it does not tell us anything about what God is like in reality, although through Faith we know that God is love. All natural phenomena in the universe observed through the senses are only a very pale reflection of God's creative powers, mere traces or footprints, so to speak, which He left behind of His creation in the inanimate world (rocks, mountains, minerals, and so forth), the animate world of plants and animal creatures, and His children, human persons. Although we do not see them through Faith, we know by His own Word in Holy Scripture of the existence of the supra-human, not supernatural creatures, which he has created such as our own Guardian Angel and various Angels which act also as special Guardian Angels for certain persons, nations, institutions, and so forth in this world. The demonic spirits, that is, the fallen angels, the devils, some of whom wander throughout the world seeking the ruin of souls, are also supra-human and, of course, invisible to us, attacking the soul through the senses and the imagination, thereby attempting to entice the intellect and the will of the soul to rebel against it Creator, our Almighty God. Thus, the expression, God the Almighty, indicates the reality of His supreme perfection. Among these attributes of His perfection, to name but a few, are perfect love, grace, beauty, simplicity, purity, truth, wisdom, prudence, obedience, mercy, justice, goodness, kindness, sweetness, generosity, fortitude, meekness, power, perserverence, compassion, grandeur, glory, and His ineffable or indescribably incomprehensible, eternal divine essence. In regard to this last statement all that our senses or our imagination can imagine is unlike Him, for all of these observable phenomena have only a participatory role in God's divine perfection. They contain only that degree of perfection which God has assigned to their specific natures, be they in the inanimate world, the inanimate planet world, the world of His animal creatures, the world of His children, human persons — or in the invisible world of His supra-human Angelic spirits — invisible to our senses except in those very rare and extraordinary appearances ordained by God when they appear in a form willed by Him alone. The appearance which they assume is not related to any material substance or composition whatever since they are pure spirits devoid of all materiality. Although He is a hidden God, as stated earlier, He is a hidden God to the soul, we know from Holy Scripture and Revelations which followed that God is always present in the soul by His grace and love, and is at the same time omnipresent, that is, that there is nothing that occurs anywhere that escapes His divine eye. God remains in the soul always, no matter how hardened the soul may be in sin.

Thus, it is God alone Who knows in what state of His grace and love each individual soul is in. No individual soul has this knowledge, and therefore we work out our salvation in fear and trembling by the grace and love of God alone. To presume to have such knowledge would be a contemptuous prideful insult of self-love or self-esteem before God Who alone possesses such omniscience or perfect knowledge.

Thus, in the "Journey of Faith" the soul is suspended literally between earth and heaven, for as it becomes detached from all of the things that bind it to this earth which appertain to the world, the flesh, or the devil, the very heart of its soul is reaching out to God unattached to all that is not of God. Because the greatest enemy of Satan, or the devil, is Faith, the soul, by the grace and love of God, wages a horrible, relentless war against the world, the flesh, and the devil; the devil, Satan, attacking the soul through the senses and the imagination at the same time, coaxes and cajoles the intellect and the will to rebel against God. While Satan is the most difficult enemy of the soul to defeat because he is so difficult to understand, it must also be understood very clearly that our very own soul itself is our own worst enemy, for much of our sinning and rebelling against God has nothing to do very frequently with the temptations which Satan brings to us. Satan does employ the world and the flesh in the war he wages against the soul which loves God, for he hates God, and the soul which loves God, with an indescribable hatred. These attacks which originate from the sin in the very heart of our soul, and form the temptation of Satan, cannot be warded off unless the soul is, literally, enclosed in the fortress of Jesus Christ; for by its own natural powers without the grace and love of Jesus Christ the soul cannot stand up against the fierce assaults directed against it. The "Journey in Faith" is a "Light Ray of Darkness," it's God that it knows - and inspired by His love and grace - relentlessly seeks a "Hidden God," despite the soul's knowledge that it believes He is in the soul by His grace and love, and is present actually by the power of His omnipresence here beside us; while at the same time He is in His heaven completely unknown to us as to His nature or essence, since His nature or essence cannot be grasped by any natural or supernatural powers which He our Creator has endowed us with. He is complete darkness to the soul - and yet He is closer to us in our soul than we are to ourselves - but He remains always a hidden God. Thus, in the constant purification of the soul by Jesus Christ, He remains hidden and elusive as the soul suffers all kinds of indescribable trials, tests, and tribulations as it longs to find Him and literally cries out in agonizing pain, torment, and anguish: Where are you hidden my God, the Bridegroom of my soul?

At this point, I must refer the reader to read prayerfully and study under the guidance of God, the Holy Spirit, this "Journey in Faith", the "Midnight" of the soul expressed by St. John of the Cross so eloquently, clearly, and with such beautiful lyrical poetry and soaring majestic prose. St. John of the Cross, it can be seen - and in fact on occasions of rare grandeur, so states himself - pleads with the Holy Spirit to guide his hand as he attempts to sharpen the clarity of some particularly soaring majestic thought which he wishes to convey to the reader. It is clear that St. John of the Cross described his soul's "Dark Night of the Soul" which culminated in the "Spiritual Marriage" or the "Spiritual Union of Love," after he by the grace and love of God had already climbed to the apex of that mystical theological state of love between his soul (the bride) and God (the bridegroom). It is from this spiritual height of spiritual development that his observations and his keen spiritual insights are presented. He warns again and again of how many souls attempting to climb to this summit of love with God backslide again and again for a variety of reasons. He expounds on these reasons with eloquent clarity, pointing out that among the chief obstacles are the soul's rebellions itself in which the inferior nature of the soul (the sensory) wages a relentless war against the superior nature of the soul (the spiritual). It (the inferior nature of the soul) seeks to covet the superior nature of the soul, or possess it, and prevent it from entering the spiritual union of love with God and consummate the "Spiritual Marriage" with God here upon earth before the soul departs from the body.

In attempting to understand the spiritual direction which St. John of the Cross is so graciously providing as drawn from his own life, it is very important to understand his exposition of the soul as being a suppositum, that is a pure spiritual entity with an inferior and superior nature possessed of the different operative faculties specified earlier in this article. In his consideration for the prayerful reader, he states that at first there will be many difficulties in understanding the spiritual directions he is presenting, but with words of encouragement states that after several readings the points of spiritual direction he is making will become clear to the faithful reader of his works who perseveres.

A second formidable enemy is the devil himself, and St. John of the Cross explains why throughout his works in extensive detail. Again in very extensive detail this masterful, saintly spiritual director describes how another formidable enemy, or enemies, are various spiritual directors themselves that the poor beleaguered soul consults as it passes through its "Dark Night of the Soul" in quest of its "hidden God." This particular section of the Saint's work in which he treats of the subject of spiritual directors, good, bad, and indifferent, is a classic work in itself, and should be must reading for all clergy and laity who bear a responsibility for the spiritual direction of others, be they in the Church, in the home, or in the outside world community, and in other areas of life.

Few Go the Distance

St. John of the Cross makes the very cogent observation that God would desire with His Sacred Heart full of love that more of His children would enter the "Spiritual Marriage" or "Spiritual Union of Love" with Him before they depart from this earth, but for a variety of reasons they do not do so. He points out as has been indicated earlier in this article that many simply do not wish to undergo the necessary suffering which will take place in the pursuance of the achievement of this "Spiritual Marriage" of the bride (the soul) with God (the bridegroom). Also, that many, many souls drawing so near to such a union of love with God, do not succeed in completely detaching themselves from all that is not God, that is anything relating to the world, flesh, or the devil. He explains in a graphic analogy that they are like birds who could soar to the heavens - just as the soul could to God - but they are held back as if by a tiny thread from the flight, a thread, be it ever so thin, which still is sufficient to keep them from flying from their perch of attachment to anything whatsoever that is not God. He also, as has been repeated, earlier, indicates clearly that the involuntary appetites in themselves are not necessarily an impediment to the achievement by the grace and love of God of the "Spiritual Marriage" with God. It is only when the involuntary appetites become transformed into voluntary ones that they become obstacles to such a "Union of Love" with God.

St. John points out in a statement fraught with profound mystical meaning (it warrants repetition) that there are souls who fervently desire to enter into the "Spiritual Union of Love" with God while they are still on this earth, but for reasons known to God alone, as he states, God does not bring them to his highest state of bliss in a love of God possible here upon this earth before our soul departs from it. He does not elaborate upon this point of spiritual direction, and it apparently has nothing to do with those whom God would welcome and embrace in a "Spiritual Marriage" of love with Him, but, rather because such persons do not wish to suffer in imitation of His indescribable, incomprehensible suffering which He endured throughout His entire life.

Before I proceed to explain briefly the third part of the "Dark Night of the Soul" in its quest - through the grace and love of God - of the "Spiritual Marriage" or "Union of Love" with God, I wish to present here St. John of the Cross' dire warning to be taken *very seriously indeed by each individual soul* of those who would wish to give the full strength of their heart, mind, soul, and body, or expressed in another way the very depths of the heart of their soul, to God. His reference is to King Solomon whom God in Holy Scripture refers to as the wisest of men that ever lived or ever will live - his wisdom was so great. And yet St. John of the Cross strongly implies that this wisest of men in the final end may have abandoned God. He points out that in his old age the wise King Solomon paid adoration to mere silver and gold statuettes which were brought to him by a number of his many wives. Of course, it is only God who knows the final truth as to whose soul has turned away from Him irrevocably. However, St. John of the Cross, a profound interpreter of Holy Scripture adds two observations regarding King Solomon which makes us tremble in holy (not servile) fear as we strive, by the grace and love of God, to work out our salvation in this vale of tears upon this earthly globe of deadly spiritual warfare. For those persons who scoff at the existence of the devil and his powers for doing evil here upon this earth, St. John of the Cross, a masterful, powerful scholar and interpreter of Holy Scripture provides and extremely extensive and detailed variety of profound insights into the nefarious, diabolic wiles and evil stratagems directed against each soul in the devil's indescribably violent hatred of God, his Creator (before his fall) following after his calamitous and cataclysmic lightening fall through pride and envy into hell.

Toward Daybreak

Now I wish to address the third part of the "Dark Night of the Soul," that is "The Communications of God to the Soul," that twilight period of night when the darkness is dissipating and twilight begins to appear, the daybreak. In this phase of the entire "Dark Night of the Soul" the soul enters the highest degree of contemplation of God that will be possible to it in this world. Thus, in such contemplation - unlike in meditation - the soul becomes passive in receiving communications from God, it becomes a listener to God's communications, rather than raising the very heart of its soul to God in a variety of ways and prayers. The soul in this state of communications from God appears to be doing nothing in prayer despite the fact that it is actually praying to God in some form or another. It hears nothing from God that it can perceive, it simply is there in God's presence in a contemplation of silence, and yet the soul knows without being able to describe this contemplation - in fact, were it to call it by name it would describe it as an "I don't know what it is." Thus, for example, in contemplation of the sufferings of our Saviour, Jesus Christ, not only during the horrible heart -rending violent assaults upon Jesus Christ in the terrible "Agony in the Garden," involving indescribably excruciating mental torture when blood and perspiration poured out through the pores of His body; or the "Scourging or Brutalization at the Pillar" when no part of his body appeared to be spared from the relentless flogging, or cutting even into the bone; or the profound indescribable spiritual suffering of soul endured during the "Crowning with Thorns" when the Creator of all that is good throughout the universe, Whom the universe cannot hold, but which He holds in the palms of His own incomprehensibly beautiful, perfect Divine Hands was crowned in mockery and made sport of by His very own children whom He had come to save; and the "Carrying of the Cross" where His human endurance was tested beyond all human endurance to which any other human being has ever been, or will be subjected to - to such an extent that Angels comforted Him to fortify Him on His way to the Crucifixion, but without taking away from His savagely brutalized body any of the full thrust of suffering He was enduring; to the final agony of the Crucifixion when Jesus Christ was literally torn apart in body and affixed to His Cross, a tree not made to fit His body against, but rather to be stretched on to and nailed down upon crying out to His Father for help as if his Father had abandoned Him, as He was dying and giving up His spirit to His Father for all of us His children. Thus, in such contemplation of the sufferings of Jesus Christ, our Saviour in His "Passion," a horrible climax to a life of 33 years, a life which was actually one of suffering throughout - incomprehensible to us from Holy Scripture itself - the soul passively receives from God communications without knowing what it is receiving, as it just passively listens while praying or not actually engaging in any form of prayer. St. John of the Cross explicitly indicates that the soul in such contemplation does not in any way, of its own accord or volition, enter upon this state of supreme contemplation of God possible upon this earth; but that rather it is only God that brings the soul into such a stage of contemplation. Nor does the soul ask of God to be brought to this high form of contemplation; instead it waits hoping that God will do so. If God does bring it to this state of contemplation, during the "Daybreak" or "Twilight" phase of the "Dark Night of the Soul," the soul may still go back and forth in meditative practices where it is prayerfully speaking to God in a variety of forms of prayer throughout the day, as opposed to the highest form of contemplation where all the communications come to the soul from God, the soul remaining passive throughout. It is thus that the soul indicates that the communications of God to it are so sublime, that while it is receiving these communications, the soul cannot describe to anyone what transformations the soul is undergoing. It is only after undergoing this profound spiritual experience, by the grace and love of God alone, when a soul has ultimately reached the state of the "Spiritual

Marriage" with God, or the "Spiritual Union of Love" with God - that is, the state, when the world, the flesh, and the devil have been defeated, and the full strength of the soul with a heart filled with God's love and grace to its full capacity is given to God, that the soul can look back, as St. John of the Cross did, and attempt to describe under the guiding Hand of the Holy Spirit, what this "I don't know what experience" it went through actually meant to it as it was going through such a spiritual transformation. It is very soon after reaching this state of "Spiritual Marriage" with God that the soul departs from the body and goes to the glory of God to see Him.

A Master

St. John of the Cross as a spiritual director, so amazingly graced by God's love was, at the tender age of about 25 selected by another remarkably great Saint, St. Teresa of Avila, who was about 52 years of age when she took him to be her spiritual director, and recommended him in laudatory terms to other aspirants in the religious community who aspired to lift their hearts up to God in love. He had an amazingly profound knowledge of Holy Scripture, and combined such knowledge to guide the soul in its terrible war of ordeal of the "Dark Night of the Soul" against its three greatest enemies: the world, the flesh, and the devil. He provides masterful expositions on the diabolic stratagems of the devil used to deceive and mislead the soul on its journey to God. It must be admitted that St. John of the Cross is not easy reading, but must be prayerfully studied, read and reread under the constant guidance of God, the Holy Spirit.

It needs to be pointed out again, as I have stated earlier, that St. John of the Cross himself quite candidly, honestly with great humility, stated that his work was not for those who simply had a "mere spiritual sweet tooth"; but did not wish to get down to the very "nitty-gritty" of the essential fundamentals of growth in the spiritual life aimed at the love of God alone above all. He points out as stated earlier above also, that because souls are so varied, and that one may differ from another by as much as 50 percent, that not everything in his collected works is applicable to each individual soul, but that each soul will find something in his works which it can profitably use as a spiritual guide. He is, in my mind, truly a spiritual director for all times, and one of especially inestimable value in today's troubled times which permeate the entire world. The Catholic Church itself in 1926, entitling St. John of the

Cross as a Mystical Doctor of Theology, emphasized his being a profoundly wise spiritual director for these our troubled times of today when good spiritual direction is so badly needed.

Spiritual Development and St. John of The Cross

Joseph P. Kozlowski

In spiritual life, many directors - saints included - catagorized the spiritual development of each individual into stages of beginner, advanced (or proficient), and the perfected. In the perfected stage, a "Spiritual Marriage," "Union of Love," "Likeness (participatory) with God" is achieved by the grace of God with the cooperation of the individual. The "Likeness (participatory) with God" that is achieved in the stage of the perfected may be described by thinking analogously of God as an indescribably lovely diamond with brilliant facets. The human soul would be one of those facets reflecting God's incomprehensible beauty.

The foundation of a person's spiritual development is laid through persevering prayer, participation in the Eucharist, reception of Reconciliation and personal prayer. Private prayers include any form of prayer which comes from the person who is trying to know and live out God's will in his or her own life. I use the phrase "any form of prayer" here because St. John of the Cross explains that each person is different in spiritual make-up and development.

St. John of the Cross makes a clear distinction between people who in their spiritual journey are in the stage of meditative prayer, and are entering or have entered the stage of pure contemplative prayer. He explains it thus: In meditative prayer, people still make use of their senses through images, forms, pictures and imagination. For example, they may call up scenes from the lives of the Holy Family, the Apostles and others who lived with them on this earth as they progressed through life. Thus, in meditative prayer such people are, in essence, making use of their senses in praying to God. They may use the external senses of sight, touch, hearing, smell, taste, and the internal senses among which include: the memory, common sense, imagination, and what is called the evaluative sense. This sense enables people to pass judgment on the goodness or evil of a course of action presented as a choice from within them.

In pure contemplative prayer, however, a person while actually praying to God, no longer makes use of any of the senses. The soul is actually completely passive, receiving the secret infusion of God's love without even realizing it. Expressed differently, the person's soul listens passively to God, as if the soul were doing nothing, while it continues in prayer. In fact, in such purely contemplative prayer, the persons praying may actually think they are wasting their time doing nothing, and may strongly desire to revert back to the use of their senses again in meditative prayer.

From what has been stated above, the questions arise: When do prayerful people know whether they have arrived at the pure contemplative stage of prayer? When, on the other hand, may they still be in the meditative stage? Or are they actually alternately going from the meditative stage of prayer to the contemplative stage, and back again to the meditative stage? All of the above may commonly happen before the stage of pure contemplative prayer is reached. I would like to sum up the answer of St. John of the Cross. He states that prayerful people will know when they have entered into the stage of pure contemplative prayer when three conditions exist in their spiritual life. The three conditions, which must be present simultaneously, are:

1. It is no longer possible whatsoever to pray using the senses cited above.

2. The person in prayer has a very strong desire for as complete a solitude in prayer at all times as it is possible to achieve in their particular state of life.

3. The imagination, although it may continue to wander in prayer, now becomes quickly recollected within the soul as though its wandering has now come under a firm discipline. (Note: The imagination, an internal sense, was one of the operative faculties of the soul hardest hit in our human nature as a result of original sin. It plays an important role in our own personal sinning through life, and plays a powerful role in intervening in our attempt to develop a good prayerful life).

If these three conditions exist and are clearly identified, there occurs a pure contemplative state of prayer to God, a "loving awareness," which is indescribable and incomprehensible because it is a secret, passive influence of God's love which surpasses all knowledge and understanding. Thus, if a person in such a stage of prayerful life were to be asked to describe or explain this secret, passive infusion of God's love, he or she would not be able to do so. That person would truthfully reply, "I don't know what it is." Yet, the "loving awareness" of it would exist in his soul without any knowledge whatsoever of how or when it entered, or when it comes and goes. (Note: See St. John of the Cross. *Collected Works*, pp. 141-143 for a detailed elaboration of this aspect of profound mystical theology.)

In conclusion, whatever forms of prayer are prayed to God, be they the Rosary or any others, these prayers are to be perseveringly prayed throughout one's life. Those individuals fortunate enough to be brought to the prayer of pure contemplation through God's love and grace, may very well be on their way to achieving the "Spiritual Marriage," a "Union of Love," or the state of a "Likeness (participatory) with God" before they depart from this earth.

I must stop at this point, for this is an exceedingly complex subject of profound mystical theology as exemplified so remarkably in *The Collected Works of St. John of the Cross*.

Acknowledgment

I am grateful to the institute of Carmelite Studies and its staff, especially Brother Bryan, business officer, for granting me permission to cite from *The Collected Works of St. John of the Cross*, translated by the Rev. Frs. Kieran Kavanaugh, OCD and Otilio Rodriguez, OCD, with Introduction by Kieran Kavanaugh, OCD: ICS Publications, Institute of Carmelite Studies, Washington, D.C. 1979.

Index

ST. FRANCIS DE SALES

ST. TERESA OF AVILA

THOMAS a KEMPIS:

Bibliography

A Companion to the Summa (Vol. I - the Architect of the Universe); pp. 1 - 457, 1945.

(Vol. II - The Pursuit of Happiness); pp. 1 - 467, 1945. (Vol. III - The Fullness of Life); pp. 1 -530, 1945. (Vol. IV - The Way of Life); pp. 1 - 4464, 1949 by Walter Farrel, O.P., S.T.D, S.T.M., Member of the Thomistic Institute. New York,Sheed and Ward.

Introduction to a Devout Life. From the French of *St. Francis de Sales, Bishop and Prince of Geneva,* to which is prefixed an abstract of his life. Frederick Postet & Co. Printers to the Holy Apostolic See and the Sacred Congregation of Rites. Ratisbon, Rome, New York, Cincinnati; pp. 1 - 367 (with Table of Contents, But Without an Index; No Date).

COLLECTED WORKS OF ST. TERESA OF AVILA

Volume One - The Book of Her Life, Spiritual Testimonies, Soliloquies. Translated by Kieran Kavanaugh, O.C.D. and Otilio Rodriguez, O.C.D. ICS Publications. Institute of Carmelite Studies, Washington, D.C., 1976; pp. 1 -406.

Volume Two - The Way of Perfection, Meditations on the Song of Songs, the Interior Castle. Translated by Kieran Kavanaugh, O.C.D. and Otilio Rodriguez, O.C.D ICS Publications, Institute of Carmelite Studies, Washington, D.C., 1980; pp. 1 - 554.

Volume Three - The Book of Her Foundations, Minor Works, the Constitutions, on Making the Visitation, A Satirical Critique - Response to a Spiritual Challenge, Poetry.Translated by Kieran Kavanaugh, O.C.D. and Otilio Rodriguez, O.C.D.. ICS Publications, Institute of Carmelite Studies, Washington, D.C., 1985; pp. 1 - 483.

THE COLLECTED WORKS OF ST. JOHN OF THE CROSS

One Volume Work (pp. 1 - 774). Translated by Kieran Kavanaugh, O.C.D. and Otilio Rodriguez, O.C.D. with Introductions by Kieran Kavanaugh, O.C.D., ICS PUBLICATIONS, INSTITUTE OF CARMELITE STUDIES, WASHINGTON, D.C., 1979
(Co).

My Imitation of Christ by Thomas a Kempis.* Revised Translation, Illustrated. Confraternity of the Precious Blood. Rt. Rev. Msgr. Joseph B. Frey, Director, 5300 Ft. Hamilton Pkway, Brooklyn 19, N.Y.; pp. 1 - 474.

---

* Although we find references in a great variety of spiritual works, histories, and so forth, as to the true authorship of *My Imitation of Christ*, Fr. John Laux, M.A. in his excellent book: CHURCH HISTORY - A Complete History of the Catholic Church To The Present Day For Upper High School & College Courses and Adult Reading (With Illustrations and Maps). TAN BOOKS AND PUBLISHERS, INC., Rockford, Illinois 61105; pp. 1 - 621 (With Appendix & Supplementary Materials, Index, and so forth; pp. 1 - 37_, has this to say about Thomas a Kempis: (p. 417) "Before the Middle Ages passed away they gave to the world 'the most beautiful book ever penned by the hand of man' -*The Imitation of Christ*. The author, Thomas a Kempis, was born in Kampen in the Archdiocese of Cologne in 1380, and he died at Zwolle in Holland in 1471. Educated by the Brothers of the Common Life at Deventer, he entered the Monastery of the Canon Regular near Zwolle. He was ordained a priest in 1413 and was subsequently appointed sub-prior. For seventy years Thomas knew no other life but that within the monastery walls. The cell, constantly dwelt in he writes, 'groweth sweet...a dear friend and a most pleasant comfort.' His favorite motto bears this out: 'Everywhere have I sought for peace, but nowhere have I found it save in a quiet corner with a little salvation in union with God', this is his whole philosophy of life. His passionate longing for the heavenly fatherland is beautifully expressed in a passage of the Third Book of the Imitation, which has been well styled a "*Gothic Hymn of Longing*."